# MAMONTOV'S PRIVATE OPERA

**Russian Music Studies**
Malcolm Hamrick Brown, founding editor

# Mamontov's Private Opera

## The Search for Modernism
## in Russian Theater

OLGA HALDEY

Indiana University Press

*Bloomington & Indianapolis*

*This book is a publication of*

Indiana University Press
601 North Morton Street
Bloomington, IN 47404-3797 USA

www.iupress.indiana.edu

*Telephone orders*   800-842-6796
*Fax orders*   812-855-7931
*Orders by e-mail*   iuporder@indiana.edu

Manufactured in the United States of
America

Library of Congress Cataloging-in-
Publication Data

Haldey, Olga, [date]
    Mamontov's Private Opera : the search
for modernism in Russian theater / Olga
Haldey.
       p. cm. — (Russian music studies)
    Includes bibliographical references and
index.
    ISBN 978-0-253-35468-6 (cl : alk.
paper) 1. Opera—Russia—Moscow—
19th century. 2. Moskovskaia Chastnaia
Opera. 3. Mamontov, Savva Ivanovich,
1841–1918. I. Title.
    ML1737.8.M67H35 2010
    792.50947'31—dc22

2009051156

1 2 3 4 5 15 14 13 12 11 10

*To* ERIK

# CONTENTS

# ACKNOWLEDGMENTS

This book is the culmination of a long road of scholarly pursuit that started almost a dozen years ago—ever since Savva Mamontov had materialized in my head, quite unexpectedly, one memorable October afternoon. I would like to note a few individuals who helped me along on that journey.

First, my thanks go to Margarita L. Mazo, who in a typically brilliant flash of inspiration first linked Mamontov and Diaghilev in my mind, and to Myroslava Mudrak, who taught me to love and even comprehend modernist art—a skill without which this project would have never been realized. To Charles M. Atkinson and Tama I. Kott, who read more versions of Mamontov-related papers, articles, and manuscript drafts than I (or they) would care to remember, I offer my deepest apologies. I am grateful to Barbara Haggh-Huglo, Dan Zimmerman, David Haas, Lynn Garafola, and Malcolm H. Brown for their helpful editorial suggestions, and to Jane Behnken at Indiana University Press for her prompt and cheerful assistance. I would also like to acknowledge the University of Maryland Graduate School, whose summer research grant was invaluable in completing the book and purchasing publication permissions for its plates.

Finally, I wish to thank Mr. Savva Ivanovich Mamontov and his colorful cohort of students, associates, allies, and critics, who even after so many years of rather close acquaintance, never failed to impress, fascinate, and inspire me. I hope I did them justice.

# NOTE ON TRANSLITERATION
## AND TRANSLATION

Throughout this book, I have used the Library of Congress system for all transliterations of Russian text, with the following modifications: я—"ya," ё—"yo," ю—"yu," ы—"y," ый—"yi." И and й are both transliterated as "i," and their combination at ends of words as "y." Proper names containing the letters above have been spelled similarly: "Yury," "Valery," "Elena," "Ekaterinburg."

In rendering proper names and places, English variants or spellings of proper names have been sought whenever possible without substantially altering the pronunciation. For example, I used "Victor," not "Viktor," "Claudia Winter," not "Klavdiya Vinter"; but "Elizaveta," not "Elizabeth," "Nikolai," not "Nicholas." Commonly accepted spellings of well-known names have been preserved; e.g., "Tchaikovsky," not "Chaikovsky"; "Alexandre Benois," not "Alexander Benois" or "Aleksandr Benua."

In captions, endnotes and bibliography, in order to facilitate catalogue searches by the readers, all Russian-language bibliographic citations conform to the unmodified Library of Congress system, not common spelling or the modified system used in the main text. The latter is used for title translations (in square brackets after the first appearance of a title), as follows: Benua, Aleksandr, *Aleksandr Benua razmyshliaet* [Alexandre Benois Contemplates]. Places of publication are rendered in their common English equivalent; e.g., Moscow: Muzyka; St. Petersburg: Kompozitor. After the first appearance, titles are referred to in their language of publication.

Within the main text, all Russian titles are rendered in transliteration at their first appearance, with common English translations to follow in square brackets, thus: *Zhizn' za tsarya* [*A Life for the Tsar*], *Maska i dusha* [*Mask and Soul*]. Thereafter, English translations are used, with the exception of journal and newspaper titles, which remain in the original Russian.

Common Western book titles appear in their original languages throughout. Western opera titles appear in their original languages, unless mentioned as part of a title in a Russian-language bibliographical citation. If that is the case, they have been transliterated using the unmodified Library of Congress system in a title, and appear in their original languages in its translation, as follows: S. K-ov, "Bogema Puchchini" [Puccini's *La bohème*].

Unless otherwise indicated, all translations from Russian and other foreign languages are mine.

# ABBREVIATIONS

## ARCHIVES

| | |
|---|---|
| BM | State Central Theater Museum named after Alexander Bakhrushin [The Bakhrushin Museum], Moscow, Russia |
| MATM | State Museum of the Moscow Academic Art Theater [The Moscow Art Theater Museum], Moscow, Russia |
| RMLAH | Museum of Literature and Art History named after Janis Rainis [The Rainis Museum], Riga, Latvia |
| RGALI | Russian State Archive of Literature and Art [Rossiisky Gosudarstvennyi Arkhiv Literatury i Iskusstva], Moscow, Russia |
| RNL | Russian National Library, St. Petersburg, Russia |
| RSL | Russian State Library, Moscow, Russia |
| SRM | State Russian Museum, St. Petersburg, Russia |
| STG | State Tretyakov Gallery, Moscow, Russia |

## SELECTED NINETEENTH-CENTURY PERIODICALS

| | |
|---|---|
| MV | *Moskovskie Vedomosti* |
| ND | *Novosti Dnya* |
| NBG | *Novosti i Birzhevaya Gazeta* |
| NS | *Novosti Sezona* |
| NV | *Novoe Vremya* |

PG    *Peterburgskaya Gazeta*

PL    *Peterburgsky Listok*

RMG   *Russkaya Muzykalnaya Gazeta*

RS    *Russkoe Slovo*

RV    *Russkie Vedomosti*

SPV   *Sankt-Peterburgskie Vedomosti*

MAMONTOV'S PRIVATE OPERA

# Introduction

Russian musical modernism has long been seen as an oxymoron in musicological discourse, and perhaps understandably so. After all, the adventurous idiosyncrasies of late Scriabin filled barely half a decade; the iconoclastic genius of Stravinsky, albeit fueled by his heritage, flourished far away from his native soil under the fashionable spotlights of Paris; and the youthful futurism of Prokofiev has been seen in some quarters as a mere surface veneer grafted upon a classical edifice.[1] Other manifestations of modernity in Russian music have been dismissed as either inconsequential or nonexistent.

Meanwhile, scholars of Russian history, literature, and visual and performing arts have never suffered from a lack of modernism to explore, as they actively discuss the various aspects of the historical-cultural phenomenon known as the Silver Age. A time period encompassing the last decade of the nineteenth through the first two decades of the twentieth century, it saw a veritable explosion of early modernist trends in philosophy, aesthetics, literature, and the arts.[2]

The discussion of the Silver Age on both sides of the Atlantic has been dominated by literary scholars, who see it as primarily the Age of Symbolism.[3] Indeed, the era saw a proliferation of prominent symbolist literati, including Valery Bryusov (1873–1924), Vyacheslav Ivanov (1866–1949), Andrei Bely (1880–1934), and Alexander Blok (1880–1922), who collectively defined the philosophical and aesthetic foundation of Silver Age art and culture, and as a consequence will figure prominently in the narrative to come. Yet painting the picture of the Silver Age with only a symbolist brush is misleading, as the history of its visual arts makes clear. Russian painters of the period followed a dizzying mosaic of trends and styles, including but not limited to symbolism, impressionism, neo-primitivism, cubo-futurism, and rayism, all of which found inspiration in Western art, yet claimed allegiance to Russian antiquity while celebrating Russian modernity. This ideological multiplicity defines the Silver Age, a cultural landscape in which numerous visions of modernity vied for prominence with each other, and in its early years—the Russian *fin de siècle*—also with the still vital realist and naturalist trends of the not-so-distant past.

The concept of reconciliation and fusion of competing visions is fundamental to the Silver Age phenomenon. At its heart was a thriving bohemian subculture of clubs, cabarets, and private gatherings, at which poets, painters, and other artists met, debated and exchanged ideas, and collaborated on joint projects.[4] For that reason, the necessarily collaborative art of theater is central to the era, and the kernels of modernism found in staged art of the period are vital to our understanding of it.

The Silver Age of theater is represented historically by the *commedia dell'arte* experiments of Vsevolod Meyerhold (1874–1940), the retrospectivism of Nikolai Evreinov (1879–1953) and his Ancient Theater,[5] and the warped synthesism of *Pobeda nad solntsem* [hereafter, *Victory over the Sun*], a futurist *Gesamtkunstwerk* created by Alexei Kruchonykh (1886–1968), Mikhail Matyushin (1861–1934), and Kazimir Malevich (1878–1935), whose 1913 premiere all but spelled out modernity on stage.[6] The music for *Victory over the Sun* was written by Matyushin, a painter, and as such has been dismissed as amateurish, and the weakest aspect of the production. Discussions of Meyerhold's and Evreinov's theaters do not count music among their accomplishments either, prompting one to wonder if in fact there was no such thing as Russian musical modernism. The present study aims to refute that persistent notion by locating and deconstructing a long-overlooked cradle of Russian artistic modernity, in which music played a prominent, indeed indispensable role—opera theater. Or rather, our subject is one particular opera theater—the Moscow Private Opera (MPO).

## THE COMPANY

The MPO was an *opernaya antrepriza*—an operatic enterprise, or a private opera company—that operated in Moscow and St. Petersburg at the turn of the twentieth century. It was created, sponsored, and directed by Savva Ivanovich Mamontov (1841–1918; plate 1).[7]

An heir to a business empire, a railway tycoon responsible for creating the transportation system that ushered Russia into the modern age, Mamontov has earned a worthy place in history as an important representative of the country's merchant capital. He received an excellent education, first with a private tutor (who taught, among other subjects, such gentlemanly pursuits as riding and fencing), then at a private school, and finally at Moscow University. He was fluent in German, French, and Italian and for a time took English lessons; he traveled widely in Europe, Central Asia, and the Middle East. His youthful diaries are peppered with Greek and Latin quotations and references to contemporary literature, criticism, politics, and the arts. Savva Mamontov grew to become one of the country's leading art patrons, who brought together three generations of the foremost Russian painters in an artist colony he had established at his country estate of Abramtsevo, near Moscow. At various times his friends and associates described this remarkable man as a talented sculptor, writer, librettist and translator, a brilliant character actor, and a born stage director. Unlike traditional art patronage, however, these gifts remained hidden from public view: Mamontov's social status obliged him to keep his personal artistic aspirations private. Not so private was his lifelong passion for theater, especially opera. In his student days he was a regular presence in his uncle's box at the Bolshoi Theater; studied his favorite works at the piano, which he played fluently; and took singing lessons in Moscow and Milan that almost resulted in a professional operatic career. Yet some still professed shock when he was revealed as both the artistic and the financial force behind the MPO, the company he led from 1885 to 1892 and then again between 1896 and 1899, during which time it became one of the most influential theatrical institutions of *fin-de-siècle* Russia. The revelation was the scandal of the social season: in September 1899, the notorious millionaire and Maecenas was arrested and put on trial for embezzling hundreds of thousands of rubles from his shareholders, only to spend them—surely an unprecedented incident in the history of jurisprudence—on an opera company.[8] Mamontov's acquittal in June 1900 brought the courthouse down in a tumultuous standing ovation. But the subsequent bankruptcy brought his association with his most important artistic project, the MPO, to a close. The company operated, under new management and with modest success, for four more seasons before being dissolved permanently in the spring of 1904.[9]

At the peak of its creative activity, however, Mamontov's Private Opera was a viable market enterprise that successfully competed with the powerful Imperial Theaters and made a major imprint on the artistic lives of both Moscow and St. Petersburg. The company employed the cream of Russia's performing forces. Among its singers were Rimsky-Korsakov's celebrated muse, soprano Nadezhda Zabela (1868–1913), and the legendary bass Feodor Chaliapin (1873–1938), whose international career was launched from Mamontov's stage. Young Sergei Rachmaninov (1873–1943) received his training as a conductor there. The company also employed at various times almost two dozen painters, among them Vasily Polenov (1844–1927), Victor Vasnetsov (1848–1926), Valentin Serov (1865–1911), Konstantin Korovin (1861–1939), Mikhail Vrubel (1856–1910), and other recognized masters.

Throughout its fifteen-year history, the MPO playbill featured over eighty-five titles. Among the foreign operas it premiered on the Moscow stage were Verdi's *Otello,* Wagner's *Lohengrin,* Gluck's *Orfeo,* Saint-Saëns' *Samson et Dalila,* Thomas' *Mignon,* Humperdinck's *Hänsel und Gretel,* and Puccini's *Les villi* and *La bohème.* The company's contribution to the history of Russian opera includes its staged premiere of Musorgsky's *Khovanshchina* and a return of his *Boris Godunov* and Borodin's *Knyaz Igor* [*Prince Igor*] to the repertory after years of oblivion. The opera composer most central to the MPO repertoire, however, was undoubtedly Nikolai Rimsky-Korsakov (1844–1908). Mamontov directed an acclaimed 1885 production of *Snegurochka* [*The Snow Maiden*] (the Moscow premiere of that opera; see plate 34), and in 1896 premiered the new, definitive version of *Pskovityanka* [*The Maid of Pskov*]. The MPO also had the honor of presenting the world premieres of no less than six Rimsky-Korsakov operas: *Sadko* (1897), *Motsart i Saleri* [*Mozart and Salieri*], *Vera Sheloga* (both 1898), *Tsarskaya nevesta* [*The Tsar's Bride*] (1899), *Skazka o tsare Saltane* [*The Tale of Tsar Saltan*] (1900), and *Kash-*

*chei Bessmertnyi* [*Kashchei the Deathless*] (1902; for the precise dates of these and other premieres, see Appendix B). As a result, the composer called the time in his creative life between 1896 and 1902 his "private-opera period," while Mamontov's enterprise earned the nickname of "Rimsky-Korsakov's Theater."

These are the known facts about the MPO; its basic "biography" has already been written.[10] The present investigation aims to interpret and contextualize these facts in order to illuminate the surprisingly deep and fundamental impact of Mamontov's company on the development of staged art in the early twentieth century, in Russia and beyond. As we shall see, the MPO revolutionized opera production by introducing major innovations in acting, directing, and design, and became a crucible for the emerging modernist trends in stage aesthetics. Reflecting the *fin-de-siècle* fascination with artistic correspondences, Mamontov saw opera as a perfectly integrated art form, to be created through the collaboration of his outstandingly talented team of performers, directors, and designers. His team echoed the spirit of the times, if not necessarily Wagnerian theories, as they strove for the ideal of a true synthesis of the arts. To achieve this goal, the MPO became a veritable school of theater design, transforming a disdained craft into a modern, internationally recognized art form, and placing a designer at the head of its production team (see chapters 3–4). The company also promoted the vision of opera as a staged drama. Almost single-handedly, Mamontov created the concept of operatic stage director, training the first generation of Russian opera régisseurs and developing novel acting and staging techniques influenced by contemporary spoken drama troupes, such as the Meiningen Theater. His approach would prove highly influential on both operatic and dramatic stages of the new century, as it impacted the work of revolutionary stage directors Konstantin Stanislavsky (1863–1938),[11] Alexander Sanin (1869–1956), and Vsevolod Meyerhold, all of whom were aware of Mamontov's work and benefited from personal interaction with him (see chapters 5–6).

Another revolutionary iconoclast whose career and artistic outlook were shaped by his early encounter with Mamontov was Sergei Diaghilev (1872–1929). The historical relationship of the MPO and the Ballets Russes and the direct connection between their leaders form one of the focal points of the present study. Savva Mamontov was a copublisher and sponsor of *Mir Iskusstva* [*World of Art*], an art journal edited by Diaghilev that united decadent painters, litterateurs, philosophers, and aestheticians, promoted the development of new artistic trends, and became a voice of the country's young modernist movement. Several of Mamontov's designers contributed to *Mir Iskusstva* while still employed at his company and later worked with Diaghilev on his Russian Seasons, a Parisian theatrical venture that would become the Ballets Russes. Diaghilev would also collaborate with the singers and stage directors connected with the MPO, producing a number of operas that were not only central to that company's playbill but thoroughly identified with it. These parallels have led leading Diaghilev scholar Lynn Garafola to view the MPO as "a musical and artistic blueprint for Diaghilev's initial Russian Seasons."[12] The present study goes further by positing the existence of a mentor-student relationship between Mamontov and Diaghilev based on their shared aesthetic views and vision of modernist staged art. This relationship resulted in Mamontov's support for the *Mir Iskusstva* journal (see chapter 4). Even more consequentially, it led to Diaghilev's adoption of both the organizational principles and the creative methodology of Mamontov's enterprise, which he implemented at his own new venture, the Ballets Russes. The final chapter of this book traces this process, as well as Diaghilev's emulation of Mamontov's position of artistic director, which allowed him to eclipse his mentor by realizing his long-held dream of conquering Paris.

### THE LITERATURE

The name of Savva Mamontov is familiar to any educated Russian. After all, his Abramtsevo estate is a museum to which schoolchildren from the Moscow region take their mandatory sixth-grade trips. Recently he even warranted a fictionalized biography in the popular series *Zhizn zamechatelnykh lyudei* [*Lives of Notable People*].[13] Yet a curious Russianist who wants to learn more about Mamontov's contribution and the significance of his most personal and arguably most important artistic project, the MPO, would encounter an interesting dichotomy. On the one hand, the multifaceted Mamontov makes an appearance in just about every study of Russian *fin-de-siècle* culture published since the 1940s, and the general impression today, at least among Russian scholars, is that the topic has literally been researched to death.[14] On the other hand, very few studies have been exclusively dedicated to Mamontov, and prior to my own work, only one thin monograph specifically focused on the MPO.[15] The existing, primarily biographical accounts furnish both facts and their interpretation for the mountains of scholarly works that feature Mamontov cameos. As a result, this larger body of literature treats the subject superficially and offers no original contribution to the study of the Mamontov phenomenon.

In addition, if our curious Russianist happens to be a musician, he or she would be disappointed to find that the Mamontov studies have been primarily the province of art historians—after all, even during his lifetime, the man's public face in the cultural world was that of an art patron who supported and employed some of the country's most outstanding painters. Understandably, in an art-historical study—even a valuable and sympathetic one such as Evgeny Arenzon's recent set of biographical essays[16]—the MPO warrants only a cursory mention, with the emphasis on its approach to visual design and no attempt at a comprehensive assessment of an opera production in all its interdisciplinary complexity. The few theater studies that mention the subject treat it in a similarly one-sided manner, addressing the issues of acting and staging at the MPO, but not music or design. When the subject matter is tackled by musicologists, the company becomes a focus of conversation primarily as a vehicle for a composer's, singer's, or conductor's art. This includes perhaps the best researched and most comprehensive Soviet-era treatment of Mamontov's company, the 1974 monograph *Russky opernyi teatr na rubezhe XIX–XX vekov i Shalyapin* [*Russian Opera Theater at the Turn of the Twentieth Century and Chaliapin*] by leading Soviet opera scholar Abram Gozenpud.[17] Gozenpud's study has undeniable merits. Among them, his attempt at drawing a broad historical-cultural context for the company's operations and his focus not merely on matters musical but also on issues of staging and design (although the author tends to borrow his evaluations of these issues from the sister disciplines) are a welcome comprehensive approach that will be developed in the present study. Yet the book's very title illustrates the skewed nature of its narrative: it portrays the MPO as merely a vessel for the great singer's art, propagating a popular misconception about the company that views Chaliapin's participation as its only claim to fame.

Gozenpud thus joins a great majority of Mamontov scholars who commonly attribute the MPO's undeniable accomplishments to the talented group of artists and musicians associated with the company. Meanwhile, they tend to dismiss Mamontov's personal artistry, denying him any individual contribution to his favorite project beyond his infectious enthusiasm and the generosity of his pocketbook. This study aims to dispel this persistent yet inaccurate notion by highlighting Mamontov's innovative work as a régisseur, and beyond that, as the Moscow Private Opera's artistic director, the creator of the overarching central concept for each production. Savva Mamontov was the heart and soul of his company; its engine, not merely the source of its monetary fuel. Without his artistic leadership, it reverted to an ordinary commercial troupe that left little mark on Russia's cultural landscape and soon perished, unnoticed and unlamented. In the same way, the Ballets Russes perished with the death of Diaghilev, whose personal artistic contribution to his company has long been acknowledged by critics and scholars.[18] Throughout this book we shall discover how, through a combination of personal charisma and targeted recruiting, Mamontov assembled a diversely talented team that together and under his guidance was able to realize his own "private opera"—his distinct, personal vision of the operatic genre as a powerful staged drama revealed through visual spectacle.

This vision stemmed from Mamontov's idiosyncratic aesthetic philosophy that was developed over the decades of his involvement with the arts. This aesthetic platform has proven to be a source of fascination and a major focus of attention for Mamontov's champions among scholars across disciplines and across the world. For the most part, their interpretations followed one of two trajectories: Mamontov was portrayed either as a defender of realism on stage, or as an ardent nationalist. The descriptions stemmed from researchers' good intentions, their desire to legitimize Mamontov within the historical canon as a part of some positive development. Different approaches to constructing that positive history inside and outside Russia have resulted in the divergences between the presented models. In Soviet scholarship, the history of the arts was typically viewed as a gradual evolution toward realism. In order to neutralize Mamontov's problematic background as a "greedy capitalist" and insert him into the canon of important—and ideologically sympathetic—artistic personalities, Rossikhina, Gozenpud, and virtually all

Soviet-era Mamontov scholars were obliged to situate their protagonist's achievements, specifically in staging and repertoire policy, within that preconceived realist framework.[19] This tradition of casting Mamontov as an adherent of realism explains the lack of Russian research before the 1990s into his connections with the aesthetic trends of the Silver Age, including symbolism, *Mir Iskusstva,* and the Ballets Russes. Links with early twentieth-century modernism would have been detrimental to Mamontov's cause in Soviet art and music history, the disciplines that treated any such links as ideologically deviant.[20]

That is not to say that scholars outside Soviet Russia offered a better-rounded and more comprehensive portrait of Mamontov's aesthetics. On the contrary, they failed to achieve this objective, equally spectacularly and for surprisingly similar reasons: their desire, with the best of intentions, to write their hero into a preconstructed positive history of Russian music. Instead of realism, the magical password to legitimacy for a Russian subject in Western scholarship has been nationalism. As a result, historian Stuart Grover's 1971 dissertation "Savva Mamontov and the Mamontov Circle," prior to my own research the only full-length study of Mamontov in a language other than Russian and the leading source of information on the subject for English-speaking scholars, is predictably subtitled "Art Patronage and the Rise of Nationalism in Russian Art."[21] The work's one-sided nationalist slant is evident and uncompromising.

In musicology, the nationalist tradition began with the first Western publication on the history of Russian music: César Cui's fantastically biased 1880 *La musique en Russie.*[22] It continued in the work of Rosa Newmarch, Michel Calvocoressi, and Gerald Abraham, the elders of Russianist musicology who were all much influenced by Cui's work.[23] They were also profoundly impacted by the equally tendentious nationalism of Vladimir Stasov, whose mantle of an unrepentant realist was, interestingly enough, inherited by Soviet scholars.[24] The nationalist interpretation of Russian music history has finally received a well-deserved mortal blow in recent years in the revisionist scholarship of Richard Taruskin. Among that ecumenical scholar's many interests, Savva Mamontov has never been at the top of the list. He did, however, make a cameo appearance in Taruskin's acclaimed tome *Stravinsky and the Russian Traditions.*[25] Although this is justifiably one of the most respected and widely read studies on Russian music, its treatment of Mamontov's contribution is still unfortunately indebted to Grover's work—at least in factual matters. Interpretively, Taruskin situates Mamontov in the context of what he calls the "neo-nationalist" movement, which he associates specifically with the visual arts. The term, with its built-in implications of "nationalism reborn," seems somewhat problematic to me, yet it takes a large step forward and away from a traditionally nationalist narrative in its emphasis on the decorative, modernist approach to art and theater. As we shall see in chapters 3 and 4, these aspects of modernist aesthetic were reflected in some of Mamontov's activities, including his Abramtsevo workshops that studied and imitated folk crafts and his opera productions such as *The Snow Maiden* and *Sadko*. Yet Taruskin is still guilty of limiting Mamontov's vision primarily to one art (décor) and a single unified aesthetic (neo-nationalism), thus excluding some of his most personal, creative, and, by his own estimation, artistically dominant projects, such as those based on ancient Greek mythology.[26]

It is not my intention to claim in this book that either realist or nationalist trends were absent from Mamontov's ideological makeup. On the contrary, their impact on his artistic philosophy and decision-making process will be analyzed in chapters 6 and 7, respectively. What I would argue, however, is that realist, nationalist, and even neo-nationalist models have all proved inadequate in assessing Mamontov's contribution due to their artificially created ideological purity. In their attempts to construct a single-issue aesthetic niche for their protagonist, Mamontov scholars were often forced to simplify his complex, contradictory aesthetic makeup, and purge from the list of his associates those deemed ideologically suspect. In addition, the primary sources used to support their arguments were treated selectively: the evidence that conformed to a preconceived theory was admitted, that which did not was downplayed, ignored, or sanitized by strategically placed cuts.[27]

The present study aims to embrace the complexities and contradictions native to Mamontov's mercurial personality as a man and an artist, an approach that is essential for understanding his aesthetics as realized in the daily operations of the MPO. These contradictions are seen not as aberrations to be explained away, but rather manifestations of an inherently transitional aesthetic environment in which, as I will argue throughout this book, Mamontov truly belongs—early Silver Age decadence. The nature of decadent aesthetics in turn-of-the-century Russia was a state of ideological flux that saw it equally embrace futurism and passé-ism; naturalism, decorativism, and transcendence. Russian decadent culture was based on collaboration and convergence of the arts, as their practitioners stumbled forward out of the dying century toward the seductive promise of modernity. That journey, full of uncertainty, fascinating discoveries, and blind alleys offers perhaps the clearest portrait of Savva Mamontov's adventures in opera. It also provides the main impetus and a starting point for the present study, underlying both its interdisciplinary premise and its goal of tracing the uneasy coexistence of numerous, often contradictory philosophies and trends that lay at the foundation of the MPO. As we shall see, the most enduring characteristic of Mamontov's company mirrored its leader's personality in its aesthetic multiplicity—both the source of its greatest strength and its most debilitating weakness.

## THE SOURCES

Let me close with a few necessary comments on the primary sources upon which this book is based. First, the reader should be forewarned not to expect stunning revelations of previously uncatalogued letters, or sensational claims of exclusive access to a newly available family archive. For decades now, the archival materials that allow us to chart Mamontov's creative persona and assess his contribution to the world of art have been for the most part (barring an occasional restoration effort) fully available to both local and foreign scholars. Their rather unique accessibility (to Russians, that is—or Westerners willing to travel) might be one reason for a common scholarly perception of Mamontov as a known quantity, and a consequent reluctance of some researchers to spend time interpreting the evidence so easily obtained. As a result, a remarkable number of important documents have been overlooked or left unexplained, in addition to the ones read tendentiously to support a predetermined point of view. Meanwhile, the materials themselves frequently resist direct interpretation, since they reflect the biases, prejudices, and singular perspectives of their authors—their own individual and often contradictory truths. This last issue is particularly relevant to Mamontov studies that rely to a great extent upon the large body of published and unpublished autobiographies.

Mamontov's charismatic personality attracted a variety of talented people in all branches of the arts into his circle of influence. Many of those people went on to build distinguished careers of their own, and to record their life stories in the form of written memoirs, some of which contain vivid recollections of their associations with Mamontov. Feodor Chaliapin, Sergei Rachmaninov, Konstantin Stanislavsky, Alexandre Benois, Vasily Shkafer, Nadezhda Salina, Pyotr Melnikov, and Mikhail Ippolitov-Ivanov are only a few memoirists whose Mamontov stories made it into print. These stories are colorful and seductively palpable. It is tempting to accept them at face value, while overlooking their venerable authors' sometimes barely concealed attempts at self-aggrandizement; their ideological agendas, professional biases, and personal grudges. For example, in art-historical scholarship, one particularly controversial memoir has been that of Princess Maria Klavdievna Tenisheva (1867–1928). Princess Tenisheva had plenty of reasons to dislike Mamontov: her operatic ambitions were thwarted by his flat refusal to admit her to the MPO stage; her Talashkino estate was established explicitly to compete with Abramtsevo's workshops and its reputation as an artistic Mecca. Yet her understandably skewed assessment of Mamontov and the MPO has been viewed as a reputable source, particularly by Western scholars.

In the musicological community, the picture of Mamontov has been significantly colored, both in Russia and elsewhere, by the recollections of one of his most important collaborators, Nikolai Rimsky-Korsakov, recorded in the composer's memoirs, *Letopis moei muzykalnoi zhizni* [*Chronicle of My Musical Life*],[28] and reflected in his voluminous correspondence with the MPO soprano Nadezhda Zabela, who, as we shall see in chapter 5, had her own axe to grind. Rimsky-Korsakov's denial of Mamontov's musicality, a consequence of both aesthetic disagreements and personal resentment, has typically been accepted as an objective and unbiased opinion of a highly respected source, leading some music scholars to patronizingly dismiss the "tone-deaf" tycoon's forays into their realm. Clearly, memoirs and correspondence cannot be read uncritically. Despite the pitfalls they present, however, if studied attentively and contextually they allow us to illuminate both Mamontov's ideas and activities, and those of his associates. As such, these sources play an important role in the present study.

Another frequently biased yet invaluable source of information about Mamontov and the MPO used extensively throughout this book is the voluminous body of reviews of the company's productions. The Russian operatic press loved talking about the MPO, observing and interpreting every success and gloating over every misstep. This coverage, mostly to be found in the "theater and music" sections of Moscow and St. Petersburg dailies, was of course never dispassionate, as ideological and aesthetic agendas colored both perceptions and commentaries. Parsing press biases in Mamontov coverage is difficult: because of the limited number of late-nineteenth-century Russian periodicals that published opera reviews, few media outlets systematically promoted a specific political or cultural agenda. Rather, individual critics were known for the views expressed, more or less aggressively, in their writings. When a certain critic worked exclusively for one newspaper (as did, for example, Mikhail Ivanov of St. Petersburg's daily *Novoe Vremya*), it acquired a reputation (in this case, conservative) similar to his. When critics freelanced, or wrote for several publications at the same time, more than one periodical would have an opportunity to expose their ideas. In addition, in order to appeal to a wider constituency, newspapers commonly syndicated the columnists with directly opposing ideological stances, while journalists were known to express widely divergent opinions about the same topic (such as the quality of a specific MPO production) depending on the style, agenda, and projected readership of a particular outlet expected to publish their work. The result was a press coverage that was volatile, unpredictable, frequently contradictory, and almost always deliciously acrimonious—a fact that delighted Mamontov, a fan of scandalous publicity (see chapter 8), and allowed me to enliven these pages with some juicy quotes I hope my readers will enjoy.

Most importantly, this confluence of conflicting ideologies and aesthetic trends completes the picture drawn by the memoir literature, archival photographs, and unpublished correspondence. Viewed in their entirety, these sources present Mamontov's company as a brilliant, messy, exciting, and conflicted artistic institution. It authored a revolutionary new approach to the operatic genre; it illuminated a path toward modernism for its numerous descendants in the world of staged art, yet so often failed to walk that path. Mamontov's innovations, some imperfectly executed or even self-sabotaged, inspired, guided, and directed a generation of artists, who appropriated, developed, and patented his ideas, and by so doing earned their places in the history books. It is time for their mentor to join them.

ONE

# The Silver Age and the
# Legacy of the 1860s

From the early days of the Moscow Private Opera through the present day, Mamontov's supporters and his detractors, his contemporaries and modern scholars have all identified one characteristic of his company that made it unique. The artistic policies, internal structure, and daily operations of Mamontov's enterprise were to a large extent driven by ideology—the aesthetic views of its leadership, most importantly Mamontov himself. As the exact nature of that ideology remains a matter of debate, it is a goal of this study to illuminate the nature of Mamontov's aesthetic platform and trace its impact on various aspects of his company's operations, as well as its relationships to its critics, competitors, and audiences. This question is crucial to understanding the role played by the MPO in the history of Russian theater at the dawn of the Silver Age.

From the moment it opened its doors, Mamontov's company positioned itself at the epicenter of the cataclysmic aesthetic shift that saw the new generation of modernist artists confront, battle, and ultimately displace their predecessors. As a result, it was inevitably drawn into the aesthetic debate that underlined that struggle, and as we shall see, its response to the issues of the debate was an outgrowth of Mamontov's personal aesthetic preferences, shaped and tested over three decades. We shall start, therefore, with an overview of the major ideological currents that guided the development of the arts in Russia from the 1860s, the time of Mamontov's personal aesthetic maturation, through the 1890s, the time of the aesthetic coming-of-age of his company.

In the late nineteenth century, as Western civilization stood on the verge of the modern era, an age-old debate over the meaning and value of art in society was once again taking center stage in the aesthetic discourse. The debate focused on the extent of art's engagement with reality. Its main issue has been summarized by Charles Harrison as follows: "Should we measure all forms of cultural production alike according to what we might summarily call their realism, [or] does the true potential of culture lie . . . in its autonomy vis-à-vis social and utilitarian considerations and in its pursuit of the aesthetic as an end in itself?"[1] Both trends of thought coexist in constant dialogue within Western cultural discourse to this day, their relative centrality to the spirit of an age in perpetual flux, continuously rethought and reevaluated. At any moment in history one of these trends may become dominant, while the other is marginalized but never completely absent from aesthetic consciousness.

As the autonomy of art, arguably, lies at the very core of modernist aesthetics, the discourse was becoming increasingly polemical in Russia and elsewhere as the new century approached. In order to position themselves within that discourse, clarifying (and perhaps simplifying) it, critics, philosophers, and aestheticians seized upon a convenient—and conventional—dichotomy, the followers of realism waving the banner of "truth" and modernist aestheticians dedicated to "beauty."[2] Naturally, to the practitioners of the arts—whether poetry, painting, or music—the issue was more complex. To them, the dividing line between truth and beauty was, at best, blurred: whatever the aesthetic affiliation, rare was an artist who would not wish his or her works to be both beautiful and relevant.

A perfect example of that complexity is the philosophy of Charles Baudelaire, creator of the first aesthetics of *modernité*. In his 1863 *Le peintre de la vie moderne,* the poet urged artists to experience and to capture the reality of their fluid and transient modern world. And yet, he was also a dedicated follower of writer and aesthetician Théophile Gautier, who had famously declared: "Nothing truly beautiful can serve any useful purpose whatsoever; everything useful is ugly . . . The most useful part of the house is the toilet."[3] With Gautier, Baudelaire proclaimed aesthetic autonomy an essential quality of true art, and beauty its highest goal. "Since Baudelaire," wrote Matei Calinescu, "the aesthetics of modernity has been consistently an aesthetics of imagination, opposed to any kind of realism."[4] And it is this side of Baudelaire's argument that made a particularly strong impact on young Russian intellectuals of the early Silver Age. His writings on the subject were quoted by heart and paraphrased in print; the following fanciful piece of Baudelairiana is typical: "The foundation of poetry lies in a man's striving for the highest beauty, and the realization of that striving is enthusiasm completely independent of . . . truth, that steering wheel of reason, for [it] is natural, too natural not to introduce a sharp, dissonant note into the dwelling of pure beauty."[5] Following Baudelaire and other like-minded artists, Russian modernist aestheticians placed the cult of beauty at the foundation of their escapist philosophy. According to Dmitry Sarabyanov, a leading Soviet-era scholar of Russian modernist art, in turn-of-the-century Russia worshipping pure beauty was a sign of the times: "Beauty turned into an all-encompassing, global category, into a deified subject. The cult of beauty became a new religion."[6] One of the leaders of this artistic trend, poet Valery Bryusov, summarized the aesthetics of his generation in a 1902 article with a characteristically controversial title "Nenuzhnaya Pravda" ["Useless Truth"], writing: "In art, imitation of nature is a means to an end, not the end in itself . . . The real world is merely a prop used by the artist to give shape to his dreams."[7] In a 1903 lecture "Klyuchi tain" ["The Keys to the Mysteries"], the poet elaborates:

> One must not, in order to satisfy knowledge and science, see in art only a reflection of life. . . . There is no art that would repeat reality. In the world around us, there is nothing corresponding to architecture and music. Neither the Cathedral of Cologne nor Beethoven's symphonies reflect our surroundings. . . . Art relates to reality like wine to grapes.[8]

The establishment of the cult of beauty as a foundation for turn-of-the-century aesthetics in Russia did not go unchallenged, initiating a heated debate between the adherents of truth and beauty. One of beauty's most visible and controversial detractors was Leo Tolstoy, Russia's greatest living writer and arguably its most revered cultural figure. In his 1898 monograph *Chto takoe iskusstvo?* [*What is Art?*], Tolstoy rejected the "false theory of beauty" as superfluous and immoral.[9] Since its true purpose, according to him, was pleasure of the privileged upper-class minority, the art of beauty was not worth the sacrifices and labor of the common people who helped to create it while providing luxurious living for an artist. As a consequence, the writer also denounced the majority of his own creative output as worthless, for in his novels the aesthetic considerations had prevailed over what he now believed to be art's true mission—serving the common good:

> More and more often, the people of high society, who see the contradiction between the good and the beautiful, exalt beauty as the highest ideal, thus relieving themselves of the demands of morality.... The substitution of the ideal of beauty, i.e., pleasure, for the ideal of morality constitutes [one of] the horrible consequences of the degenerate art of our time.[10]

Tolstoy's rejection of the aesthetic independence of art and his denigration of the cult of beauty as moral depravity had a mixed reception in Russia's intellectual circles, from unbridled enthusiasm to silent embarrassment to outrage. As we shall see, the outrage was expressed primarily by younger intellectuals, who exalted instead the transcendent philosophy of their own idol, Vladimir Solovyov (1853–1900). While similarly concerned with the questions of the nature of goodness and the promotion of righteousness, Solovyov equated the search for beauty with the search for the salvation of the world. Beauty to him was an idea that objectively existed in the material world—an extension of the Word becoming flesh. As embodied perfection, it was not a means to any end and did not serve any purpose, because it was in itself the goal toward which the world must strive. Goodness and truth, while accepted as important concepts in Solovyov's philosophy, were described as merely steps toward that goal, meaningless without beauty: "Beauty is . . . a realization in material forms of that very ideal meaning which, prior to that realization, is called Goodness and Truth. . . . [They say that] goodness does not need beauty. But in that case would not goodness itself be incomplete?"[11] Solovyov's "mystic realism"—his belief in the materiality of ideas, as well as objects—differed in its subtlety and sophistication not only from the utilitarianism of "true" realists but also from the *au-delà* idealism of the new generation. Unsurprisingly, his acolytes would tend to read his writings somewhat selectively, appropriating some passages and reinterpreting others as needed to support their own aesthetic platform—beauty, exalted as the highest ideal. The early works of Nikolai Berdyaev (1874–1948), another important philosopher, and a representative of the 1890s generation much influenced by Solovyov, contain a pointed reference to the truth-beauty debate under consideration here. In an essay published in 1907 but probably written earlier, Berdyaev wrote: "[We] must accept an *independent meaning of beauty* and artistic creativity in human life. *Beauty is an ideal goal of life,* elevating and ennobling a man. We accept the idea of the independent meaning of beauty, understanding in it the *self-purpose* of beauty."[12] According to Berdyaev, this "theoretical aesthetics that under no circumstances would consider art a reflection of reality" defined the foundations of a movement that, in retrospect, stands as one of the most significant artistic trends of the Russian Silver Age, namely, symbolism.

### SYMBOLISM AND DECADENCE

Symbolism, a movement that, to quote Bernice Rosenthal, "sought to transcend mundane reality through beauty and aesthetic creativity," was one of the most enduring artistic trends of the Silver Age, and one of the earliest manifestations of modernism in the Russian arts.[13] Just as Russian symbolism in many respects resembled its French counterpart, the term "symbolism" in Russia, as in France, was not immediately accepted. Throughout the 1890s and into the early 1900s the label preferred, particularly by critics of the movement, was "decadence." In critical and scholarly discourse, the term "decadence" has acquired multiple meanings, and has been classified variously as a philosophical concept and an artistic style, as well as a particular aesthetic movement.

The idea of decadence as an ideology of degeneracy and decay was discussed by a variety of the nineteenth-century writers, ranging from Désiré Nisard, who in 1834 first expanded the usage of the term beyond the history of the Roman civilization and applied it to the romantic movement, to Friedrich Nietzsche, who condemned its "desire for weakness" and used it to critique the music of Wagner.[14] The negative connotations attached to the term included its associations with creative decline, pessimism, bohemian lifestyle, amorality, and sexual deviance. Ironically, all these pejorative labels appeared to have been validated on the pages of *À rebours,* an infamous novel by Joris-Karl Huysmans that would become an instant classic of decadent literature as well as a favored straw man for the movement's detractors. The 1884 publication of *À rebours* is commonly seen as the birth of decadence as an artistic movement, soon given a voice on the pages of the poetic journal *Le décadent*, launched in 1886. As the title of the journal makes clear, Paul Verlaine and other radical literati who contributed to *Le décadent* did not shy away from the controversial term. On the contrary, they used it for self-identification and publicity, and by so doing transformed it from an insult into a slogan. In their polemical writings, the editors of *Le décadent* specifically targeted the prevailing view of decadence as cultural decline; instead, they saw and portrayed themselves on the cutting edge of modernist aesthetics. Like Charles Baudelaire before them, they defined decadence as an "awareness and acceptance of modernity":

> The true decadent will not only try to harmonize his work with the most outstanding features of modern civilization but will also resolutely and courageously express a progressive creed, a firm belief in what Baju calls "*la marche ascensionelle de l'humanité.*" In other words, the decadent is in the avant-garde.[15]

The editors of *Le décadent* thus discussed their movement primarily as an attitude toward contemporary life. They seemed reluctant, however, to point to the characteristics of decadence as an artistic style. Scholarship since has been equally hesitant to define the stylistic trend of decadence, pointing to the vague and fluid nature of the term, noting the history of its usage as a pejorative label, and assigning various aspects of the phenomenon to other aesthetic trends such as aestheticism, art nouveau, and symbolism, among others. In a notable exception, John R. Reed in his monograph *Decadent Style* offers a thorough classification of stylistic decadence. Its characteristics include the cult of beauty, distaste for the quotidian, fascination with an object of art for its own sake, individualism, escapism, and an obsession with the decorative and the ornamental. Fascinated by the remote past and disenchanted by the present, the decadents sought to refashion nature into an elegant ornamentation of the artist's own self. As Reed notes with respect to Aubrey Beardsley, "All of experience [is] reduced to design, but a design that is, in itself, compelling."[16] According to Brooks Adams' *Law of Civilization and Decay* (1896), decadent style prefers "lavish ornament to purity of form";[17] that is, it concentrates on the surface details of an art object at the expense of its underlying structure, sometimes to the point of the utter dissolution of the latter. Thus, according to Paul Bourget's oft-quoted critique of decadent poetry: "A decadent style is one where the unity of the book decomposes in order to give place to the independence of the page, where the page decomposes in order to give place to the independence of the phrase, and the phrase in order to give place to the independence of the word."[18] Reed's analysis of the deconstructive nature of decadent style closely resembles Robert Morgan's discussion of musical modernism as realized specifically in the early atonal works of Schoenberg.[19] In both cases, the shift of significance from background structure to surface detail lies at the foundation of the style as it dissolves the boundaries of traditional forms—a parallel that once again reveals decadence to be an important aspect of modernity.

In turn-of-the-century Russia, a strong association of decadence with modernity was arguably the reason for the invariably derogatory application of the term in critical discourse. Widely and indiscriminately, it was used to denigrate early modernist trends in literature and the arts. And since the Russian critics rarely parsed their terms, a follower of aestheticism, impressionism, decadence, art nouveau, or any other *fin-de-siècle* movement—indeed any artist with a demonstrated predilection for a modernist philosophy or technique—would be typecast as a decadent. In hindsight, it seems paradoxical that while decrying the modernity of the decadent style, the majority opinion in Russia wholeheartedly embraced the vision of decadence as cultural decline, expressed in Max Nordau's infamous treatise *Degeneration*.[20] In polemical discourse, decadence would be described as a kind of a contagious disease, and the decadents portrayed as dangerously sick men spreading the infection among the weak-minded. Leo Tolstoy once warned: "It is a mistake to pay so little attention to the decadents; this is a sickness of our time, and it deserves serious scrutiny."[21] On the pages of the Russian press, the terms *dekadentstvo* [decadence], *vyrozhdenie* [degeneracy], and *upadnichestvo* [decline], used as synonyms in Nordau's book, were interchanged with similar frequency.

Another favored insult was "symbolism"—possibly because the symbolists were the most active and well-organized among Russian "decadents." It is unlikely that most critics concerned themselves with discerning and qualifying the similarities and differences between the two movements and their corresponding artistic styles. Valery Bryusov, for instance, accepted the synonymous use of "decadent" and "symbolist" as a matter of course, albeit hinting at the possibility of discriminating between the two terms. That possibility, however, proved fascinating to the scholars of the period. Thus, according to Reed, decadence and symbolism share an ideological foundation: "Both use prominent symbols, reject the inelegant contemporary world, and stress the longing for another sphere of being—aesthetic, ideal, even supernatural."[22] The difference between the two is that the symbolist approach to the realization of that common philosophy is more radical and experimental. In other words, Reed views decadence and symbolism as two adjacent, sequential steps on an aesthetic-historical continuum, with the belief in the suggestive and transformative power of art present in both styles but expressed more strongly in symbolist poetics.

While this hypothesis accounts for the interchangeable use of the two terms by scholars and critics, both in Russia and in France, it does injustice to the subtle differences of emphasis and interpretation seen in the writings of the period dedicated to the common subjects of fascination, such as the meaning of beauty and the role of art. These subtleties are reflected in the usage of the two terms in modern studies of Silver Age aesthetics, in which "symbolism" is employed as a general, all-encompassing stylistic category, with "decadence" as its temporal qualifier. For example, literary scholars distinguish between the two generations of symbolist poets in Russia: the decadent symbolists of the 1890s and early 1900s, such as Bryusov, Konstantin Balmont (1867–1941), Dmitry Merezhkovsky (1865–1924), and Zinaida Gippius (1869–1945), who assigned to art primarily decorative and escapist functions (i.e., Reed's "decadents"); and the mystic symbolists of the later 1900s and 1910s—Andrei Bely, Alexander Blok, and Vyacheslav Ivanov, who emphasized the theurgic, transformative power of artistic creativity (i.e., Reed's "symbolists").[23] Although the writings of the mystics (specifically Ivanov) will be touched upon in later chapters, it is the generation of the decadents with which this study is primarily concerned.

The decadent symbolists, led by Valery Bryusov, adopted the motto of art for art's sake, called for decorating the world, and promoted the use of symbols to gain knowledge of its mystery and free the imagination of individual artists to transcend reality in their work. In his 1894 book *Russkie simvolisty* [*Russian Symbolists*], Bryusov declared his solidarity with his French counterparts, recognized decadence as the foundation of symbolist poetics in Russia, and claimed, similarly to *Le décadent,* that symbolism was a progressive, modernist trend, albeit not an exclusive form of "poetry of the future."[24] Bryusov believed that the only worthy subject matter for art was the glorification of beauty; truth was to be left to the newest inventions of scientific progress, portrayed in his writings as the icons of an aggressively utilitarian bourgeois modernity opposed to an aesthetic modernism of the artistic world. "Let us leave representation of reality to photography, to the phonograph—the innovations of technicians," he wrote.[25]

### THE MIR ISKUSSTVA GROUP

Bryusov's ideas on decadence and symbolism (published either under his own name or a pseudonym, "Aurelius") reached his audience via a variety of printed media—newspapers, literary journals, and self-published booklets in his hometown of Moscow and elsewhere. One of the most important and powerful outlets for his views, however, turned out to be an art journal. The St. Petersburg-based *Mir Iskusstva,* which published his bombshell, "Useless Truth," also opened its pages to poetry and criticism by Merezhkovsky, Balmont, Gippius, and other decadent literary figures. The Mir Iskusstva group was a loosely defined "cultural 'club' of artists, literati, musicians, and aesthetes"[26] led by the then little-known art critic and collector Sergei Diaghilev (1872–1929) and his more illustrious partner—painter, critic, and art historian Alexandre Benois (1870–1960). The group organized annual exhibitions of modern art and sponsored regular concerts of contemporary music. Arguably its most significant achievement, however, was *Mir Iskusstva,* the journal published between 1898 and 1904. A bright, edgy, and irreverent forum for the country's most innovative talents in literature, philosophy, and the arts, the journal quickly established itself as the voice of Russia's young modernist movement by uniting the most illustrious representatives of literary decadence with the painters and aestheticians of the Russian *style moderne.*[27] Each contributor had the option of participating in editorial work, as well as submitting reviews, position articles, and plates.

The first issue of *Mir Iskusstva* appeared in October 1898. It opened with the aesthetic platform of the group, outlined by Diaghilev, the journal's editor-in-chief, in a series of articles under the common title "Slozhnye voprosy" ["Complex Questions"]. One of these complex aesthetic questions was the polemic between the followers of truth and beauty in art, tackled by Diaghilev in an essay "Vechnaya borba" ["Eternal Struggle"]. Calling his young contemporaries a "generation seeking beauty," Diaghilev branded Leo Tolstoy an ungrateful servant and enemy of art, who had slapped it in the face by rejecting its intrinsic value and reducing it "merely to one of the Christian virtues." Diaghilev believed the great power of art to be contained "precisely in its self-purposefulness, self-usefulness, and most importantly—its freedom," and concluded with a declaration of the group's aesthetic principles: "A creator must love beauty alone."[28]

The allegiance to the cult of beauty and pure art proclaimed in Diaghilev's essay placed the Mir Iskusstva group squarely into the decadent camp—to the great delight, as we shall see, of its detractors. Ironically, Diaghilev found the label of decadent infuriating: he shared the common view of the term as indicative of moral degeneracy and creative decline and devoted the entire inaugural essay of "Complex Questions" to building a defense against the "alleged decline" of new art by portraying it as progressive and modern.[29] The argument could have been lifted directly from *Le décadent* or from the pages of Baudelaire, whom Diaghilev quoted on multiple occasions in his editorials. He also revealed his allegiance to the aestheticians of beauty by eagerly joining in criticism of their ideological opponents, the realists. Yet most tellingly, he and his Mir Iskusstva colleagues joined forces not against the multitude of Western-European utilitarians, but rather mined their own aesthetic heritage in search of convenient straw men. They found plenty: just as in France, Germany, or England, the debate between truth and beauty had an extensive and convoluted history in Russia, going back at least half a century.

Despite ridiculing the aesthetics of truth as worn-out and old-fashioned, Diaghilev and his fellow decadents understood the necessity of confronting it in order to overcome its powerful sway over the tastes and opinions of the Russian public. In a sense, they had to face their own past, their mentors—an older generation of writers, painters, and musicians who came of age during the triumph of realist aesthetics in the 1860–70s, and some of whom were instrumental in bringing about that triumph. Some giants of the realist age, such as eminent critic and art historian Vladimir Stasov (1824–1906), were still active and highly influential in the 1890s. Others—prominent literary critic Vissarion Belinsky (1811–48) and renowned writer and publicist Nikolai Cherny-shevsky (1828–89), among others—inspired posthumous reverence. As part of a mounting rebellion by the young modernists against "[their] teachers, [their] enemies," as Diaghilev aptly put it,[30] poet, philosopher, and future member of Mir Iskusstva Dmitry Merezhkovsky attacked Belinsky's brand of "literary criticism grounded in sociology" in a 1892 essay *Prichiny upadka i novye techeniya v russkoi literature [The Causes of the Decline and the New Trends in Russian Literature]*.[31] Diaghilev himself, with the impertinence of youth, issued a pointed challenge to Chernyshevsky in "Eternal Struggle," writing: "The unhealthy figure [of Chernyshevsky] is not yet digested, and our judges in art still cherish at the back of their minds that barbaric image that dared to touch art with unclean hands and thought to destroy or at least tarnish it."[32]

As the passionate arguments sampled above make clear, it is impossible to appreciate the magnitude of the aesthetic shift that inaugurated the Silver Age without first addressing the foundations of an entrenched ideology against which the decadents were fighting. Let us therefore turn our attention to the history of the realist doctrine whose confrontation with and eventual triumph over aestheticism defined the ideological landscape in Russia of the 1860s—the time when our story begins.

### REALISM VERSUS AESTHETICISM: 1840S–60S

The birth of realist ideology in Russia can arguably be traced to a radical naturalist school of literary criticism that developed in St. Petersburg in the mid-1840s. Led by Vissarion Belinsky, naturalist critics believed that literature should be dedicated to an unflinching depiction of reality: social background, details of the environment, and the grim everyday life of its characters. Reality itself was viewed as the protagonist of a novel or a play, while human beings represented merely aspects of that reality. By way of examples, the naturalist school singled out for praise the writings of Nikolai Gogol and selected early works of Fyodor Dostoevsky (e.g., *Bednye Lyudi [Poor Folk]*), seen as depicting, in Belinsky's words, the *khudozhestvennaya statistika* [artistic statistics] of contemporary Russia.[33] After Belinsky's death in 1848, his argument continued to be promoted by the younger generation of realist critics grouped in the mid-1850s around the St. Petersburg literary journal *Sovremennik*. This second wave of realist criticism took its cues from the pages of perhaps the most widely read and most important master's thesis in Russian history, Nikolai Chernyshevsky's notorious *Esteticheskie otnosheniya iskusstva k deistvitelnosti* [*Aesthetic Relations of Art to Reality*], defended and published in May 1855. Chernyshevsky then proceeded to apply the theoretical premise of his thesis to specific literary works in a series of essays, *O gogolevskom periode v russkoi literature* [*On Gogol's Period in Russian Literature*], published in *Sovremennik* in 1855–56. These were followed in the late 1850s and early 1860s by an extremely popular series of *Sovremennik* articles penned by talented journalist Nikolai Dobrolyubov (1836–61); after his untimely death, the banner of realism was carried, arguably, to its furthest extreme by Dmitry Pisarev (1840–68), the author of a radical 1865 work, *Razrushenie estetiki* [*The Destruction of Aesthetics*].

Developing the ideology of Belinsky's naturalism, mixed with the materialism of Feuerbach, and the rationalism of the English utilitarians, Russian realists outlined their own version of utilitarianism. In *Aesthetic Relations,* Chernyshevsky stated that "for a fully developed intellect there is only the true, and no such thing as the beautiful." He viewed art as inherently inferior to the reality that it imitates, either "as is" (the real) or "as should be" (the ideal), calling upon it cheerfully to admit its inferiority the way science does. In what became a wildly popular slogan, he declared: "the beautiful is life," and saw art of the future as a precise description of reality, in the manner of history and sociology.[34] Chernyshevsky argued that faced with a choice between a picture of an apple and an actual object, a person would invariably prefer the latter; or, as his followers were fond of saying, Raphael and Shakespeare are worth less than a good pair of boots.[35] Dobrolyubov and other critics expanded on Chernyshevsky's militantly black-and-white aesthetics by focusing on the concept of art's usefulness. They declared art valuable when it documents real life, but only to the extent that it carries a message, a purpose, and serves social change via education of the people. Fyodor Dostoevsky—who, like many of Russia's best poets and novelists, including Ivan Turgenev, Afanasy Fet, Ivan Goncharov, and at the time, Leo Tolstoy, protested the extremism of the realists—summarized their position in his journal *Vremya:*

> Utilitarians demand from art a direct, immediate, concrete usefulness that adjusts to circumstances, submits to them, and does so to such a degree that if at a certain time society works on resolving, for example, a certain question, art (according to some utilitarians' doctrine) must have no other goals than to resolve that same question.[36]

What particularly angered Dostoevsky and ensured the paucity of good writers in the realist camp in the early years of the debate was the critics' position that in judging the value of an artwork, quality should be viewed as an incidental side effect, secondary to function. A badly written novel, Dobrolyubov argued, could be considered worthwhile if it is a faithful mirror of life; yet even a highly artistic literary work lacks value if it fails in its realist mission. As Dostoevsky noted in his critique of Dobrolyubov's works,

> Without openly attacking *khudozhestvennost* [artistry], utilitarians at the same time completely reject its necessity. "As long as the idea is evident, as long as the purpose for which a work is written is evident—that is enough; and artistry is an empty business, of the third rank, almost unnecessary." . . . We have noticed that they take special pleasure in raging against a literary work whose main attribute is its artistry.[37]

The favored target of the critics' "rage" was the poetry of Russia's literary icon, Alexander Pushkin (1799–1837), whose six-volume complete edition made its inaugural appearance in 1855, the year of Chernyshevsky's thesis. The edition immediately became both a lightning rod for the realist thunderbolts, and a rallying point for the Russian aesthetes, their opposition. The realists dismissed Pushkin's works as elitist, old-fashioned, useless "album trifles" (a term coined by Dobrolyubov), and proclaimed them inferior to those of Gogol, who ideally fulfilled their ideological expectations. The aesthetes clarified their own position by rushing to Pushkin's defense. In response to Chernyshevsky's Gogol essays mentioned above, writer, critic, and notable aesthete Alexander Druzhinin (1824–64) proclaimed art for art's sake that group's motto.[38] Dostoevsky who, as we have seen, aligned himself philosophically with the aesthetes, declared:

Art is its own purpose and must be justified by its very existence. There should be no question of "usefulness" in art. . . . Writers, poets, painters, and actors must not be concerned by anything quotidian or current—be it politics, the internal life of the society to which they belong, or even some burning national issue—but only with *high art*. To be concerned with anything but art is to humiliate it, drag it down from its heights, and mock it.[39]

The debate between the realists and the aesthetes reached the peak of intensity between the late 1850s and mid-1860s. As the sample opinions above indicate, it was vehement, polarizing, and absolutely uncompromising. The two camps showed no desire to engage each other's arguments or even to acknowledge the enormity of the gray area between the stark black-and-white extremes of their entrenched positions. This tradition of aesthetic absolutism began with Chernyshevsky, who declared in *Aesthetic Relations* that "truth is unitary; there cannot be different ways of perceiving truth, and by extension reality: there can be only one way, to which the force of reason must ultimately bring everyone."[40] In addition, the high passion shown by the Russian aestheticians and unheard of anywhere else in Europe where similar arguments also took place has another explanation: in Russia, the allegedly artistic debate acquired clear political overtones. With all public debate stifled by the stringent censorship of the repressive Nikolaian era (1825–55), liberal Russian intellectuals from Belinsky on used literature and literary criticism to evaluate the appalling social conditions in their country and call for reform, while getting around the censor by supposedly depicting or discussing fictional characters. For example, Dobrolyubov's celebrated essay on Alexander Ostrovsky's play *Groza* [*The Thunderstorm*] expressed the critic's outrage at the oppressive reality of what he famously called "the dark kingdom" of provincial merchant life, while ostensibly showcasing the plight of the play's unfortunate heroine.

After the ascension of Alexander II in 1855 offered the prospect of political and economic reform, realism was increasingly portrayed by its practitioners and seen by its consumers as more than an aesthetic choice—rather, as an urgent and necessary political stand. The more precise the literary depiction of the horrific reality, the argument went, the more readers would thirst for change. As a result, the participants in the supposedly innocuous debate about the nature of art and beauty split along the ideological fault lines: progressive realism versus conservative aestheticism. Thanks in part to the considerable polemical talents of Chernyshevsky, Dobrolyubov, and Pisarev, the realists succeeded in winning over public opinion by painting their opposition as elitist reactionaries who did not care about their social responsibilities, while draping themselves in the fashionable rhetoric of liberalism. The cream of Russia's radical intelligentsia came to feel "virtually obliged to accept the arguments [Chernyshevsky] made in his essay: the volume had acquired something like the force of intellectual law."[41] By ca. 1870, the most influential realist critics had either died or departed from the scene, but the damage, as they say, was done. Prose short stories and ideological novels championed by the realists replaced poems and plays of the aesthetes as main vehicles of literary expression. In all artistic endeavors, the evidence of an author's social consciousness was demanded by the strict "censorship of the left."[42] Pushkin lost; the aesthetes with their pure-art idealism were forced out of the ideological mainstream.

By that time, realism was also on its way toward becoming the prevailing ideology in artistic fields other than literature and criticism. Most notably, the dominance of historical and mythological subjects in the French-based curriculum of the St. Petersburg Academy of Fine Arts prompted thirteen young painters to officially secede from their alma mater in 1863. Forfeiting the prestige and security enjoyed by the members of the artistic establishment, they created, in 1870, an independent, radical exhibition society, *Tovarishchestvo Peredvizhnykh Vystavok* [Association of Traveling Exhibitions], and became known as the *Peredvizhniki,* or the Wanderers. The subjects chosen by the Wanderers paralleled the naturalist school in literature by exposing the drunken poverty of the lower classes, the corruption of state and church officials, the dark side of patriarchal family relations, and other social ills.[43] Years later, painter Ilya Repin (1844–1930), arguably the most talented among the group, recalled repentantly in his "Pisma ob iskusstve" ["Letters on Art"]:

> The Hellenes of art who traced their lineage to pure Phidias, Praxiteles, Apelles, and Polygnotus, to Botticelli, Raphael, Titian, and Veronese reborn in Italy in the fifteenth century, were toppled. Their regal composition, that necessary sphere for expressing the greatest spirit of the gods, seemed now a cold stylization; the serenity of their graceful lines an artificial study; the harmony of the whole was explained by the lack of

means. . . . "Art for art's sake" was a banal, shameful phrase to an artist; it smelled of some kind of lechery and pedantry. Artists were forced to teach and moralize to society, so they would not feel like spongers, lechers, or other such nobodies. "Raphael himself isn't worth a penny," [said] a hero of that time, Bazarov.[44]

According to Repin's memoirs, the Wanderers believed that their art should have a moral center: "In our [work], morality ruled everything; that virtuous old maid subordinated everything to her power and allowed nothing but charity and tendentious journalism."[45]

In the musical world of St. Petersburg, realist ideology paralleling that of the Wanderers was represented by the so-called Moguchaya Kuchka [Mighty Handful; hereafter the Kuchka], or the "New Russian School of Composition," analogous to the "New Russian School of Painting," as the Wanderers were called.[46] All three terms, incidentally, were coined by Vladimir Stasov, a mentor and self-appointed spokesman for both groups and a staunch believer in their supposedly common purpose.[47] In his essay "Perov i Musorgsky" ["Perov and Musorgsky"], Stasov drew a parallel between the two artists as characteristic representatives of their respective circles, who practiced the ideology of socially conscious art by faithfully representing the truth of its darker aspects, i.e., through realism:

> Both Perov and Musorgsky, with complete sincerity and incorruptible truth, expressed in their works only that which they saw with their own eyes, which existed in reality, and did not waste their time thinking up fantasies and idealisms. [Their characters are] recreated with the truth that can rarely be found in art, and even less so in music.[48]

Indeed, the ideology of the Kuchka was initially formulated on the premise of the so-called "musical truth." The catchphrase, coined by young Modest Musorgsky in relation to the group's idol, the older-generation composer Alexander Dargomyzhsky (1813–69), might perhaps be more appropriately applied to Musorgsky's own early works.[49] It was Musorgsky who, in an oft-quoted 1872 letter to Stasov, best articulated the aesthetic approach that, by this time, had become the prime ideological current in all the Russian arts. He wrote: "The artistic representation of beauty alone, in the material sense of the word, is coarse childishness, the infancy of art." Instead, the composer proclaimed the faithful imitation of the speech patterns in colloquial Russian—that is, a detailed representation of everyday reality—"the true mission of an artist."[50]

The ideological war against the aesthetics of beauty waged by (and increasingly, on behalf of) the Wanderers and the Kuchka in the late 1860s and 1870s was not confined to the privacy of art studios and publishing houses. It took place on theatrical stages, at exhibitions, in concert halls, and most visibly and importantly, in the press. According to a leading historian of Russian art, Elizabeth Valkenier, "precisely because the situation in Russia up through the 1880s offered so few other options, the artistic scene was viewed not as a field for the free play of different styles and subject matters but as a battlefield."[51] Stasov, in his role as one of the battlefield's most powerful generals, demanded that the Russian arts be both "truthful"—that is, realist—and increasingly, nationalist. His call for a defined national style has been traced to his dismay at the condescending reception by the Western critics of the "inferior" and "derivative" Russian art exhibited at the 1862 London International Exhibition, the first World Fair in which Russia participated.[52] Meanwhile, the plea for the country's return to its unique "national path" was also part of an important and increasingly influential philosophy in Russia that developed during the 1840s and '50s in parallel with the realist doctrine—the philosophy of the *pochvenniki*.

### THE *POCHVENNIKI* AND THE MAMONTOV FAMILY CIRCLE

The *pochvenniki* [men of the soil] was a diverse group of Slavophile-leaning intellectuals clustered around the literary journals *Moskvityanin*, *Vremya*, and *Epokha*. The *pochvenniki* believed that the early eighteenth-century reforms that westernized Russia under Peter the Great represented a catastrophic mistake that made the country lose its way. Modernization and westernization would lead only to the corruption and decadence that they perceived as rampant in their contemporary Europe. Instead of following in its wake, they called for Russia to rediscover its own unique identity founded, they believed, on its traditional connections to the East and on Orthodox Christianity with its promotion of the communal spirit, or *sobornost*.[53] The model of this so-called "Russian Idea" was located in the heartland of Russia, literally in its *pochva* ("soil"; hence the term *pochvenniki*). The established way of life in Russian villages, ruled by the *obshchina* ("community," or "commune"), was offered as the ultimate blueprint for the future political organization of the country.[54] The Slavophile views were based on the idealized, romantic Herderian notion of the "folk"—the wisely naïve village populace, pure of heart, uncorrupted by urban civilization, and preserving "the soul of the nation" in their mythology, arts, and culture.[55]

The views of the *pochvenniki* ran contrary to those of the realists who saw Russian village life as anything but idyllic. Rather, it was to them a gloomy, backward, horrifying symbol of their country's problems—political, social, and cultural—and was to be portrayed as such in literature and the arts. Stasov, ever the revolutionary, shared that notion, which is why he had never accepted the basic premise of the *pochvenniki*'s national idea, although he did agree with their advocacy of the nationalist inspiration for the Russian arts. Besides, as a staunch defender of the realist truth, he could never have officially allied himself with the aesthetic platform of the *pochvenniki*. For instance, writer, publicist, and one-time editor of *Moskvityanin* Apollon Grigoriev (1822–64), the movement's founder and one of the most prominent and idiosyncratic aestheticians of the period, was a pointed critic of the "materialism and utilitarianism" of Belinsky, Chernyshevsky, and their disciples.[56] In his writings, Grigoriev never openly embraced aestheticism, yet his vision of art as an organic and intuitive expression of its creator's emotions rather than a faithful description of "real life," and his absolute commitment to the "ideal of Art . . . in an age that turned violently against art and aesthetics"[57] placed him firmly on the side of the aesthetes in the truth-beauty debate. It also allied him with the Dostoevsky brothers—Mikhail, owner of *Vremya* and *Epokha,* and Fyodor, who served as editor and leading contributor to both.[58] A relentless critic of Dobrolyubov and the realist aesthetics, Fyodor Dostoevsky shared Grigoriev's belief in the primacy of beauty, both in art and in daily life. This belief was crystallized in his much-quoted diary entry, *krasotoyu mir spasyotsya* [the world shall be saved by beauty], and realized in one of his most significant literary achievements, the novel *Idiot* [*The Idiot*].[59] In one of his articles for *Vremya,* Dostoevsky wrote:

> Art has its own wholesome, organic life and consequently basic and unchanging laws for that life. Art is just as much a necessity to man as food and drink. The need for beauty, and for creativity that expresses it, is in-

separable from man, and without it he perhaps would refuse to live. Man yearns for it, finds and accepts beauty *unconditionally,* simply because it is beauty, and bows before it with awe without asking what it is used for, and what could be bought with it. And perhaps, the greatest mystery of artistic creativity lies in that the image of beauty created by it immediately becomes an idol, *unconditionally....* Beauty is a part of everything healthy—that is, the most alive—and is a necessary requirement of a human organism. It is harmony; it is a condition of peace; it represents the ideal for man and humanity.[60]

Together with the concept of *sobornost,* the cornerstone of Slavophile thought (the term *Slavophile* came to replace *pochvennik,* which was rarely used past 1860), Dostoevsky's philosophy of art would inspire the work of Vladimir Solovyov and, through him, shape the transcendentalism of Vyacheslav Ivanov and the mystic symbolists. Thus, in some respects, the Slavophile movement served as a harbinger of Silver Age aesthetics.

While the power base of the realist movement was composed primarily of the St. Petersburg liberal intelligentsia and university students, the majority of the prominent *pochvenniki* came from the Moscow merchant circles. After the reforms of the 1860s plunged Russia into the long-delayed industrial age, the emerging big capital gradually increased its influence over the country's economic and cultural life during the second half of the nineteenth century. Influential Moscow businessmen, instrumental in the development of Russia's native industry and the modernization of its economic policies, habitually expressed Slavophile views that extended beyond their business practices. For example, the "silk king" Fyodor Chizhov (1811–77), one of the strongest critics of foreign influence on Russia's economy, was an impassioned advocate of the Slavophile cause in the arts. A student of art history, specifically traditional Russian icon painting, he became a friend and patron of one of the greatest Russian painters of the 1840s, Alexander Ivanov (1806–58), who based his work on that tradition.[61] Millionaire wine seller Vasily Kokorev (1817–89) who, like Chizhov, frequented the Slavophile literary and artistic salons in the 1850s–60s, gathered an excellent collection of Russian paintings at his home and opened it to the public.[62] One of the first private collections of that kind in the country, Kokorev's gallery predated and possibly inspired the work of Pavel Tretyakov (1832–98), whose family also belonged to the Slavophile circles, and whose collection, deeded to the city of Moscow in 1882, is known today as the State Tretyakov Gallery.

The *pochvenniki* dominated Moscow's intellectual and artistic landscape at the time when the first-guild merchant, millionaire wine seller, and railway industrialist Ivan Fyodorovich Mamontov moved his family there from Siberia. Upon their arrival, the Mamontovs quickly established cordial social and familial relationships with prominent Slavophiles. Ivan Mamontov was a close friend and business associate of Kokorev and Chizhov, and a relative of the Morozovs, the Ryabush-inskys, the Alekseevs, and the Tretyakovs. Among frequent visitors to his house were the Aksakov family of writers, father Sergei (1791–1859) and his sons Konstantin (1817–60) and Ivan (1823–86); historian Mikhail Pogodin (1800–75) who, after the death of Apollon Grigoriev, replaced him as the editor of *Moskvityanin;* and other prominent *pochvenniki.* Such was the atmosphere in which Ivan Mamontov's second son, Savva, grew up. He was in his early teens when the family arrived in Moscow, and there began the development of his aesthetic views, which will be discussed in detail in the following chapter.

TWO

# Serving the Beautiful

Growing up in his father's house, Savva Mamontov was exposed to the
Slavophile ideology on a daily basis. His youthful diaries reveal that he
was well versed in their politics, and clearly admired Kokorev and Pogodin.[1] Savva was evidently an avid reader; copies of *Vremya, Moskvityanin,*
and *Russkaya Beseda* (another Slavophile publication), as well as books
by Sergei Aksakov, whom he revered, were freely available to him. A
lifelong relationship with Fyodor Chizhov—a mentor and father figure—
had a particularly lasting effect on him, shaping the business philosophy
of the future railway tycoon. Savva Mamontov grew to become one of
the country's leading nationalist businessmen, whose unwillingness to
allow foreigners to establish control over Russia's heavy industry would
eventually lead to the crash of his financial empire. His contemporaries
also credited him with creating the foundation for the country's railway
transportation system, which provided for its resource-based economy's
survival during World War I.[2]

While the Slavophile influence on Mamontov's business practices is
indisputable, it does not necessarily follow, as Grover assumed, that his
nationalism spread beyond the office doors.[3] Fyodor Chizhov, businessman cum art historian, was certainly a role model for him. We might
also speculate, for instance, that Savva's interest in folklore, ranging from
fairy-tale subjects for paintings to village crafts (see chapter 3), could
have been influenced by the reverence for the "folk" that the *pochvenniki*
had inherited from Herder. There is no documentary evidence, however,
to confirm such a hypothesis. Mamontov's Westernized sympathies, on

the other hand, can be clearly discerned in his aesthetic views, artistic taste, and lifestyle. Fluent in several languages, he traveled extensively throughout his lifetime and demonstrated encyclopedic knowledge of, and unbridled enthusiasm for, Western European art and culture.

Perhaps a balance to the Slavophile influence in his house was provided by the Westernized stance of some members of the 1860s realist movement, to which he was exposed while a student at the Moscow University.[4] While the majority of the important realist critics were based in St. Petersburg, young Savva Mamontov and his fellow students had plenty of opportunities to attend public lectures on the subject and read *Sovremennik* and other realist publications sold in Moscow bookstores. During his university years, Savva also acquired first-hand experience of realist theater by joining the Sekretarev drama circle led by Russia's two leading realist playwrights, Alexander Ostrovsky (1823–86) and Alexei Pisemsky (1820–81).[5] Together with his classmates, some of whom, including Glikeriya Fedotova, would become prominent dramatic actors, Mamontov performed in excellent productions directed by Ostrovsky himself.[6] The Sekretarev plays were attended by the cream of Moscow society and reviewed by the most respected media outlets of both capitals.[7] Such attention given to an admittedly amateur troupe can be only partially attributed to the personal involvement of a famous playwright. More important, perhaps, is the fact that prior to 1882, the Imperial Theaters enjoyed a royally decreed monopoly on both drama and opera productions in Russia. Informal, private circles like the Sekretarev provided the public with its only alternative to the repertoire choices and staging practices of the so-called *kazna,* or *kazyonnaya stsena* ("the crown stage," that is, the state-owned theater companies, such as the Maly Drama Theater). Mamontov thus already had a taste of this alternative at the dawn of his artistic career while at the same time immersing himself in the aesthetics of truth. In the early 1860s, realism was still a radical new idea, not universally accepted and thus all the more attractive to a curious young student. By the end of that decade, however, realism became the mainstream ideology in Russia, and the aesthetes appeared soundly defeated. As Repin recalled in his "Letters on Art": "Pure art was pushed to the background as something useless, dulling perception, and in any case, it was understood only by a few veteran aesthetes. Artistic success belonged to Trutovsky's illustrations of Krylov's fables."[8] Meanwhile, Savva Mamontov's aesthetic education took a surprisingly unconventional turn.

## THE ROMAN FRIENDS

In the late 1860s, Mamontov and his family started spending a large part of the year abroad, mostly in Italy. While in Rome, they befriended a number of Russian artists who met at the houses of Mark Antokolsky (1843–1902), arguably Russia's finest sculptor of the period, and the Prakhov brothers, art historian Adrian (1846–1916) and eccentric philosopher, poet, and publicist Mstislav (1840–79). Mamontov began a serious study of sculpting in Antokolsky's studio, became an accomplished tour guide to the city's art galleries and ancient ruins, and publicly proclaimed "living in art" his true vocation.

The subculture of the Roman colony—a Rome-based group of expatriate Russian painters, sculptors, art historians, and musicians—must have provided an astonishing change for the young Muscovite. From his teen years, both at home and at the university, he witnessed daily heated political debates over Russia's present misery and future path. In Rome he saw Russian intellectuals who deliberately removed themselves from the social and political concerns of their day. Equally oblivious to their country's historic mission envisioned by the Slavophiles and to the social agenda thrust upon the arts by the realists, these artists lived abroad, painting the ruins of the Colosseum instead of their native towns and villages. In both theory and practice, Mamontov's new Roman friends actively cultivated the ideology of the aesthetes that in Russia of the time would have been considered decidedly retrograde.

Savva Mamontov soon became one of the most enthusiastic proponents of the ideas endlessly discussed by his new friends, particularly Mstislav Prakhov. With his idealistic nature, Mstislav presented both a source of admiration and a target of endless jokes: the group's ideal of "living in art" he understood literally. Mamontov's 1874 letter from Moscow to a close friend and fellow Roman, painter Vasily Polenov, contains a colorful description of him: "Mstislav Prakhov is still staying with me; he is walking on clouds, smelling heavenly flowers, and only wears pants because it's cold. Oh, oh, oh, what an idealist, I've never seen anyone like that." Nevertheless, for a railway magnate kept away from Rome and art by mundane business affairs, the idealist's presence was indispensable, as Mamontov himself testified, adding: "Thanks to him I still keep my feelings on a necessary elevated plane, for otherwise I would soon truly become no better than any shopkeeper."[9]

Mstislav Prakhov's aesthetic views can be discerned from a rarely quoted portion of Polenov's well-known letter to Mamontov in which the Roman days are remembered:

> At the time when the aesthetic was thrown out of art, and the doctrine of tendency was established in its place, [Mstislav Prakhov], in his naïve idealism, had the courage to swim against the current and quietly but firmly assert the aesthetic as a necessity to human beings, not only to potential artists, but as one of the most essential foundations of human existence.[10]

The "tendency" mentioned by Polenov refers to the so-called tendentious art of the 1860s: art with a social function, the art of truth, not of beauty. Both Prakhov and Mamontov, according to their friend, followed a different ideology—the ideology of the aesthetes whom Savva had heard Dobrolyubov ridicule while at Moscow University. Mamontov's interest in aestheticism, perhaps sparked initially by reading Dostoevsky and Apollon Grigoriev, was undoubtedly fueled by his relationship with his Roman friends, and by the early 1870s had formed the foundation of his personal aesthetic views. From now on, quoting Soviet musicologist Abram Gozenpud, "he sought not so much truth, but rather beauty in art."[11]

Despite frequently being accused of Mstislav Prakhov–like idealism by friends, critics, and researchers,[12] Mamontov, a student of Chizhov, always exhibited a very practical, hands-on approach to art. An artist, not a philosopher by nature, he was rarely satisfied with mere rhetoric and understood his new aesthetic creed not as an abstract fantasy, but as a call to action. According to Polenov, Mamontov "grabbed on" to the Romans' aesthetic ideals, which he understood "not theoretically, but with the senses," and immediately began to put them into practice.[13] In the spring of 1870, Mamontov purchased a country estate, Abramtsevo, near Moscow—a former family nest of the Aksakov family he knew since childhood. At Abramtsevo, he succeeded in creating his own artist colony—a Mecca for painters, sculptors, musicians, literati, and other intellectuals. With Mamontov and his Roman friends as the founding members, this informal group became known as the Mamontov Circle. It organized a variety of artistic activities, from painting sessions and architectural projects to collective readings and amateur theatricals (these will be discussed in detail later in the book). Finally, in 1885, the circle branched out, actively participating in Mamontov's new venture, the Moscow Private Opera.

The company became Mamontov's favorite child, for as both director and patron he was finally in a position to project his aesthetic views directly to his audience. Until recently, research published both in Russia and elsewhere has offered, alternatively, realism[14] and nationalism[15] as the core of Mamontov's aesthetics that was to be implemented at the new theater. However, as we have seen, the sources for these labels are the divergent yet equally one-dimensional views of Mamontov propagated by his detractors, apologists, competitors, and, most unfortunately, scholars who, perhaps with the best of intentions, painstakingly constructed alternative histories of Mamontov's enterprise molded to their personal notions of progress. What dooms these accounts is their insistence on ideological uniformity: the real Mamontov was much too complex to be labeled; his aesthetic views were unsystematic, fluid, and full of contradictions. Selective reading of the primary sources that supported earlier studies cannot therefore do justice to his often frustratingly inconsistent yet remarkable aesthetic vision that laid the foundation for the MPO. Viewed for the first time in their entirety, these still largely unpublished materials form the basis for the following discussion.

## MAMONTOV'S AESTHETIC PLATFORM

Savva Mamontov's colorful personality creates an obvious impediment to any attempt to reconstruct his theoretical views and outline his aesthetic platform. Mamontov was not an abstract thinker. He conceived but never wrote a treatise on his aesthetic views and teaching methodology (his "school," as he called it); his literary style, while often lofty, is rarely sophisticated. An infinitely practical man, he despised empty rhetoric, saying: "I passionately love art, consider it a great gift from God, and hate it when there is empty *talk* . . . around it—all this seems so trifling to me; in a word, unworthy."[16]

At the same time, he was also a teacher. "You look upon any young artist employed at the Private Opera as your student," wrote an alumnus of Mamontov's "school," gifted stage director Pyotr Melnikov (1870–1940). "I also came to the troupe as such a student, and for this I am deeply and sincerely grateful to you."[17] The warmth of this remark is characteristic of the extraordinary level of adoration Mamontov inspired in his students. "Great teacher," "master," "prophet in art" are only a few of the many epithets peppering their letters, as well as the letters from people who never actually worked for Mamontov (some had never even met him), but considered his aesthetic principles a foundation for their own work. Typical is this telegram to Mamontov in commemoration of the twenty-fifth anniversary of his company, an event widely celebrated in Moscow. Its author, the great stage director and the collaborator of Diaghilev and Stanislavsky Alexander Sanin, enjoyed free access to the MPO performances and rehearsals early in his career as a beneficiary of an open-door policy Mamontov had instituted for his friends, colleagues, and talented protégés: "Today the brightest thoughts, the most precious tender feelings go to you, dear splendid artist, teacher, to your inspirational creative genius, to its mighty power, breadth, and eternal youth. [I] venerate, love, remember, thank [you], bow down low."[18]

The role of the MPO as a studio theater—a "school for Russian operatic forces"[19] with an expressed goal of employment and training of singers, directors, and designers—will be explored in detail in chapter 8. But some of the basic premises of Mamontov's aesthetic "curriculum" need to be examined here, as they vividly illustrate his own views. To start with, he considered the intellectual and aesthetic development of opera singers to be an essential part of their training, and believed that the educational establishment failed in its responsibility to the younger generation:

> Not everyone will understand what I with deep conviction say about art, and the majority (God forgive them!) will even brush it aside. . . . It doesn't matter to me, but it matters to the young—they will suffer and will be thrown back into the same soup; that means that another generation could be lost. . . . Large institutions (conservatories, art schools) are stuck in the same routine, and there is no one to awaken the consciousness of the young and their love for pure art (turn around—tremble—the Safon-

ovs rule!).[20] But it is necessary to hammer and break through the crust tirelessly and persistently—this is a sacred duty for the people warmed by the heat and illuminated by the divine light of art.[21]

Believing himself responsible for the minds and souls of his students, Mamontov saw it as his "sacred duty" to speak to them at length on the subject of aesthetics. Fortunately for us, when he could not do so in person, he maintained diligent correspondence. His aesthetic views can therefore be discerned from these written conversations with students (mostly singers and stage directors) and associates (composers, designers, the company's repertoire advisor Semyon Kruglikov, and other close allies). Most of these letters are still unpublished. This is understandable: few of Mamontov's correspondents are giants of Russian cultural history who received attention in separate studies (indeed, even his own position as such is still a matter of debate). What is most fascinating about these neglected epistolary treasures, however, is the amount of attention paid by Mamontov and his students to their company's aesthetics and its artistic mission. In addition, the letters do not read as official business transactions between an employer and his employees: the correspondents share a common set of references, terminology, and favorite colloquialisms, demonstrating an intimate tone of confidence and friendship. A fragment from Pyotr Melnikov's letter shows how much value Mamontov's students placed on these exchanges: "I value your letters very much, and preserve them carefully. In them you are the person whom I and many others love, and who is not known nor even suspected not only by the masses, but also by the majority of the people interested in art and theater."[22]

There are elements of patronizing, fatherly didactics, and pep-talk in Mamontov's letters, especially when circumstances prevented him from directly participating in the staging of an important production. "Arise, fire up, get up and *show* everyone that in both of you there is a sacred fire that I have noticed! . . . [Show] that my school brings life to art,"[23] he urged the singers for one such production, adding in another letter: "I trust your word that you would stand up for the Private Opera and for my principles."[24] According to the memoirs of Mamontov's students, he steadfastly went about instilling in them his artistic philosophy (what he referred to as his "school" or his "principles") from their first day with the company.[25] Naturally, aesthetic issues often constitute a subject of their letters to him. It is logical to assume that it would be in the young singers' best interests to tell their mentor (and, we need not forget, their employer) exactly what he wanted to hear—that is, to express his own aesthetic views in the language that he would use, and in the wording pleasing to him. Consequently, whether or not we could prove that the views expressed in the letters of Mamontov's students are indeed what they truly believed, we can in fact define their teacher's aesthetic platform as it was reflected through their eyes.

We should also expect a large chasm between the beautiful rhetoric of the letters and the reality of what was practically implemented in the daily operations of a market enterprise struggling to reconcile its ideology with its business interests. This discrepancy will be a subject of a detailed investigation in chapter 7. The following section exclusively treats Mamontov's aesthetic theories, set in the context of the continuing struggle between realism and modernism on the Russian operatic stage of the early Silver Age.

### THE "CAUSE" AND THE MISSION

As we know, from the late 1860s the Russian intelligentsia saw realist truth as the primary aesthetic trend of their time, its ideological mainstream: Musorgsky would not be alone in calling it "the true mission of an artist."[26] Mamontov's correspondence reveals that he and his troupe also believed that they had a mission. It is represented in their common vocabulary by the word *delo*—a word with a double meaning in the Russian language, translated alternatively as "business enterprise" (for example, *otkryt svoyo delo*—"to start one's own business"), or as "mission" or "cause" (for instance, *delo zhizni*—"a life's mission"). In the former meaning, the MPO was itself a *delo*, that is, an enterprise. In the latter, the word figures prominently, for example, in Russian political phraseology, as in a popular slogan: *nashe delo pravoe, my pobedim* [our cause is just, we shall be victorious]. Savva Mamontov and his students used the word frequently as a part of a phrase, *delo iskusstva* [the cause of art], as in the following excerpt from Mamontov's letter to César Cui: "I believe that I can take from you much that would help me intellectually to move the cause of art that is the joy of my life."[27] They also liked to play on the double meaning of *delo* in their letters, using the word for "business enterprise" in a sense of an ideological cause, or mission of that enterprise. Their correspondence is full of references to "our cause," "our common cause," "our dear cause," and "our beloved cause." Here is an excerpt from a congratulatory note by Melnikov writing from Paris on the occasion of Easter and the company's recent triumphs:

> I rejoice with all my heart in the success of the cause, the great cause that you have, with God's help, begun so successfully. As one of the good wishes for the holidays let me wish for the least amount of dirt and mundane sleet to stick to this radiant cause, and that nothing should dull your eternal, powerful energy and good will to serve the beloved cause.[28]

Love and work for the cause was Mamontov's daily charge to his troupe. To one of his most loyal disciples, singer and stage director Vasily Shkafer (1867–1937), whom we shall meet often on the following pages, he wrote: "I rejoice with all my heart that you are working hard—be happy in it, for this is necessary for the pure and noble cause. . . . Love art, work sincerely for its cause, spit in the face of banality and gossip . . . cause, cause, and cause."[29] The students, in turn, pledged their lives to the cause. For some of them, that cause was the company itself—its continued survival, its success, and their own daily work as part of it (indeed, the word *delo* may also be translated as "work").[30] More sophisticated minds such as Shkafer's, however, were better able to articulate the meaning of *delo* as the aesthetic platform implemented by the MPO, as its own "true mission" in Musorgsky's words. "My whole soul will belong to the cause, to the artistic objectives that you have placed at the foundation of this wonderful company," Shkafer wrote to Mamontov at the very beginning of their collaboration.[31] A year later, he added: "Our common cause, our task has become so close and dear to me that I see meaning, goal, and purpose in human life; I believe that staged art is not an idle man's folly, and that our work is a true cause, a serious task with a great future."[32]

Mamontov and his associates took a strongly idealistic approach to their cause. For instance, their service to it was supposed to be anonymous: quest for personal glory was to be avoided and despised. Mamontov himself led the way by adamantly refusing to publicize his association with the company (one of the worst-kept secrets in Moscow's artistic circles, as his trial would reveal),[33] and publicly admitted his role only years after its demise. Members of the press corps were persuaded to play along, and would typically discuss Mamontov's involvement without mentioning his name.[34] He gave no signed interviews about the upcoming productions, nor did he allow his artistic contribution to be acknowledged on playbills (with a single notable exception, to be discussed below). Indeed, the MPO's "official" figureheads were his associates, company administrators Nikolai Krotkov and Claudia Winter: in its early years, the company was known as Krotkov's Private Opera (1885–92), later as Winter's Private Opera (1896–1900). According to a company insider, painter and architect Ilya Bondarenko (1870–1946),

> Mamontov did not like to advertise his name. There was this story: after a brilliant, spectacular performance of *Sadko* the audience shouted: "Mamontov! Mamontov!" Savva Ivanovich left the theater . . . Sitting always in the director's box on the left, he was always afraid that someone would call: "Mamontov," and then he would tell me: "Let's go home."[35]

Apart from being anonymous, service to the cause of art was to be an altruistic endeavor: while commercial success was sought as a measure of access and prestige (see chapter 7), financial viability was sacrificed, if need be, to artistic interest: as we shall discover, some of Mamontov's most important productions, such as Gluck's *Orfeo*, brought little into the coffers.

From the first days of the Moscow Private Opera through the present day, both Mamontov's apologists and his detractors claimed to have discovered the ideological principles of his enterprise. Their assessments have been known to contradict each other, and have not always aligned with the reality of their protagonist's creative endeavors. For a clearer view of Mamontov's ideology, I suggest tapping into a somewhat obscure source that might perhaps come closest to the truth. It is a series of "program letters" by Vasily Shkafer who, inspired by his mentor's idealism, set out to outline the company's aesthetic platform in writing. A representative excerpt follows:

> Life, light, and warmth must reign in a theater of true creativity. It is not an opera-selling venture, where artisans entertain and amuse an idle crowd of their peers for a set fee. Here, *something sublime* takes place; with its help, a man may know the great truth of life, and know himself

... We must be proud that in our humble lot we have the joy to demonstrate that a Russian opera theater is no variety show, that it lives by the pure ideals of art and rejoices in everything that serves the high ideals of creativity.[36]

The creative atmosphere of the MPO that was highlighted so poetically in Shkafer's letter differed from both the business-like management of other commercial opera companies and the suffocating bureaucratic straitjacket of the Imperial stage.[37] Shkafer was well acquainted with the former, after working for several provincial enterprises; in another "program letter," he wrote:

Our theater of the Russian Private Opera is given a huge, great task, and we, the young actors, the workers of this stage, must come together into an unbreakable unity, so that with a common effort we can clean up the atmosphere of the old circus theater where art is for sale, and where there is nothing but crudeness, lies, and falsehood.[38]

After experiencing the Mariinsky stage—with its excellent singers, chorus, and orchestra undoubtedly the brightest jewel in the Imperial crown—Feodor Chaliapin in his memoir compared it to Mamontov's company as the "luxurious sarcophagus" to the "lovely green field full of simple fragrant flowers."[39] Another peculiarity of the MPO was, of course, its pedagogical aspect. As Shkafer pointed out, "the theater of the Russian Private Opera is an exceptional institution—a kind of academy, with its own rules and regulations."[40]

## THE PURE ART OF THE MPO

Clearly, Mamontov and his "academy" of idealists shared a common cause, a mission. A number of Soviet scholars have claimed that this mission was aligned with the aesthetics of truth—the realist cause of the 1860s. Yet, while the realists believed that art must awaken people to the horror and ugliness of everyday life in order to shock them into action, Mamontov did not accept the social function of art, at least not in a traditional sense. "There is no need to make people face *the difficult, the desolate, the depressing*. Life itself will make sure to offer each his share of terror and decay," he wrote to his cousin and younger colleague, Konstantin Stanislavsky,[41] adding: "there is only one consolation—live in art; . . . *seek beauty and joy*—there lies all the happiness of our lives."[42] By thus contrasting the joy and beauty of art to the depressing truth of life, Mamontov positioned himself against the realist current, echoing instead the escapist philosophy of the Silver Age. Indeed, we might wonder whether symbolist philosophy and literature of the early 1900s influenced his letter, dated 1908. To place Mamontov's aesthetics within the framework of the developing ideology of the decadents described in chapter 1, it will be helpful to consider his earlier correspondence.

The first thing we encounter is the motto adopted by Mamontov back in the 1870s and printed on the MPO playbills, programs, and stationery since 1885: *vita brevis, ars longa* [life is brief, art is lasting]. In Russian, the opposition is even more pointed: *zhizn korotka, iskusstvo vechno* [life is short, art is eternal].[43] The idealist in Mamontov led him to teach his students, first and foremost, to love art and to serve it selflessly, with firmness and perseverance, with purity and sincerity. "I demand service to art that I myself serve with an open heart," he declared.[44] In a note to Stanislavsky after the triumphant opening night of the Moscow Art Theater, an institution almost as indebted to Mamontov's aesthetics as the Moscow Private Opera, Mamontov wrote: "Warmly and sincerely happy about last night's success; I firmly believe that the cause into which one puts one's soul and love cannot help but bring a positive result. One needs serenity, strength, and perseverance. A bureaucrat, able beyond reproach, remains dry and formalist; art permits neither. It needs to be loved."[45] Mamontov's students got the message and sometimes remembered it, at least in their rhetoric, long after their mentor stopped paying their salaries. As late as 1910 Vasily Shkafer, about to accept a prestigious appointment as the chief stage director of the Bolshoi Theater, wrote to Mamontov the following:

> My soul is pure before you, my spiritual father who has been and remains in my artistic life the carrier of the high ideals of art. Your precepts are sacred to me, and in my further artistic career I will strive honestly and firmly to stay on the straight path of serving the beautiful.[46]

The ideals of loving and serving art would, of course, remain mere words unless based on what Mamontov called "artistic taste"—knowledge, understanding, and appreciation of art. According to Bondarenko's memoir,

[Mamontov's] deeply artistic nature, sensitive to aesthetic representations, understood art as an essential element of culture. It is no wonder that he . . . wrote into my album: "A man who understands art may consider himself happy."[47]

Mamontov insisted that his students read; that they attend theater, lectures, concerts, and exhibitions of contemporary art. He served enthusiastically as their personal guide through art galleries, and talked constantly about artistic matters.[48] Melnikov recalled:

> In the company of Savva Ivanovich, in daily conversations with him that circled constantly around art (he even wrote a play about it once, titled *Okolo Iskusstva* [*Around Art*]), theater, music, singing, opera, painting, and sculpture, all of us, without noticing it, learned a lot and got a real education.[49]

Young singers, enthralled by their mentor's charismatic personality, listened, memorized, and swore by his opinions. To quote his highly emotional protégé, soprano Alevtina Paskhalova:

> You are the teacher in art, I have always known it and still do, and you also know how highly I value your opinion . . . May God give you good health and joy, and to spend summer well, so later, with fresh strength, you may continue teaching us about art and understanding its beauty. You are its true and, one may say, its only servant.[50]

Years later, Stanislavsky—never an employee but evidently a self-professed student—invited Mamontov to the dress rehearsal of one of the Moscow Art Theater's signature productions, Maurice Maeterlinck's *L'Oiseau bleu*. In an oft-cited but rarely interpreted note, he wrote: "I would like very much to see you at the theater tomorrow, as my teacher of aesthetics."[51]

So what was Mamontov's aesthetic creed, never published as a philosophical treatise but gradually formulated in his correspondence and daily conversations with an adoring circle of young disciples? After all, the precept "to love, understand, and serve art" is merely a pretty platitude that could be applied to the realists of the 1860s just as easily as to the decadents of the 1890s. Unlike the realists, however, Mamontov clearly equated art with beauty, rather than with truth: "serving art" meant, in Shkafer's words, *sluzhenie prekrasnomu* [serving the beautiful]. It is possible that Shkafer's words were his own: in both letters and published memoirs, he demonstrated a rather sophisticated personal philosophy, although it was, by his own admission, strongly influenced by Mamontov. Let us look, therefore, to another piece of correspondence: a brief, little-known telegram from Alevtina Paskhalova on the occasion of Mamontov's name day; that is, a kind of a birthday card. It reads: "Congratulations on your saint's day. [I] wish you many years of good health. Let your motto 'art for art's sake' be preserved for a long time, along with your precept, 'serving beauty.' [Your] grateful, sincerely devoted Paskhalova."[52] What is most remarkable about this telegram is the identity of its sender. Not a poet, a philosopher, an art historian, or even an erudite stage director like Shkafer, Paskhalova was a young girl who came from the provincial town of Saratov to study singing at the Moscow Conservatory. According to her memoirs, she knew no one remotely artistic in Moscow prior to meeting Mamontov in 1894 and singing Zerlina in his home production of *Don Giovanni*.[53] She was unsophisticated and seems not to have done much reading. Her vocabulary, syntax, and grammar leave much to be desired (in fact, I had to make corrections for the telegram to be intelligible). Consequently, there is little probability of her coming up with the motto *iskusstvo dlya iskusstva* [art for art's sake] on her own, or even picking it up from the symbolist literature of the day. Paskhalova's letters to Mamontov suggest an intimate friendship with her teacher, a kind of father-daughter relationship—a relationship that Mamontov seems to have encouraged. When writing to her, he used second person singular, rather than plural, with no patronymic; even his closest associates, Melnikov and Shkafer, were not addressed that way. She often signed her letters "your Sparrow," a nickname invented for her by Mamontov and known to few in the troupe. Paskhalova comes across as enthusiastic, eager, and probably infatuated with her mentor. It would seem only natural that she should memorize his favorite sayings ("your" motto and precept, she says) and repeat them word for word, revealing to us her teacher's aesthetic philosophy in his own language.

Thus, instead of "art as a representation of reality" (a realist motto), Mamontov preferred "art for art's sake" as his own. As we have seen, he was not unique in adhering to that principle: in the 1890s the demand for the autonomy of art expressed in Valery Bryusov's writings, as well as in Sergei Diaghilev's "Complex Questions," became the foundation for the emerging Silver Age philosophy. It is revealing that the motto of the Mir Iskusstva group formulated by Alexandre Benois—*svobodno iskusstvo, skovana zhizn* [art is free, life is fettered]—is not that far removed from Mamontov's "life is short, art is eternal." And while Benois himself, as we shall see, would not be thrilled by his association with Mamontov, his friend and colleague Diaghilev, who had recognized their shared aesthetic values, welcomed the collaboration, the sources and consequences of which will be explored later in this book.

## MAMONTOV AND ANTIQUITY: *ORFEO*

An aspect of Mamontov's artistic philosophy that perhaps separates him the most from the realists, placing him instead at the cutting edge of evolving modernist aesthetics, was his obsession with classical antiquity, particularly Greek mythology. For Mamontov, as for the decadents, idealized images of the ancient world were symbols of pure, eternal beauty—the essence of art. He was an expert on ancient art[54] and evidently an avid collector: according to *Russkoe Slovo,* one of the rooms of his Moscow mansion was decorated and furnished in the style of Pompeii, complete with authentic artifacts.[55] True to his practical approach to his own idealist philosophy, Mamontov was involved in at least four projects with a Hellenic theme, all of them in collaboration with his closest friend Vasily Polenov, a painter who specialized in mythological, Biblical, and historical subjects.

The first such project was a dramatic tableau vivant, *Afrodita [Aphrodite]*, produced for the All-Russian Congress of Artists that took place in Moscow in 1894, and that Mamontov co-chaired. The opening tableau in a series titled "The Ages of Art," *Aphrodite* boasted an elaborate stage set, with costumes and music by Polenov, and featured Stanislavsky as a Greek sculptor who recited a poem written by Mamontov; the latter also directed. The main theme was appropriate: "The ages will pass, devastating storms will fall upon the future generations, but the beauty of Aphrodite['s statue] will endure forever."[56] The second Hellenic collaboration between Mamontov and Polenov was the 1897 MPO production of Gluck's *Orfeo.* The first two acts of Nikolai Krotkov's opera *Ozherele [The Necklace]* staged in December 1899 (see chapter 4) were also set in Ancient Greece (that is, the Greek colonies in Southern Italy during the

Hellenistic period). Finally, in 1905 Mamontov and Polenov embarked upon *Prizraki Ellady* [*The Phantoms of Hellas*][57]—an opera both composed and designed by Polenov to a text by Savva Mamontov and his son Sergei, a minor symbolist poet and dramatist. While the score of this work did not survive, it is known to have been completed in 1907, to be produced and published by Mamontov soon afterward.[58] There is also a record of its being performed in 1924.[59] Archival materials suggest the existence of at least two more incomplete projects with an Ancient Greek theme in which Mamontov was involved around the turn of the century, with various collaborators.

The most significant of Mamontov's Hellenic projects was, undoubtedly, *Orfeo*—a production viewed by a number of scholars as a *chose manquée*. There are valid reasons for such an assessment: *Orfeo* never generated much success; in fact, it mostly played to an empty house. In addition, the lead singer—Mamontov's protégé, mezzo-soprano Maria Chernenko—was sharply criticized in the press for the deficiencies in her vocal production and inability to use her naturally strong voice. More detrimental to *Orfeo*'s reputation among scholars, however, was its supposed ideological incongruity within the constructed histories of Mamontov's aesthetics. For instance, as the production has no connections to the ubiquitous Russian nationalism, it lacks interest for Grover, whose work ignores Mamontov's Western influences. Rossikhina dedicates a whole chapter of her book to *Orfeo*, but only to document the opera's misfortunes without any attempt at reconstructing its aesthetic *raison d'être*. Her rationale is equally clear: the main premise of her monograph is the triumph of realism on the Russian operatic stage, which again makes *Orfeo* irrelevant. Even Gozenpud, generally the most tolerant of the Soviet scholars to Mamontov's decadent leanings, believed that *Orfeo* "did not coincide with the *magistralnaya liniya* [main trajectory] of the Private Opera's development."[60] He did, however, acknowledge the significance of this production as a reflection of Mamontov's aesthetic views, the fact that makes its analysis indispensable to the present discussion.

Indeed, *Orfeo* was one of Mamontov's favorite creations. It was his only signed work throughout his association with the company: for the first and only time, he allowed his name to be acknowledged on programs and playbills as a codirector of a production, sharing credit with

Polenov. Mamontov incurred a great financial loss in order to stage the opera and keep it onstage. Despite its lack of financial success or— initially—critical acclaim, he was proud of the production and considered it his personal aesthetic creed or, in his own words, an attempt "to teach the Moscow public a lesson in aesthetics."[61] Among Mamontov's associates, there was no unanimous support. Polenov, after complaining about the production's lack of polish at the dress rehearsal and lobbying Mamontov in vain to replace Chernenko as the lead, actually boycotted the premiere.[62] Shkafer, meanwhile, was predictably ecstatic:

> [An *Orfeo* audience member] probably felt himself imperceptibly flying away from that gray, mundane, banal life to some other world, the world of wondrous dreams, and [his] eyes shed a tear of joy and exaltation that seized [his] heart. Crudeness and harshness involuntarily disappeared in such moments, the heart wanted love, caresses, *forgiveness.* The best, the loftiest feelings of man won over the animal, and he was close to the ideal created by God. This is the main goal and purpose of theater.[63]

The supporters hoped that St. Petersburg would be kinder to *Orfeo* than its hometown of Moscow, which, despite Shkafer's rapture, was left cold by it. They were right, as Melnikov testified:

> I was sure that St. Petersburg would appreciate the stylishness of your production, that bright talent penetrating the whole performance of the opera, filling every movement of the characters on stage—in a word, all that covers the impression of the whole production with a beautiful mist, and makes one think that one did not spend time in a theater, but simply saw a divine ancient dream, undisturbed even for a minute by crude reality.[64]

It is understandable that Mamontov's *Orfeo* might prove puzzling to a Soviet scholar like Rossikhina. Both the subject matter and the ideology of this "divine ancient dream, undisturbed even for a minute by crude reality" are completely alien to the realist mentality of the 1860s. And, apparently, of the 1890s, as the following outburst from Vladimir Stasov demonstrates:

> Five years ago, in 1893, I. E. Repin started his sermon on "art for art's sake," and his persecution of "topic" and "content" in painting. This interesting doctrine had its followers. Perhaps, some of those gentlemen began to follow that cult independently of Repin; perhaps, in the hearts of some

of them there already lived the sprouts of sweet passion for "thoughtless-ness" and "meaninglessness," for lack of subject and lack of substance—perhaps! Perhaps, they were all born as those "Hellenes," those classical Greeks from the times before Christ's birth, so that the only thing in the world that exists for them is "beauty," and they could not care less about anything else![65]

This article by Stasov was published on 24 February 1898—two days after the MPO began its first tour of his native city of St. Petersburg. Gluck's *Orfeo* was featured prominently on its playbill. As we shall see, Stasov loved Mamontov's work, although he completely misread some of its ideological foundations. He wrote several articles in support of the company; none mentioned the existence of *Orfeo*.

Stasov was always known for his astuteness: he knew his ideological opponents and wrote scathing critiques of the events and aesthetic currents that were sufficiently noticeable to cause him concern. From the quotation above, it is evident that he recognized the fact that classical antiquity was becoming an increasingly popular subject as the new century approached. Prominent in the works of the French symbolists, it was now appearing in Russian literature, visual arts, theater, and music, and not only by those authors whom Stasov could easily dismiss as inconsequential young decadents. To cite just a few examples from the operatic world, Sergei Taneev's *Oresteia,* based on a play by Aeschylus, dates from 1895, while Rimsky-Korsakov's *Servilia,* on an Ancient Roman subject, was written in 1901. Even Rimsky's 1896 masterpiece *Sadko,* despite the Russianness of its subject, was portrayed by its contemporary press as a revival of an ancient Slavic myth: "I felt as if I was transported into the ancient times of Perun and Dazhdbog, and spent several hours living in that epoch. . . . A deep love for antiquity is very much felt throughout the entire opera."[66] It appears that the success of *Orfeo* in St. Petersburg (*pace* Stasov) may be partially explained by the fact that the symbolists fascinated with antiquity had a stronger power base in the northern capital than in Moscow. The idealism and escapism of Hellas appealed, for instance, to the members of the Mir Iskusstva group, for whom the myths of Ancient Greece would become a favored theme of easel paintings and theatrical projects.[67] Furthermore, St. Petersburg symbolists were strongly influenced by the ideas on ancient drama discussed in Friedrich Nietzsche's cult opus, *Die Geburt der Tragödie.* Nietzsche's description of the eternal struggle between Apollo and Dionysus, his ideas of a synthesis of the arts, his interpretation of Wagner's music dramas, and his vision of the communal art of the future that would resurrect the spirit of ancient tragedy by merging artists with their audience appealed to many Silver Age poets, writers, and philosophers. Symbolist writings are filled with references to antiquity: a 1908 essay by poet Andrei Bely titled "Teatr i Sovremennaya Drama" ["Theater and Modern Drama"], with its numerous references to Greek tragedy (in a Nietzschean interpretation), is a good example.[68] As the followers of Solovyov, mystic symbolists such as Bely were particularly engrossed in the subject, as evident also from the works of Vyacheslav Ivanov, who wrote several scholarly treatises and numerous articles on the subject of Dionysism.[69] The potency of the Orphic myth to the mystic symbolists, who regarded it as a symbol of the eternal power of beauty, art, and music, is difficult to overestimate. Indeed, in Vladimir Solovyov's well-known poem *Tri Podviga* [*Three Heroic Deeds*], the highest form of heroism is that of Orpheus, who leads Eurydice, a symbol of beauty, out of Hades. In 1912, Vyacheslav Ivanov, a Solovyov disciple, wrote a preface to a series of books on mysticism published by *Musaget;* the series was entitled *Orfei* [*Orpheus*].[70] It is a remarkable illustration of Savva Mamontov's sensitivity to the issues and subject matters most significant to the history of Russian symbolism that, while he certainly cannot be counted among Vyacheslav Ivanov's mentors or acolytes, he did choose the myth of Orpheus as his personal aesthetic statement.

## MAMONTOV AND REALISM: *BORIS GODUNOV*

As we have seen, Vladimir Stasov, that scourge of Hellenism, did not find Mamontov's production of *Orfeo* particularly inspiring and, master of the ideological narrative that he was, he conveniently neglected to acknowledge its existence. Instead, he publicly exalted the feature of the MPO playbill that most endeared the company to him, despite its leader's questionable leanings. That feature was the prevalence in the repertory of Kuchkist historical dramas, still commonly viewed as the essence of operatic realism. The productions of Rimsky-Korsakov's *The Maid of Pskov*, Musorgsky's *Khovanshchina* and *Boris Godunov*, Borodin's *Prince Igor*, even Alexander Serov's *Rogneda* and Tchaikovsky's *The Oprichnik*

(Stasov's ideological quarrels with their authors notwithstanding) all provided stimulation for his essays. Years later, the same productions also laid the foundation for Rossikhina's study that cast Mamontov in a leading role as the realist standard-bearer of Russian theater.

The dominance of Kuchkist operas in Mamontov's repertoire is undeniable. And while, as we shall see in chapter 7, it can partially be explained by the pressures of the commercial marketplace, it is equally undeniable that Mamontov liked many of the Kuchkist works he staged and willingly invested his energy and artistry in creating the innovative productions Stasov so enjoyed. At the Moscow Private Opera, as in the larger cultural universe it inhabited, realism coexisted with emerging modernism—uneasily, perhaps, but for the most part peacefully. Yet it is characteristic of Mamontov's personal aesthetics that whenever a conflict arose between the two ideologies in a production that he staged, truth would always defer to beauty—a principle amply demonstrated by the production history of *Boris Godunov*.

Soon after the MPO premiere of Musorgsky's masterpiece on 7 December 1898, Mamontov wrote a letter to Rimsky-Korsakov, who had authored the new edition of the score. This well-known and much interpreted document, first published in Andrei Rimsky-Korsakov's five-volume biography of his father, focused specifically on the penultimate tableau of *Boris Godunov*, the scene near Kromy. Mamontov wrote:

> [The Kromy scene] made a grave impression upon me during the dress rehearsal. One must be fair to Mr. Lentovsky, who directed the staging. He made the scene of the rowdy mob disgustingly realistic. There were axes; stakes; crude disheveled peasants tearing [the boyar] Khrushchev's coat to pieces; screaming females. . . . I decidedly protested and demanded that this scene be cut altogether.[71]

Since the Kromy scene, a depiction of a popular uprising, has been viewed as the ideological center of the opera by Soviet musicologists, Mamontov's reputation was in serious trouble. Several scholars chastised him for misunderstanding Musorgsky's realist *chef-d'oeuvre* and underestimating the ideological significance of the scene.[72] Meanwhile, Abram Gozenpud defended Mamontov from being branded a decadent reactionary by citing the naturalist staging of assistant stage director Mikhail Lentovsky (1843–1906) as the main cause of the conflict.[73] By so doing, the researcher aimed to reposition the argument about the controversial letter and portray its author as a defender of true, "progressive" realism against the decadent excesses of "pathological naturalism," thus minimizing the damage the document had done to his legacy.[74]

At first glance, Gozenpud's theory seems plausible. The extremes of naturalism—a fashionable trend in turn-of-the-century drama theater that was gradually making its way onto the operatic stage—often provoked Mamontov's harsh criticism for their lack of beauty and artistry. His attitude is revealed in a number of public comments made in the late 1900s and 1910s about new operatic productions by the naturalist stage directors Nikolai Arbatov at the Solodovnikov Theater, Konstantin Mardzhanov at the Svobodnyi Theater and, to Mamontov's dismay, MPO alumnus Pyotr Olenin (see plate 26) at Zimin's Private Opera. In his review of Mardzhanov's 1908 production of Musorgsky's *Sorochintsy Fair*, which featured live farm animals, Mamontov protested such excessive verisimilitude as unnecessary, anti-artistic, and even "educationally harmful"—that is, sending to the audience the wrong message of truth, instead of beauty.[75] Five years later, after sitting through Mardzhanov's bedroom-centered *Belle Hélène*, he expressed horror at its "creativity founded on cynicism," concluding: "Clearly, these people have no understanding of staged art."[76]

As these outbursts demonstrate, Mamontov had a problem with stage naturalism, believing that it violated the code of beauty. However, Gozenpud's portrayal of realism and naturalism as two contradictory and opposing aesthetic forces—one progressive, the other decadent—does not align with Mamontov's views. To him, naturalism was merely a stronger form of realism. Indeed, that is how the movement was perceived by the critics and aestheticians of the time, both inside and outside Russia. *Boris Godunov* was staged as a realist drama. As we shall see in chapter 5, Feodor Chaliapin in the title role created a masterpiece of psychological characterization with Mamontov's knowledge, guidance, and support. If the problem Mamontov had with the scene near Kromy was limited, as Gozenpud suggested, merely to the degree of naturalism in staging, he could have simply restaged the offending scene—and he initially did. But finally, despite Rimsky-Korsakov's protestations, the Kromy scene was permanently excised from the MPO production of *Boris Godunov*, as is evident from the reviews of the company's 1899 St. Petersburg tour.

It appears that witnessing Lentovsky's overly realistic staging of the scene brought home to Mamontov how significantly his own aesthetic views diverged from what he believed to have been Musorgsky's. Indeed, the unexpected aesthetic "culture shock" could have been the cause of his letter to Rimsky-Korsakov in which, after discussing his Kromy problem, Mamontov went on to focus on the broader issues of realist ideology, both Kuchkist and that of the Wanderers. He wrote:

> All great people make mistakes, hold biases in tribute to their times. Those were the times of emphasizing heavy realism; it was necessary to thrust gaping wounds into one's face, point to rotten foot-wraps, and paint vomiting drunkards. At that time, Repin . . . went to an anatomic theater to watch blood flow in order to portray that horror in his painting of Ivan the Terrible with his murdered son. Thank God, this time is past; art is moving away from the pathological and seeks touching and elevated feelings elsewhere. Grief, suffering, poverty will sooner find empathy in the hearts of the people educated on the basis of sensitive comprehension of beauty . . . than by offending their sense of harmony with the stench of pus and the stale air of a peasant's house overflowing with foul language. Such is my conviction, and I follow it in my work for art.[77]

It is remarkable that Mamontov's squeamishness about the Kromy scene may in fact have aligned with Musorgsky's opinion after all. According to the controversial memoirs of his poet friend, Count Arseny Golenishchev-Kutuzov, the composer was allegedly uneasy about the scene's realistic ugliness and approved, even applauded, conductor Eduard Napravnik's decision to cut it from the opera's Mariinsky Theater premiere.[78] Moreover, in a fascinating twist of fate, Musorgsky's change of heart about the Kromy supposedly resulted from the influence of Golenishchev-Kutuzov's own philosophy of unapologetic aestheticism— the same philosophy that made the poetic count a minor hero of the Silver Age, and that engendered Mamontov's own reaction to the graphic violence of the Kromy.

Mamontov, of course, could not have known about Golenishchev-Kutuzov's memoirs, as the manuscript did not resurface until the 1930s. Instead, he knew and trusted, along with many others, the Stasov-conjured persona of Musorgsky the realist, as ironically Mamontov scholars would later trust their protagonist's realist image that we shall witness Stasov construct with equal determination.[79] Thus unaware of the authorial blessing of his approach to the Kromy scene, Mamontov faced a familiar artistic dilemma that surfaced every time a realist opera was staged by his company. He acknowledged the need to preserve and relate an aesthetic message built by the composer into his work, but at the same time seemed to have been repulsed by that message. Instead, he saw the operatic genre as a beautiful, colorful, indulgent, escapist—in a word, decadent—spectacle, as witnessed particularly by his love of myth and fairy tale, including Rimsky-Korsakov's *Sadko* and *The Snow Maiden,* his favorite opera.

It has frequently been remarked that a rejection of realism by the Silver Age artists led to their enthusiastic embrace of the world of fantasy. Myth and fairy tale were central to the Russian symbolist aesthetic—truly, Calinescu's "aesthetic of imagination." Similarly, to Mamontov and his associates, theater—even when representing history—was primarily a fantasy world. They saw the creation of "the world of wondrous dreams," illusion, and make-believe—"the beautiful mist" of *Orfeo*—as "the main goal and purpose of theater." Theater could also be the world of witty, elegant fun, joyous entertainment: Mamontov's partiality to comic opera and operetta is well documented. Yet, as a wondrous dream or a fun spectacle, it was not to be a faithful mirror of reality. Reality was the everyday, and the everyday meant either ugliness or boredom: "Beware of mediocrity and boredom in the theater," Mamontov wrote to Shkafer, echoing the escapist fantasies of the decadents.[80]

## VISIONS OF ARTISTIC TRUTH

The aesthetic shift from reality to fantasy we have been observing is brought into sharp relief by analyzing the changing meaning of a catchphrase ubiquitous in Russian art criticism during the period in question—*khudozhestvennaya pravda* [artistic truth]. From the 1860s on, it was a beloved slogan of realist critics, used to exalt the art of the Wanderers, the Kuchka, and evidently the MPO. As late as 1897, an unrepentantly Kuchkist MPO supporter described what he perceived to be the company's objectives in the following ecstatic dithyramb: "[Its goal], a declared motto of the Russian School of Dargomyzhsky, is 'artistic truth!' Truth in the text, the music, and the acting; truth in the overall impression created by these elements together; the truth of life;

psychological, quotidian, and historical truth!"[81] Such a hymn to "artistic truth," understood in the realist meaning of the term as "truth in art," would have done Stasov proud back in the 1860s. Thirty years later, however, it must have sounded curiously anachronistic. Indeed, Stasov's comrade-in-arms, the Kuchkist composer and critic César Cui, stated in an 1899 *Novosti Dnya* interview that true realism in opera was impossible due to the nature of the genre, and that he would never strive for it in his own compositions.[82] The catchphrase "artistic truth" was still as popular with the critics in the 1890s as in the 1860s, but the emphasis had shifted overwhelmingly from the veracity to the artistry of representation. Witness, for instance, Shkafer's recollection of the very first MPO production he ever saw—the 1896 revival of *The Snow Maiden:* "A lovely, fragrant, wonderful spring fairy tale was gradually unfolding before my eyes. . . . It was all so poetic, so unexpectedly and deeply touching and exciting. I all but cried out from the wondrously joyful feeling that swept over me. I was in ecstasy! I saw artistic truth on stage."[83] The poetic spectacle Shkafer described was certainly no representation of daily life in a Kuchkist sense: "artistic *truth*" was replaced by "*artistic* truth," in which the beautiful prevailed over the real. Several years later, the great modernist stage director Vsevolod Meyerhold, whom we shall meet frequently on these pages, used the same phrase "artistic truth" when discussing the influence of Feodor Chaliapin, the Mamontov company's brightest star, on his own idea of symbolist theater. He wrote: "In Chaliapin's acting, there is always *truth,* but not the truth of life—a theatrical truth. It is always elevated above life, this somewhat decorated artistic truth."[84]

The reenvisioning of "artistic truth" seems to have begun in the late 1880s. Characteristically, Stasov immediately sensed the new emphasis on artistry in the use of the phrase, and rebelled against what he perceived to be essentially its opposition to the realist vision. Enjoy the following expansive diatribe (italics are added for emphasis):

> I believed that our current aesthetes could surprise me no longer. . . . [Their recent article states:] "Everyone remembers the relatively recent time when so-called realism was the prevailing direction in Russian art. . . . Naked truth—that was the motto of that movement; naked truth in technical devices; that is, in precise representation of reality, in drawing, in composition, in color, without any artifice, without a certain style and

school, without beauty . . . However, the dominance of that school was relatively brief. It soon demonstrated its lack of substance; it contained no seeds of development. The element of realism gradually widened, and *the concept of artistic truth and beauty* entered it. Since then, Russian art has entered upon a new path. . . ." You read this and don't believe your eyes. Has the New School of Painting truly exited the stage; has realism—its main tone and goal—revealed itself to be false and has given way to something else, have "scenes from daily life of the people lost interest in the eyes of a contemporary Russian artist"? No, on the contrary, our realist school is alive and well, it flourishes as well as one could wish.[85]

As we have seen, Mamontov's aesthetic principles, based on "the concept of artistic truth and beauty," were part of a growing ideological current. First noticeable in Russia's cultural landscape in the mid-1880s (the MPO first opened its doors in 1885; the Stasov quotation above is from an 1887 article), it openly challenged the mainstream aesthetics of realism in the 1890s, and by mid-1900s replaced it as a dominant ideology. This new aesthetic, based on the concepts of art for art's sake and transformation of the world through the power of beauty and creativity, became the ideological foundation of the Silver Age. Despite their differences, the early symbolist artists and poets, including those affiliated with Mir Iskusstva and, to a great extent, with its ideological descendant, the Ballets Russes, shared these fundamental beliefs. Savva Mamontov's Moscow Private Opera proved to be a potent force that developed these early modernist ideas and propelled them into the twentieth century.

## MAMONTOV AND MODERNITY

As we have seen, Mamontov's artistic views thus closely paralleled the emerging aesthetics of the Silver Age—amazingly and uniquely so, for a man brought up in the 1860s. The question suggests itself: can we in fact go as far as calling Mamontov a modernist? The answer is difficult and perhaps impossible to provide. Just as the MPO was a place of convergence for the old and the new, Mamontov's philosophy is contradictory, containing elements of both. Still, from the information available to us, his aesthetic views and artistic tastes were most closely aligned with those of the first generation of Russian modernists—the decadent symbolists. Indeed, his cult of beauty and belief in the autonomy of art echo the philosophy of his friend Valery Bryusov. On the other hand, while Mamontov's faith in the transformative power of art mirrors some ideas of the "mystics," overall his views bear little resemblance to the eschatology of Vyacheslav Ivanov.

In the world of visual arts (see chapter 3), Mamontov loved and promoted many early Silver Age trends: the impressionism of Konstantin Korovin and Isaac Levitan (1860–1900), the *style moderne* of Valentin Serov, and the proto-symbolist mysticism of Mikhail Vrubel and Victor Borisov-Musatov (1870–1905). *Golubaya Roza* [the Blue Rose], the first organized group of Russian symbolist painters, initially called itself *Alaya Roza* [the Scarlet Rose] in honor of Savva Mamontov, who had once written a Beauty and the Beast–like fairy tale by that name. The later painterly styles, however, were alien to Mamontov's artistic sensibility: like many representatives of the early, decadent period of the Silver Age, he would never accept the avant-garde.

Similarly, in theater Mamontov was fascinated by the symbolist experiments of Vsevolod Meyerhold and the Moscow Art Theater (see chapter 6). It is hardly a coincidence that Stanislavsky called Mamontov his "teacher of aesthetics" while personally inviting him to a Maeterlinck production. But the more avant-garde theatrical ideas were clearly foreign to Mamontov. For instance, in his opinion, futurist attributes on stage (such as machinery) contradicted the ideals of pure art.[86] In one of his reviews, he wrote: "Of course, it is hard to predict what [Olenin's new production] might look like. But judging by the tendencies displayed in Musorgsky's *Boris* we may expect brave inventiveness and novelty, such as . . . a phonograph, an automobile, some new limericks, and other laughable arguments having little to do with pure art."[87]

Throughout his career as both artist and critic, Mamontov continuously searched for that elusive and precarious balance between reality and dream world. It is revealing that Reed discusses just such an in-between aesthetic position as one of the major characteristics of the "self-consciously transitional" decadent style, an illegitimate offspring of aestheticism and naturalism,[88] while Sarabyanov analyzes it as a feature of the Russian *style moderne*.[89] To Mamontov's great chagrin, some of his contemporaries evidently agreed, gleefully throwing at him the insulting label of "decadent."[90] Yet he certainly deserved that reputation in his role as a theorist of art. And arguably, his choice of art form as its practitioner was equally damning. Indeed, few artistic endeavors at the time could rival the self-consciously passé-ist reputation of opera, with its escapist pageantry, its aristocratic old-world glitter, its seductively bohemian lifestyle, and its fascination with its own glorious history. The only other genre that could match opera's famed degeneracy was ballet—particularly in Russia where it was justifiably viewed as a playground for the rich and decadent. It is a testament to the power of decadent aesthetics in the country that one of its first openly acknowledged modernists, Sergei Diaghilev, chose to make first opera and later ballet his own personal playground.

Both Mamontov and Diaghilev, of course, found the accusations of decadence distasteful and offensive. At the root of their protests, however, was a belief that the term, which to them spelled creative impotence and obsession with the past, was inaccurate and misrepresented their shared aesthetic position. The two would have much preferred being called "modernists," for in their approach to art, their common passion was novelty. Both insisted that art that did not strive for constant development was doomed to stagnation.[91] Like Diaghilev, Mamontov tirelessly searched for the new faces: new performers, new artists, new composers, and new music. "I must search for new . . . operas. But where to find them?" he once exclaimed in desperation.[92] He tirelessly pushed his students to change, to develop, and to perfect their roles. "Talent dies without development. Why would you want to be an artist *near* art?" he wrote to Shkafer and Maria Chernenko.[93] In this respect his most talented student, Chaliapin, was to him a source, early on, of infinite joy, and ultimately of disappointment. "Where is his old desire to work, to perfect himself, to move forward?" Mamontov asked one interviewer.[94] And to another, he stated: "Today, F. I. Chaliapin remains the same wonderful artist and singer, but he no longer exists as a living artistic force. Today he does not strive to move forward, like before."[95]

According to the sources cited by his biographer Mark Kopshitser, to his dying day Mamontov attended every new theatrical production (even those of which he disapproved) and art exhibition, at which his sharp eye, good judgment, and an ability to spot talent remained valuable.[96] His correspondence is full of battle rhetoric: he "fights" for the new, organizes "military assaults" against the establishment, and so on. His students and associates clearly saw his hunger for the modern as an important part of his artistic persona. For instance, Shkafer in his memoirs compared his mentor to another MPO stage director, Mikhail Lentovsky—the same Lentovsky mentioned above in connection with *Boris Godunov*. As Shkafer suggested, the differences in their directing styles were merely a reflection of their divergent aesthetic views, specifically with respect to their approaches to modernity, which in Mamontov's case strongly resemble Diaghilev's: "Mamontov the aesthete greedily grabbed for the 'new,' wished to go forward by whatever means necessary. M[ikhail] V[alentinovich] Lentovsky was filled with the past of the old theater, and he accepted the edgy 'new artistic searches and revelations' with great difficulty."[97] Similarly, in a letter congratulating Mamontov on his name day (the same occasion on which Alevtina Paskhalova sent her telegram), Semyon Kruglikov painted a colorful picture of Mamontov the artist-revolutionary. Like Paskhalova, Kruglikov appears very sincere in his admiration. But even if he was merely trying to please his friend and employer, we may still assume that the language used in his note would have been agreeable to Mamontov and might have even reflected his own vision of himself. Kruglikov wrote:

> Revolution is a horror, but in the best sense of the word it exists in any striving forward, and any champion of progress is, to some extent, a revolutionary. And you are a revolutionary, and what a revolutionary! One of the most insistent and impatient ones: you forever strive for the new and new shores, whatever obstacles appear on your way. . . . You are an enemy of conservative mold and conservatory stagnation; you are an innovator by your very nature, your intellectual outlook, and your artistic impulses. The French revolutionaries used to sing "Ça ira." But it is not enough for you to see that something you wish for, at some later time *will go forward.* You demand it now, this minute; you are only happy when it is already *going forward,* and your song is "Ça va." Apparently, that's why you are [called] Savva.[98]

In light of Mamontov's love of modernity, and his and Diaghilev's shared passion for decadent staged art forms, it may appear strange that Mamontov chose to employ his talents in the service of opera—a genre that few believed had a future—while ignoring ballet, which Diaghilev embraced and made into a staple of the early-twentieth-century modernist repertoire. Of course, Mamontov's personal abilities and predilections would partially explain that: a trained *bel canto* singer and actor, he was certainly no classical dancer. He did incorporate some relatively untraditional choreography into his productions (for example, in tableau 6 of *Sadko*). His interest in stage movement was profound and paralleled early Ballets Russes experiments; it will be the subject of a separate discussion in chapter 4. However, he apparently did not see the independent genre of ballet as suitable for implementing his artistic ideals, believing it somewhat empty and shallow, devoid of serious meaning. As he commented in 1904,

> To feed the public cute, varicolored little ballets does not achieve the goal. A trifle remains a trifle, however prettily colored. Give me classical operas, produced and performed with strict artistry, that make me tremble with awe; give me stylish, happy, brightly and energetically performed comic operas, without the luxuries but with artistic meaning and brilliance—I will take off my hat and bow low.[99]

Mamontov's statement predates the first productions of the Ballets Russes. At age sixty-eight in 1909, he would have been too frail to travel to Paris to see it perform. It is hard to predict whether or not Mamontov would have considered Diaghilev's productions ideologically shallow (undoubtedly, some of them would have attracted his criticism). But it is certainly possible that the enormous number of second-rate ballets Mamontov saw at the Bolshoi Theater throughout his lifetime lowered the genre's value in his estimation. Perhaps his preference for opera stemmed from his love of literature that demanded poetry to accompany the music. Perhaps he simply did not realize the enormous possibilities of the genre. As it happened, he believed opera to be the perfect vehicle to transmit his aesthetic ideals to his audience.

### THEATER AS SCHOOL; THEATER AS CHURCH

As mentioned above, Mamontov's artistic philosophy abounds in contradictions. One such contradiction was a coexistence in his mind of the belief in the autonomy of art and the need to "teach" it to the public. Mamontov wanted to educate his audience about beauty, to teach it a lesson in aesthetics, and to raise the level of its cultural awareness. Indeed, according to Melnikov, "the original program of the Private Opera [was] the development of public taste."[100] As Mamontov wrote to Shkafer in the aftermath of his arrest, "If I must still be active in life, much will be completely changed, to come closer to the ideal, to what is necessary for raising the level of public understanding."[101] He was especially anxious about the younger audience; if he failed to convert them, another generation would be lost. He aimed to attract young people to the theater by providing reduced-price and even free morning performances, and justified it as follows: "The morning audience is the most *interesting* (*this is young Russia craving development*—these are not fancy dandies and simpering ladies bored with everything) . . . Morning performances must be packed with people—*this must be the law for the Private Opera* [as] an *educational, cultivating* institution."[102]

In this regard, the idea most wholeheartedly approved by Mamontov's Soviet apologists (and most remote from Diaghilev's vision) was his idea of creating the so-called people's theater; that is, a theater that, in both its repertoire and its prices, would cater to poor and lower middle-class audiences. Here is an excerpt from his interview with *Russkoe Slovo:*

> Let us not forget that the stage is not an entertainment for the rich or a show for amusement-seeking persons with the capital, but a school, a platform from which pure and noble art flows to people. . . . People need music, people love opera—for me this is an incontrovertible fact . . . That is why I express a warm wish for the construction in Moscow of a grandiose building of the People's Opera in which thousands could be accommodated for a mere 10–15 kopecks.[103]

This quotation in particular played in Mamontov's favor after the revolution: researchers interested in his work found an opportunity to rescue him from being labeled a capitalist. Instead, his name was placed into the so-called "fellow traveler" category, which allowed some research to be done as early as the 1940s. What was understandably left out of the Soviet literature was the fact that, while the idea of enlightenment of the masses was present in his mind, his curriculum did not include raising his audience's class consciousness—the goal of the Kuchkists, the Wanderers, and the literary critics of the 1860s. Mamontov's agenda was the development of the public's aesthetic taste—its sense of beauty, rather than of social responsibility. In this sense, his aesthetic position is again opposed to that of the realists. Instead, it has a lot in common with the views of early-twentieth-century modernists and their understanding of the purpose of theater.

Specifically, Mamontov's beliefs in the transformative powers of staged art align with the ideal of "theater as church" expressed by the mystic symbolists[104]—a group that advocated Vladimir Solovyov's "free synthesis" of art and religion.[105] As a hedonist and far from a devout Christian who was once called "the sun worshipper,"[106] Mamontov could never have fully accepted Solovyov's synthesis, but he did see art as a type of worship, often claiming, as Solovyov did, that "religion is declining and art ought to fill its place."[107] His letters and those of his students are filled with quasi-religious phraseology and references to the sanctity of art. "Art—that's our religion!" exclaimed Mikhail Vrubel.[108] "Raise the spirits of talented people; call them to noble heights. Be an apostle, and everyone will love and respect you," Mamontov wrote to Shkafer.[109] And to Stanislavsky: "May God help you firmly and decisively to lead the sacred cause of art, and may He send you people who will support you fully and firmly."[110] In the following excerpt from one of his "program letters" mentioned above, Shkafer expressed a hope of transforming theater into a temple of art—a popular idea enthusiastically shared by the symbolists of both generations.

> The theater of the Russian Private Opera serves the future, and in the present it must direct all its energy, all its strength to keeping the bright, the pure, and the joyous that have descended, blessed, and transformed an ordinary theatrical enterprise into a *temple of art*. Here everyone has felt the sanctity, the purity; the ideals of the good and of the truth.[111]

Notice how Shkafer links the ideals of pure beauty and art professed by Mamontov and his associates with *dobro* [the Good] and *istina* [Truth, in a higher, more sublime sense of the word than *pravda*, the truth of the realists]. This is another echo of Solovyov's philosophy as expressed in his 1889 essay, "Prekrasnoe v Prirode" ["The Beautiful in Nature"]:

> Beauty ... is not an expression of any meaning, but only the ideal meaning, it is an *embodiment of Idea*. ... Looked at, specifically, from the point of view of its internal unquestionable nature, as absolutely desirable or allowable, Idea is Good; from the point of view of the particular definitions embraced by it, as a mental content for the mind, Idea is Truth; finally, from the point of view of perfection as a completeness of its realization, as actually sensed in a felt existence, Idea is Beauty.[112]

Mamontov never denied that theatrical enterprise was a business, and earning a living was a part of it. Yet, he had little tolerance for people who, in his own words, "cling to art" as a way to make money, but lack talent and dedication to serve its sacred cause. "All that mediocrity, those little people; it is not given to them to look up, to absorb *the flight of angels on high*," he said,[113] and in another letter added bitterly:

> Everyone [at the Imperial Theaters] thinks only about pay raises and pensions, and no one cares about art. It appears that a man possesses not five but six senses. The first five (sight, hearing, touch, taste, and smell) require development, and the sixth is *banality* that requires annihilation. While with rare exceptions banality reigns everywhere, the sermon about pure and sublime art would be considered idle talk, and the people serving it, shallow.[114]

Konstantin Stanislavsky was apparently Mamontov's favorite partner in conversations about art as a new religion. "You know, of course, that I love you very, very much for your love of art. Believe me that it is a great cause, a high sermon," he wrote to the young director.[115] With Stanislavsky Mamontov shared his most daring and advanced views about the purpose and meaning of theater. In one letter, filled with biblical references, he expressed sentiments very similar to some of Solovyov's ideas, and at the same time typical of his own way of thinking:

> In the eyes of the majority in our social circle, you and I are a pair of eccentrics, maybe even mentally deranged people. But in that derangement of ours, something sacred, noble, and pure exists that saves society from becoming like animals and calls it toward the ideal. In the early days, such [people] would be hanged or stoned to death, but now the times are different: now respectable people merely shrug their shoulders. But the masses still absorb something, and whatever is absorbed nothing can poison. Through the ages, art has had an irresistible influence upon men, but in our time, I think, due to the shakiness of other aspects of the human spirit, it would shine even brighter. Who knows, maybe, theater is fated to replace the sermon?[116]

Mamontov's views on the role of theater in modern society adhere very closely to the symbolist writings of the 1890s and early 1900s. Like him, the symbolists sought to transcend reality through beauty and art, despised naturalist theater, and avoided social and political stands in their work. Indeed, Mamontov's words in his letter to Stanislavsky seem to echo those of symbolist writer Alexei Remizov, who believed that "theater is not a copy of human degradation; theater is a cult, a liturgy in whose mysteries, perhaps, Redemption is hidden."[117] Like Mamontov, the symbolists "envisioned a theater that would assume the psychological and social functions formerly served by religion."[118] Still, Mamontov believed that while artists-worshippers influenced the audience through their service by instilling tender and sublime feelings and inspiring it to strive for the ideal (or for the "noble existence," in Solovyov's words), the audience itself was passive, reactive to the artist as creative agent. Never in his wildest dreams would Mamontov have gone as far as the mystic symbolist writers, Georgy Chulkov (1879–1939) and Vyacheslav Ivanov, who, in the later 1900s, wanted to bridge the gap between an artist and his audience by making everyone in the theater equal participants in a common liturgy. Then again, other symbolists disapproved of their radicalism just as much as Mamontov would have. Perhaps, in the final analysis, his aesthetic principles did not move far beyond the threshold of the new century. Nevertheless, absorbing throughout his long life the diverse ideas of realism, Slavophilism, and art for art's sake, by the 1890s Savva Mamontov developed his own personal philosophy that ideologically and aesthetically echoed that of the Russian decadents, and thus truly belongs to the Silver Age.

In the remainder of this book, we shall investigate how philosophy translated into practice by tracing the impact of Mamontov's decadent aesthetics on specific policies he promoted in various aspects of his artistic endeavors. We begin with a creative field that gave Mamontov the most exposure as part of Russia's cultural canon, yet also arguably marginalized him the most by making him the exclusive property of art historians—his lifelong commitment to the visual arts. Mamontov's involvement with Russia's leading painters, sculptors, architects, craftsmen, illustrators, and other artist members of the Abramtsevo Circle is the subject of the following chapter.

# THREE

# Echoes of Abramtsevo

The best-known aspect of Savva Mamontov's colorful career is undoubtedly his role as a Maecenas.[1] The tradition of sharing a part of
one's wealth with one's countrymen while exalting one's own name
through charity work or art patronage had deep roots in Russia's business circles, to which the Mamontov family belonged.[2] In the late nineteenth century, art patronage was viewed as both a noble, respectable
pastime and good business practice by the Moscow capitalist elite.
Theater historian Konstantin Rudnitsky explains: "Moscow entrepreneurs and businessmen, while risking substantial sums of money for
the sake of art and education, wished at the same time to glorify their
own names. The *Tretyakov* gallery, the *Mamontov* opera company, the
*Shchukin* collection, the *Bakhrushin* museum were founded."[3] A variety
of well-wishers, from Vladimir Stasov[4] to an anonymous admirer whose
letter is preserved among Mamontov's papers,[5] compared him to his
brother-in-law Pavel Tretyakov, whose charitable gesture of donating
his gallery to the city of Moscow brought him widespread admiration
and respect. Meanwhile, in a letter quoted in the previous chapter, Mamontov described himself to Stanislavsky as an "eccentric" in the eyes
of his social circle, an accusation that was never leveled at Tretyakov.[6]
Indeed, contrary to Stuart Grover's assertion that involvement with
the arts helped further Mamontov's business interests,[7] Vasily Shkafer
described in his memoirs a rude reprimand his mentor once received
from finance minister Carl Witte for "babying some opera company"
instead of paying attention to his railroads.[8] Evidently, there was some

aspect to Savva Mamontov's artistic activities that broke the unwritten code of the socially acceptable; something that distinguished him from other patrons.

In the great tradition of the Russian merchant class, Mamontov considered it his duty to provide financial support to artists. Like Shchukin, Morozov, and Tretyakov, he commissioned and bought their works; he was also in the habit of discretely supplying numerous cash loans that would never be repaid. However, his motivations differed substantially from those of other representatives of his social circle who considered supporting the arts their social, religious, or patriotic duty. Ilya Bondarenko, one of the beneficiaries of Mamontov's patronage, pithily defined its unique quality in his memoir, writing: "[Others] *collected art*. Savva Ivanovich *created* art. That is a significant difference, and that is where his advantage lies."[9]

In his assessment, Bondarenko was not thinking only of Mamontov's work as a sculptor, although this talent—acknowledged, developed, and promoted by as sharp a critic as Mark Antokolsky—brought him much-desired (and well-deserved) public recognition late in life (see plate 5). Nor was Bondarenko's judgment specifically addressing Mamontov's four decades of experiments in ceramics and majolica, for which he would be awarded gold medals at two consecutive Paris World Fairs. Mamontov was a gifted sculptor, but certainly not one of Antokolsky's rank; and his majolica designs, while original, lacked Vrubel's vision. If his artistic endeavors were limited to sculpting and ceramics, Mamontov's place in the history of the Russian arts would remain, if respectable, rather modest.

What made Mamontov's activities unique (and in his social circles, likely rather inappropriate) was his ability to create art around him; he made it happen. His associates from different artistic fields described in their letters and memoirs the unbridled energy and enthusiasm of the "magician" who could break through their writers' block, laziness, or depression. For instance, MPO soprano Nadezhda Zabela, who would prove to be one of Mamontov's severest critics (see chapter 5), once wrote to him: "Somehow you are surprisingly able to settle things, to make people act, and to turn them toward their true path; you were a big help to me in this way."[10] Painter Victor Vasnetsov, the creator of the *Snow Maiden* designs, marveled at Mamontov's "ability to uplift and to build creative enthusiasm" around him: "working with [Mamontov], it was easy to fly up to heavenly clouds."[11]

Mamontov's ability to inspire, described by Vasnetsov, became evident even in the early days of his friendship with the members of the Roman colony. In the 1870s, when business commitments prevented him from spending as much time in Rome (and later Paris, where some Romans would migrate) as he would have liked, he kept in touch with his friends by writing to them directly or through his wife, Elizaveta, who during that time lived permanently in Italy. As this correspondence reveals, Mamontov carved a twofold niche for himself as a member of the group: creating art (as a sculptor) and supporting artists (through commissions and direct financial aid). Somewhere in between these two activities, however, lay his true and increasingly evident mission— supporting his friends by inspiring (and later, as we shall witness, directing) their creativity. Back in Moscow after his first extended trip to Italy, Mamontov wrote the following to Elizaveta, who was still in Rome: "Overall, to my great pleasure I note that my heart is drawn towards our Roman friends even more strongly than before; and fool that I am, I was afraid I would dry up ... What is Morduch [Antokolsky] working on? Please, describe in detail. Is Basil really not painting *comme il faut*? Whip him up, it's your responsibility!"[12]

During that time, Mamontov's friendship with "Basil"—Vasily Polenov—grew deep; he also became closer to Polenov's former classmate and Paris roommate, Ilya Repin. In letters to Polenov, Mamontov discussed his personal artistic frustrations, related news from Rome, and of course demanded detailed accounts of both painters' time in Paris: "Tell me, at least in secret, what you are doing, i.e., what you and Repin are painting—I promise I won't tell. For I am interested, as God is my witness. I am sculpting happily; pity that nothing [good] is coming out but I'm still sculpting ... For Christmas I was in Rome, of course."[13]

By the mid-1870s, however, Mamontov was growing dissatisfied. While still visiting Rome and Paris regularly, he began a persistent campaign to convince his Roman friends to return to Russia. "Ah, damn it, how wonderful it would be if Repin, Morduch, and yourself could really be in Moscow; what a good, active, artistic life we would lead," he wrote to Polenov.[14] He further enticed the artists during their intermittent visits to Moscow by creating ideal working conditions for them: renting studios, helping with the sale of their works, organizing open lectures and publicity. But it was his country estate of Abramtsevo that would finally bring them back, becoming the Russian artistic Mecca, and eventually the crucible for the Moscow Private Opera.

## THE MAMONTOV CIRCLE

The "Abramtsevo" or "Mamontov Circle," as it came to be known among Russia's intellectual elite, was an informal group that united, over more than a thirty-year period, three generations of the greatest Russian artists. Apart from Polenov, Repin, and Antokolsky, its members included the Vasnetsov brothers, Victor and Apollinary (1856–1933), and Vasily Surikov (1848–1916), all usually affiliated with the Wanderers. The artists of the next generation included landscape painters Ilya Ostroukhov (1858–1929) and Isaac Levitan; Mikhail Nesterov (1862–1942), whose passion lay in religious subjects; and sculptor Paolo Trubetskoy (1866–1910). Most importantly, Repin and Polenov's students—Valentin Serov, Konstantin Korovin, and Alexander Golovin (1863–1930)—joined in, as well as the maverick genius Mikhail Vrubel. In the 1890s, these artists would lay the foundation for modernist art in Russia: Korovin would become its Manet, Golovin its Pissarro, Serov its Cézanne, and Vrubel its Van Gogh.[15] Finally, the youngest members of the Mamontov Circle—painters Victor Borisov-Musatov, Pavel Kuznetsov (1878–1968), Nikolai Sapunov (1880–1912), Sergei Sudeikin (1882–1946), Nikolai Ulyanov (1875–1949), and Kuzma Petrov-Vodkin (1878–1939)—would grow to be major representatives of symbolism in Russian painting.

The artists of the Mamontov Circle exhibit an enormous variety of styles and techniques, ranging from traditional realism to impressionism, symbolism, and neo-primitivism. What brought them together was the unique personality of Savva Mamontov. Indeed, his name figures so prominently in many painters' biographies that it is not surprising to find it more frequently in the works of art historians than those of musicologists. From 1873 onward, Mamontov's Abramtsevo was a summer retreat where painters lived for months, resting and working in spacious studios or on beautiful natural locations around the estate. In winter, similar hospitality was provided at Mamontov's Moscow mansion. Guests could be personally invited by the host or introduced by an intimate of the circle. In the latter case, Mamontov and the rest of the group apparently needed to approve the newcomer before he or she became a permanent fixture at their gatherings: according to art historian Dora Kogan, since the Roman days, the circle called itself "the family" and jealously guarded against "invasions by outsiders."[16] Visitors to Abramtsevo enjoyed an opportunity to discuss their art, finding inspiration, appreciation, and sophisticated criticism in their colleagues, as well as their host. "I love asking for [Mamontov's] advice," Repin once wrote to Serov. "He is a sensitive person—smart and artistic."[17]

The list of Mamontov's hand-picked guests was not limited to artists. Discussion topics covered, apart from purely painterly matters, music, poetry, drama, philosophy, politics, and religion. Members of the circle modeled for each other and made art together. "Repin, Vasnetsov, and I have sculpted [portraits of] each other; and now the three busts are triumphantly displayed. You'll see them when you get here," Mamontov wrote to Polenov from Abramtsevo.[18] Pyotr Melnikov, an intimate of the circle, recalled Repin painting Mamontov as his *Nikolai-Chudotvorets* [*Nicholas the Miracle Worker*].[19] The host's children modeled for numerous masterpieces by Polenov, Serov, Nesterov, and Victor Vasnetsov, including the latter's *Tri Bogatyrya* [*Three Knights*] and a Serov classic, *Devochka s Persikami* [*Girl with Peaches*]. For the younger members, Mamontov would organize field trips abroad—to France, Italy, and Spain— and to the Russian North that he saw as an untapped treasure chest for landscape painters. Among the results of Korovin's trips, Melnikov listed "his famous *Ispanki* [*Spanish Girls*] that used to hang in Savva Ivanovich's study, and the equally famous *Severnaya Idilliya* [*Northern Idyll*] in his living room."[20]

One of the most important communal projects of the Mamontov Circle was the 1882 construction of the Abramtsevo church, often viewed by scholars as the group's inauguration as an artist colony.[21] Members of the circle effectively created the building from scratch: from the architectural design, masonry, and carpentry to icon painting and floor mosaics. An outgrowth of the work conducted by Vrubel, Victor Vasnetsov, and Adrian Prakhov in Kiev, where they were commissioned to restore St. Cyril's Cathedral, this project was an indication of the future that lay ahead for the group. Another such indication was *domashny teatr* [home theater]—amateur theatricals initially mounted during Christmas holidays at the Moscow house, and later also at Abramtsevo during the summer. At first merely entertainment for the children, these productions eventually grew into more serious artistic endeavors, becoming the main focus of the group's collective creativity. As such, they also became public affairs, performed in the presence of invited dignitaries from the Moscow intelligentsia, with printed programs, newspaper advertising, and official press reviews. Productions of the Mamontov Circle included spoken dramas, operettas, and spoofs (some of Mamontov's own creation), as well as operatic scenes and even complete operas. The whole circle participated in designing sets, costumes, lighting, and makeup, as well as singing, acting, dancing, playing the piano, and anything else required by the stage director, Mamontov (a small orchestra for the operas would usually be the only hired help). According to Vasnetsov, it was considered inappropriate to refuse an assignment due to a perceived lack of talent or experience—both were acquired and developed in practice.[22]

Mamontov's home theatricals were the first practical experience of his painter friends with designing for the stage. At the Academy, set design was taught for a single semester on paper and models, without taking into account the peculiarities of theatrical perspective that required a designer to adjust his vision to a much larger canvas and a greater distance in order to create the necessary illusion.[23] Those who learned that skill on their own became professional decorators. As such, they rarely if ever returned to the easel, and were derided, often justly, as mere artisans by their colleagues. Mamontov provided his painter friends with their first opportunity to experiment—in an informal atmosphere, without the pressure of a paid job or demand for perfection—with transferring their techniques from an easel onto a backdrop. In the large study of his Moscow residence and the Abramtsevo ballroom, the Russian school of theater design was born. Its radically innovative approach to the painterly medium would revolutionize Russian stage production and, in the flamboyant designs of the Ballets Russes, would take Europe by storm and influence modernist art for years to come.

The collective creativity of such diverse artistic personalities as those composing the Mamontov Circle was only possible, of course, because the collaborators had a common aesthetic platform that would unite them, despite their differences, for a single creative purpose. This platform was their allegiance to the philosophy of art for art's sake, developed by the founding members during their tenure in Rome and Paris and enthusiastically embraced by the younger generation. Mamontov and his artists also shared another, more practical interest, noted by Elizabeth Valkenier: "[At] Mamontov's Abramtsevo circle . . . decorative aspects of art were of primary importance."[24] This fascination with the decorative and the ornamental resulted from the circle's continuous in-depth study of Russian folk art. Abramtsevo boasted woodcarving, furniture making, and ceramics workshops, where the traditional crafts were resurrected and even taught to local villagers. Apart from working in these workshops, the artists also studied traditional pottery painting, costumes, toys, and the form of woodcut printed miniature called the *lubok*,[25] as well as medieval architecture and icon painting, putting their knowledge to the test in the construction of the Abramtsevo church. Apparently, each artist would try his or her hand at multiple crafts. Some exhibited particular preferences, such as Maria Yakunchikova and Elena Polenova's study of traditional embroidery, the Vasnetsov brothers' interest in icon painting, also shared by Vrubel, and the latter's enduring fascination with majolica. As will be evident from the discussion below, the Mamontov artists' study of folklore did not have as its purpose a faithful, realistic copying of folk art, but rather an absorption and aesthetization of its motifs and techniques.

The philosophical and artistic agenda of the Mamontov Circle—its allegiance to the aesthetics of pure art, its interest in the decorative, formalist aspects of art (a central characteristic of the decadent style) as well as the imaginative application of folk motifs in the works of its members—opened a new page in the history of Russian art. It is on that page that we first discern the word "modernism." Why then have scholars on both sides of Russia's borders so consistently propagated a myth of Abramtsevo as a power base of the Wanderers?

## MAMONTOV AND THE WANDERERS

As we have seen, the Wanderers' call for an artist "to learn higher obligations, dependence on the instincts and needs of his people, and the harmonization of his inner feelings and personal strivings with the general striving"[26] was alien to Mamontov and his circle. They refused to accept a Russian artist's supposed obligation to give up creative freedom in order to take a stand on social and political issues, as the leader of the Wanderers, Ivan Kramskoy (1837–87), once put it in a letter to Ilya Repin.[27] Instead, they adhered to Dostoevsky's demand for the works of art "without a preconceived tendency, produced solely because of an artistic urge, dealing with strictly neutral subjects, [and] hinting at nothing tendentious."[28] Nevertheless, a common misconception about Mamontov as a supporter of the Wanderers and their ideology prevails in much secondary literature. In a glaring example, respected American scholar Glenn Watkins managed to conflate the two groups in both of his widely acclaimed studies of musical modernism. The following fascinating ideological mélange is excerpted from his *Pyramids of the Louvre*:

> At Mamontov's estate at Abramtsevo near Moscow, a colony of painters, composers, singers, actors, architects, art historians, and archaeologists, who dubbed themselves "The Wanderers," threw the first challenge to the official Petersburg Academy of Art, which had dominated taste since the time of Catherine the Great in the mid-eighteenth century. In an attempt to define an art that was useful to the people, they rejected, not unlike Herder in Germany, the Western aesthetic of "art for art's sake" and sought to formulate an art based on their Russian national heritage.[29]

Here, Watkins mistook the Abramtsevo Circle for the Association of Traveling Exhibitions; alluded to the Wanderers' secession from the Academy, which occurred a decade prior to Mamontov's purchase of Abramtsevo, as a part of its history; and even conflated the divergent philosophies of the realists, Slavophiles, and aesthetes. Unfortunately, he also completely misrepresented Mamontov's aesthetic platform to his wide readership.

The roots of the scholar's confusion lie in the fact that the formative years of the Mamontov Circle overlapped with the creation of the Wanderers Association. Many of the Abramtsevo artists were also card-carrying members of the Association, or at least participated in its annual exhibitions. This apparent aesthetic contradiction is easy to reconcile, however, if we realize that "The Wanderers," as an ideologically unified organization with the single purpose of serving society the truth about itself, has always been an illusory concept. The illusion was carefully constructed and maintained, in cooperation with Kramskoy, and not always by praiseworthy means, by Vladimir Stasov, the group's self-appointed spokesman. As Valkenier astutely observed,

> Stasov expended not only his energies but also considerable cunning to create ("shape" would be a more exact word) a certain public image that did not always correspond to the painters' preferences and aspirations. In fact, he did not hesitate to distort their views in order to promote his own vision of a Russian school of painting that was both national and civic-minded.[30]

A good example of Stasov's promotion of the realist public image of an artist without the latter's knowledge or consent is the critic's relationship with Ilya Repin. Repin started his career as Stasov's favorite realist. However, in the early 1870s, after spending time at the Roman colony and later settling in Paris on a three-year Academy scholarship, his views on art and the mission of an artist began to alter. Early in his Paris tenure, now a close friend of Polenov, the Prakhov brothers, and Mamontov, Repin wrote an alarming letter to Kramskoy: "When will [Russian art] fight its way out of the fog?! It's a misfortune that terribly fetters it with barren accuracy in . . . techniques; and in its ideas, with rationalized concepts drawn from political economy. How far removed poetry is from such a situation!"[31] Despite Repin's changed attitude toward the aesthetic and social mission of the Wanderers, Stasov managed to pressure him into painting works with a correct realist message for at least another decade (*Kryostnyi Khod v Kurskoi Gubernii* [*Religious Procession in Kursk District*] dates from 1883). The critic also succeeded during that time in manipulating the public into believing in the Repin that he had created. He fought bitterly against any of the artist's friends who dared to attempt a different approach to his output. Thus, in his *Novoe Vremya* article dated 8 January 1877, Stasov responded furiously to the threat posed by Adrian Prakhov, who had suggested that Repin's talent might allow him to paint, apart from the endless barge haulers, other subjects as well.[32] Only in the 1890s did Repin, by then a respected member of the Academy with a voice of his own, finally dare to set the record straight, publicizing his views (from the safety of Paris) in a series of essays titled "Letters on Art." Stasov never forgave him. Predictably enough, Soviet art historians who created the posthumous image of Repin faithfully followed Stasov's portrait of the artist. They ignored "Letters on Art" and other writings, in which Repin stated his preference for art for art's sake over realist truth and defended the value of painterly technique over moralizing content. They also purged his biography of any personal connections that could jeopardize his retouched realist image. Among the names conveniently forgotten were those of Adrian Prakhov and Savva Mamontov.

Repin was not the only Wanderer who managed occasionally to escape Stasov's prescriptions on what form and content were suitable for art. Another of the critic's pet projects was sculptor Mark Antokolsky, whom he exalted as a true realist for his statue of Ivan the Terrible.[33] In 1872, Antokolsky rebelled against Stasov's stifling tutelage and the path that the critic had chosen for him by adamantly refusing to follow his Ivan with a statue of the eighteenth-century rebel peasant leader Emelyan Pugachov. In his defense, the sculptor wrote to Stasov: "I no longer want to spoil other people's nerves with my art, to arouse bile . . . and hatred among people. This is the consequence of tendentiousness [in art], and I have given it up."[34] Antokolsky's letter dates from a year when the Roman colony was particularly active, holding regular gatherings at his studio. Conveniently, Antokolsky's refusal to accommodate Stasov's demand for the Pugachov statue freed him to work on another commission—from Mamontov who, by contrast, left the choice of subject matter up to the sculptor. The statue of Christ profaned by the crowd that would later grace Mamontov's study (see plate 2) was one of Antokolsky's masterpieces, and an image completely different from what Stasov would have him project.

As we can see, despite the pressure to conform, Russia's most talented artists found ways to affirm their independence from the demands of realist ideology. However, Kramskoy and Stasov still held the trump cards: starting in 1870, the annual exhibitions of the Wanderers Association were the most prestigious venue for Russian artists to display their works outside the Academy. Consequently, they represented the only public market available for them to sell their paintings, receive new commissions, and thus make a living as professionals. According to Valkenier, by the late 1870s the process of selecting the paintings for these exhibitions became exceedingly prescriptive, rejecting any work that did not conform to the Wanderers' narrow vision of art: the exhibits now consisted almost exclusively of realist "genre" paintings, while any experiment with form and color was disallowed. The artists had two choices: to starve, or to compromise by painting genre works for the exhibitions, while privately creating art more personal in content and more advanced in technique, in the hope of one day finding an outlet for it. Savva Mamontov gave his artist friends a third option. His keen eye, excellent taste, and little patience "for either moral or critical realism"[35] made him an ideal judge of their experiments. His vast capital and willingness to invest it in art created a one-man market for the works that could not fulfill either realist or academic expectations. Finally, Mamontov's social position as a recognized authority on art, a popular host to Moscow's intellectual elite, and a brother-in-law to Russia's most steadfast collector of native art, Pavel Tretyakov, provided the artists he supported with de facto recognition, valuable connections, and much-needed exposure.

Not everyone could partake of Mamontov's generous patronage, however. He was highly selective in his friendships. Thus, despite dutifully attending the exhibitions, this apparent insider of the Wanderer circles was never close to Kramskoy (or to Stasov, for that matter). Instead, he preferred the liberal wing of the Association—the artists with a broader view of their mission, a more beauty-oriented aesthetic outlook, and a keener interest in and tolerance for technical innovation. In the 1870s, Mamontov's intimates included Antokolsky, Repin, and particularly Polenov, who, as the most sophisticated and the least "realist" of the Wanderers, was an object of Stasov's pointed disdain. During the 1880s, Mamontov also became close to Vasily Surikov, who at that time had just discovered art for art's sake and was much taken with the new techniques of color usage he had observed while visiting Polenov in Rome. Mamontov was equally particular about the works that he bought. There is no record of his ever purchasing a Kramskoy, a Perov, or a Makovsky, but, according to a letter to Polenov, he was "passionately happy" to have acquired several sketches by Fyodor Vasiliev (1850–73).[36] The early death of this talented landscape painter unfortunately prevented him from becoming a Levitan of the 1870s. In retrospect, the association of such a true decadent with realist circles seems a curious misunderstanding on both sides.

Perhaps the most instructive case of Mamontov's role in creating an outlet for the new post-realist trends born within the Association is his relationship with and patronage of Victor Vasnetsov. At the beginning

of his career, Vasnetsov was a typical representative of the realist movement, his paintings sympathetically depicting the poor and the desolate
of Russian society. By the late 1870s, however, he began taking his subjects from ancient Slavic history, myths, and fairy tales—a tendency that
alarmed Stasov and Kramskoy but deeply intrigued Savva Mamontov
when Vasnetsov was introduced to him by Repin.

The new Vasnetsov was considered a traitor and was boycotted by
the realist-affiliated students at the Moscow College of Painting, Sculpture, and Architecture. Two Wanderers threatened to resign from the
Association if Vasnetsov's canvas *Posle Bitvy Knyazya Igorya Svyato-
slavicha s Polovtsami* [*After the Battle of Prince Igor with the Polovtsy*]
(inspired by the twelfth-century epic *Slovo o Polku Igoreve* [*Tale of Igor's
Campaign*], newly translated by Mstislav Prakhov) was accepted by the
selection committee; when it was eventually exhibited, Stasov refused to
review it. The critic was even more infuriated by the *Bitva Russkikh so
Skifami* [*Battle of the Russians with the Scythians*], which, with its openly
anachronistic subject matter, offended his concept of the historical painting as a representation of the truth. Stasov branded Vasnetsov's fairy
tales "unsuccessful trumped-up stories," his *Tri Tsarevny Podzemnogo
Tsarstva* [*Three Princesses of the Underground Kingdom*] "dry wooden
idols" lacking soul and inspiration,[37] and his masterpiece, *Alyonushka*
a "whiny, ugly, and sentimental figure completely unnatural for [the
painter's] talent."[38]

In his extensive treatise titled *Dvadtsat Pyat Let Russkogo Iskusstva*
[*Twenty-Five Years of Russian Art*], the critic declared that "all those
bogatyri, at a battlefield, at a crossroads, in magical flight, in thought,
etc., were completely worthless when created by Russian painters."[39]
Despite the apparent generality of his critique, every single subject on
Stasov's hit list was a reference to a painting by Victor Vasnetsov. Indeed,
the painter's name appears in the very next sentence: the critic called the
style of Vasnetsov's works on "gray Russian antiquity" unrecognizable,
while later in the treatise praising his early, realist canvases such as *S
Kvartiry na Kvartiru* [*From Apartment to Apartment*], *Chai v Kharchevne*
[*Tea at a Diner*], and *Preferans u Chinovnika* [*The Card Game*] as "the
painter's best."[40] Meanwhile, Mamontov encouraged his protégé, paid
for his studio and living expenses, bought his works, and commissioned
new ones. Indeed, two of the *bogatyri* paintings dismissed by Stasov as

worthless, *Vityaz na Raspute* [*A Knight at a Crossroads*] and *Kovyor-Samolyot* [*Magic Carpet*] as well as *Alyonushka* and *The Three Princesses*, all at one time decorated the walls of Mamontov's Moscow mansion (see plate 3). Mamontov also brokered outside commissions for the painter, including a prestigious one from the History Museum for the frescos depicting the Stone Age—a work that even Stasov grudgingly admired.[41] Mamontov would remain close to Vasnetsov for the rest of his life, and the artist would become one of the most important collaborators on his patron's theatrical projects.

In her definitive work on the Wanderers, Valkenier explains Stasov's disapproval of the new trend in Vasnetsov's career by suggesting that the painter "started to glorify the wrong historic tradition."[42] She believes that in the critic's view, Vasnetsov's topics were too ancient to be of relevance to contemporary society, with their legends of good princes running contrary to the modern orientation toward the poor and, more importantly, ignoring the true realities of history. That is, Valkenier still considers Vasnetsov a painter with a historical orientation, comparing him to another Abramtsevo insider, Surikov, whose best-known works, *Boyarina Morozova* and *Utro Streletskoi Kazni* [*The Morning of the Streltsy Execution*], feature scenes from seventeenth-century Russian history. It is characteristic, however, that while there were several canvases by Vasnetsov in Mamontov's house, there were none by Surikov.[43] It is also important to note that Stasov never had a problem with Surikov's understanding of history. It appears that the critic was worried not by the fact that Vasnetsov was abandoning genre paintings for historical subjects, but by his new approach to those subjects. The direction the painter was taking, away from proper realist storytelling toward legends and fairy tales—that is, from history toward mythology—is what Stasov probably feared the most.[44] Yet, that new direction was precisely what Mamontov admired and supported. He used both his personal encouragement and his considerable resources to promote Vasnetsov's "stylized primitivism"[45] that would later so intrigue the Mir Iskusstva artists that they felt compelled to launch their journal with an issue dedicated to the painter.

Victor Vasnetsov was one of only a few painters of the older generation whose work was accepted (sometimes grudgingly) by Mir Iskusstva, and featured in their eponymous journal. In general, starting in the late 1870s, the relationship between the original Wanderers, by now a powerful establishment in their own right, and their younger colleagues supported by Mamontov, became increasingly strained. Serov, Korovin, Vrubel, Nesterov, Levitan, and other young painters detested the realists for their rejection of individual artistic expression and their preoccupation with socially relevant content at the expense of technique. To Sergei Diaghilev, for example, the restrictive manner in which the older Wanderers enforced the "monopoly on artistic taste they had come to think was their birthright to exercise"[46] indicated a lack of sincerity he demanded of modern art in "Complex Questions."[47] To Vrubel, the subordination of artistic freedom to social causes meant a rejection of art and an assault on its audience:

> [An artist] must not become a slave: he has his own original, special cause in which he is the best judge; the cause he must respect, and not denigrate its significance by using it as a tool of tendentious journalism. To do so is to deceive the public: playing on its ignorance, to steal from it that special pleasure that separates the spiritual state in front of an artwork from that in front of an unfolded newspaper. In the end, this could even lead to a complete atrophy of the need for such pleasure. It would mean stealing the best part of life from a person![48]

Another point of generational contention was access to and acceptance of contemporary Western art. While the older painters admired the dramatic, realistic story-telling of Hans Makart (1840–84) and Jan Matejko (1838–93), the younger ones studied the Pre-Raphaelites, built an uneasy relationship with the impressionists, and adored the French symbolists, particularly Pierre Puvis de Chavannes (1824–98). Even the more liberal Wanderers such as Repin parted ways with their students on that issue: the conflict that led to Repin's departure from the *Mir Iskusstva* editorial board was sparked precisely by the journal's scathing criticism of Matejko.[49] But the most problematic issue between the realists and their successors, as Valkenier points out, was the spirit of intolerance and bureaucracy that reigned in the Wanderers' selection committee charged with choosing works for the annual exhibits and accepting new members into the Association:

> The older painters were loath to encourage the young and very grudgingly admitted them first as exhibitors in the annual shows and then to full membership in the Association. Serov gained membership in 1894 after

several years of exhibiting; Korovin was never admitted, even though he had nine works accepted by the jury between 1889 and 1898; and Vrubel never made it past the jury. While these painters, now recognized as masters of Russian art, were being slighted, many a mediocre Salon talent long since forgotten . . . was readily admitted to the exhibits and to the Association.[50]

Even card-carrying Wanderers such as Repin, Polenov, and Vasnetsov suffered from that approach. In addition, thanks to the Association's restrictive by-laws, which gave only its founding members votes on the selection committee, the liberal Wanderers had no opportunity to help their younger colleagues. By the 1890s, the need for change was imminent. And as usual, Savva Mamontov was the driving force behind that change. A long-standing and active member of the Moscow Society of Art Lovers, in 1895 Mamontov, together with Polenov, wrote the mission statement and by-laws of a new exhibition society. The Moscow Association of Artists [Moskovskoe Tovarishchestvo Khudozhnikov], or MAA, established in 1893 but officially registered in early 1896, was a Moscow equivalent of the St. Petersburg Society of Artists, established in 1890.[51] Both organizations appeared in response to the suffocating atmosphere created by the merger between the dried-up remnants of the Wanderers threatened by the emergence of new artistic styles, and their former adversaries at the Academy:

> For a few years now, the former difference between the two chief camps of our artists—the Wanderers and the Academicians—has been disappearing, like a brook in the sand. [The Wanderers'] genre has mellowed and crumbled; a stamp of mediocrity and weariness is upon it. On the other hand, genre has also found its place among Academic painters.[52]

The new exhibition societies attempted to present an alternative for young artists who essentially had no place to exhibit their innovative works in public. Mamontov's involvement in the Moscow organization included a place on the admission committee, as well as chairmanship of the jury that both selected the works and awarded annual prizes. His guidance is discernable in the MAA's more liberal policies, as compared to the Wanderers and even to its counterpart in the northern capital. Its primary goal, stated in the founders' official registration request, was to ensure that "with the creation of the MAA, a large number of artists would be freed from the influence of the Wanderers Association, which pressures [them] with its one-sided direction."[53] The admission process for the new members was refreshingly democratic: closed ballot of the general assembly. Despite the MAA's apparent anti-Wanderer stand, no styles were excluded from its exhibitions, the only criterion being artistic quality of the work, as judged by the selection committee. Works ranged from traditional realist genre paintings to the newest trends presented by the adherents of art for art's sake, with an emphasis on landscape and a preference for "coloristic painterly style, as opposed to the dry narrative of the late Wanderers."[54] A remarkable innovation of the MAA was its practice of exhibiting decorative crafts alongside easel painting and sculpture. The practice was established at the Sixth MAA Exhibition in February 1899 and subsequently became the norm. The MAA policy of concurrent exhibition of arts and crafts was unprecedented in the history of Russian arts. The two genres were traditionally separated not only by style and technique, but also by their "unwritten hierarchy," the crafts commonly being dismissed as artisan fare of marginal importance.[55] The practice of equating the artistic value of easel and crafts was a legacy of Abramtsevo, and one can hardly overestimate its significance for the development of the décor-obsessed Russian *style moderne*.

The Moscow Association of Artists thus essentially offered a historical transition point from the exclusively realist exhibits of the Wanderers in the 1870s and 1880s to the modernist annuals organized by Diaghilev starting in 1898 under the banner of Mir Iskusstva, in which realist works were no longer welcome. Ensuring an occasionally awkward coexistence of widely divergent artistic trends (from realism to symbolism) in the same show was a Mamontov trademark. In 1894, the First All-Russian Congress of Artists took place in Moscow. Among its goals were resolving the conflict between the older and the younger generation, discussing the new trends in contemporary Russian art, and providing safeguards for its continuing development. According to the press reports, the congress delegates did not progress far beyond a declaration of principles. Yet, Mamontov's active participation in its organization (he also supervised the exhibitions, tableaux vivant, and other artistic activities accompanying the congress) speaks volumes of his position in the 1890s as a living bridge between the old and the new aesthetics in the arts.

As mentioned earlier, Mamontov's relationship with the arts of the late 1900s and 1910s was complicated. At his age, it was probably difficult for him to adjust to the lightning pace of innovation. Mamontov was especially upset about the fate of talented older painters like Repin and Polenov, whose legacies were now predictably neglected by younger artists and ignored by audiences. In one letter to Polenov, Mamontov expressed dismay at the poor publicity for his old friend's latest show, and grumbled that instead, "everyone ran to the exhibition of the stupid Blue Rose (the latest word in artistic insolence)—but why?"[56] Mamontov defended his old friends as best he could, in private correspondence and in the press. Half-serious, half tongue-in-cheek, he wrote to Polenov:

> I have already made my debut as a journalist. Well, they haven't beaten me up yet, but it would probably end this way, for I am no good at singing praises, and to the contrary point out weaknesses. A little article about sculptor Trubetskoy turned out well. I want to write about Repin and Polenov, and what I write is my own business: I am not going to ask for their advice. But seriously, it is wrong to keep silent about the people who have worked so long and hard.[57]

Pressed by Paris Opéra Comique director Albert Carré (1852–1938) to procure designs by a younger artist, rather than supplying those by Vasnetsov, for its 1908 production of *The Snow Maiden,* Mamontov responded testily: "When one can profit from the work of Vasnetsov or Polenov, one has no need of Korovin or Bilibin."[58] The latter response needs to be judged in the context of the falling-out between Mamontov and Korovin over the artist's shameful behavior during his patron's arrest and trial.[59] Their (still largely halfhearted) reconciliation would not be forthcoming for several years. As a consequence, Mamontov, also clearly offended by Carré's assessment of Vasnetsov's work, cannot be expected to be completely objective in his recommendation. Similarly, in an interview two years later, while publicly acknowledging Korovin as a wonderful artist, Mamontov expressed his doubts about his more daring formal experiments, judging them to be an empty pursuit of fashion.[60]

Mamontov was even less enthusiastic about cubo-futurism and other avant-garde trends in nonrepresentational art: to him, such art lacked sincerity, as well as beauty. For example, while not particularly excited about Fyodor Fedorovsky's impressionist designs for the 1913 production of *The Sorochintsy Fair* (see chapter 2), Mamontov did find the following saving grace: "The only joy is that [the sets] do not reflect the latest disgraces—all those cubisms, futurisms, rayisms."[61] He was not alone in his rejection of these radical artistic movements: Alexandre Benois, the artist and aesthetician of the Mir Iskusstva group, that cradle of Russian modernist art, consistently opposed the avant-garde in his published works.[62] In fact, the foresight that Mamontov demonstrated in his support for modernist art is unparalleled by anyone of his generation. For instance, as made clear by his letter quoted above, he disapproved of the direction that his protégé artists, the Blue Rose group, took after 1907. Yet he did champion their earlier work. Blue Rose member and future constructivist Georgy Yakulov (1884–1928) worked at Mamontov's ceramics workshop. Nikolai Sapunov and Sergei Sudeikin were granted theater commissions (see below). The leader of the group, Pavel Kuznetsov, was employed as an interior designer of the Yaroslavl train station in Moscow. That building was created by architect Fyodor Shekhtel (1859–1926), the greatest representative of the Russian *style moderne* in his field and another intimate of the Mamontov Circle during its later years.[63] According to his nephew's memoirs, Mamontov also commented favorably on the set designs created by the future neo-primitivist star Kuzma Petrov-Vodkin for the Nezlobin Theater's revival of a signature MPO production, Tchaikovsky's *Orleanskaya deva* [*The Maid of Orleans*].[64]

The most impressive demonstration of Mamontov's allegiance to contemporary art is his discovery, lifelong financial support, and untiring promotion of Mikhail Vrubel. Before Mamontov, Vrubel was an unknown quantity in Russia's artistic circles. As noted above, he never made it past the jury for any of the Wanderers' exhibitions; he was not any luckier at those of the Academy. In his single official commission—participation in the restoration of St. Cyril's Cathedral in Kiev, supervised by Adrian Prakhov—he was not permitted to work on figures, but rather was given the unglamorous job of "designing ornamental panels on the lower side walls of the church."[65] Of course, those who wanted to slight the artist with this restriction could not have foreseen that, as Dmitry Sarabyanov points out, "Vrubel's work on ornament that started in the 1880s at St Cyril's [would] in many ways direct the development of the mature *style moderne*," with its particular attention to the decorative and the ornamental.[66] Nevertheless, the painter's work was sufficiently anonymous for Stasov (to Diaghilev's great delight) to misattribute his designs to Victor Vasnetsov.[67]

It was Mamontov's efforts that introduced Vrubel to Russia's artistic community as well as to the general public. By doing so, he enormously influenced the development of Russian art of the early twentieth century: according to Camilla Gray, Vrubel, more than any other artist, was an inspiration to the Russian avant-garde.[68] The first public display of the painter's work took place at the All-Russian Exhibition in Nizhny Novgorod in the summer of 1896. Mamontov, the art director for the Fair, commissioned Vrubel to create two huge mosaic panels, *Mikula Selyaninovich*, inspired by a Russian folk epic, and the symbolist *Printsessa Gryoza* [*Dream Princess*]. After the works were unanimously rejected by the selection committee, Mamontov proceeded to erect a separate pavilion for exhibiting them, just beyond the fair grounds, in order to bypass the committee's prohibitive order. The scandal created by this affair made the public flock to see Vrubel's notorious works—something the committee obviously did not anticipate. Mamontov, however, did expect this reaction, and exploited it to promote his favorite artist.[69]

In his memoirs, Chaliapin, who had first met Mamontov at the Nizhny Novgorod Exhibition, recalled his mentor taking him to Vrubel's pavilion. The singer described Mamontov "teaching" Vrubel to him: explaining his works' advantages over the realist ones by pointing out the depth and emotional impact of the panels, and guiding him though the rough terrain of the artist's modernist technique.[70] Chaliapin was clearly not an exception; Mamontov must have "taught" Vrubel to all his students who would later work closely with the painter at the MPO.

In Mamontov's theater Vrubel was allowed to work on his favorite subjects. He designed water scenes and costumes for Rimsky-Korsakov's fairy tales and was able to project his lifelong obsession—his Demon— onto the stage by designing the sets for Anton Rubinstein's opera based on Mikhail Lermontov's eponymous poem. Mamontov also introduced the artist to ceramics and majolica. Working in the majolica workshop at Abramtsevo helped Vrubel to develop his characteristic color palette with its signature peacock blues.[71] It also gave him an opportunity to continue experimenting with thick, decorative, complex, multidimensional surface patterns first evident in his illustrations for the 1890 edition of Lermontov's *The Demon* (see plate 7).[72] In addition, the tile patterns and majolica sculptures Vrubel created earned him the gold medal at the 1900 Paris World Fair, thus allowing the wider world of art its first glimpse of his unique artistic style.

As we have seen, from the early 1870s Savva Mamontov's activities as a patron, a leader of the Abramtsevo artist colony and the Mamontov Circle, a public figure, and a recognized authority on art among Moscow's intellectuals made a significant impact on the development of post-realist art in Russia. In his position, Mamontov aimed to bridge the generation gap between the most talented and progressive wing of the Wanderers and their successors, as well as to support and promote Vrubel and other representatives of early modernist art of the 1890s and early 1900s. Mamontov's most valuable contribution to the birth of Russian *style moderne,* however, was the opportunity to experiment in stage design that he offered his painter friends by involving them in the daily operations of his enterprise, the Moscow Private Opera. Their groundbreaking work for theater is the focus of the next chapter.

# FOUR

# Visual Impressions

In retrospect, Mamontov's decision to commission easel painters to design his operatic productions seems natural: he had access to Russia's premier artistic forces and would certainly want to benefit from it. In reality, the idea was unprecedented, at least in the Russia of Mamontov's time. There, easel and design were viewed as two professions no less different than, say, painting and singing. After the initial reports came in, stating that at the MPO, "the execution of set designs has been entrusted not to typical decorators-artisans, but to painters," the common reaction was widespread amazement coupled with understandable skepticism.[1] As *Russkoe Slovo* critic Alexander Gruzinsky put it: "clearly, not every decorator is an artist, nor can every artist-painter necessarily make a good decorator—this much is obvious."[2]

Not only did the skepticism subside, but Mamontov's innovation fundamentally altered the role of the designer on the Russian stage, both dramatic and operatic. The Moscow Art Theater was the first to follow in Mamontov's footsteps, when its leader Stanislavsky employed an MPO alumnus, painter Victor Simov, as his chief decorator. The Imperial stage was not far behind. Soon after his appointment as the new head of the Moscow crown theaters, Vladimir Telyakovsky (1860–1924) secured Konstantin Korovin's designing talent for the Bolshoi, and upon his transfer to St. Petersburg as the director of the Imperial Theaters, added Alexander Golovin to the Mariinsky staff. In 1905, Vsevolod Meyerhold employed the three youngest painters of the Mamontov Circle, Nikolai Sapunov, Sergei Sudeikin, and Nikolai

Ulyanov, to design the Povarskaya Studio productions (see chapter 6). Finally, Sergei Diaghilev used Serov, Korovin, Golovin, and a number of St. Petersburg–based artists in his Parisian Russian Seasons, later making these painters' designs an integral part of the Ballets Russes. Thus, appointment of easel painters as set designers, unheard of before Mamontov, would become commonplace within two decades after the MPO first opened its doors.

Another fundamental change brought about by Mamontov's new approach concerned the perceived value of design works. Previously, stage sets were prized less for their quality and more for their utility, including adaptability to productions other than their own. The most useful were generalized settings—a Renaissance palace, a medieval castle, a rococo boudoir—that could be taken out of storage as needed after having been located by literally browsing the Imperial Theater catalogue.[3] The individuality of each particular project obviously suffered as a result. Indeed, whenever a production-specific design was judged too unique to be reused, it would habitually be destroyed or recycled. Unfortunately, such fate befell the set from one of Mamontov's own productions, the tableau vivant Aphrodite, created for the art program of the All-Russian Congress of Artists (see chapter 2), which was never returned either to designer Polenov or to stage director Mamontov after the show. A letter to Polenov, in which Mamontov comments on the disappearance of the Aphrodite set, illustrates both his personal philosophy and his distaste for the status quo: "I believe that your Aphrodite and Orfeo are real masterpieces that truly belong in a museum. And do you know that your Aphrodite is tyu-tyu [gone]? The museum's night watchmen must have used it for foot wraps."[4] The lack of independent artistic value placed on the sets by most theaters also meant that preparing separate designs for each new production was a luxury—even for the state-supported Imperial stage, let alone for cash-strapped private enterprises. Yet this was common practice at the MPO, a fact noted with incredulity by critics such as Gruzinsky, who, in the review cited above, discussed "completely new sets" being prepared for the MPO's production of Prince Igor.[5]

Mamontov's tireless promotion of his approach and the success of his company gradually led to a more widespread acceptance of the new practice: stage sets began to be viewed as independent artworks that really did "belong in a museum." Previously rarely mentioned outside theater reviews, they started attracting attention as distinct *objets d'art,* equal to painting and sculpture. Stasov dedicated a whole section of his article "Moskovskaya Chastnaya Opera v Peterburge" ["Moscow Private Opera in St. Petersburg"] to the work of Mamontov's designers, and made the *Snow Maiden* sets the centerpiece of a Victor Vasnetsov feature published in the inaugural issue of his journal *Iskusstvo i Khudozhest-vennaya Promyshlennost [Arts and Crafts]* in October 1898. That article, in which the designs were analyzed in a manner previously reserved for easel, also included color plates of the artist's sketches—a laborious and expensive process, still rare in Russia at the time. The only other journal to use color plates was Stasov's competition, Sergei Diaghilev's *Mir Iskusstva,* launched simultaneously with *Arts and Crafts* with its inaugural issue also dedicated to Vasnetsov. Naturally, Diaghilev the decadent was an enthusiastic convert to Mamontov's design-friendly philosophy (as we shall see, the personal relationship between the two might have had something to do with it as well). Earlier that same year, Diaghilev featured the designs of Victor Vasnetsov's brother Apollinary for the MPO production of *Khovanshchina* at the first Mir Iskusstva exhibition alongside conventional easel, and later published their source sketches in his journal.

Mamontov's decision to involve painters in the work of his company caused stage design, previously viewed as an inferior and nonartistic occupation, finally to be ranked equal with easel. It is significant that Mamontov's approach to the value of design paralleled his attitude to the decorative crafts reflected in the exhibition policies of the Moscow Association of Artists discussed in chapter 3. Together with the folk-influenced crafts, theatrical design would become one of the most important stylistic experiments of the Russian *style moderne.*[6]

### THE PRODUCTION TEAM

Another of Mamontov's innovations concerns the way his designers' talents were utilized at his company. Each production was assigned from its earliest phase either to a single painter, or to a team of painters who in this case would work together on the same scenes rather than dividing the work between them. This seemingly logical method was rarely adhered to at Russia's "model stage" and Mamontov's main competitor—the Imperial Theaters. There, whenever new sets were ordered, several decorators would be hired to work separately on their assigned tableaux, perhaps to speed up the process. For instance, *Novosti Dnya* named as many as five decorators on the production team of the 1897 Bolshoi revival of Glinka's *Ruslan i Lyudmila* [*Ruslan and Lyudmila*], each responsible for a specific scene.[7] Mamontov's designers, on the other hand, were responsible for the production as a whole. This responsibility included but was not limited to sketching and painting the sets. An artist or a team of artists who designed the sets would also create sketches for costumes and stage accessories; personally supervise hair, makeup, lighting, and special effects. The result of this approach was a production that created a unified, harmonious visual impression—a characteristic frequently commented on by the press.[8] For instance, in his review of the MPO production of Saint-Saëns's *Samson et Dalila*, St. Petersburg critic Vladimir Baskin noted: "The opera is staged with particular care. Here, it is not only the highly characteristic sets and costumes that transfer the spectator into the legendary Biblical epoch and create the necessary atmosphere, but also the lighting—a feature that rarely creates a theatrical illusion on our stages."[9] The critic did not venture a hypothesis as to how the theatrical illusion he described might have been achieved, noting only that it was an attribute of many MPO productions.

The methodology of creating a unified visual impression would become a subject of thorough study only when it was revealed to be an integral part of the Ballets Russes phenomenon. Arnold Aronson describes it as follows: "The costume was made to work harmoniously with the setting and, in many cases, the designs . . . virtually fused the two together so that the costumes might be seen as moving fragments of scenery. For such visual unity to be achieved, costumes and sets were usually designed by the same person."[10] Until recently, Diaghilev scholars habitually declared this practice to be unique to the Ballets Russes—a perception supported by reference publications such as the *Grove Dictionary of Art* and the *International Encyclopedia of Dance,* from which the above quotation is derived. The history of this misconception dates, predictably enough, to Diaghilev and his team, who clearly understood the unique value of this innovative production method and wished, consequently, to secure their exclusive rights to it in the public eye. This desire is easily traceable through the Ballets Russes memoir literature, in which the method is emphasized as that company's trademark. Here, for instance, is an excerpt from the recollections of choreographer Serge Lifar: "A painter . . . will be entrusted with all the artistic details. Not only will he be made responsible for providing the designs for both sets and costumes, he will also be expected to design all the properties and other accessories: in a word, to be responsible for the whole scenic presentation . . . down to its smallest details."[11] As we have seen, Lifar could have easily been talking about the MPO, whose designers worked in a manner identical to Diaghilev's. Indeed, another Ballets Russes insider, Alexandre Benois, rarely inclined to give Mamontov's company credit for any of Diaghilev's innovations, in his article dedicated to Korovin called the artist's stage work "the first example of a set and costume designer united in one person, which resulted in amazing, never before seen harmony."[12]

Indeed, the MPO design team frequently assumed a leading role in the creative process: not limiting themselves to the visual aspect, the painters would often assume part of the stage-directing duties as well. The latter has proved one of the best-documented aspects of their work, due to an abundance of memoir literature on the subject: Mamontov's singers found being directed by the designers an unusual and rewarding experience, and frequently commented on it. During its early years, the company did not even have a stage director on its staff: in a table of the MPO premieres Vera Rossikhina compiled for her monograph, she listed "Mamontov and the painters" in the directing column for the 1885–87 time period. During these first seasons, Polenov and Victor Vasnetsov participated most actively in the company's work, utilizing the multifaceted experience they had acquired in the Abramtsevo theatricals. Specifically, the codirecting of Dargomyzhsky's *Rusalka* must be credited to Vasnetsov. According to lead soprano Nadezhda Salina, apart from creating an amazing backdrop for the underwater act, he personally decorated the singer with garlands of water lilies, and staged the mermaid dance and pantomime. The painter also created the groundbreaking personality of the mad Miller for act 3. When Anton Bedlevich, who sang that role, rebelled against his torn shirt and disheveled hair and changed his costume just prior to his entrance, Vasnetsov reportedly personally restored his artistic vision with the help, among other things, of some floor dust and a quantity of flour.[13] This amusing anecdote related by Salina clearly demonstrates the altered power structure at Mamontov's enterprise: the leadership role that in an opera company traditionally belonged to a singer was transferred instead to a director-designer.

After his company reopened in 1896, Mamontov for the first time began employing and training professional stage directors for his productions (see chapter 5). As a result, the directing duties of the designers—at that time, primarily Korovin, Serov, and Vrubel—correspondingly diminished. However, they apparently still participated in the rehearsal process, at least in an advisory capacity. Stage director Pyotr Melnikov, who first worked with Korovin at the MPO and later for years at the Imperial Theaters, recalled the artist's similar level of involvement from his Bolshoi years: "[Korovin] was never involved in stage directing [while at the Bolshoi]. But during the rehearsals, while watching a performance, he would occasionally make such fabulous comments, and often give amazing advice. A true theatrical genius!"[14] Feodor Chaliapin's memoirs contain perhaps the most detailed information on the painters' participation in the MPO operations. The singer's association with Mamontov's designers was so close and long-term that it even became a subject of a separate study.[15] In both *Stranitsy iz moei zhizni* [*Pages from My Life*] and *Maska i dusha* [*Mask and Soul*], Chaliapin gratefully acknowledged the great influence the painters had on his artistic development during his time with the company. Specifically, he noted their assistance in illuminating the inner world of his characters by altering their outward appearance; Platon Mamontov and other memoirists also frequently commented upon it. The history of the transformation of one signature Chaliapin role will serve as a good illustration.

As one of the most enduringly popular operatic characters on the Russian stage, Gounod's Mephistopheles was expected to look a certain way. He was always portrayed as a restless creature with dark hair, a goatee, a costume à la Henry IV complete with a short cape, a French beret with a red feather, small horns made of foil, and the manners of a provincial Harlequin. This was the image Chaliapin had been taught to present while at the Mariinsky Theater, where tradition was respected above all else (see plate 14). Instinctively dissatisfied, the singer rebelled against the cliché during his 1896 Nizhny Novgorod debut with Mamontov's company; but without a new concept in his mind, he failed his part altogether.

The first step toward creating a new Mephistopheles was Chaliapin's work with Polenov on changing the character's external image. The result of their work, first presented during Chaliapin's Moscow debut in the fall of 1896, was striking and original: Polenov's Satan was a blond. A visiting Swedish painter, Arnold Zorn, testified that Western Europe had never seen nor heard the role in that way.[16] Polenov's vision helped Chaliapin shed some of the preconceptions acquired by observing and performing at the Mariinsky stage. However, the transformation of Mephistopheles did not stop with this first success: Chaliapin was displeased with the costume that still imitated a seventeenth century French chevalier with a feathered beret (see plate 11). Three years later, a reviewer of a Moscow daily *Novosti Dnya* noted: "The artist inserted several new little details in the part of Mephistopheles, which was performed as always with rare artistry. Thus, contrary to tradition, Chaliapin sang the whole of act 3 in a black costume, and it certainly made an impression."[17] The black costume referred to by the critic is probably the one preserved in an extant 1897 photograph (see plate 15). The difference is striking, both from the Mariinsky's and from Polenov's versions of the character. Chaliapin finally rejected the blond hair, the beret (although he kept the feather), and opted instead for a simple black cloak that enveloped his figure like a pair of wings, presenting a terrifyingly quiet creature—unhurried, powerful, sarcastic, and condescending. This was an image he would explore in the future, both in *Faust* and later in Boito's *Mefistofele*; the image borrowed from Goethe's poem and, arguably, rather inappropriate for a French opera. Baskin pointed out this perceived stylistic discrepancy in his review of Chaliapin's performance, saying:

> Mr. Chaliapin pays serious attention to the demonic side of the character; this is of course very good, but he overlooks the fact that the *French*, operatic Mephistopheles is much different from Goethe's original, and this difference is revealed particularly in his outward appearance, manners, dexterity, gracefulness, etc. In this aspect, Mr. Chaliapin seems to be moving in the wrong direction, by presenting him as rather angular, sometimes sharp and even rude, for example, in the scene with Siebel in act 2. Such a Mephistopheles would perfectly satisfy us in Goethe's tragedy, but not in a French opera.[18]

As the critic's reaction makes clear, Chaliapin's Mephistopheles was shaped contrary to operatic tradition. The new image was created in large part by his outward appearance—his costume, makeup, and stage movement. It would be impossible for Chaliapin to create the image without going to the designers first: all costumes were executed according to their specifications. Just as the blond 1896 Mephistopheles was a creation of Polenov, the final version betrays an unmistakable influence of Vrubel, whose image of Goethe's character was realized in his 1896 *Faust* triptych.[19] In later years, the singer's continuously evolving interpretation of his favorite character conformed even more closely to Vrubel's vision (compare plates 8 and 16).[20]

During his tenure at Mamontov's company, Chaliapin was also influenced by the eschatological visions of Vrubel's Demon: in 1899 the artist completed *Demon Letyashchy* [*The Demon in Flight*], and immediately started working on *Demon Poverzhennyi* [*The Demon Cast Down*] characterized by his wife as "a modern Nietzschean."[21] A year later, already a Bolshoi Theater superstar, Chaliapin appeared in the title role of Rubinstein's *Demon* [*The Demon*]. The baritone part was prohibitively high for the singer, but the image held too powerful an attraction. It was the image that caused Nadezhda Salina as Tamara to faint at the premiere without finishing the final duet,[22] and that was recognized immediately by both critics and audiences as "Vrubel's Demon."[23] Savva Mamontov appeared to have recognized it too. It is revealing that in 1900, despite his bitterness over Chaliapin's defection to the Bolshoi, he sculpted a bust of the singer, the only portrait of him he ever made. It was his portrait as the Demon.[24]

Apart from their involvement in directing, the designers participated in virtually every aspect of the company's operations—everything at the Moscow Private Opera had to be "artistic." For example, after a disastrous January 1898 fire all but destroyed their building, the Solodovnikov Theater, its interior was completely redesigned. A cold, drafty former warehouse, the subject of constant press complaints, was transformed into a true "temple of art," as attractive as it was comfortable. This was the work of Mamontov's artists: Vrubel created the new curtain and ceiling panel, with Bondarenko in charge of architectural design. Even more characteristic is the artists' contribution to the publicity for the productions, such as designing playbills and program covers. For instance, *Novosti Dnya* reported on "the programs decorated with Mr. Vrubel's original vignettes," sold at intermissions during the premiere of *Orfeo*.[25] The following season, another critic noted a certain affinity between the images on the MPO printed programs and the impression created by the enterprise as a whole—a unity undoubtedly sought and promoted by Mamontov and his designers:

> One of the indications of the approaching opening night was a product offered at the Kuznetsky Bridge shops, and worthy of the enterprise itself in the artistry of its production. We are talking about the colored printed program covers created by painter M. A. Vrubel. The drawing is successfully conceived and beautifully executed. At the front, Bayan is playing his *gusli;* the mermaids behind him are engrossed in listening against a backdrop of a wonderful Russian landscape. To the right, the words: "Russian Private Opera" and the year "1898" are drawn in capriciously decorative letters.[26]

This description of Vrubel's drawing is reminiscent of the playbills and printed programs created by Polenov, Vasnetsov, Korovin, and Vrubel himself for the theatricals of the Mamontov Circle, still preserved at the Abramtsevo Museum (see plate 6). These designs are characterized by a particular attention to decorative patterns: frames, ornaments, and fancy lettering—the typical features of *Mir Iskusstva* covers and vignettes, some of which were to be created by the same artists. These features would later be analyzed by art historians as signature elements of the Russian *style moderne* book illustration. Abramtsevo artists such as Elena Polenova were in fact the pioneers of that genre, described by Sarabyanov as one of the most significant and innovative Silver Age art forms.[27]

## COLLABORATIVE PROCESS

Clearly, the painters were involved in every aspect of daily operations at the MPO, from visual design to directing to advertising. This required their extensive, regular interaction with singers, stage directors, conductors, machinists, stagehands, as well as with Mamontov himself. Such collaboration was practically nonexistent in an opera theater of the day, which made the creative process inefficient and frustrating. Rimsky-

Korsakov's dismal experiences with the 1894 Mariinsky production of *Mlada* occasioned an unusually bitter outburst in the composer's autobiography that practically begged for a Mamontov to intervene:

> Set design, costume design, stage machinery, directing, and music sections move in the Russian Imperial opera in different directions, and there is no person at the Directorate who coordinates them all. Every one of these sections knows only its own affairs, and would more readily stab others in the back than collaborate with them. When an opera is to be produced and everything should come together, it turns out that much does not fit; but despite that, no one considers himself responsible for the actions of another.[28]

During 1896–99, the MPO staged seven of Rimsky-Korsakov's operas, four of them world premieres. Here, unlike at the Imperial Theaters, the composer was able to benefit from the methodology developed by Mamontov and his team that had ensured their success: productions were created by a community of artists, actors, musicians, and stage directors during intensive brainstorming sessions.

A particularly revealing illustration of this method is the 1897 world premiere of Rimsky-Korsakov's masterpiece *Sadko*. The production became one of the Moscow Private Opera's greatest artistic successes, as well as its greatest public-relations coup. Initially offered to the Directorate of the Imperial Mariinsky Theater in St. Petersburg, *Sadko* was rejected by the theater's selection committee; in a famous statement the tsar, who traditionally had a final say in determining the repertoire of what was after all his court theater, requested something a little more cheerful. Offended, Rimsky-Korsakov severed his connections with the Imperial Theaters for several years, which opened the door for Mamontov to lobby for the rights to the score through a mutual friend, Semyon Kruglikov, who managed to secure Rimsky-Korsakov's approval.[29] The subsequent staging and resounding success of *Sadko* at the MPO was perceived by Russia's political liberals as a triumph of private initiative over the Imperial bureaucracy, essentially as a victory of modern capitalism over outdated feudal law. The plot of the opera, "a parable of free enterprise, capitalism *avant le mot*,"[30] exalted these very virtues personified by its resourceful merchant hero, which certainly helped bolster the above-mentioned reading and made the production by a private company particularly appropriate. *Sadko* brought long-awaited legitimacy and prestige to Mamontov's enterprise. It was now unconditionally acclaimed by public and press alike as an institution of great cultural significance that promoted the neglected output of Russia's most important living composer.

The true source of the MPO's success, meanwhile, lay beyond the attraction of a scandal and the quality of the score. In his memoirs, Ilya Bondarenko, who witnessed Mamontov's work on *Sadko,* called the process "a truly communal action."[31] Young Vasily Shkafer, who had joined the company as an assistant stage director just a few weeks before the rehearsals began, recalled the first group session on the opera in his memoirs. With most of the troupe present, an impromptu sight-reading of the score was punctuated by the designers voicing their ideas on sets, costumes, and makeup and followed by a collective discussion of stage directions and special effects.[32] More often than not, the preliminary work on a production was taken out of the theater building altogether. Instead, it occurred around Mamontov's tea table or at the country dacha of his companion, the troupe's mezzo-soprano Tatyana Lyubatovich. That practice, later to be systematized by Stanislavsky, is a standard for drama troupes to this day. It is described in Bondarenko's memoirs as follows: "Nightly tea parties, starting at 8:00 PM, always occurred in the presence of Chaliapin, the painters Korovin and Serov; Vrubel came by; and here at the tea table, plans for future productions were discussed, future stage images were sketched."[33]

Collective creativity and decision-making resulted in an infectious spirit of camaraderie that reigned at the company during the height of its success. The team members not only worked together: they lived, ate, entertained, took vacations together, and roomed together in Paris, where they were sent by Mamontov for their annual summer study tours.[34] Those unsuited to this atmosphere did not stay with the company long; according to Bondarenko, this was the fate of stage director Mikhail Lentovsky, employed during the 1898–99 season: "In all productions of Mamontov's Russian Private Opera the collectivity principle always ruled, but Lentovsky absorbed this collectivity principle the least; he was the least comfortable with it. He could not fit in and left soon after."[35] Interestingly enough, one of the reasons for Lentovsky's departure was his conflict with Serov and other MPO painters. Evidently he adamantly refused to bend his work to their vision, and as a result his life at the company quickly turned complicated. In a letter to Mamontov, Lentovsky complained bitterly that his employer had effectively thrown him to the wolves by declining to take his side against the designers.[36] The incident demonstrates once more the role of the painters in the company's power structure, as well as the importance of the collaborative process in its effective operation. To quote another Mamontov employee, singer Varvara Strakhova, the best MPO productions represented "a product of collaboration between an artist-musician and an artist-painter, assisted by the creative ideas of their 'silent' director Savva Mamontov."[37]

In light of the previous discussion, it is easy to see why the concept behind *Mir Iskusstva* would have appealed to Mamontov. The result of a creative collaboration between artists, musicians, critics, poets, writers, and philosophers, the journal was a great illustration of the collectivity principle to which he himself subscribed. And just as the methods of Mamontov's early Abramtsevo productions would be applied and developed in the professional atmosphere of the MPO, the Mir Iskusstva group transferred their experiences with the journal to other artistic ventures, most notably theatrical ones. Alexandre Benois' description of their work on the ill-fated Mariinsky commission for Delibes' ballet *Sylvia* may serve as a good illustration; it is notable that out of the five artists mentioned, two—Korovin and Serov—were former members of Mamontov's team:

> Some of us have taken possession of the dining room; others were busy in [Diaghilev's] study, while even the back rooms were strewn with drawings and sketches. I . . . had just sketched the plan of the décor for the first act; Lanceray was occupied with the third act. . . . Korovin was working at the second scene of the second act; Bakst had been entrusted with creating Orion's cave and almost all the costumes; even Serov, carried away by the general enthusiasm, had started on a sketch of the principal satyr.[38]

In her monograph on the Ballets Russes, Lynn Garafola discusses the creative process employed in the creation of *Sylvia* as a "professional strategy" that would be used in the productions of Diaghilev's enterprise.[39] The collaborative methodology that the researcher dubbed "the committee style"[40] was viewed by Parisian audiences of the Ballets Russes as an exciting innovation, and was compared favorably to the status quo. Critic Valerian Svetlov wrote:

How different things are in the new Diaghilev ballets. Composers, painters, ballet masters, authors and those interested in the arts come together
and plan the work to be done. Subjects are proposed, discussed, and then
worked out in detail. Each makes his suggestions, which are accepted or
rejected by a general consensus of opinion, and thus in the end it is difficult to say which individual was responsible for the libretto, and what
was due to the common effort. . . . So too with the music, the dances: all
is the result of this collective effort. . . . Thus, both artistic unity of design
and execution are achieved.[41]

The MPO was obviously an unknown quantity in Paris; after all, even
in Moscow its professional secrets would not be publicly revealed until
years later. It is all the more remarkable then to witness Svetlov's account
of Diaghilev's practices outlining Mamontov's collaborative methodology with such uncanny precision.

### SYNTHESIS OF THE ARTS

At the conclusion of his report, Svetlov formulated the ultimate goal of
the creative method he described as "artistic unity of both design and
execution." Indeed, the collaboration between the MPO artists, musicians, and stage directors who collectively shaped each production,
guided by the unifying artistic vision of the supervising designer, aimed
at just that. In the process, it contributed to the realization of perhaps
Mamontov's most cherished aesthetic ideal—synthesis of all the arts on
the operatic stage.

The nature of opera as a perfectly synthesized artistic medium was
indeed the reason for Mamontov's fascination with the genre, despite its
complexity and great expense. He saw opera as the perfect art form, and
believed that the conventional understanding of it as primarily a musical work was inherently flawed. In a letter to Shkafer, he protested:

Musicians follow the performance of the notes, but *no one ever talks* about
the *total harmony of the role as a whole* . . . That's why life, brightness,
brilliance, and enchantment are paralyzed on the operatic stage—there
is no continuous current, it keeps being interrupted . . . What is this? This
is stupidity, a lack of development, and a lack of understanding of stage
aesthetics. . . . A B-flat is a good thing, but [not if] it falls onto a wounded
soul, onto an artistic feeling hurt by a shattered illusion.[42]

Unfortunately, Mamontov's distrust of "B-flats" would bring him into a dangerous conflict with Rimsky-Korsakov, Russia's most venerable living opera composer and one of the MPO's most important assets. Throughout his career, Rimsky-Korsakov had always been firmly convinced that music, indeed singing, was opera's structural dominant, while other aspects of its production were relatively unimportant.[43] Self-professedly "sight deaf," he was reluctant to discuss "painterly and visual matters" related to his operas—even Vrubel's designs, despite his close friendship with the artist and his wife, Nadezhda Zabela.[44] He was not, and would not be, included in the collaborative process of Mamontov's enterprise beyond occasionally conducting the orchestra. For the production of his operas, he demanded flawless execution of musical details and nothing else, and would not accept any consideration of staging or design taking precedence over the precise realization of the score. Forgetting his own frustration over the production of *Mlada* only four years earlier (see above), the composer faulted Mamontov for relegating music to a secondary position in his search for a perfect artistic synthesis, and once complained furiously in a letter to Kruglikov: "To [Mamontov], visual impressions are precious, and to me aural ones."[45]

Mamontov, just like Diaghilev, has often been accused of privileging the visual aspects of his productions over the aural ones.[46] In all honesty, he frequently invited such criticism. Six days before the premiere of *Orfeo*, a production plagued by purely vocal problems, an oblivious Mamontov wrote to Polenov: "The opera runs pretty well, beautifully and smoothly. Orfeo and Euridice are very graceful figures, but Amour's image is still not working—the costume needs rethinking."[47] Characteristically, the appearance of the singers and not their voices is the subject of discussion; it is remarkable that Polenov, a painter, was evidently more concerned with the vocal aspects of *Orfeo* than Mamontov, a former singer. On the other hand, unlike Polenov, who begged him for a few extra rehearsals, Mamontov understood that a voice, unlike a costume, could not be reinvented in a week, and the show (particularly a charity event like the premiere of *Orfeo*) had to go on.

Ideally, the visual and the aural were equally important to Mamontov, as the unified aesthetic impression created by the synthesis of all artistic media was the professed goal of each production. In letters to

Shkafer, he discussed the unique nature of the operatic genre, in which every word, every movement, every facial expression should be perfectly in tune "with every measure" of the musical score,[48] and described his favorite opera, *The Snow Maiden*, as "a masterpiece of unity between text and music."[49] Indeed, at the Moscow Private Opera, the visual concept realized in design and staging was supposed to enhance the impression created by the music, an approach rare outside the MPO's walls. Witness, for instance, Gruzinsky's comparison between two productions of Alexander Serov's *Rogneda* after that opera, staged by Mamontov in 1896, was revived at the Bolshoi the following year:

> Comparing the Bolshoi Theater production of *Rogneda* to what we have seen and heard last year on the Solodovnikov Theater stage, we should note the following. Bold, decorative sketches created by the painter, Korovin, wonderfully suited the energetic musical brush strokes with which *Rogneda* is written, resulting in a complete correlation between the internal content of the composition and its external realization. Our aesthetic sensibility, somewhat offended by the harsh musical colors, is kept in this state also by the intelligent staging, resulting in an overall unity of impression. But among the sets by [the Bolshoi's chief decorator] Mr. Waltz (unquestionably excellent in their own right), [Alexander] Serov's music felt out of place—it was too crude.[50]

Mamontov's designers—Polenov, Serov, Korovin, and Vrubel—were known for their sensitivity to all facets of operatic music. To their boss, however, "music" in opera primarily meant singing. At least, vocal technique and role interpretation (solo, ensemble, and choral) were the only musical aspects of opera production in which he was personally involved (see chapter 5). Meanwhile, the orchestra pit was left squarely in the hands of the conductor.[51]

The MPO employed a number of conductors over the years (see plates 29, 30, 31). Most were experienced, competent professionals trained to work under pressure with highly complex scores (even Rimsky-Korsakov grudgingly acknowledged that much in his memoirs).[52] According to press reviews, some (Vladimir Zelyonyi, Giuseppe Truffi) were better interpreters than others (Eugenio Esposito, Enrico Bevigniani, Alessandro Bernardi). None were acknowledged for their musical genius; and only one was noted for his musicianship and great potential. This was the young Sergei Rachmaninov, who worked as an MPO assistant conductor and pianist during the 1897–98 season. Rachmaninov was indeed a great musician. Unfortunately, in 1897 he had absolutely no experience conducting opera and was forced to learn on the job; by the time he could be useful to Mamontov, he no longer worked for him.[53]

Similarly, the MPO orchestra was competent, but not first rate. The best Moscow instrumentalists worked at the Bolshoi Theater: as a state-sponsored institution, it was able to offer them tenure contracts with full benefits including sick leave and a pension plan, something no private enterprise could match. Furthermore, typically for any private opera company, Mamontov's orchestra employed a relatively small number of full-time musicians. The parts for rarely used instruments were arranged for those available, guest-performed, or omitted (a fact that considerably displeased Rimsky-Korsakov in the production of *Sadko*—understandably so, given the intricacy of the opera's orchestration).[54] Most tellingly, while it was acceptable to replace or cancel an opera due to a singer's illness or the sets not being ready on time, no MPO production was ever canceled or delayed because the orchestral parts were not adequately rehearsed.[55]

To be fair, Mamontov did consider the quality of the MPO orchestra to be a shortcoming. Toward the end of the 1898–99 season he reported to Rimsky-Korsakov an increased number of musicians and the addition of new instruments.[56] He also hired a new conductor, Tchaikovsky's student Mikhail Ippolitov-Ivanov (1859–1935), who combined an education and musicianship comparable to Rachmaninov's with professionalism stemming from many years of opera conducting experience in Tiflis. Presumably, Mamontov's plan was to raise the quality of musical execution at his company to the level of the other aspects of its operations in order to achieve the balance necessary for a true synthesis of the arts.[57] But overall, throughout his association with the company, Mamontov discussed specifically musical issues of opera production very little. Perhaps the innovator in him did not feel that what he called "the performance of the notes" required his attention as an artist, for unlike in staging and design, no new word was to be said there.

Thus, Mamontov's approach to the operatic genre was untraditional and arguably, problematic. He saw opera first and foremost as a staged spectacle, a fusion of the visible, if not exclusively the visual—singing, acting, movement, sets, costumes, props, makeup, lighting, special effects, and so on. Mamontov was keenly aware of the uniqueness of his view, which he on one occasion formulated as follows:

> However good [the music] is, without the *spectacle* it would end up on the shelf of oblivion after the second night. Why? . . . Apart from the charm of the music, [opera] demands classic *beauty of characters;* powerful, soul-absorbing *acting; sets* and *costumes* enchanting with their charm; a strict artistic style—in a word, a perfectly unified *spectacle* . . . The beauty of *sound* combined with *the beauty of poetry, strictly beautiful movement,* the *power of acting,* and the enchanting *beauty of color and design*—this is something that has *never yet been achieved!*[58]

In all productions that he personally directed, Mamontov strove for the elusive ideal of this "perfectly unified spectacle." His work did not go unnoticed by the press. *Novosti Sezona* described the 1897 production of Musorgsky's *Khovanshchina* as a perfect, truly amazing blend of "excellent staging, excellent casting . . . masterful sets, accessories, and costumes."[59] Reporting on the company's St. Petersburg production of Borodin's *Prince Igor,* Baskin noted: "The directorate of the Muscovites apparently cares a great deal about the unity of impression, remembering that opera is a synthesis of all the arts; that is why serious attention is paid here to the visual aspect as well as to the music itself."[60]

A particularly telling comment comes from Ivan Lipaev's review of Puccini's *La bohème,* one of Mamontov's most personal works as a stage director: "The ensemble is amazing, starting with wonderful sets by Korovin and ending with many accessories."[61] What is most notable in Lipaev's remark is a word used to describe the performance: "ensemble." Normally, this term would be utilized by theater correspondents to define the interaction of actors in spoken drama; it was frequently used in this manner in relation to Mamontov's goal of fusing singing and acting in his productions (see chapter 5). Lipaev, however, clearly expanded his usage of the term to include Korovin's set designs for *La bohème.* In *The Snow Maiden,* another signature Mamontov production, the "rare, harmonious, artistic ensemble" Lipaev described in his review referred to sets, costumes, accessories, lighting, and staging, as well as the musical performance.[62] As the quoted reviews demonstrate, the term "ensemble" in relation to Mamontov's company took on a new meaning, indicating the harmonious blending of all elements of a production. It is in this meaning, increasingly common by the early twentieth century, that the term would habitually be employed by critics and scholars of Diaghilev's Ballets Russes.

Despite favorable press reviews, Mamontov was restless and dissatisfied, even with his favorite productions, *Orfeo* and *La bohème*. Undaunted by his arrest in the fall of 1899, he was determined to create his perfect spectacle, even if he had to direct it from his jail cell.[63] *The Necklace,* an opera with a Hellenic theme written to his own libretto by a friend, minor composer Nikolai Krotkov, and designed by Vasily Polenov, premiered in Moscow on 27 December of that year. The process of conceptualizing the production from afar forced Mamontov finally to verbalize his ideas and goals, which he outlined in a series of letters to Shkafer, who both directed and starred in the work. Mamontov's most profound aesthetic statements quoted throughout this book were made in connection with this project, including those addressing his approach to synthesis of the arts. He wrote:

> The music, the true beauty of singing, the power of acting, the beauty of stage movement, the beauty of set designs. . . . This is what *The Necklace* is, in my opinion—it is the *beginning of a new trend* in art. Musicians need to feel and understand that in the art business their communication with *artists* would elevate both; they need to realize that, however good a *musical* creation is, on stage, *without* an artist, it would vanish.[64]

After opening to lukewarm interest and disappointing reviews, *The Necklace* broke, cancelled after only two performances. The critics predictably (and not without merit) branded the libretto "a mixture of naïve sentimentality with the fog of decadence and mediocre symbolism."[65] They were equally unflattering about the quality of the music. How justified they were in that respect we will never know for sure: unlike the libretto, the score of the opera did not survive. Yet it is clear that Krotkov's mediocre talent was unlikely to rise to the tremendous aesthetic challenge posed by his librettist Mamontov. And as Mamontov himself would discover, to his immense disappointment, even with an artist, but without a musician at the helm, his artistic creation "vanished" just as surely.

Mamontov's dream of a perfectly synthesized operatic spectacle could not be realized in *The Necklace.* Sergei Diaghilev was luckier: he had Stravinsky (rather than Krotkov) to complement Fokine, Bakst, Benois, and Golovin. With his own creative team complete, Diaghilev would be able to achieve in his Ballets Russes the balance between the arts that eluded his predecessor. The result, as they say, was history:

> The Firebird, being the result of an intimate collaboration between chore-ography, music, and painting, presents us with the most exquisite miracle of harmony imaginable, of sound and form and movement. The old-gold vermiculation of the fantastic backdrop seems to have been invented to a formula identical with that of the shimmering web of the orchestra . . . Stravinsky, Fokine, Golovin in my eyes are but one name.[66]

### THE WAGNERIAN CONNECTION

The ecstatic outburst quoted above, from an anonymous reviewer of *The Firebird,* is just one example of the enormous wave of enthusiasm that surrounded Diaghilev's early Parisian productions. A common topic of discussion in the public and the press was the idea of a synthesis of the arts that seemed to have been, for the first time, perfectly realized by the Ballets Russes. At the time, that idea was commonly viewed as an extension of the Wagnerian concept of *Gesamtkunstwerk,* and as a result, any attempt to implement art synthesis was judged through the Wagnerian prism. The following discussion traces the influence of the Wagnerian discourse on Diaghilev studies and Silver Age scholarship, and investigates the possibility of a Wagnerian connection in Mamontov's approach to synthesis of the arts.

Diaghilev's audiences believed his productions to be superb realizations of the Wagnerian ideal. His exotic tours de force, *Cléopatre* and *Schéhérazade,* were discussed in the press as the true *Gesamtkunstwerke,* indeed superior even to Wagner's original: "[*Cléopatre* is] a dream-like spectacle beside which the Wagnerian synthesis itself is but a clumsy bar-barism," declared Camille Mauclair.[67] This view of the Ballets Russes was carefully and deliberately crafted by its insiders. For instance, Alexandre Benois argued in his review of the company's 1910 season that Diaghilev had achieved the *Gesamtkunstwerk* "only dreamt about" by Wagner.[68] Prince Lieven in his memoirs could not "imagine any spectator who does not feel after experiencing *Petrushka* that mood of exalted satisfaction, which can be given only by a great complete work of art."[69]

Positioning themselves as the heirs to the *Gesamtkunstwerk* dream was vital to Diaghilev and his crew: it allowed them to attract to their theater the crème de la crème of the Parisian intellectual and artistic elite, most of them acknowledged acolytes of the Bayreuth Master. And marketing consideration aside, Diaghilev's team was not entirely disingenuous in their self-proclaimed Wagnerian connection. It was a personal choice, as well as a sign of the times; it was also a part of their intellectual heritage. The history of Russian Wagneriana has been written,[70] and is in any case outside the scope of this book; yet a brief summary here might be useful.

According to Rosamund Bartlett, by the time the complete *Ring* cycle finally appeared in Russia in 1889, the country's intellectuals were well versed in Wagner's theories. Already in the 1860s, despite the fact that the treatises of the Dresden revolutionary were barred from publication, "over 225 articles and reports were written about the composer in the Russian press."[71] Many were sparked by the composer's concert tour of St. Petersburg and Moscow in 1863 and by the St. Petersburg premiere of *Lohengrin* in 1868. The bitter Wagner war that was to rage in the Russian press for the next several decades involved, on the composer's side, Apollon Grigoriev, the venerable writer Vladimir Odoevsky, and Wagner's main champion, composer and critic Alexander Serov. The opposition presented an intriguing combination of opposites: on the one hand, conservatives like Feofil Tolstoy, who asserted the supremacy of Italian opera; on the other, Dargomyzhsky, the Kuchka, and Vladimir Stasov who, from their own realist and nationalist perch, opposed Wagner and the Italians with equal vigor.[72]

The next significant phase of the Wagner polemics in Russia was inspired by the first Bayreuth Festival in 1876, which was exhaustively discussed in the Russian press by respected correspondents exhibiting a wide variety of views. Among the critics officially dispatched to cover the festival by their respective media outlets were the "Russian Hanslick," Hermann Laroche; the venomous Kuchkist César Cui; and their perhaps most objective colleague Pyotr Tchaikovsky, then a reporter for the Moscow daily *Russkie Vedomosti*. Finally, the 1889 guest tour of Angelo Neumann's German Opera, which performed, in addition to two Wagner concerts, four sets of the *Ring* in St. Petersburg and two in Moscow, was covered and discussed in the press with equal intensity.

It appears that by 1898, the year of *Mir Iskusstva*'s founding and Mamontov's first tour of St. Petersburg, Wagner was gradually gaining acceptance in Russia's capital as a significant opera composer, if not a popular one. His operas were being offered by touring foreign troupes, and were also slowly finding their way to the Imperial stages of both capitals. However, as will be discussed in chapter 7, barring the idiosyncrasies of the 1860s debate (such as the personal animosity between Alexander Serov and Stasov that added much fuel to their Wagner polemics), the three-way disposition of the "Wagner war" of 1898 was curiously similar to that of 1868, thirty years earlier. Even some of the "generals" (for instance, Stasov and Cui) remained at their posts. The Wagnerian camp, for its part, lost a faithful field marshal in Alexander Serov; it did, however, gain Sergei Diaghilev.

The Mir Iskusstva members knew and admired Wagner's music; Diaghilev himself was an avid fan. It is difficult to say, however, whether his pronouncement, "not only have we accepted Wagner, we love him passionately," made in the last of the "Complex Questions" editorials, referred to Wagner's scores or to his aesthetic ideas, including *Gesamtkunstwerk*.[73] The group certainly believed it their job to popularize the latter. Henri Lichtenberger's trendy 1898 Wagner digest, *Richard Wagner: Poète et penseur*, was translated and published in installments in *Mir Iskusstva* under the title *Vzglyady Vagnera na Iskusstvo* [*Wagner's Views On Art*]. Friedrich Nietzsche, whose *Die Geburt der Tragödie* was daily reading for the *Mir Iskusstva* editorial board, was represented on the pages of the journal not by that classic volume, but by a translation of his monograph *Richard Wagner in Bayreuth*.[74]

Savva Mamontov, of course, read the journal he sponsored, including its Wagner articles. Since the composer's theories are never mentioned in his extant correspondence, there is no hard evidence that Mamontov was aware of them prior to these *Mir Iskusstva* publications. However, such ignorance is hardly possible. Back in the 1860s, Apollon Grigoriev's promotion of Wagner's ideas in several influential Slavophile journals (including his reprints of Alexander Serov's essays) would certainly have been readily available to him. Mamontov missed Wagner's 1863 visit to Moscow; ironically, at that time he was studying Italian *bel canto* in Milan. However, as a man avidly interested in all artistic and intellectual currents of his time, he could not have missed the press polemic between Alexander Serov and Vladimir Stasov over *Lohengrin* that was making waves in the music world in 1868. There is also no evidence that Mamontov ever visited the Bayreuth Festspielhaus. But it is highly unlikely that, as a friend of Nikolai Rubinstein, who was a member of the Moscow *Wagnerverein*, and an intimate of the Moscow Conservatory circles, he would not have been familiar with Tchaikovsky's coverage of it.

As for Wagner's music, Mamontov did know some of it. He staged *Lohengrin* at the Private Opera in February 1887, and later claimed to have staged *Tannhäuser* as well (no evidence of this production is available). He also apparently considered producing *Siegfried* and *Die Walküre* at the MPO during the 1898–99 and 1899–1900 seasons. The reasons for his contemplating the *Ring* productions (thwarted by the lack of suitable forces), however, might have been more ideological and commercial than aesthetic (see chapter 7). There is also documentary evidence that *Tristan* and *Parsifal* were under discussion for possible inclusion in the 1899–1900 season repertoire. The initiative was Melnikov's, who suggested, interestingly, that instead of reviving *Lohengrin,* in which "nothing new could be said," Mamontov ought to "stage *Parsifal* or *Tristan und Isolde,* both wildly famous yet completely unknown" in Russia.[75] While Melnikov's assertion regarding *Tristan* was not entirely accurate (the opera was unknown in Moscow, but it was premiered in St. Petersburg in March 1898 and staged at the Mariinsky the following year), the production of *Parsifal,* if realized, would indeed have been the Russian premiere.

We do not have access to Mamontov's reply, so it is unclear whether or not he knew these works, or what he thought about his assistant's proposal. However, Melnikov's discussion of the operas, including MPO casting possibilities, without mentioning their author's name or the voice types needed to perform them indicates that he expected his addressee to have at least some knowledge of the works. It is unknown whether Mamontov would have pursued Wagnerian projects further had he stayed at the helm of the company after 1900; the composer's increasing popularity would probably have impacted his decision. Personally, however, Wagner was not Mamontov's favorite. As late as 1910 he would admit in an interview: "Still, I just don't understand Wagner," illustrating his statement with an amusing anecdote about falling asleep midway through a performance of *Die Walküre* at the Paris Opéra.[76]

While some of Wagner's theoretical ideas, especially his view of a synthesis of the arts as a vehicle for serving drama, paralleled Mamontov's own approach to stage directing (see chapter 5), Mamontov's understanding of art synthesis, despite its seemingly Wagnerian rhetoric, likely stemmed from other sources. One of these sources, tentatively suggested by Rossikhina, was the amateur theatricals of the Mamontov Circle in which artists from different fields exchanged and blended their ideas as well as performed the tasks outside their own areas of expertise (such as Vasnetsov's acting, Korovin's singing, and Serov's belly dancing).[77]

But even outside Abramtsevo, it is hard to disagree with Taruskin, who states that "it is high time to stop ascribing to Wagner's influence every turn-of-the-century manifestation of the tendency to mix artistic media or see union as their highest aim."[78] Synthesis of the arts proved to be one of the most potent ideas floating through the cultural universe of the *fin de siècle*. Already Charles Baudelaire viewed a systematic effort to break down conventional boundaries between the arts as the main characteristic of decadence. After centuries of artistic specialization resulting in some subjects "belonging to painting, others to music, others to literature," Baudelaire observed a radically different principle taking hold in contemporary art: "Is it an inevitable result of decadence that every art today reveals a desire to encroach upon neighboring arts, and the painters introduce musical scales, sculptors use color, writers use the plastic means, and other artists, those who concern us today, display a kind of encyclopedic philosophy in the plastic arts themselves?"[79] In his own creative works, particularly in the famous poem *Correspondences* (which made as much impact on Russian decadents as it did on their French counterparts), Baudelaire revealed his allegiance to the very same principle. Meanwhile, in Germany, Nietzsche in *Die Geburt der Tragödie* called for the return to ancient drama that united all the arts and discussed Wagner's role in that process. And in Russia, Vladimir Solovyov believed art to be a theurgy—"divine agency of revelation and prophecy," with the power to transform the world.[80] In order to achieve its goal, all branches of the arts needed to be combined, and therefore the highest, most synthetic and thus most theurgic of the arts had to be theater, which was to become the temple of the new art-religion.

Solovyov and Nietzsche proved potent sources of inspiration for the mystic symbolists—Alexander Blok, Andrei Bely, and Vyacheslav Ivanov. According to Rosenthal, Ivanov studied Wagner's ideas of music drama and art synthesis, but in his 1909 book *Po Zvyozdam* [*Lodestars*] discussed them as merely the first step toward harnessing the power of theurgic art.[81] He believed that Wagner's greatest achievement was his attempt to recapture in his music dramas the lost sense of collectivity (*sobornost*) between art and the people, present in ancient rites and to some extent in Greek tragedy but lost to the modern world.[82] As mentioned in chapter 1, the concept of *sobornost*, much debated by Solovyov and other philosophers, became a cornerstone of mystic symbolism. So it is interesting to note Ilya Bondarenko's description of Mamontov's production of *Sadko* as "a truly *sobornoe deyanie* [communal action]."[83] Writing in 1941, Bondarenko deliberately applied to an MPO creation the term used by Ivanov in his calls for the synthesized art-religion of the future. Considering the fact that in Stalinist Russia it would have been politically astute to avoid any such connections (for the safety of the writer as well as of the cause he promoted), we must conclude that the ideological link between Mamontov and Russian symbolism was extremely important to Bondarenko. He was, incidentally, one of Mamontov's closest friends during the 1900–10s and perhaps was privy to his opinions about the symbolists that were not preserved either in correspondence or in the press.

Ivanov himself, of course, could not have considered Mamontov's company as a vehicle capable of realizing his ideals of *vse-edinstvo* [all-unity]; after all, it no longer existed by the time he started developing his ideas. Instead, he placed his hopes in Alexander Scriabin's colossal *Mysterium*, the plans for which are partially accessible in the extant sketches for its *Predvaritelnoe Deistvo* [*Preparatory Act*]. The description of this synthesized music drama turned religious rite provides us with an (admittedly vague) picture of the complete synthesis of the arts (music, poetry, visual arts, dance, drama, even architecture) organized into a type of liturgy:

> In this artistic event there will not be a single spectator. All will be participants. . . . The cast of performers includes, of course, an orchestra, a large mixed choir, an instrument with visual effects, dancers, a procession,

incense, rhythmicized textual articulation. . . . The form of the cathedral, in which it will all take place, will not be of one monotonous type of stone, but will continually change, along with the atmosphere and motion of the *Mysterium*. This of course will happen with the aid of mists and lights, which will modify the architectural contours.[84]

Unlike Ivanov, Mamontov never viewed himself as a theurgist. Instead, like Bryusov, Diaghilev, and other decadents, he was a self-professed hedonist: not trying to transform the world, he preferred to decorate it. While he apparently admired Scriabin's music ca. 1908 and was aware of his theosophical ideas,[85] no information is available about his opinion of the composer's late style. It is all the more remarkable to read, in the Moscow daily *Kurier,* the following description of the premiere of Mamontov's *Orfeo:* "The production of *Orfeo* was thorough, from the artistic set designs to the interesting staging, even to the extent of burning sacrificial incense in the auditorium, all of which helped to enliven Gluck's slightly old-fashioned opera."[86]

This review of *Orfeo*—a production that, as we have seen, was conceived as a realization of Mamontov's aesthetic creed—does put his concept of synthesized opera production conspicuously in line with Scriabin's own description of *Mysterium*. And lest we wonder about the significance of this single episode as an illustration of Mamontov's views, theatrical projects he realized and contemplated in the later 1900s may shed some light on the issue. In a letter to Polenov regarding a scene from *The Phantoms of Hellas,* Mamontov advised his collaborator not to introduce too much coloratura into one of the female parts, reminding him that "since a dance is going on at the same time, [it] will be very difficult to perform."[87] As this remark suggests, singing and dancing were to be merged in the new opera, for which Mamontov was not only librettist but also author of the overall artistic idea. Even more remarkably, one week after that letter, Mamontov wrote to Polenov again, describing a new project he had conceived based, unsurprisingly, on yet another Greek myth. He wrote: "I have translated *Yabloko Razdora* [*The Apple of Strife*]. This could be a very beautiful, noble piece, but not in operatic form, but in some new one. There is ballet here, melodrama, singing—in a word, a new form. It may offer fascinating beauty."[88] Clearly, *The Apple of Strife,* if realized, would have been a remarkably innovative work that fully abandoned traditional operatic forms in order to achieve a complete synthesis of the arts. It certainly would have placed Mamontov squarely in the modernist camp.

## MAMONTOV AND THE DECADENTS

None of the actual MPO productions were quite as radical as *The Apple of Strife* of Mamontov's imagination. Nevertheless, the press routinely accused the company of modernist bias, and its leader of breeding, shielding, and disseminating everywhere the seeds of "his beloved decadence."[89] As we have seen, Mamontov, despite his aestheticist philosophy, his interest in and support for modernist art, his cutting-edge theatrical experiments, and his openly bohemian lifestyle, did not see himself as a decadent any more than Sergei Diaghilev did.[90] Yet his work, especially the décor of his productions, was all too often charged with decadent leanings. For instance, according to *Russkoe Slovo,* Konstantin Korovin was "commonly nicknamed" a decadent as early as 2 November 1896 (the date of Alexander Gruzinsky's comment in that paper).[91] Mikhail Vrubel's decadent affiliations dated from earlier still: young journalist and future renowned realist writer Maxim Gorky (1868–1936), in his report on the 1896 Nizhny Novgorod Exhibition, described Vrubel's panels exhibited there by Mamontov as "a direct reflection of that fashionable malaise named decadence."[92]

Although Korovin and Vrubel were not the only MPO artists afflicted with Gorky's "fashionable malaise,"[93] the press criticism was typically aimed at the pair as the designers with the most exposure. Their work was perceived as the face of the Moscow Private Opera design team. Indeed, Korovin's creative touch, on the level of overall concept and/or execution, can be identified in almost every Mamontov production between 1896 and 1899. Vrubel rarely designed sets at that time.[94] His art, however, more than that of any other painter, represented the face of the company: his signature decorative vignettes graced programs and playbills, and his arresting images were also exhibited on the Solodovnikov Theater curtain and ceiling panel.[95] It was Vrubel's work that was the primary target of a feuilleton whose author declared the building's "decadent" interior design an example of "not even art spared for art's sake."[96] Apparently, Vrubel's "decadent" sets were similarly unable to attract anything but criticism: they were routinely described as "an-

noying" and "anti-artistic."[97] His imaginative ornaments once reportedly evoked "a feeling of disgust by their resemblance to a pack of giant
rats" in a *Novosti Dnya* critic, who then proceeded to caution the artist
on his use of "decadent painterly techniques."[98]

The charge was not to be taken lightly: the Russian operatic press
of the 1890s used the accusation of decadent or symbolist tendencies
as a harsh and comprehensive indictment of a theatrical venture. It is
interesting to observe how Moscow journalists adjusted their tone depending on their general attitude toward the MPO and its leader. Thus,
a wicked *Russkoe Slovo* feuilleton dedicated to Mamontov's arrest in
September 1899 depicted his partiality for decadent art as one of the
fatal character flaws that led to his downfall. As the author sarcasti-
cally pointed out, "only a few steps appear to separate the Solodovnikov
Theater from the Taganskaya Prison," the new home of the ubiquitous
"chief of railroads, millionaire, Maecenas, art patron, and planter of
decadent art."[99] Similarly, if the critics wished to censure a particular
Mamontov production, sharp comments on its decadent designs would
abound in the reviews. On the other hand, if a specific production
was to be commended—an increasingly common occurrence as the
company's popularity and support in the city grew—the critics often
preferred to avoid discussing its set designs altogether. Alternatively,
the "decadence" of the décor might be downplayed: the sets would be
described as "very bold and a little decadent"[100] or exhibiting "a slightly
decadent bias."[101] Finally, a critic might issue a halfhearted compliment
like the following: "The designs are splendid, although not free of the
usual symbolist slithering."[102]

The "decadence" of Korovin and Vrubel's designs referred primarily to their innovative painterly techniques. Unlike the worldly, sophisticated Parisian elite that would later flock to see Diaghilev's productions, the majority of Mamontov's audience comprised conservative
middle-class Muscovites who in the 1890s were only minimally exposed
to contemporary European art.[103] Instead, they would have been familiar with the work of two local artistic groups, the Academy painters
and the Wanderers. Despite differing in their choice of subject matter,
these groups shared a generally traditional approach to form, color,
and painterly technique.[104] As a result, thick textures, rough, broad
brushstrokes, and strikingly unusual color combinations employed

by Mamontov's decadent painters, along with their experiments with perspective, and their preference for color over shape shocked many of their spectators.

According to press accounts, the public apparently experienced the visual culture shock produced by the designs as a sense of incompleteness, an impression of a sketch rather than of a serious, finished work.[105] For example, according to Gruzinsky, the *Khovanshchina* sets, although "wonderfully conceived," were "executed clumsily, perhaps even with *deliberate carelessness*."[106] Similarly, washed-out colors and vague shapes of objects portrayed on the backdrops were increasingly noted as characteristic of the "decadent" painterly style. A correspondent of the St. Petersburg daily *Novoe Vremya*, for instance, indicated in his 1898 review of the company's tour that the sets, while announced as being "new, just recently painted" on the playbills, looked "pale and worn out." He finally concluded: "Clearly, the artists who created them are drawn toward the decadent style of painting."[107] In a review published by the same critic two weeks later, no hesitation was displayed: "It is difficult to approve of the decadent, as if worn-out style of the set designs, although their composition is original," he wrote.[108] Indeed, the qualities that the conservative *Novoe Vremya* reporter found so hard to approve were equally disturbing to that newspaper's avowed enemy, Vladimir Stasov. In a section of his essay "The Moscow Private Opera in Petersburg," which treated the company's designers, Stasov addressed the "unfinished" quality of the sets and, notably, attributed it to time constraints. According to the critic, the problem lay in the fact that the great artistic ideas of Mamontov's painters were executed in a hurry: "Justice requires us to note that frequently the *composition* of the sets in Mamontov's theater is better than their execution: this has occurred, probably, only due to the hurried nature of the work and thus the occasional lack of time for the completely detailed, precise, and perfect execution of the *composition* on such huge canvases."[109] Justice requires us to note that the sets Stasov was discussing in his article were not first unveiled during the company's 1898 St. Petersburg tour. Instead, they were already utilized for a period ranging from two months (*Sadko*) to several years (*The Snow Maiden*). Any rush job would certainly have been corrected by that time, especially considering the fact that winter months were normally a low season for Mamontov's designers, since premieres rarely occurred after the Christmas holidays, and particularly taking into consideration the enormous significance attached to the troupe's first visit to the capital. The "incompleteness" Stasov noted in his essay was most likely the result, either of the critic's own (mis) understanding of the artists' modernist techniques or of his attempt, in a desire to support Mamontov's enterprise, to explain away the unusual characteristics of its designs and thus protect it from the accusations of decadence.

## HISTORICISM AND STYLIZATION

Stasov had a good reason for coming to (what he thought was) the defense of the MPO: he held Mamontov in high esteem and considered him an ideological ally. Yet as seen in chapter 3, whenever Stasov put his formidable influence behind a cause, he was relentless in ensuring that the cause "behaved" in line with his expectations, or at least making certain it was publicly presented as such. In his discussions of Mamontov's enterprise, therefore, the critic deliberately sought out and praised the qualities that he himself considered admirable, while ignoring or explaining away the others. With respect to visual design, Stasov's battle cry was historicism.

In Russian theater criticism of the 1890s, historicism was understood as fidelity to historical accounts in all details of scenery, costumes, accessories, and so on. It was an accepted style for designing all stage productions, dramatic and operatic, and particularly those based on a historical subject. The historicist approach to design was viewed as a progressive trend;[110] the Imperial Theater productions that did not adhere to it were criticized as obsolete. An art historian by trade, Stasov used his considerable clout to demand so-called "archeological exactness" from all historical productions he reviewed.[111] The critic had his own reasons for raising the historicist banner: to him, a precise rendition of historical details was a realization of the idea of truth on stage.[112] In his well known critique of the Mariinsky revival of Glinka's *Ruslan,* which condemned the production as "an example of tastelessness, senselessness, and ignorance" on the part of decorators and costume designers, Stasov described the sorcerer Chernomor and his attendants as "some kind of crowd of beggars and invalids in torn clothes." Prince Svetozar evidently looked like a janitor, and sorceress Naina like "a witch from a street puppet show." As an example of a "correct" staging of *Ruslan*, the critic offered the 1867 Prague production directed by the Kuchka's leader Mily Balakirev. The designer of the Prague *Ruslan* was art historian and archeologist Gornostaev, who earned Stasov's approval by possessing, "apart from fine taste and painterly talent . . . a very solid art-historical knowledge" with a special expertise in ancient Russian art.[113] It is noteworthy that Stasov defined *Ruslan* as a fairytale opera, yet issued the same demand for authenticity in its designs that he would for a real historical subject.

Having accepted Mamontov as a comrade-in-arms and having observed a great number of historical operas on his playbill, Stasov naturally expected the idea of historical authenticity to be preserved on the MPO stage. The critic reviewed the company's productions in accordance with this assumption. He pointed out various details in the *Streletskaya Sloboda* [*The Streltsy Compound*, act 3] set from *Khovanshchina* that in his opinion "truly resurrected the old Moscow," and approved the recycling of a *Maid of Pskov* set for *The Oprichnik* as "permissible and lawful, for both operas depict the epoch of Ivan the Terrible." Vasnetsov's *Berendei Palace* from *The Snow Maiden* (see plate 9) was described as not only poetic, but also full of "old Russian truth."[114]

Some of Stasov's observations on the historical approach evident in the company's productions are clearly on target. As we shall see in chapter 6, Mamontov was influenced to an extent by the historicism trend. He accepted the need for historical research in staging operas set in the past, as evident from a *Russkoe Slovo* report on the production of Verstovsky's *Askoldova Mogila* [*Askold's Tomb*]: "Historical costumes have been prepared for the opera. Set designs, armor, and all the accessories have been created from sketches by well-known painters."[115] In applying historicism to his productions, Mamontov saw an additional benefit of avoiding traditional operatic clichés: an unconventional setting of Gounod's *Faust* in a medieval German town is a good example of his approach. Unlike Stasov, however, he did not limit himself by history, as is evident from his reaction to some historicist productions he would witness in his later years. Platon Mamontov recalled the following outburst from his uncle, after attending a historically informed performance of *Evgeny Onegin* [*Eugene Onegin*]: "They should have at least given us beauty, Uncle Savva said, instead of putting charwomen on stage and saying that the landowners always had those in the old days! Know-it-alls! They forgot all about Tchaikovsky!"[116]

The reference to beauty, even at the expense of the historical truth, is of course characteristic of Mamontov's thinking. His aesthetic priorities were markedly different from Stasov's, and while in historical operas such as *Boris Godunov, Khovanshchina,* and *Rogneda* their visions might have overlapped, they diverged noticeably in dealing with fairy tales or mythology. To Stasov, as we have seen, the historical approach was just as necessary for staging Glinka's *Ruslan* as, for example, the same composer's *Zhizn za tsarya [A Life for the Tsar]*. Mamontov, on the other hand, turned to a different idea in designing his legends and fairy tales: the symbolist idea of *uslovnost*—idealization, or stylization.

The Russian decadents of the Silver Age embraced stylization as an essential quality of the new theater, opposed to the outdated realism and appropriate particularly for a realization of ancient myth. Valery Bryusov, for example, concluded his 1902 manifesto "Useless Truth" with a call for all artists to move away from "the useless truth of the modern stage to the conscious *uslovnost* of ancient theater."[117] It is unsurprising, therefore, that the first time we encounter the idea of *uslovnost* in Mamontov's correspondence, it happens to be in relation to Gluck's *Orfeo*.

In a letter to Polenov in which Mamontov first brought up the subject of *Orfeo,* he made the following request with respect to its designs: "Compose the sets in a strict classical style. It seems to me that they must be done in completely light-colored, stylized tones, especially paradise (i.e., the Elysian Fields)."[118] In another letter later that month, he confirmed: "The picture should be very *light* and overall somewhat *uslovnaya* [stylized]."[119] Mamontov was sufficiently pleased with the results of Polenov's work to suggest a similar approach for his *Necklace*. He wrote to the painter: "The visual aspect [of *The Necklace*] is not complex but requires a noble artist such as yourself; that is, the same tone needs to be presented here as that which you managed to lift so incomparably high in *Aphrodite* and *Orfeo*. The same pure, noble, and somewhat stylized Greece."[120]

A rare group photo of the final apotheosis from the 1897 production of *Orfeo* offers an illustration of Mamontov's concept of *uslovnost* (see plate 35). In the center of the composition is an idealized ancient

Greek temple (rather than a specific building) set against the backdrop of an idealized Mediterranean landscape. An ahistorical approach is evident here. Its cause, however, was not ignorance, which would have been Stasov's habitual charge. Polenov's knowledge of classical ancient art and architecture was impressive. He traveled extensively in Greece and the Middle East, and frequently used minutely realistic details of his experiences in his mythological and Biblical works exhibited—and lauded—by the Wanderers. In his designs for *Orfeo,* the painter could have easily used specific locations and monuments.[121] Instead, he chose to disregard the possibility of a realist reading and follow Mamontov's request for a stylized treatment of his subject.

Victor Vasnetsov demonstrated a similar approach to Russian antiquity in his acclaimed designs for act 2 of Rimsky-Korsakov's *Snow Maiden—Berendei's Palace* (plate 9), which earned such high praise from Stasov as an example of "old Russian truth." Taruskin, meanwhile, called Vasnetsov's design the first major post-realist, post-Wanderer departure in Russian painting, and endorsed a Silver Age reading of it as the first page in the history of Russian modernism.[122]

Interestingly, these two contradictory assessments refer to the very same feature of *Berendei's Palace*—its indebtedness to a thorough knowledge of folk art that its author had accumulated in Abramtsevo workshops. Despite what Stasov evidently believed, Vasnetsov did not approach the *Snow Maiden* sets as a realist, by copying traditional models, although such a method would have been completely acceptable—after all, the production did, to Stasov's delight, use original or precisely imitated village costumes. Instead, the painter absorbed traditional designs he had studied, and created his own artistic variation on them, spinning "a novel poetic system" from "old peasant folk motives."[123] For example, the ornaments decorating the palace walls that so excited Stasov are highly atypical for Russian folk architecture; on the other hand, they were commonly used in traditional brocaded and embroidered clothing.[124] Folk embroidery patterns observed at an Abramtsevo workshop were thus "translated" into a different artistic medium, so that "the traditional vocabulary of ornamental forms was enlarged, and this in turn paved the way for a new plastic system."[125]

This aesthetization of folklore evident in Vasnetsov's *Snow Maiden* designs may also be discerned in Vrubel's majolica, Elena Polenova's book illustrations, and the work of other Abramtsevo-affiliated artists. Indeed, it would become one of the fundamental principles of the Russian *style moderne*. As such, it found a particularly concentrated manifestation in the flamboyant Ballets Russes designs by Leon Bakst. Similarly to Vasnetsov's, Bakst's designs never claimed "archeological exactness" while managing to look authentically "Russian" to their audiences—a clear example of Diaghilev's company adopting a crucial design concept developed at Mamontov's enterprise.

One of the most far-reaching applications of this approach at the MPO was Korovin's 1897 set designs for Rimsky-Korsakov's *Sadko*. The sets attracted much criticism at the time for their flattened, two-dimensional appearance that seemed to ignore basic laws of painterly perspective. A diligent student of Polenov and an excellent easel painter, Korovin chose to abandon the accepted approach to theatrical design, which called for creating the illusion of three-dimensional reality on the backdrop. Instead of the real world, he searched for inspiration in old art forms, such as traditional icon painting and the *lubok* prints (see chapter 3, n.25). Both genres long fascinated Mamontov's artists, particularly due to their use of flat, perspectiveless space:

> The artists in Savva Mamontov's Circle paid close attention to the perspectival conventions of the old icon painters and miniaturists. In their sketches and finished works, they were inspired by the dynamic patterns in icons and miniatures, asymmetrical architectural compositions, repeated motifs, strong contrasts between wide surfaces and deep narrow openings, arabesques and bright colors—in short, the plastic vocabulary—of the old Russian masters.[126]

A unique photograph of the Torzhishche [the Marketplace, scene 4] from Mamontov's production of *Sadko* clearly illustrates Korovin's approach (see plate 36). The buildings on the left side of the stage are two-dimensional (note especially the roofs); there is no shading or any other attempt to create an illusion of depth. There is no blending of colors; the artist even abandons his signature fragmented brushwork for thick, rough, "primitive" brushstrokes imitating a child's drawing. An aesthetic application of the *lubok* style, this manner would later become typical of the Russian neo-primitivists Mikhail Larionov, Kuzma Petrov-Vodkin, Natalia Goncharova, and young Kazimir Malevich—the artists who, despite an acknowledged influence of Cézanne and Matisse, had always traced the main source of their inspiration to Russian *lubok* and icon painting.[127] Perhaps even more telling are the sails of the ships on Korovin's backdrop: their stylized shapes, borrowed from the *lubok,* would emerge in the paintings and book illustrations of Ivan Bilibin and Wassily Kandinsky.

It is perhaps unsurprising that Larionov, Goncharova, and the Russian Cézannistes—indeed a majority of the Russian avant-garde artists of the early twentieth century—would start their careers as students of Konstantin Korovin. By the time they finish their training in the late 1900s and early 1910s, their work, though still cutting-edge, would receive philosophical justification, get placed in the context of similar artistic trends in the West, and find its audience. In 1897, however, the use of the *lubok* as a source for formal experimentation was a completely novel idea in Russian painting. It was equally unusual in stage design, and Korovin, of course, chose the controversial approach deliberately. Like Rimsky-Korsakov, he was facing the challenge of finding a comparable realization in a different artistic medium of the ancient Russian folk legend of Sadko. And like the composer, who turned for help to ancient folk poetry and original epic melodies, the artist tapped into the oldest layer of folk painterly tradition available to him, and assimilated this tradition into a modern creative vision of his subject. Realized in Mamontov's production, this vision turned out to be remarkably compatible with Rimsky-Korsakov's score.

The structure of *Sadko* is epic in its proportions; its loose dramatic intrigue; its juxtaposition of sweeping tableaux separated in time and space; and its characters, which symbolically represent Christianity and paganism, the realm of the real and the world of fantasy. With its tendency toward portraying its characters and its worlds as carefully crafted doubles, mirrors of each other, the music of *Sadko* has its own iconic quality, its own two-dimensionality.[128] The composer here created two contrasting soundscapes: one of the legendary "real," rendered via the adaptation and stylization of folk music and Orthodox chant, another of the equally legendary "unreal," realized through the artificially designed symmetry of octatonic scales and augmented triads.[129] People and creatures occupying these soundscapes are their reflections—just as intangible, and just as symbolic and profoundly meaningful as the faces of saints on the old icons and the figures in the *lubok* prints.

The composer himself seems to have been acutely conscious of the decorative, "designed" quality of his music for *Sadko* and other so-called fantastic operas—of their underlying artifice. In a letter to Nadezhda Zabela,[130] Rimsky-Korsakov described his fantastic operas as lacking "humanity" (that is, realistic drama), and their compositional process as "coloring in the little boxes" (i.e., design patterns), as opposed to the "free painting" typical of a more traditional work like *The Tsar's Bride*.[131] The tone of the letter suggests that the composer considered the decorative two-dimensionality of *Sadko* to be a stylistic weakness. However, Korovin's reading, realized in his designs for Mamontov's production, accepted and affirmed the perspectiveless quality of the music with an equally flattened *lubok*-inspired décor, thus not only asserting the ancient folk roots of the plot, but also proclaiming the opera's modernity, almost against the wishes of its author. A strikingly novel reading such as this was of course unlikely to find a favorable reception in a conservative majority of Moscow critics and audiences. It was, in effect, an artistic creation for its own sake. But at least one reviewer, Nikolai Kashkin, in his report on *Sadko*'s premiere for the Moscow daily *Russkie Vedomosti,* commented favorably on Korovin's designs, finding his approach original and appropriate for a folk epic.[132]

## STYLIZATION IN STAGE MOVEMENT

Thus, in designing the MPO productions, Mamontov and his artists aesthetically "translated" their ancient Greek and Russian models via the use of *uslovnost,* or stylization. True to their principle of creating a unified visual impression for each production, they went beyond sets, costumes, makeup, and props, and applied the same aesthetic standards to stage movement. Consider, for example, the following comment by a reviewer of *Orfeo*: "One had to invest much work in order to lend every single movement of the masses the fluidity and harmony necessitated by the Greek character of the opera, and we must admit that this work was crowned with complete success. . . . The movements of the masses in act 1 and tableaux 3 and 5 displayed that very fluidity and harmony."[133] The phrase *plavnost i garmonichnost,* translated here as "fluidity and harmony," suggests an image of unified, synchronized, and ultimately deliberate, predetermined, stylized gestures and movements of the chorus—the image diametrically opposed to the so-called "individualized crowd" of realist operas on which Mamontov's enterprise made its reputation.[134]

The principals of *Orfeo* were evidently moving in a similar manner, with every gesture carefully choreographed by Mamontov himself. This stylized stage motion, blended with the stylized sets, was in fact central to the artistic conception of that production, dictating its other aspects, including casting. Thus, as we have seen, mezzo-soprano Maria Chernenko (plate 35, front center) might not have been the best choice for the leading role from a purely musical standpoint. However, the singer's rare talent for expressive gesture made her indispensable in a part conceived essentially as vocalized pantomime. Indeed, *Orfeo* was not the only example of Mamontov integrating his unique choreography into an operatic production. For instance, in Saint-Saëns's *Samson et Dalila*, every moment of Delilah's role was again carefully choreographed for Chernenko.

More significant still is the case of Alexander Serov's *Yudif* [*Judith*]— a production designed by its composer's son, a Repin student, an Abramtsevo insider, and perhaps one of Russia's most original modernist painters, Valentin Serov. The stage movement for a leading character, Holofernes, portrayed by Feodor Chaliapin, was choreographed two-dimensionally in a simulacrum of ritualized figures in profile postures that Serov had found in albums of ancient Assyrian bas-reliefs. The same images also served as models for the opera's sets and costumes (see plates 12, 13). In his memoirs, Ilya Bondarenko described how the bas-relief idea was born: "His arms spread, [Serov] walked around the dining room like a true Assyrian, bending over and staring with bulging eyes. Mamontov approvingly stressed that the movement should be much sharper than in the book illustration, since one would need to make allowances for the stage."[135]

In his discussion of Chaliapin's interpretation of Holofernes, Abram Gozenpud, again with the best intentions of protecting Mamontov and Chaliapin, toned down the radical nature of Serov's modernist approach, claiming that the singer "created a realistic image, despite the stylized character of poses and movements."[136] Since according to Dmitry Sarabyanov "a combination of the stylized and the natural, the real" was a distinct trait of the Russian *style moderne*, the two aspects of the production need not be perceived as mutually exclusive.[137] Yet Gozenpud apparently viewed them as such. And possibly, so did Chaliapin—a fact that may shed light on an intriguing little mystery that surrounds the singer's work on *Judith*.

The MPO premiere of *Judith* took place on 23 November 1898. By mid-December, Chaliapin declared that he would no longer perform the role of Holofernes, ostensibly to concentrate on Musorgsky's *Boris Godunov*, which premiered on 7 December. The singer's decision—unprecedented for Mamontov's disciplined troupe—has never received a satisfactory explanation. Clearly, the part of Boris is larger, more prominent, and musically superior to that of Holofernes. But perhaps other factors might have been involved. As we shall see in the next chapter, Chaliapin's primary focus was always the drama of his roles. While concerned with costume, hair, makeup, and other details of his character's appearance, the singer considered the visual aspect a means to realizing the overall dramatic concept, which at this early stage of his career leaned toward the then-fashionable psychological naturalism. As a result, Chaliapin might have found that Serov's stylized approach, deliberately restrictive of his range of motion, contradicted his current interests, realized to such a great extent in Musorgsky's character.

Later, during his tenure at the Imperial Theaters, the restless Chaliapin returned to *Judith*, which was revived with his participation in 1911. According to Gozenpud, in the Mariinsky version, "the elements of stylization, only outlined in the earlier production, became stronger. Some critics even doubted the legitimacy of such an approach to Alexander Serov's opera."[138] Among the elements that strengthened the stylized tone of the production were its ballet scenes, choreographed by Michel Fokine to create living bas-reliefs. The critics also observed that the movements of singers on stage were evidently patterned after those of the dancers. They failed to notice, however, that the result was the same stylized "fluidity and harmony" that Mamontov had first envisioned in his unique operatic pantomimes.

It is notable that Mamontov's concept of signification through choreography was applied exclusively in the operas whose plots were based on (broadly defined) myth—whether the ancient Greece of *Orfeo*, the eschatology of *The Demon*, or the Biblical Oriental exotica of *Samson* and *Judith*. He wanted to capture in motion the essence of myth—its ephemeral, preternatural quality. The team of symbolists running Diaghilev's

Ballets Russes was convinced that the outdated genre of opera could not capture that quality; to them, it could only be revealed in ballet. The ritualized dance of the nymphs in Nijinsky's *L'aprés-midi d'un faune* was a realization of their vision—which makes it particularly intriguing to speculate whether that production might have been partially influenced by Mamontov's *Judith*. Act 3 of that opera was included in the Ballets Russes' inaugural 1909 season, with Chaliapin in the title role offering essentially the same interpretation he had developed at the Moscow Private Opera. The sets were painted anew under Valentin Serov's supervision, while all costumes and accessories, according to press accounts, came directly from Mamontov's 1898 production.[139] To be sure, that last idea may have come to Diaghilev as an afterthought: the Imperial Theaters refused to rent their costumes for his risky venture. The choice, however, was not arbitrary: with Fokine's stylized dances, Chaliapin's ritualized movement, Serov's Assyrian set designs, and Mamontov-approved costumes and props, Diaghilev's Parisian *Judith* became a true realization of Mamontov's decadent dream.

## MAMONTOV AND DIAGHILEV

The resurrection of Mamontov's *Judith* on Diaghilev's stage was certainly a unique experiment. Yet Diaghilev scholars have noted numerous connections between the Moscow Private Opera and the Russian Seasons, a theatrical venture that would become the Ballets Russes. For instance, Serov, Korovin, and Golovin—the designers trained at Mamontov's company—collaborated with Diaghilev on his Parisian productions. Operas presented as a part of the Russian Seasons, including *Boris Godunov, The Maid of Pskov, Sadko, Maiskaya noch [May Night], Prince Igor,* and *Khovanshchina,* as well as *Judith,* were all central to the MPO repertoire, and indeed directly identified with the company. Diaghilev's lead singers, Chaliapin and tenor Dmitry Smirnov (1881–1944), started their careers under Mamontov's tutelage.[140] Finally, we have already witnessed stage director Alexander Sanin, creator of Diaghilev's spectacular *Boris Godunov,* publicly acknowledging Mamontov as his mentor.[141] Nevertheless, few researchers who have recognized these facts have attempted to explain them as anything more than a series of historical coincidences. Lynn Garafola went furthest in calling the MPO "the musical and artistic blueprint" for Diaghilev's Russian Seasons, but she stopped short of establishing any firm connections between Mamontov's enterprise and the Ballets Russes beyond their sharing of repertoire and personnel.[142]

As we have seen, however, there are numerous points of ideological convergence between the two companies and their leaders. These include, but are not limited to, an adherence to the art for art's sake philosophy, a striving for the realization of a synthesis of the arts through a collaborative creative process, and the fostering of a unified visual impression for each production; a guarded stand on realism, and a rejection of unqualified historicism; and, finally, a reliance on stylization in staging and design. It is possible that Garafola's caution, apart from a natural inclination to place her own hero in the limelight, stems from a paucity of documentary evidence that proves that the correspondences between the two enterprises are more than coincidental. Both in Russia and elsewhere, scholars from various disciplines drew parallels between Mamontov and Diaghilev. Most commonly they cite Mamontov's co-sponsorship of the journal *Mir Iskusstva* during its first year of publication, as well as discussing his designers' collaboration with Diaghilev on his various ventures, including the Ballets Russes. Garafola went so far as to hint at a similarity in the methodologies of the two companies, which she linked to the egalitarian traditions of Russia's merchant enterprises.[143] But until now, researchers have always avoided discussing personal connections between Mamontov and Diaghilev. The reason was a lack of information: archival evidence is scarce, memoir literature conflicting and confusing, and no typically prolific correspondence between the two men has been preserved. Russian art historian Eleonora Paston, in a paper read at a Diaghilev conference, declared with frustration that the subject still awaited its researcher.[144] Meanwhile, there are documents available—some unpublished, others published but never interpreted—that shed fresh light on the hitherto poorly understood friendship between Mamontov and Diaghilev.

First of all, the Pickwick Club on the Neva—a circle of young St. Petersburg intellectuals who would give birth to Mir Iskusstva—was no secret to Mamontov. In Benois' *Vozniknovenie Mira Iskusstva [The Birth of Mir Iskusstva]*, Mamontov's nephew Yury Anatolievich is listed as an active member of this circle between 1890 and 1892.[145] His uncle must have been aware of this. He frequently visited his St. Petersburg relations, while Yury was friendly with his Moscow cousins, as well as Mamontov's painters. In a photograph taken at Abramtsevo in 1888, he is pictured with his brother Mikhail, Sergei Mamontov, Ilya Ostroukhov, and Valentin Serov (see plate 4). In fact, it is possible that it was from Yury Mamontov that Serov and Korovin first heard the name Benois.

As for Diaghilev, the evidence preserved at the State Russian Museum indicates that in the fall of 1897 he was actively engaged in preparing the first Mir Iskusstva exhibition. It would take place in St. Petersburg in early 1898 and include paintings by Moscow artists, of whom the great majority were at that time working for Mamontov. In October–November 1897, Diaghilev frequently visited Moscow in order to select the paintings to be exhibited. His adventures there are chronicled in his correspondence with Alexandre Benois. In a letter to Benois dated 8 October, Diaghilev asks: "What do you think of Vrubel?"[146] Mikhail Vrubel, as we remember, was Mamontov's favorite painter and protégé; even though after his 1896 marriage to Nadezhda Zabela he no longer lived at Mamontov's house, he still had a studio there. Meanwhile, the artist's name had never before entered Diaghilev's correspondence; Benois apparently did not know him either. It is logical to assume that Diaghilev met Vrubel in Moscow that fall. It is equally plausible that they must have been introduced by Mamontov, who was actively involved in the preparation of the exhibition, as he not only employed the artists Diaghilev surveyed, but personally owned many of their works.

Another letter from Diaghilev to Benois from that period concerns one of Mamontov's designers, Apollinary Vasnetsov. This is the earliest surviving letter in which Diaghilev directly mentions Mamontov by name. He writes: "Mamontov has promised Apollinary's set designs."[147] The designs in question were those for Musorgsky's *Khovanshchina*, in rehearsal at the MPO since October 1897. Whether it was the need to see those sets that first brought Diaghilev to Mamontov's theater, or whether he saw them by chance during one of his visits and later decided to borrow them for the exhibition, is immaterial. More important is the fact of his presence in the theater during *Khovanshchina*'s rehearsals.[148]

While in Moscow, Diaghilev would also have had a chance to observe the rehearsals of *Orfeo* that premiered on 30 November 1897, three weeks after *Khovanshchina*. He left no direct comment on Mamontov's production, but the following remark in one of the "Complex Questions" articles is noteworthy: "Not only have we accepted Wagner, we love him passionately, but that does not prevent us from eternally admiring *Don Giovanni* and adoring *Orfeo*."[149] The mention of *Orfeo* in this context might pass unnoticed except for the fact that Diaghilev would have had no opportunity to familiarize himself with the opera other than watching it at Mamontov's theater. Prior to the MPO production, *Orfeo* had never graced Russia's professional operatic stages; a few student performances at the conservatories took place well before Diaghilev's arrival in the capital. The score was available, but there would have been no reason to study it: in the 1890s, Russian music lovers were not interested in *Orfeo*. It was not considered representative of Gluck's mature reformist style (unlike *Alceste* and the Parisian operas) and was viewed as tedious and old-fashioned. Even Rimsky-Korsakov once remarked to Zabela: "*Orfeo* is boring, and no one needs it."[150] To place *Orfeo* on the same artistic level with Wagner's music dramas, adored by the Russian symbolists, and Mozart's *Don Giovanni*, immortalized by Mir Iskusstva's beloved E.T.A. Hoffmann, Diaghilev needed more than just to have known the opera. He needed to have seen *Orfeo* in a new, modernist light—an opportunity that at the time could have been provided only by Mamontov's innovative production.

Despite Diaghilev's professed adoration, Polenov's sets for *Orfeo* did not make it to the Mir Iskusstva exhibition. Neither did Korovin's *lubok*-inspired designs for *Sadko*—they could not have been ready in time. They would, however, be displayed in St. Petersburg on the last day of Diaghilev's exhibition: on 22 February 1898, *Sadko* opened the MPO's triumphant inaugural tour of the Russian capital, during which Korovin's sets made a deep impression on the Mir Iskusstva artists.[151] Halfway through the tour, another historic occasion took place: on 18 March 1898, the publishing agreement for Diaghilev's journal was signed. Scholars, used to Mamontov's fabled generosity, never before questioned the reasons for his involvement with *Mir Iskusstva*. Meanwhile, the timing was rather inopportune: Mamontov was on the verge of bankruptcy, his financial empire was in tatters, and his primary responsibility—the Moscow Private Opera—still required his attention. Still, he enthusiastically committed a substantial sum of money in order to launch *Mir Iskusstva*, rather than spending it on his business or his opera company. Indeed, if he did have that much money to spare, Mamontov could have chosen to sponsor Stasov's realist journal *Arts and Crafts:* it appeared simultaneously and in open and direct competition with Diaghilev's decadent publication, and was desperate for funding. I would argue that Mamontov's reasons went far beyond those of a generous patron. Rather, his philosophical and artistic principles, vastly different from Stasov's, had much in common with the ideological platform of *Mir Iskusstva,* while his personal friendship with Diaghilev gave him an added incentive to support his initiative. Furthermore, there is evidence to posit the existence of a mentor-student relationship between Mamontov and Diaghilev, based on their shared aesthetic views and vision of modernist theater. The nature of that relationship, which would lead Diaghilev to use Mamontov's company as a model for his Ballets Russes, will be discussed in detail in chapter 8. In the meantime, we shall turn our attention to an issue that rivaled stage design in its centrality to Mamontov's conceptualization of operatic genre—the issue of opera as drama.

PLATE 2. Mamontov and artists in his study; *left to right:* Ilya Repin, Vasily Surikov, Mamontov (*at the piano*), Konstantin Korovin, Valentin Serov, Mark Antokolsky. Antokolsky's statue of Christ is at the background. Mark Kopshitser, *Savva Mamontov,* plate 16.

PLATE 1. (*facing page*) Savva Mamontov. BM, photography division; used by permission.

PLATE 3. Dining room in Mamontov's Moscow mansion; Victor Vasnetsov's *Magic Carpet* is behind Mamontov on the wall. Mark Kopshitser, *Savva Mamontov,* plate 29.

PLATE 4. A gathering at Abramtsevo, 1888; *left to right:* Valentin Serov, Sergei Mamontov, Ilya Ostroukhov (*at the piano*), Mikhail Mamontov, Yury Mamontov. Mark Kopshitser, *Savva Mamontov,* plate 31.

PLATE 5. Savva Mamontov at his studio (1910s). Mark Kopshitser, *Savva Mamontov,* plate 74.

PLATE 6. A playbill for the play *Black Turban* (designer—Victor Vasnetsov; text—
Savva Mamontov). Mark Kopshitser, *Savva Mamontov*, plate 51.

PLATE 7. Mikhail Vrubel, *Tamara's Dance* (1890). Mikhail Vrubel, *Perepiska. Vospominaniia o khudozhnike*, plate 34.

PLATE 8. Mikhail Vrubel, *Mephistopheles
and His Acolyte* (1896). Abram Raskin,
*Shaliapin i russkie khudozhniki*, 50.

PLATE 9. Victor Vasnetsov, set sketch for "Berendei's Palace," *The Snow Maiden* (MPO, 1885). Militsa Pozharskaia, *Russkoe teatral'no-dekoratsionnoe iskusstvo kontsa XIX–nachala XX veka*, plate 7.

PLATE 10. Vasily Polenov, set sketch for "Euridice's Tomb," *Orfeo* (MPO, 1897). Militsa Pozharskaia, *Russkoe teatral'no-dekoratsionnoe iskusstvo kontsa XIX–nachala XX veka,* plate 8.

PLATE 12. Valentin Serov, a costume sketch for Holofernes, *Judith* (MPO, 1898). Ekaterina Grosheva, ed., *Fëdor Ivanovich Shaliapin: Literaturnoe nasledstvo*, 1: opposite 385.

PLATE 11. (*facing page*) Vasily Polenov, a costume sketch for Mephistopheles, *Faust* (MPO, 1896). Ekaterina Grosheva, ed., *Fëdor Ivanovich Shaliapin: Literaturnoe nasledstvo*, 1: opposite 128.

PLATE 13. Chaliapin as Holofernes, *Judith* (MPO, 1898). Ekaterina Grosheva, ed., *Fëdor Ivanovich Shaliapin: Literaturnoe nasledstvo*, 2: opposite 176.

PLATE 14. Chaliapin as Mephistopheles, *Faust* (Mariinsky Theater, 1895). Ekaterina Grosheva, ed., *Fëdor Ivanovich Shaliapin: Literaturnoe nasledstvo*, 2: opposite 72.

PLATE 15. Chaliapin as Mephistopheles, *Faust* (MPO, 1897). Ekaterina Grosheva, ed., *Fëdor Ivanovich Shaliapin: Literaturnoe nasledstvo*, 2: opposite 72, verso.

PLATE 16. Chaliapin as
Mephistopheles, *Faust*
(Bolshoi Theater, 1912).
Abram Raskin, *Shaliapin i
russkie khudozhniki,* 51.

PLATE 17. Chaliapin as Varangian Trader, *Sadko* (MPO, 1898). Ekaterina Grosheva, ed., *Fëdor Ivanovich Shaliapin: Literaturnoe nasledstvo,* 2: opposite 161.

PLATE 18. (*facing page*) Tsvetkova as the Snow Maiden (MPO, 1896). BM, photography division; used by permission.

PLATE 20. Zabela as Volkhova, *Sadko* (MPO, 1898). BM, photography division; used by permission.

PLATE 19. (*facing page*) Tsvetkova as Ioanna, *The Maid of Orleans* (MPO, 1899). BM, photography division; used by permission.

PLATE 22. Strakhova as Marfa, *Khovanshchina* (MPO, 1897). BM, photography division; used by permission.

PLATE 21. (*facing page*) Zabela as the Snow Maiden (MPO, 1897). Mark Kopshitser, *Savva Mamontov,* plate 60.

4051.

А. М. ПАСХАЛОВА
оп. „Снѣгурочка"

PLATE 24. Lyubatovich as Carmen (MPO, 1896). BM, photography division; used by permission.


PLATE 23. (*facing page*) Paskhalova as the Snow Maiden (MPO, 1898). BM, photography division; used by permission.

PLATE 25. Bedlevich as Khan Konchak, *Prince Igor* (MPO, 1896). BM, photography division; used by permission.

PLATE 26. Olenin as Rangoni, *Boris Godunov* (MPO, 1898). BM, photography division; used by permission.

М. Д. ЧЕРНЕНКО
„Княгиня" въ оп „Русалка.

PLATE 28. Shkafer as Kabil, *The Necklace* (MPO, 1899). BM, photography division; used by permission.

PLATE 27. (*facing page*) Chernenko as the Princess, Dargomyzhsky's *Rusalka* (MPO, 1898). BM, photography division; used by permission.

PLATE 29. Enrico Bevigniani. BM, photography division; used by permission.

PLATE 30. Vladimir Zelyonyi. BM, photography division; used by permission.

PLATE 32. *La bohème,* act 1 (MPO, 1897); Rodolfo (*left*)—Sekar-Rozhansky.
BM, photography division; used by permission.

PLATE 31. (*facing page*) Iosif (Giuseppe) Truffi. BM, photography division; used by
permission.

PLATE 33. *Boris Godunov,* act 2 (MPO, 1898); Boris—Chaliapin, Shuisky—Shkafer. BM, photography division; used by permission.

PLATE 34. Cast photo, *The Snow Maiden* (MPO, 1887); The Snow Maiden—Salina. BM, photography division; used by permission.

PLATE 35. *Orfeo*, act 3 apotheosis (MPO, 1897); (*center*) Orfeo—Chernenko, Euridice—Negrin-Schmidt, Amour—Klopotovskaya (*with a bow*). BM, photography division; used by permission.

PLATE 36. (*facing page*) *Sadko*, scene 4, "The Marketplace" (MPO, 1897); Sadko—Sekar-Rozhansky, Lyubava—Rostovtseva. BM, photography division; used by permission.

PLATE 37. Cast photo, *Mandarin's Son* (MPO, 1900); *first from left*—Lossky, *second from right*—Stavitskaya. BM, photography division; used by permission.

PLATE 38. (*facing page*) *Tale of Tsar Saltan*, finale (MPO, 1900); décor—Mikhail Vrubel. BM, photography division; used by permission.

PLATE 39. Old Judge, "Idyll." *Shut* 13 (1899), 8–9.

PLATE 40. Old Judge, "Boundless Joy." *Shut* 4 (1900), 8–9.

# FIVE

# Opera as Drama

As we have seen, Savva Mamontov's name virtually never graced the Moscow Private Opera's playbills. As founder and patron of the company, he was certainly never on its payroll; indeed, he had no official job description within "Mrs. Winter's private operatic enterprise."[1] In the memoir literature, we see many references to Mamontov as "the guiding spirit" of his company,[2] the creative center of each production, whose mere presence in the theater galvanized the cast into producing their best work in rehearsal or performance.[3] Yet, while poetic and flattering to our protagonist, these descriptions are admittedly vague, and make one wish for a simple declarative statement on what exactly Mamontov did at the company, apart from keeping it financially afloat.[4] The next two chapters of this book take as their starting point just such a simple declaration from a former employee whose legacy is rarely associated today with opera theater. Looking back at his brief tenure at the MPO, Sergei Rachmaninov recalled: "Mamontov was a born stage director."[5]

It is notable that Rachmaninov did not exactly mean the title as a compliment, but instead as a wistful indictment of Mamontov's comparative lack of interest in "purely musical" matters. This, of course, is a familiar accusation that a number of Mamontov's associates, from Polenov to Rimsky-Korsakov, made in reference to his view of opera as a colorful spectacle rather than a piece of music that just happens to be staged. A number of surviving archival documents demonstrate, moreover, that Mamontov craved not only visual brilliance, but also—and perhaps more so—powerful drama. This view is clearly revealed in his comments on *The Tsar's Bride*—an MPO production that he was forced to relinquish, after his arrest in September 1899, to Rimsky-Korsakov's supervision. In a letter to Shkafer regarding poor audience turnout for the third performance of the opera, Mamontov wrote:

> Sincerely happy for the success of *The Tsar's Bride*. [But] what happened is what I was afraid of. From the third night on, the ticket sales have weakened. The music is probably wonderful, the staging apparently is also successful, the vocal performance is also good, but is there a *powerful* talented performance of the *drama*? Musicians sometimes put this issue on the back burner. So, strict musical judges are pleased, while the audience keeps yawning.[6]

The creation of the powerful drama on stage that Mamontov considered so necessary for the production's success was to him a responsibility of the stage director. He viewed that position not as that of a "stage manager," whose role was limited to coordinating singers' entrances and exits, but in a radically modern light as a true author of a staged production, who led rehearsals, designed mises-en-scène, coached the soloists, as well as coordinated other aspects of the work.[7] There were virtually no precedents in Russian opera theater for such a novel job description, and thus no model for Mamontov to follow.[8] Unsurprisingly, his conceptualization of the stage director's role developed in parallel with his views on synthesis of the arts and in the same familiar environment of Abramtsevo. Theater, as we have seen, was important to the regulars of the Mamontov Circle, starting with the "Mamontov Drama Nights" led and documented by Mstislav Prakhov in the late 1870s and culminating in the full-length 1882 performance of Ostrovsky's *The Snow Maiden* that became the group's aesthetic manifesto.[9] It was in these home theatricals that Mamontov—long a frustrated actor and a reliable dramatist and librettist of the Circle—first took upon himself the stage director's role. Outside the walls of Abramtsevo, he would wear the same mantle for the 1894 production of *Aphrodite* and the 1880 concert performance of Schumann's *Manfred,* a joint production of the Maly Drama Theater and the Moscow Conservatory.[10] Informed by these experiences, the coming-of-age of Mamontov the stage director arrived with the Moscow Private Opera, where his artistry reached a new level of complexity and sophistication.

## MAMONTOV AS STAGE DIRECTOR

Mamontov's contemporaries valued his MPO stage directing work very highly. His associate Pyotr Melnikov declared it exemplary, indeed "artistically ideal, for I believe you have no rivals in this field."[11] The critics evidently agreed; Evgeny Petrovsky of *Russkaya Muzykalnaya Gazeta,* an important St. Petersburg monthly, once lamented the modesty of the company's playbill that "conceals the name of the truly gifted artist responsible for the Moscow Opera's general staging."[12] Both the press and the general public tended to pick up quickly on which productions benefited from Mamontov's close supervision and which did not. A telling example of the difference is provided by the 1898 production of Rimsky-Korsakov's *May Night.* The opening performances of the opera gave every indication of a flop: the dull, humorless acting was particularly lamented by the press, as well as by the company's insiders such as Semyon Kruglikov, who was keeping the composer apprised of the fate of his work. A few days later, both Kruglikov's letters and the press reviews began to report a remarkable transformation: *May Night* suddenly became a hit. Apparently Mamontov was away on business during the final rehearsals and opening night; after returning to Moscow, he completely restaged the opera. Kruglikov described the result as follows: "In staging, *May Night* runs so much better it's unrecognizable; . . . all the performers are finally in place. [The soloists are] not just better than before, but simply very good; the crowd scenes are full of life and of purely Mamontovian original movement."[13] As evidenced by Kruglikov's letter, Mamontov's presence and involvement in the staging of Rimsky-Korsakov's opera made a significant and recognizable difference to its fortunes. What the letter does not tell us is exactly how this miracle was accomplished—what it was about Mamontov's directing that was able to produce such spectacular results.

One relatively accessible source of information on the subject is the memoirs of MPO troupe members, which provide at least some anecdotal evidence of Mamontov's methodology and techniques. He watched rehearsals from the back of a room (the large study in his house or the theater auditorium), observing each mise-en-scène as a whole, as if studying a painting. When correcting a tone, pose, or gesture of a single performer, he might limit himself to a brief comment while still seated, using sharp, palpable, visually arresting imagery to elucidate the internal motivations of a character; he could also come on stage to demonstrate. Bondarenko recalled a rehearsal of *Vrazhya sila* [*Power of the Fiend*]:

> A talented artist, Olenin, performing the role of Eryomka, was lounging elegantly in a chair. Mamontov couldn't stop himself and shouted through the whole theater: "Olenin, don't sit like a duke!" Suddenly everyone jumped to attention. Mamontov flew up onto the stage and demonstrated how a simple Eryomka should sit, discarding the learned, fake-classical poses.[14]

Whenever a new mise-en-scène was to be created, or an existing one adjusted, Mamontov would, as a rule, work on stage, personally demonstrating and explaining his reasons for the change. He was extremely demanding, and could keep the singers on stage for hours, until a scene worked exactly as planned: the dress rehearsal of *Sadko* went on until dawn. At the same time, his charisma, enthusiasm, and brilliant demonstrations inspired the cast, resulting in few complaints.

> For each role he could find its specific, characteristic attributes of appearance, facial expression, and voice, and could briefly but clearly create the whole portrait of a character. He could show some characteristic movement typical for this character, and in this movement, in the intonation and the facial expression, the image was instantly revealed, became clear and understandable. Using these special means, he could describe a character, and analyze it in detail. The face of Savva Ivanovich was extremely animated; the face of a true, slightly neurotic artist who could express, in his voice, hands, and body anything he wanted to show.[15]

Unfortunately, no Mamontov-directed productions can be reconstructed in their entirety: the *montirovochnye knigi* [rehearsal books] that he occasionally used (for example, for *The Necklace*) did not survive. Indeed, few such books existed in the first place: unlike that of the methodical Stanislavsky and the meticulous Meyerhold, Mamontov's idiosyncratic stage directing was based on improvisation and a spontaneous, live creative process. Consequently, many scholars have dismissed his work as amateurish, random sparks of inspiration, rather than an established, systematic methodology. Platon Mamontov, himself a professional opera director, disagreed, mounting a vigorous defense of his uncle's principles in his memoir. Throughout that manuscript, he attempts to reconstruct the method behind the MPO's directing madness, emphasizing the long-term planning and careful research that went into each production. For example, he highlights Savva Mamontov's insistence on acquainting the performers with the historical, cultural, and stylistic contexts of an opera, to promote a better understanding of each character's development and relationships with others within the drama.

> Before each new production Uncle Savva gathered all the participants and started the work with a complete, detailed introduction to and discussion of the entire piece using the piano-vocal score, with all the parts performed by the appointed singers. This was accompanied by explanations; specifically, he brought the performers' attention to the requirements and suggestions of the composer. He touched upon the epoch, style, and artistic aspect of the work according to its libretto. He asked the painters involved in a production to acquaint the performers with their plans and ideas on visual design.[16]

Platon Mamontov's memoir aims to portray Mamontov's methodology as a stable system strictly implemented in each production from the earliest days of the company. This idealistic representation is contradicted by the archival documents that trace a complicated, tortuous, long-term process of establishing the new position of stage director, outlining its fields of responsibility, and determining the necessary areas of expertise. In September 1897 Vasily Shkafer, newly appointed as MPO stage director, anxious to understand the limits and requirements of a job that he had never held before and that, in effect, did not exist in any of his former places of employment, wrote Mamontov a letter. Unfortunately, only a fragment of this interesting document survives, but it appears that the letter was Shkafer's attempt to summarize his job description, as he understood it after a long face-to-face discussion with his boss. He wrote:

> When staging an opera, not only a new, never before performed one, but also an old one, played according to the ubiquitous, often absolutely senseless, set-in-stone traditions of the crown theaters, a stage director should first of all not only acquaint the participants with the general picture of the drama, but include as far as possible every character, every detail that could play a role in the dramatic as well as musical aspect. (It is important that not only the conductor is in agreement with the stage director, but

that the two complement each other). The chief stage director has to present to the actors all existing literature on the discussed subject, as well as sculpture and painting, the necessary associates of staged art.[17]

At first glance, Shkafer's letter echoes Platon Mamontov's rosy picture above.[18] However, the future and the conditional are used much more often in the document than the present tense, and the ideas are outlined in the manner of what should be (rather than what has been) done. That is, the letter presents the position of stage director at the Moscow Private Opera as a plan to be implemented, rather than an established system to be preserved. Indeed, Shkafer goes on to critique the current approach to probably the most complex MPO production to date—Musorgsky's *Khovanshchina*, which was in active stage rehearsal at the time of writing and was apparently plagued by problems. Singers had difficulties not only rendering the composer's subtle declamation but also comprehending the nature of their characters, and they had a very vague idea of the historical events in which these characters were to play such a pivotal role. According to Shkafer, Mamontov's work with the soloists, his explanations and demonstrations, while wonderful, were insufficient for most performers to "penetrate" this complicated work. Shkafer wrote:

In *Khovanshchina* [Mr. Petrov], apparently without any understanding of the character of Shaklovityi, gave the impression that he had no knowledge of what kind of person that Shaklovityi was, and was just singing beautiful notes, without any inner sense, without a sign of penetrating the role. In this case you, Savva Ivanovich, . . . demonstrated and explained his role to Mr. Petrov as probably no other man of art could (I am speaking of contemporary ones), and yet—there was still no Shaklovityi in Mr. Petrov's singing. I believe that before approaching the role, even at the first reading, Mr. Petrov needed to learn not only Shaklovityi's history, but that of the whole musical drama of *Khovanshchina* with all its characters, and to do this with the conviction that this is the *primary* objective, and only later to begin reading the notes and develop the character in music and acting.[19]

Shkafer's letter clearly demonstrates that, as of fall 1897, the background research hailed by Platon Mamontov as fundamental to his uncle's approach to stage directing was still in its infancy. Indeed, it is entirely possible that a trip to the settlement of the Old Believers near Moscow, organized by Mamontov for the *Khovanshchina* cast in order to study a major group of characters that populate Musorgsky's opera, was a direct result of Shkafer's critique.

This is not to suggest that a systematic method of directing an opera production was absent at the MPO. But it is important to recognize the true pace of its development during the three seasons that saw Mamontov at the head of the company: slowly, by trial and error, learning from mistakes and turning weaknesses of specific troupe members into advantages. This included the weaknesses of Mamontov himself: specifically, his widely acknowledged dislike for the daily grind of drilling and polishing required in mounting a theatrical production. This "big picture" attitude, accompanied by an often blatant disregard for details, frustrated and infuriated even Mamontov's admirers, such as Stanislavsky.[20] Shkafer recalled:

> Mamontov, with his artistic nature, could not and did not like to work thoroughly—to figure out the details. To bury himself in the depths of research, to create slowly, step by step—he could not and most importantly did not like to do that, preferring to sketch out, quickly and energetically, with wide brushstrokes, a characteristic contour, the skeleton of the production, throwing in it a few colorful spots.[21]

Apart from throwing light on Mamontov's strengths and weaknesses as a stage director, what is most fascinating about Shkafer's account is his reference to the MPO staging methodology as a three-step process: preliminary research; creation of characters and mises-en-scène; and finally, practicing and polishing the details. Shkafer suggests that Mamontov's talent as a stage director laid primarily in character and scene design, that is, the second phase of the process. He had no patience and, even more likely, no spare time in his busy schedule for the painstaking, time-consuming research and drilling. These he left to Melnikov and Shkafer—two frustrated young singers he trained to be his assistants.

## MAMONTOV'S ASSISTANTS: THE THREE-PHASE STAGE DIRECTING MODEL

During its first period of operation (1885–92), the MPO did not have a stage director position. Pyotr Melnikov's, therefore, was the first name listed under "régisseur" on the company payroll. He started working for Mamontov in May 1896 during the Nizhny Novgorod Exhibition, and shared stage directing duties with his employer during the reopened MPO's first season. Vasily Shkafer joined the enterprise as a stage director in the fall of 1897, replacing Melnikov, who from then on was based primarily in Paris. During the 1898–99 season, Shkafer pulled double duty as a singer and stage director; at the same time, Mamontov was still directing productions; Melnikov paid a visit in November for some directing work; and yet another stage director, Mikhail Lentovsky, was appointed for the season. This complicated and seemingly illogical arrangement has passed unnoticed by researchers: the changes were reported but the reasons behind them were never analyzed. Meanwhile, the evidence suggests that early in the 1897–98 season, Mamontov developed a three-phase stage directing model and began implementing it at the MPO. The model was constructed for a team of three directors, whose functions were precisely defined and interdependent. Indeed, the model was designed specifically for Mamontov, Melnikov, and Shkafer to work together, dividing their duties to utilize each stage director's strengths to the best advantage. The following section elucidates the roles of Melnikov and Shkafer within Mamontov's directing model, as well as clarifying the role played by Mikhail Lentovsky.

The son of a Mariinsky star, Pyotr Melnikov was raised backstage. He received an excellent education, possessed an encyclopedic knowledge of history, literature, visual arts, and music, and was intimately acquainted with the inner workings of opera theater. Melnikov's first dream was to follow in his father's footsteps as a singer. However, their shared range (bass-baritone) only underscored the wide discrepancy in their vocal abilities. Being a Melnikov and knowing he would be constantly compared to his father, Pyotr could not afford to be a mediocrity. After meeting Mamontov, Melnikov turned his ambition to stage directing: as he once wrote to his employer, "While studying singing now, I still view it as my final goal to learn every detail of the theater business, so in time I may lead a troupe of my own."[22] Pyotr Melnikov would indeed become a prominent opera director, working at the Bolshoi and Mariinsky theaters and after 1920 at the Riga National Opera in newly independent Latvia. He would also be invited, together with the renowned avant-garde drama director Nikolai Evreinov, to direct productions of the

Paris Private Opera in 1928, and have the honor of staging the premiere of Rimsky-Korsakov's *Skazanie o nevidimom grade Kitezhe* [*Legend of the Invisible City of Kitezh*] at La Scala in the 1930s.[23] Throughout this distinguished career he consistently acknowledged that it was his first job at Mamontov's enterprise that shaped his artistic future.

Melnikov's strength as a stage director, evident to Mamontov since their collaboration during the 1896–97 season, increased dramatically after Melnikov's move to France the following summer. Fluent in several languages, an avid reader with an eye for detail, now with access to the best European theaters and libraries, he was an invaluable asset for preliminary research, and was utilized by Mamontov in that capacity. Melnikov's letters from Paris are filled with historical details, literary references, costume ideas, and makeup tips. Comfortable in all branches of the arts, he easily communicated with the company's designers (one of them, Konstantin Korovin, would become his colleague at the Imperial Theaters for more than a decade), and, just like Mamontov, was able to realize in his creative thinking the synthesis of the arts the MPO was striving to achieve. Admiring and respecting Mamontov as the "professor" to whose classes he returned time and time again,[24] Melnikov in turn was accepted for his independent, creative mind and was allowed to voice his opinions on casting and mises-en-scène for new productions. He could be rather critical and, again just like Mamontov, paid attention to the dramatic essence of each character. In one of the letters Melnikov made the following comment on *Khovanshchina* casting: "In my opinion, only Sekar should have sung Golitsyn. He himself in real life is a true Vasenka Golitsyn, and his foreign accent would be totally in place here. He is the only one who could more or less portray a *barin*."[25]

Both strong personalities, Mamontov and Melnikov occasionally found it hard to work together. Increasing tension would sometimes lead to a blowout and a temporary cooling down in the tone of their correspondence, soon revived by yet another project. At other times the two directors saw eye to eye, their collaboration reflected in the mises-en-scène of a completed production, as evident in the following comment Melnikov made about *The Maid of Orleans*: "I felt a small satisfaction after I found out recently that you took my little staging ideas into consideration. Believe me: therein lies the final satisfaction for a man who loves the cause for its own sake."[26] Melnikov and Mamontov also discussed repertoire plans and exchanged thoughts on new projects (their Wagnerian ideas were mentioned in chapter 4). It is to Melnikov that Mamontov would send his new libretto *V dvenadtsatom godu* [*1812*]. Melnikov, for his part, reported on the productions he saw in Paris and sent scores of newly published Western operas, with particular fondness for Massenet.

Unlike Melnikov's, Shkafer's letters do not contain repertory lists, casting advice, or mise-en-scène suggestions; his role within the enterprise and his relationship with its leader appear to be quite different. A provincial, less illustriously educated than Melnikov, Vasily Shkafer studied singing all his life. A weak lyric tenor, he was fortunate to have as his teachers Darya Leonova, Musorgsky's friend and best-known interpreter, and Fyodor Komissarzhevsky, a former Mariinsky principal and teacher of Stanislavsky and of his own daughter Vera, Russia's most famous dramatic actress of the 1900s. Both mentors taught Shkafer much about drama and declamation, but little about hitting the high notes, so essential to a traditional operatic career. Despite subsequent study in Italy, the young singer's professional life was unremarkable until he first saw the MPO production of *The Snow Maiden* in September 1896, fell in love with the theater, and resolved to get a job there one day.[27] In the fall of 1897, Vasily Shkafer put his singing career on hold and joined Mamontov's company as its official "régisseur"—in reality, an assistant stage director.

As with Melnikov earlier, Mamontov took Shkafer on as a student, discovered his strengths and weaknesses, and skillfully used both to his advantage. While Melnikov was a good researcher but his actual stage experience was limited to what he learned at the MPO, Shkafer had worked for several provincial troupes, including the respected Tiflis Opera. There, he observed and participated in stage rehearsals, and understood both the necessity for and the methodology of the final, polishing phase of preparing a production. Mamontov also discovered in his young protégé the talent of a character actor, not unlike his own (character roles would indeed become Shkafer's specialty as a singer), and as a consequence, a talent for demonstration. Hard-working, modest, and soft-spoken, Shkafer lacked Melnikov's arrogance and independent streak. Yet while this lack of assertiveness and creative independence was Shkafer's main weakness as a stage director, he related easily to the singers and had a gift of communicating Mamontov's directing ideas without "remaking them after his own mold" (a fault of which Melnikov was frequently accused).[28]

In his "program letter" quoted earlier in this chapter, Shkafer laid out the duties of the company's "chief régisseur"—that is, Mamontov's own function within the three-phase stage directing model. In another letter dated from the same period, September 1897, he offered a detailed description of what he thought his own duties would entail:

> You, Savva Ivanovich, are an authority figure in front of your artistic audience; you make certain demands of them all, and at the same time give them a certain plan of action, and in rehearsals you are a judge of that plan. My role, as far as I am trying to understand it, appears to me as follows. First of all, I must be a nice, good comrade to all those creatures great and small who are related to our cause. I must be the closest, most necessary person who takes care of all the needs and questions of the artists that are related to staging; that is, I should always be "at their service." . . . Furthermore, I must work out in detail those plans, those artistic tasks given by you to each performer; that is, I should shed light from all angles on the work required. My duties should also include a passionate desire to engage any employee in the idea upon which this company is founded, and which you and all those standing at the helm of our cause intend to realize.[29]

Shkafer's letters provide a wonderful illustration of the three-phase stage directing model. With Melnikov involved in preliminary research, and Mamontov in mise-en-scène creation and determining the general direction of a production, Shkafer's role involved the execution of the artistic principles developed during the first two phases of the creative process: there was no better man for the drilling and polishing phase. This was the essence of his work during the 1897–98 season; the following years, when he started appearing as a singer, his duties would be curtailed for the productions in which he participated. For instance, Melnikov came from Paris to direct *Eugene Onegin*, in which Shkafer performed his single lyrical role of Lensky. *The Maid of Orleans*, in which he was cast in the character role of Charles VII, was directed personally by Mamontov. In other cases, Shkafer would limit his directing work to the episodes in which he himself participated. This apparently happened with *The Tsar's Bride*—the press discussed Bomely's scenes (particularly the one with Lyubasha in act 2) as the only dramatically compelling moments in the opera. Similarly, Kabil's scenes were reportedly the single bright spot on the otherwise gloomy horizon of *The Necklace*.

One of Shkafer's most important singing roles at the MPO was Mozart in the world premiere of Rimsky-Korsakov's dialogue opera *Mozart and Salieri*, in which he performed alongside Chaliapin. According to Shkafer's memoirs, Mamontov allowed the two singers time and freedom to, as the singer put it, *sygratsya* [learn to play together]—that is, to develop their own onstage "ensemble"—before voicing his suggestions.[30] Indeed, *Mozart* may be viewed as the first independent directing work of Shkafer's creative life. Like Melnikov, he would make stage directing his career, starting at the Novy Theater, replacing Melnikov at the Bolshoi, and retiring in 1924 as the chief régisseur of the Mariinsky.[31] Always eager to acknowledge his debt to his mentor Mamontov, Shkafer wrote to him years later: "After being in your school for a year, I can somehow sense the very kernel of the goal—how to achieve and on what to build the success of an opera production. This is especially clear to me after starting my own work in the field of stage directing. It is fascinating work."[32]

As we have seen, the MPO three-phase stage directing model was based on collaboration and division of responsibilities between Mamontov, Melnikov, and Shkafer. A question easily suggests itself: if the triumvirate worked so well, what would have been the reason for inviting Lentovsky into the company? In order to answer it, we need to assess both his personal qualities as a stage director and the timing of his introduction to the troupe.

Mikhail Lentovsky was an anomaly among Mamontov's employees. He was not a young, novice performer, but an experienced and rather notorious entrepreneur who had specialized primarily in operetta, with several—now defunct—enterprises to his credit. As such, he was not in a position to become Mamontov's student, to be reshaped in his mentor's own image, as were Shkafer and (partially) Melnikov. In late fall 1898, when the new director joined the company, Mamontov's business empire was in trouble and required his constant attention in order to forestall the disaster that would eventually strike. The amount of time he could devote to the MPO began to diminish correspondingly. Meanwhile, the company's projects became increasingly more ambitious, including such enormously complicated works as *Judith*, *The Maid of Orleans*, and *Boris Godunov*. Apart from the complex psychological makeup of their main characters, all three operas involved large crowd scenes, difficult and time-consuming to stage. It appears that Mamontov may have intended that Lentovsky replace him in the triumvirate by taking over the second stage-directing phase, so that only the general artistic guidance would be left to Mamontov himself.

Initially, the two stage directors shared the responsibility for *Judith* and *Boris Godunov*, Mamontov working with the soloists and ensembles and Lentovsky staging the crowd scenes. The result was disastrous: a talented man in his own medium, Lentovsky lacked Shkafer's gift of absorbing and interpreting Mamontov's ideas. He also appeared to possess a Melnikov-like arrogance, without the latter's education, sensitivity, artistic taste, and ability to communicate with the designers, which resulted in a conflict with Serov and his colleagues.[33] An individualist director, Lentovsky had trouble adjusting to—or even comprehending the purpose of—the teamwork inherent in the three-phase model. In a letter to Mamontov he complained that in agreeing to join the company, he expected the staging to be "unquestionably" his own domain.[34] Moreover, the directing styles of Mamontov and Lentovsky differed so radically that their productions, instead of exemplifying the company's goal of harmonious art synthesis, appeared fragmented and disintegrated. As a result, rather than spending less time at rehearsals, Mamontov was forced to spend more, restaging Lentovsky's crowd scenes, such as the Kromy of *Boris Godunov* (see chapter 2). For *The Maid of Orleans*, Lentovsky's duties were limited; by the end of the season, he was gone.

Although Lentovsky's tenure with the MPO proved to be a mistake, it reveals Mamontov's desire to see his stage directing model function independently, without his involvement. As it happened, after he was removed from the company due to his arrest and bankruptcy (see introduction, n.8), and its leadership was transferred to the MPO's administrator Claudia Winter and its new conductor, Mikhail Ippolitov-Ivanov, the three-phase model gradually disintegrated. Melnikov had little in common with the new administration and left, giving up stage directing for several years before landing a job at the Bolshoi. Shkafer found it difficult to carry the whole model on his own as efficiently as before and was eventually forced out as well. While the model functioned, however, the MPO offered exciting and innovative directing work, studied attentively by Stanislavsky and Sanin, who both frequented the rehearsals. The work of Mamontov and his assistants was even more closely observed by those to whom it was addressed—the singers. Several of them, while never actually directing for Mamontov's company, benefited from his personal coaching and expertise. They would go on either to direct occasionally, like Chaliapin, or even to give up singing entirely and become, like baritone Pyotr Olenin and bass Vladimir Lossky (see plate 37), important stage directors in their own right.

Thus, the Moscow Private Opera, which we have already recognized as a training ground for Russia's theater designers, also educated the country's first generation of professional opera directors. One of the core ideas they would absorb at Mamontov's company and later incorporate into their own work was that of the artistic ensemble, a rare and prized quality on the operatic stage of their day.[35] Indeed, the principles of artistic ensemble laid the foundation for the MPO opera as drama; it will be discussed in the following section.

### THE ARTISTIC ENSEMBLE AND "THE STAR"

A lively, engaging interaction between the characters—that is, artistic ensemble in the traditional sense of the term[36]—was an absolutely necessary attribute of dramatic art to Mamontov from the Abramtsevo days. At the MPO, he particularly enjoyed directing the projects that allowed him to re-create that atmosphere of camaraderie on stage. To accomplish it, he would typically work with the cast together, as a group—shaping dialogue, creating stage business, and otherwise facilitating the onstage relationships between the singers (see plate 32).

The concern for ensemble revealed in Mamontov's rehearsal techniques is also evident in the larger issues of company policy, particularly in the approach to dealing with the stars. In the mid-1880s, the early days of the MPO, Mamontov made it a rule to invite famous European singers to participate in his productions alongside the Russian cast. While financially viable, the idea had ruined his dream of artistic ensemble: guest performers had neither opportunity nor desire to interact with their colleagues on stage. The issue proved a source of increasing frustration for Mamontov, contributing to his eventual decision to fold his venture in 1892.[37] After its resurrection four years later, the number of foreign stars at the MPO was sharply reduced, limited to a few guest appearances per season and never resulting in a long-term contract, a common practice at the Bolshoi.

Yet the MPO did employ one singer who clearly operated in a star capacity—Feodor Chaliapin. A separation from the ensemble was inevitable: however carefully he was integrated into the group by a stage director, the singer's magnetic stage presence would make him stand out, precluding the possibility of onstage harmony that could only be created if all performers were perceived as equals. Memoirs and press reviews that discussed the productions in which Chaliapin had participated could not help but focus almost exclusively on him. For instance, Shkafer (though contradicted by some other eyewitness accounts) declared in his autobiography that "Chaliapin reigned alone" in the *Khovanshchina* production. The observation applies even more to *Boris Godunov*, an opera whose dramatic structure centers so intensely on its protagonist (particularly in Rimsky-Korsakov's edition, which reverses the order of the final scenes). Press accounts did address the artistic ensemble created by Mamontov in this production. "The choice of artistic personnel was good," wrote Kashkin, "and consequently there was good ensemble."[38] César Cui concurred, saying: "*Boris* is performed very together, with an excellent ensemble."[39] Still, there was no denying the obvious: Chaliapin did stand out. Indeed, it appears that in staging operas dominated by a single male protagonist with the right voice range, Mamontov cleverly used Chaliapin's dominant position within the cast. His separateness from other performers and their desire to "play up" to him would thus strengthen, rather than ruin, the dramas in which he portrayed charismatic rulers or spiritual leaders such as Boris, Dosifei, or Holofernes. This way, the singer could have the story built around him without distorting its meaning. Consequently a clearly star-dominated production would achieve an otherwise impossible ensemble, as evident from a striking photograph depicting a scene from *Boris Godunov* (see plate 33).[40]

Chaliapin's name has proved a magnetic attraction to Russian critics and music lovers ever since his MPO days. Indeed, one of the most enduring and damaging myths plaguing Mamontov's enterprise implies that the singer's participation was both its single claim to fame and its sole means of survival—the reason, perhaps, why he is given a somewhat disproportionate amount of attention in the Mamontov literature.[41] It is unquestionable that Chaliapin's departure for the greener pastures of the Imperial stage spelled trouble for the company: the singer was an inspiration to its cast, as well as a box-office attraction. But his popularity came at a price: the Chaliapin cult that increasingly began to dominate the public's relationship with the MPO had its downside. There were screaming fans who interrupted performances demanding that their idol encore literally every note he sang. There was also the increasingly star-like attitude of the singer himself, which occasioned the following ironic diatribe from *Novosti Dnya*'s sharp-witted Petersburg correspondent:

> Chaliapin is truly becoming an idol of Petersburg ladies and young girls. This is a unique, unprecedented case in the history of the arts. Chaliapin laid the foundation for the type of the "cutie-pie bass." Up to this point, as we know well, there were the "cutie-pie tenors" or, less frequently, the "cutie-pie baritones"; there were no cutie-pies yet in the bass clef. And here he comes, and with his mighty octave sends the hearts aflutter.[42]

Most importantly, however, in a company that prided itself on its collaborative creative process that privileged no one, Chaliapin required (and increasingly, expected) special treatment. Apart from the need to stage some productions around his personality, his presence at the MPO affected the repertoire policy itself: Chaliapin was the only member of the troupe who could justifiably boast in his memoirs of Mamontov's promise to stage any opera he wished.[43]

After Chaliapin's impending departure became public knowledge toward the end of the 1898–99 season, the Moscow press corps salivated over the prospect. Reporters proclaimed that the singer's loss would be disastrous for the MPO, wondered why the administration was letting its major asset go, and predicted its impending doom as a result of such shortsightedness.[44] However, had Mamontov stayed with the company, its transition to a post-Chaliapin era might have proved smoother than the critics imagined. Mamontov's plan, reported to Rimsky-Korsakov by both Kruglikov and Zabela, was to strengthen the ensemble quality of the troupe even more:[45] now that the star was gone, compromises were no longer necessary.

While Mamontov certainly regretted losing a great actor in Chaliapin, the misfortune of losing a great voice—a most significant loss to any opera company—did not seem to trouble him much. Such an attitude seems to invite accusations that, driven by a vision of his personal *Gesamtkunstwerk*, Mamontov put the artistic ensemble (both visual and dramatic) above the musical one. Cui, perplexed by his favorite director's interest in a modern opera he hated, wrote: "I think that you, Savva Ivanovich, are more touched by the plot and dramatic performance than by the music itself."[46] Rimsky-Korsakov's conflict with Mamontov, as we have seen, revolved around the composer's belief that "aural impressions" were not "precious" enough to the MPO. The situation changed radically in the fall of 1899: Mamontov was gone, Ippolitov-Ivanov was in charge, and Rimsky-Korsakov himself was directly involved in the production of his operas. "As a student and friend of Rimsky-Korsakov's," noted Gozenpud, "Ippolitov-Ivanov was guarding his interests. For the conductor, the question of musical ensemble stood at the forefront."[47] Unfortunately, it did so at the expense of the artistic ensemble: according to press reports, any intent of harmoniously fusing music, drama, and design was gone.[48]

Earlier we saw Ivan Lipaev use the term "ensemble" when discussing synthesis of the arts in Mamontov's productions. Indeed, the dramatic ensemble was to Mamontov one of the necessary ingredients of art synthesis. Singers interacting, playing off each other, and working together in harmony on stage was a part of the same ideal that compelled singers and stage directors to work together with designers and everyone else involved in a production. As a result, acting and staging considerations often informed Mamontov's decisions on the visual design of the production, particularly with respect to stage movement, his special concern. In his letters and sketches addressed to Polenov regarding the designs for *Orfeo* and *The Necklace,* the projected movement of the characters is built into the set design. For example, the shape of Euridice's tomb was constructed for Orfeo to lie on and embrace; Daphne's "column" in act 3 of *The Necklace* was designed to mirror Chernenko's figure and posture at the moment when her heroine turns to stone. Similarly, dramatic concerns often played a role in what would traditionally be considered purely musically motivated decisions in opera production: casting.

## CASTING

Mamontov's casting decisions frequently generated heat: he was criticized by the press, as well as by some of his employees, for misjudging singers' vocal abilities and for the bad habit of offering leading roles to unqualified beginners. *Peterburgsky Listok,* for example, blamed the young, inexperienced performers with their "weak student-caliber" voices for the low attendance during the company's 1899 St. Petersburg tour, and recommended a change in casting policy if the troupe ever wished to visit the capital again.[49] An author of one wicked *Novosti Dnya* feuilleton even had two fictional opera buffs, Vasenka and Petenka (that is, little Vasily and little Pyotr), declare their intention to establish "a Society for Protecting Inexperienced Artists from Responsible Parts" among the MPO audience, saying:

> Pray, is this nice? These young people are barely ready to start school, but instead, in front of an audience of fifty or so, with indescribable desperation they sacrifice themselves for the sake of art that is completely alien to them. Comes a high note—their voices break off; comes a scene—it's a pain to watch. Thus, a spectator could get completely exhausted: he has to jump out of his skin applauding, for, God forbid, there could be a suicide right there backstage. To each his own temperament! Some operatic child sings like that once, twice, and then would just go off and kill himself. Positively, some things should be spared for art's sake—a human life, for instance.[50]

Even Shkafer, perhaps forgetting his own humble beginnings, noted in his memoir that Mamontov's "weakness for stage art and young actors often made him disregard the strictly musical side of a performance."[51] In order to probe the justice of such criticism, it would be instructive to examine Mamontov's main casting criteria by focusing on his two most controversial decisions, both heatedly discussed at the time they were made.

The first of these much-debated cases got Mamontov into hot water with Rimsky-Korsakov at what seemed to be the highest point in collaboration between the composer and his director. During the company's 1898 St. Petersburg tour, for the performance of *The Snow Maiden* that was supposed to take place under the composer's baton, Mamontov replaced the composer's favorite Nadezhda Zabela in the title role with a beginner, our old friend Alevtina Paskhalova (see chapter 2). Despite Rimsky-Korsakov's strenuous objections, Paskhalova appeared in two performances, on 16 and 20 March. The role was returned to Zabela toward the end of the tour, for the third and final performance of *The Snow Maiden* on 13 April, soon after a personal appeal by Stasov, who had requested to hear the opera again with Zabela as the lead.[52] While the opera itself might have been repeated for the critic's benefit, it is highly unlikely that Stasov's letter influenced Mamontov's casting decision, succeeding where Rimsky-Korsakov himself had failed: the composer's good will was far more vital to the MPO's fortunes. The real reason for Zabela's reinstatement was rather mundane: the tour was not originally expected to last beyond Easter, and Paskhalova, a senior at the Moscow Conservatory, was only allowed a short leave of absence. By the time the decision to extend the tour was made, she had already returned to Moscow, had resumed her classes, and was therefore unavailable for the final performance. Zabela, who knew and had performed the role before, was a natural choice to replace her.

Mamontov's decision to cast Paskhalova as the Snow Maiden was criticized both by Rimsky-Korsakov's acolytes and by many scholars who accepted the composer's interpretation of it as the whim of a rich despot who cared nothing for music or the arts.[53] What we have learned about Mamontov's personality and aesthetic views reveals this explanation to be simplistic and unjust. The history of the MPO demonstrates time and again that, if the decision to cast Paskhalova had indeed been merely a whim, a spur-of-the-moment flash of misguided inspiration, Mamontov would have allowed himself to be persuaded to change his mind.[54] The fact is, as Evgeny Arenzon correctly pointed out, Zabela was not the company's "official" Snow Maiden: the role belonged to the troupe's leading soprano, Elena Tsvetkova. The only reason for the casting question to be on the agenda in the first place was Tsvetkova's temporary leave of absence between November 1897 and September 1898. In a letter to Mamontov regarding the success of *The Snow Maiden* in St. Petersburg, Melnikov mentioned the inability to showcase her performance at the capital as the single disappointment of the tour. "It still upsets me that we could not show the Blossom in this role," he wrote. "This is a great hole in [the production]. Our Little Blossom is so crystalline, pure, and touching in this role that one is involuntarily brought to tears."[55]

The Snow Maiden was Tsvetkova's signature part at the MPO. The reason for Zabela's expected appearance in it during the St. Petersburg tour was the fact that she was hired as Tsvetkova's understudy and temporary replacement, taking over her major roles such as Olga in *The Maid of Pskov* and Mimi in *La bohème*. Paskhalova's participation in the production, on the other hand, was a kind of working audition: she would officially join the troupe only in the following season. Contrary to rumors, she was not actually a new discovery for Mamontov. In his letter quoted above, Melnikov noted: "I have been convinced once again by little Paskhalova's participation that you don't forget your old friends, a surprisingly constant trait of yours." The remark hinted at the first time Melnikov had met Mamontov—and Paskhalova: the two sang together in an amateur production of *Don Giovanni* that Mamontov directed in the early 1890s, with Melnikov in the title role and Paskhalova as Zerlina.[56]

As we can see, therefore, Mamontov knew Paskhalova well, saw her on stage, worked with her as a director, and understood her capabilities. It is very hard to believe that he would jeopardize the company's first tour of the capital by casting a singer he knew would not fit the part. Mamontov's reasoning becomes clear after a careful analysis of the extant photographs of the MPO's three Snow Maidens (see plates 18, 21, 23). While Tsvetkova's and Zabela's photos show a similar concept of the role, Paskhalova's image differs radically from both: her Snow Maiden is not a grown woman but a mischievous adolescent. According to the press, if there was a fault with Tsvetkova's rendition, it was her presentation of the character in the prologue and the opening acts:

> Miss Tsvetkova creates a sympathetic image of the Snow Maiden, graceful and well thought out. But there is too much sensibility in her singing, instead of a childlike carefree attitude disturbed only by fleeting moments of sadness. Only at the end is true feeling awakened in the Snow Maiden, and here Miss Tsvetkova's tone was exactly right. What was lacking was a contrast with the opening.[57]

The critics (in this case, Kashkin) argued that Tsvetkova's Snow Maiden (plate 18) turned into a passionate woman too early, well before the final scenes.[58]

Zabela—an expert on "fantastic creatures" and a wonderful Sea Princess in *Sadko* (see plate 20)—was more likely to bring the necessary coldness to the role, but her interpretation (which Mamontov surely knew after she had worked for him for three months) was still that of a grown woman (plate 21). Mamontov wanted a child. It is possible that in Tsvetkova's absence he attempted an experiment—a completely different visual and dramatic solution for the story. We must not forget that

*The Snow Maiden* (first the play, then the opera) had been his obsession since as early as 1882. The casting of Paskhalova (plate 23) was not the decision of an impresario or a despotic patron, but of a stage director. An opportunity to realize a radically new dramatic concept was too enticing: it outweighed any consideration of voice quality, stage experience, or backstage politics.

The second fierce casting battle (this time in-house, since Mamontov's initial concept never reached the stage) occurred over the role of Ioanna (that is, Joan of Arc) in Tchaikovsky's *The Maid of Orleans*. Two performers were considered for the role: Chernenko and Tsvetkova. The discussion took the vocal ability little into account: both singers were viewed as reasonably suitable, though they were still expected to have some problems with the notoriously awkward part. Even the fact that Chernenko was a mezzo-soprano was not an issue, since the composer created two versions of the role—one for a higher and another for a lower voice. The argument over casting had to do primarily with the dramatic aspect of the role of Joan of Arc: Mamontov and his associates were debating the choice of image for the heroine. Zabela, aware of the dispute, in a letter to Rimsky-Korsakov pointed out the seeming irrelevance of purely musical concerns to Mamontov's decision-making process:

> Savva Ivanovich and I are talking a lot about the new operas that are going to be staged. He has all of twenty-three titles written down, out of which Cui's *Angelo* and Tchaikovsky's *The Maid of Orleans* will most likely be staged. Particularly the latter, because Savva Ivanovich is dreaming about what an outstanding character Chernenko could create, although it is still completely unknown whether or not this part would suit her vocal abilities.[59]

In the spring of 1898 when the production was first discussed, the role was apparently intended for Tsvetkova. Kruglikov mentioned in one of his letters that Mamontov seemed to like the idea of seeing in this role "not the heroically constructed physique of a performer, but our tender, fragile Mimi with her soft, luminous eyes. Even the main idea wins this way: the power is in the spirit, not the muscles."[60] Over the summer, however, an intense debate erupted between Mamontov and Melnikov, who was in Paris doing the preliminary research for the opera, with the latter favoring Tsvetkova and the former Chernenko for the role. Mamontov's letters unfortunately did not survive, so his argument will have to be reconstructed from Melnikov's responses. Evidently, Chernenko was supposed to create an image of a warrior maid: "You write that the foundation of this character is strength and heroism. . . . You insist on Ioanna being *grande et molto belle,* writing that 'here we need strength, powerful energy, and most importantly *talent and exaltation.*"[61] Melnikov did not share that view: in his opinion, the strength of the heroine was to be spiritual, rather than physical. "The foundation of this character is mystery," he wrote:

> It was the inner power that only on a few occasions, like a momentary flickering fire, lighted up this fragile childlike body with its colossal strength, and even more with the impossibility of even a simple supposition of any unusual power in that very ordinary vessel, impressed everyone around it so much that her people demonstrated the heights of bravery, and the enemy ran, subdued by the single unimaginable fact, without a moment's thought of raising a hand against its perpetrator. According to history, Ioanna never even held a sword.[62]

The debate over Ioanna's image is perhaps peripheral to this discussion. What is most illuminating, however, is that both Mamontov and Melnikov constructed their arguments around the dramatic image that each of the performers would produce. Other candidates for the role were discussed from the same point of view: when Melnikov in the same letter suggested another soprano to sing the heroine, he commented on her coldness on stage, which would "suit Ioanna wonderfully." Even the inspiration for both "warrior" and "mystical child" images of the Maid came from spoken drama traditions—respectively, German and French. Melnikov wrote:

> There are two interpretations of [this character]. The first is German, developed not by Schiller but by German actresses, of whom I have seen five or six. It is like some grenadier who has lost all femininity, and charges into battle with her hair down, which is the only circumstance making the audience suspect a female body under the armor. . . . I believe more and more each day in the second, purely French, *modern* interpretation of the Maid. It is a fragile child's body (Ioanna is burned at nineteen); there is nothing unusual in her face—and only at moments of need inspiration transforms her completely—to the point where the people around her worship her as a saint.[63]

While Melnikov's sympathies were clearly with the French interpretation, which led him to severely criticize Maria Ermolova's acclaimed performance at the Imperial Maly Theater's production of Schiller's *Die Jungfrau von Orléans*, Mamontov admired that performance. Indeed, he was much more familiar with the German interpretation of the character than Melnikov who, by his own admission, only saw second-rate productions by provincial troupes.[64]

Eventually Mamontov and his assistant felt they needed to arrive at a compromise. Melnikov actually suggested they create two different Ioannas, one for each performer; "and if the music sometimes ends up being too powerful for either of them, *qu'importe! Nous jetons un rayon de lumière!*" he half-jokingly added. Instead, Mamontov created a fusion of two images in a single performer—Elena Tsvetkova.

The fact that the role was given to Tsvetkova suggests the French interpretation. Meanwhile, extant photographs of the singer in costume (the only visual images of the production still in existence—Polenov's sets did not survive) show a breastplate and a helmet, with the hair worn down, rather than plaited in childlike tresses as Melnikov suggested, indicating the German reading (see plate 19). The idea proved a success: a new operatic image created by merging two interpretations of the character, both taken from spoken drama, emphasized Ioanna's internal complexity, which in turn focused attention on her moral dilemma. Soviet musicologist Abram Gozenpud cited *The Maid of Orleans* as "one of Mamontov's best directing jobs."[65] The production also became Tsvetkova's personal triumph as an actress: Ippolitov-Ivanov, who conducted one of the performances, recalled her interpretation touching him so much that his "eyes impulsively filled with tears, and [he] was forced to conduct from memory because [he] could not see the score at all."[66]

## MAMONTOV AS A SINGER'S COACH

At the MPO, sensitive casting was viewed as a necessary first step in a long process of character development. One of the most important aspects of Mamontov's activity as a stage director was his coaching of the singers. As we have seen, this work has routinely been dismissed, even by Mamontov's most ardent partisans, as being limited to a few insightful comments from the back of the hall. Archival evidence indicates, however, that for the productions in which he was most deeply involved, Mamontov's work with singers was very thorough and surprisingly comprehensive. Elena Tsvetkova, acclaimed by the critics as an outstanding actress capable of dramatic power equal to Chaliapin's, was only one of many Mamontov singers who benefited from his expertise. Ippolitov-Ivanov recalled that Mamontov "worked through the role of Ioanna with the outstandingly talented Elena Yakovlevna Tsvetkova down to the last gesture, pose, and facial expression . . . approaching the part as a sensitive psychologist."[67] Note the level of detail observed by the conductor in the process of Tsvetkova's coaching. A trained singer himself, Mamontov understood the specifics of operatic performance. When necessary, he taught his students singing, including the basics of the Italian *bel canto* style.[68] More often, however, he outsourced voice lessons (for which he contentedly footed the bill) to foreign coaches, while he concentrated on the rarely taught and more elusive subjects: diction, phrasing, acting, characterization, and stage movement. This last aspect was particularly important to him, as we have seen—both for shaping a character and for creating a "complete illusion" of synthesized stage spectacle.

The benefits of Mamontov's coaching were not limited to artists in leading roles, but rather extended to the whole troupe—that is, to any singer willing to invest the time into studying with him. Those who took to his lessons with particular diligence were known to move up in the troupe (to the great chagrin of their more traditionally minded rivals, as we shall see). Among these were two of the troupe's second-tier mezzo-sopranos, Maria Chernenko and Tatyana Lyubatovich.[69] While both suffered from deficiencies in their vocal production, reviewers were often willing to overlook the problems, mesmerized by the compelling stage characters they created. Chernenko's Orfeo was one such image: Baskin commented on the singer's plasticity, classic simplicity, and beauty of movement, and emphasized these qualities as absolutely necessary for a mythological subject.[70]

One of Lyubatovich's signature roles was Carmen—the role in which Mamontov first saw her at the Tiflis Opera in 1884 (see plate 24). The reviewers of *Carmen* noted deficiencies in Lyubatovich's voice; however, all stressed her exceptional dramatic gift; the most frequently used adjective for her performance was "intelligent."[71] Lipaev was particularly impressed with Lyubatovich in this role, focusing on her in his two-page *Novosti Sezona* review of the production:

> Miss Lyubatovich performed the title role of Carmen. She understood Carmen's dramatic situation positively splendidly. Exceptionally sensitive acting, as well as makeup and facial expressions, all spoke for the artist. Overall, Miss Lyubatovich is a positively wonderful Carmen. However, this part includes much purely romance singing, for which the vocal power of the venerable artist was not always sufficient. This deficiency, however, does not diminish in the least her characteristic and solid interpretation of the heroine.[72]

A memorable character created at the MPO by both Chernenko and Lyubatovich was Saint-Saëns's Delilah. Tatyana Lyubatovich's interpretation was universally praised, her power as an actress rendering the problems of the shaky middle register negligible:

> Miss Lyubatovich recreated the ancient heroine with plasticity, but at the same time underscored the treachery and hatred in her character, the characteristic features that are rarely brought to the forefront by other performers of Delilah. This is that much harder to accomplish due to the music [that] has nowhere marked or portrayed these traits in Delilah. Bringing forth the needed shading here depends entirely on the actress. This is a fine nuance, rarely achieved.[73]

After Lyubatovich could no longer sing the part, Maria (Masha) Chernenko provided a worthy replacement. Indeed, mastering the drama of the role under Mamontov's coaching came naturally to her; it took another year for her voice to catch up. In anticipation of the opera's revival in 1900, Mamontov wrote to Shkafer: "Make Masha study the part now (she's probably forgotten it), and do it well, sensibly. She has acted it very well before, and now she can also sing it better. . . . If the question were raised about a different Delilah—God forbid, then it would be filth. Here an image and acting, plasticity is necessary."[74]

Mamontov's fascination with Chernenko (see plate 27), whom he discovered at the Conservatory and hired, first as a chorister and later as a soloist, has been a puzzle to both his contemporaries and scholars.[75] Some presumed a romantic involvement (an accusation commonly brought forth whenever Mamontov made a controversial casting decision regarding a female singer).[76] Others deplored the waste of time and energy in Mamontov's intent of "making a Chaliapin" out of Masha Chernenko,[77] an "awakening Galatea" to his Pygmalion.[78] The only person who seemed to have understood Mamontov's obsession with the singer was Pyotr Melnikov. In an insightful letter, he wrote:

> Let us put the voice aspect aside: it speaks for itself, and it is certainly important, but it does not represent everything you look for in your employees. Masha has little of the mature, independent, and direct stage talent; but she has something else that may be dearer to *you* than any original talent. She has a wonderful ability to absorb everything she is shown, and moreover, to sincerely represent someone else's ideas. You have personally parted forever with singing and the stage, but you live through personalities such as Masha's, as if she were your reflection in a mirror. You create a certain role; Chaliapin cannot interpret it the way you understand it, for he already has his own interpretation; outside it he is insincere, and therefore bad. But Masha presents a particularly suitable subject, capable of preserving much of your own reading, which would live on even beyond yourself and therefore, leave its mark on art.[79]

Melnikov is likely correct, at least partially: the stage was Mamontov's unrealized ambition, a lacuna all the more difficult to accept because of his unquestionable talent (he could certainly have become a Stanislavsky, if not a Meyerhold). Nevertheless, Maria Chernenko, whom Mamontov expected to mirror his demonstrations, was apparently an exception, rather than the rule. While demonstrating multiple interpretive possibilities for each role, he would demand independent thinking and creativity, rather than imitation.[80] Whether or not his students were able to move beyond the teacher's vision, creating their own interpretations of their characters depended on their abilities. Some borrowed the original wholesale, as Melnikov observed in relation to Anton Bedlevich's performance of Ivan Khovansky in *Khovanshchina*: "Bedlevich's first entrance is interesting, and this is your achievement: at every moment I saw you, and there are some instances when you yourself were on stage, your own figure."[81] Others, like Chaliapin, absorbed and built upon the image demonstrated during a study session, coming up with their own distinct readings. This was Mamontov's goal: the method of character analysis that he taught his singers was a tool they could apply to their future parts. As Paskhalova once observed, "working on a single role with [Mamontov] means learning to play other roles."[82] As a result, the MPO—a school of stage directing and design that also emphasized acting and aesthetic education—became a widely recognized, highly respected, and sought-after training program for singers, with good job prospects upon graduation (more on this in chapter 8), and an increasingly selective admissions policy.

## MOLDING A SINGING ACTOR

In his above-quoted letter that assessed the potential qualities of Mamontov's ideal recruits, Melnikov was astute to observe that vocal ability, although desirable, was not necessarily the primary criterion for choosing an MPO employee. Indeed, in a letter to Shkafer, Mamontov gave the following characterization of one of the troupe's sopranos: "Gladkaya is not a bad singer, but unfortunately she completely lacks talent, and would never, ever be able to arouse the audience—God decided that, and not us."[83] Since the subject of his criticism was not the singer's voice, Mamontov evidently did not consider good singing much of a talent. "She has a wonderful voice, but there is some kind of silt in her brain," he complained about Gladkaya, a future Mariinsky star, adding: "The girl sang all the notes correctly, of course, but understood nothing."[84]

Mamontov considered stage presence an absolutely essential inborn talent, and looked for it in every new employee. "Without it," he wrote, "a singer does not rise above a good artisan; with it, even without an adequately polished voice and with undeveloped musicality (but with its necessary presence, however), an artist already becomes noticeable."[85] He believed that intellectual and artistic development, another necessary quality, could be acquired through diligent work, as long as good will and a desire to learn were present. This was one of the reasons for his closeness to Shkafer—a singer who refused to limit himself to narrow "tenor concerns."[86] In letters to Shkafer, Mamontov laid out his understanding of drama on the operatic stage. Using singers such as Marie van Zandt and actors such as Sara Bernhardt and Jean Monet-Sully to illustrate his point, he called for a truly Wagnerian fusion of opera and drama:

> Look at Monet-Sully, how he grabs you and *won't let go* even for a second, making you follow his thought, a passing motion of his hand, his face, his eyes. In drama, this is completely in the hands of a performer, but in

opera, a performer absolutely must connect all these movements with music, with every measure. The deeper a performer fuses the internal impulses of his character with the sound of the voice and the orchestra, the stronger the impact on a listener's soul. In this harmony lies the *great mystery* of a staged operatic creation.[87]

To achieve this perfect harmonious blend of drama and music, Mamontov conceived of a new type of singer—"an artist-singer," or, using the term coined by his follower Stanislavsky, "a singing actor." As Shkafer recalled, the MPO put forth "a new task, unusual for an opera singer, to become an 'actor' and to learn acting on stage the same way they do in spoken drama."[88] The task was indeed unusual: at conservatories and especially at private opera studios, acting tended to be given short shrift; at best, young singers were advised to imitate their elders. "Where, from whom could we learn the real thing?" Shkafer exclaimed.[89] He himself, even with the school of Leonova and Komissarzhevsky under his belt, was still unaccustomed to acting. Mamontov had to use all his influence with his student (particularly strong because of his brilliant success with Chaliapin) to convince him and the others to "try it out":

> You must step over the barrier called "a bit ashamed." Step over it! You'll see! Do you know where to a large degree Chaliapin's *huge* acting success comes from? Talent? Yes, but no one knows what that is. The brain? Yes, but that is not enough. He has a great *desire* and at the same time *decisiveness* to *be affected and to act out on stage*. Such bravery and decisiveness bring much. Try it out.[90]

One of Mamontov's demands of his singing actors was to conceptualize a role as a whole, including the moments they were not singing or even present on stage. He treasured every moment of an operatic drama, including those in which a singer was silent; the dramatic current of a character's development was not to be interrupted. He outlines his position, typically, in a long letter to Shkafer:

> I want to prove that the singer's influence upon the operatic audience is not limited only to the moment when he is singing, that is, presenting a word and a sound . . . No, an uttered word should be completed with a movement, a facial expression, and it is possible that for several seconds or even a whole minute (an eternity on stage!) of an orchestral interlude the singer is *only* acting, and here in silence the most powerful moment of the role is being developed. This happens in opera all the time. And do

you know how often artists ignore it? . . . This is most often a sin of the conservatory boys and girls, since . . . their acting teacher for the most part is a complete idiot. That's why life, light, brilliance, and inspiration are paralyzed on the operatic stage—there is no continuous current, it keeps being interrupted. This stupidity reaches such a state that conservatory-trained ladies (I have often witnessed it) in strong dramatic roles allow themselves to adjust their costumes and hairdos during the rests in their parts, and the men even walk into the wings to spit. What is that? That is idiocy, ignorance, and a lack of understanding of stage aesthetics.[91]

To a modern sensibility, Mamontov is stating the obvious. Yet acting during the rests in a musical score was rarely attempted on the operatic stage of his time. This made critics all the more attentive and eager to point out that some of the most captivating moments of MPO productions occurred when performers were not singing. For example, rave reviews were occasioned by the act 2 finale of *The Maid of Pskov,* the entrance of Ivan the Terrible into Pskov—according to the score, an orchestral interlude. Similarly, one of the highlights of Elena Tsvetkova's interpretation of Mimi in *La bohème,* according to the press, was her exit in the finale of act 3—another moment of pure pantomime.

Every MPO singer who studied with Mamontov was expected to develop his or her acting ability, to become a singing actor. A natural model for emulation suggested by their mentor was, of course, spoken drama. Mamontov's students were expected to regularly attend the Maly Theater, as well as the Moscow Art Theater after it opened in the fall of 1898. Those staying in Paris on Mamontov's summer scholarships (among them Chaliapin, Sekar-Rozhansky, Shkafer, Melnikov, Chernenko, Eberle, Galtsyna, and Lyubatovich) were particularly recommended the Comédie Française. "I am diligently attending the Comédie Française," wrote Melnikov, "and see it as a university for myself and my fellow actors."[92] Shkafer poured out his impressions in an excited missive—his first from Paris:

> On my very first day, Pyotr [Melnikov] and I set off for the Comédie Française, where we saw an excellent production of *Ruy Blas.* Since you, Savva Ivanovich, know this institution better than I do, it only remains for me to say with what envy I watched this group of actors, who, with their hard work, love, energy, serious attitude, and faith in themselves, their sacred, pure, and lofty vocation in life, serve art, move it forward, and offer a vivid example for people like us—still uncertain, stumbling, searching

for support, etc. Obviously, such institutions are created through decades, even centuries, and, who knows, maybe our not yet sufficiently powerful soil will also bear such fruit. Sitting in that institution, I invariably flew to our dear motherland, and thought constantly of you, Savva Ivanovich, and of your child—the Private Russian Opera.[93]

It is characteristic that Shkafer compared the French drama troupe to the MPO. The young stage director was clearly searching for a frame of reference for Mamontov's theater that at the time had no equivalent on the Russian operatic or, prior to the debut of Stanislavsky's troupe, dramatic stage. Some singers found it easier than others to adjust to the new environment. The former shared and supported Mamontov's goals; the latter considered them bewildering and even incompatible with the foundations of operatic art. To elucidate Mamontov's concept of the ideal singer for his troupe, let us compare the approaches to their work demonstrated by two of his most talented employees, both of whom would leave their mark on the history of opera—Feodor Chaliapin and Nadezhda Zabela-Vrubel.

## "I WANT TO BE A MUSICIAN": NADEZHDA ZABELA

Both Chaliapin and Zabela are important names in the history of Russian music. While Zabela's post-Mamontov career was less illustrious than Chaliapin's, she has earned an impressive reputation of her own as a great musician, and particularly as Rimsky-Korsakov's legendary muse. It is also well known that while Chaliapin enjoyed a privileged status in Mamontov's troupe, and his presence had a significant influence on repertoire choices, staging, and design, Zabela's position was more difficult and more controversial. Chaliapin had every opportunity opened to him by Mamontov; Zabela and her patron Rimsky-Korsakov both felt, not without merit, that she was often ignored by her director. The composer wrote: "This systematic *neglect* of an artist such as yourself is truly astonishing."[94] It would be easy to accept Zabela's explanation of her predicament by a personal antipathy on Mamontov's part. This theory, however, does not bear close scrutiny. On a personal level, Mamontov liked Zabela well enough to play matchmaker to her and Mikhail Vrubel, and even to finance their honeymoon in Switzerland. On a professional level, he employed her at the Panaev Theater, a St.

Petersburg operatic venture that he had sponsored in 1895–96, and later hired her as Tsvetkova's replacement at the MPO for the 1897–98 season. Although their artistic differences soon became apparent, Mamontov renewed her contract after Tsvetkova's return in the fall of 1898. Besides, any conflict with Zabela would have been most unpleasant to him, as it would directly affect her admirer, Rimsky-Korsakov, as well as Vrubel, Mamontov's own beloved protégé. In reality, Zabela had every chance to earn a position among the female cast equal to Chaliapin's among the male singers. What prevented that from happening was the fact that her attitude toward her own job and the company's mission differed markedly from Mamontov's. The distinction is apparent in a series of letters Zabela wrote to Rimsky-Korsakov during the time of her association with the MPO.

From Zabela's correspondence with the composer, it is evident that she viewed herself as a singer, rather than an actress. To her, studying a part meant primarily learning the music, not learning about the character. She rarely referred to it as "a role"—a term borrowed from spoken drama, which Mamontov and his associates preferred.[95] Characteristic is Zabela's reaction to receiving a section of the *Tsar's Bride* score. "The Adagio from the aria is wonderfully beautiful, and can showcase the voice and ability of a singer in the best possible light," she wrote to the composer. "I am now singing it every morning and evening, and want to achieve a complete *cantabile*. God knows if I can do it; I have a great desire to perfect myself."[96]

In her "desire to perfect" herself, Zabela resembled many of her colleagues at Mamontov's company. Yet while they wanted to perfect their acting abilities, her aspirations lay in another direction: "I want to understand all the nuances, and to be not just a singer but a musician."[97] Zabela believed that the dramatic possibilities of an operatic production should stem exclusively from the choice of a vocal range. Discussing with Rimsky-Korsakov her desire to sing Kupava in the MPO *Snow Maiden* production, she voiced her doubts about her suitability for the part, not, however, in terms of the openly dramatic character of the role, but in terms of voice quality. "Actually, a lyrical soprano could also sing [Kupava]," she wrote, "but it is true that if Tsvetkova sings the Snow Maiden and I do Kupava, it would not be very interesting, for the voices are very homogeneous."[98]

Acting did not appeal to Zabela; indeed, she viewed Mamontov's push to "act out on stage" as embarrassing and unacceptable. Mamontov realized that. While he valued her voice and musicianship, he apparently began to feel, as time went by, that her attitude went against the basic principles of his company. The singer, however, never seemed to understand his position; after a performance of *A Life for the Tsar*, she wrote to Rimsky-Korsakov: "The part of Antonida seems to work very well for me; for some reason it is considered difficult but for me it is amazingly easy. Even S. I. [Mamontov] graced me with a compliment in the following form: 'Still, what a beautiful voice you have!' What does that 'still' mean, I wonder?"[99] Another characteristic episode occurred at the performance of *May Night*, in which Zabela was cast in the role of Pannochka—a drowned girl turned water nymph. The singer reported it as follows: "I was singing [Pannochka] without the little wreath, and did not act the corpse; of course Savva Iv[anovich] was displeased, sarcastic, and before my entrance kept inviting me to the second quadrille because he was convinced that I looked like I was going to a ball."[100]

According to Zabela, only superior vocal prowess justified a singer's appearance on stage. Consequently, she had much to criticize in Mamontov's approach that took into account acting ability, visual appearance, movement, and many other factors. To her, the idea of casting a weaker singer who looked and acted the part, as opposed to a superior singer who did not, seemed anti-musical: "I am convinced again today that the Private Opera has nothing to do with music."[101] Her reaction to the casting of Koltsov as Sadko (see n.51, above) was perhaps the harshest of all the employees (to be fair, she was the one who had to sing duets with him . . . ). And while Mamontov's choice in that case was indeed unfortunate, it is characteristic that Zabela never even considered that it might have been informed by factors other than vocal ability. Similarly, she did not believe that any production could succeed without the voices: "I wonder how *The Maid of Orleans* fares: neither Chaliapin nor Sekar participate in it, and the whole weight of this, they say, weak opera will be carried on Tsvetkova's weak little shoulders, and of course Stavitskaya in the role of Agnes."[102]

Faithful to the Italian tradition in staging, Zabela also had little sympathy for Mamontov's notion of artistic ensemble. In response to Rimsky-Korsakov's letter in which the composer mentioned Mamontov's intent of building his productions around the ensemble rather than star performers, she wrote: "I'd like to know what this 'caring about the ensemble' means. It seems that S. I. means by it to throw away all the good soloists and make the troupe out of the most green, inexperienced youths who don't know how to sing in time."[103]

Yet, despite her reluctance to act and her occasional blatant refusal to follow the stage director's instructions (for example, regarding her costume and acting in *May Night*), Zabela remained in the troupe. In order to neutralize her discord with the rest of the ensemble but still utilize her voice and sensitive musicality to the best advantage, Mamontov made sure to keep her away from the roles that focused on acting while casting her whenever solid *cantilena* was required. While discussing the prospects for the role of Iante, a young Greek princess in *The Necklace*, he suggested the following: "I am thinking that Khrennikova seems heavy for Iante. Really! She is very sweet; has a fresh, excellent voice, but it is really a dramatic soprano. Can she create a light, delicate Greek girl, won't she be heavy? I wonder. Better give it to Zabela. She will sing clearly, correctly; and God knows there is not much acting there."[104]

Similar reasoning prompted Melnikov to suggest that Zabela be cast in the trouser role of Prince Charming ("if she's not bowlegged") in Massenet's *Cendrillon*, which he was planning to direct.[105] Among other roles with "not much acting" given to Zabela were Michaela in *Carmen* and Euridice in *Orfeo*. The latter was certainly a very important assignment: as we have seen, it was Mamontov's signature production. Zabela, however, was unimpressed, complaining to Rimsky-Korsakov about participating in an opera that was not attracting audiences (i.e., *Orfeo*), or about singing a secondary part:

> Our opera company can't seem to get opened. We are rehearsing a host of operas, among them *Carmen,* which has never been a box-office hit. For some reason I am singing Michaela, although we have a whole host of young singers who beg to sing this role, but you see, they are cast as Tatyanas and Marguerites, and I am singing Michaela for some reason.[106]

The "host of young singers" encroaching on her territory was a source of constant anxiety to Zabela. By the fall of 1898, the company employed nine sopranos: Mamontov never refused entry to his "apprenticeship program" to anyone with abilities, so there was clearly a shortage of work for all. More and more, Zabela's letters were filled with venom about Mamontov promoting young and, in her opinion, inexperienced singers. She was particularly incensed about Anna Stavitskaya (see plate 37), who had joined the company during the 1898–99 season and attracted the director's attention because of her obvious ability and desire to act:

> They say that on the Imperial stage young singers are given no path, but here, poor little old ladies like us have no life because of the newcomers. Particularly dangerous is Stavitskaya, declared by S. I. to be a genius, a second Duse etc.; her name is already printed in large type. I have heard her in *Onegin,* and with all my desire to find something special in her, found nothing. I even find that she gives a surprisingly wrong type of Tatyana; ... as for singing, she is not bad but not good either, her voice is small, shaky, with a cat's timbre. And still S. I. gradually gives her all the lyrical parts; he did not get to your operas yet, but I already anticipate that soon she will be singing the Maid of Pskov, Sheloga, and maybe even the Sea Princess, while I am singing Michaela and Euridice.[107]

Interestingly, Zabela was jealous even of the purely dramatic roles that held little musical interest to her personally but in which Stavitskaya's small voice was no deterrent while her acting ability was a plus. She wrote: "I am happy I was not cast as Agnes [in *The Maid of Orleans*] because I consider her part boring, but S. I. views it as interesting, which is why he has given it to Stavitskaya."[108] Zabela believed that Mamontov's casting principles resulted from pure favoritism, occasionally supporting her opinion with a variety of rumors always abundant in theater life. For example, after Cui's *Angelo,* due to be staged in 1899, was postponed until the following season, she explained it to Rimsky-Korsakov as follows: "*Angelo,* I think, will not run at all, because it seems that Cui declared that he did not wish a mezzo-soprano to sing Katharina. What would be the fun for S. I. to stage an opera in which none of his favorites participates?"[109] César Cui himself held a different view, however. In a letter to Mamontov he agreed that it would be more advantageous to schedule his first Moscow premiere at the beginning rather than the end of a season, so that audiences would have more time to become acquainted with the opera.[110] He also enthusiastically endorsed Mamontov's choice of personnel, including the mezzo-soprano, writing: "Your casting appears splendid to me. I value Chernenko's talent highly. It's a pity about Chaliapin but, well, it can't be helped. I don't know Olenin at all, but since you chose him for Galeofa, I don't doubt that he is a talented artist."[111]

Clearly, Zabela felt possessive about any soprano role given to another performer, but particularly about the Rimsky-Korsakov operas in which she was singing, especially *Sadko*. Commenting on a performance of the opera, she wrote to Rimsky-Korsakov: "Even van Zandt appreciated this music; . . . so much that she wants to sing the duet of the Sea Princess with Sadko in concert. Here's another rival for me, and this one is truly very dangerous, although she could hardly sing this part with as much love as I do."[112]

Her position as favorite singer of Russia's most eminent living opera composer was a source of great pride to Zabela. "I am only in A-major [i.e., happy] when I am singing," she wrote to him; "when my voice sounds very good; when you are listening to me, and I feel that you are very pleased."[113] Unfortunately, this distinction also made her feel superior to and separated from the other performers, whom she believed to be jealous of her success. As evident from the memoir literature, it was customary for the MPO employees (including Chaliapin) to drop by the theater every day, even when they were not scheduled for a performance or a rehearsal. Zabela was the exception: she would not appear unless personally summoned, or unless there was a Rimsky production she wanted to hear; the internal life of the company did not interest her. "I haven't been to the theater since *Sadko*," she wrote to the composer, "and would probably go only Friday for *Mozart*. What would I do there? They don't want to know me, they don't let me sing, and I don't want to know them."[114] One of the most remarkable illustrations of Zabela's attitude was a letter she had sent to Rimsky-Korsakov on 11 December 1898. It reads: "[My bad mood] has now passed, mainly because for a long time now, for almost a whole week, I haven't been to the [theater] but stayed at home; and I don't want to know what is going on there, and how our homegrown divas printed in large type are distinguishing themselves."[115] What is remarkable about this letter is the date: four days after the premiere of *Boris Godunov*, a major event in the life of the company, which Zabela, despite her professed admiration for Chaliapin and with complete disregard for the work of her comrades, had clearly boycotted.

Thus, having entered the MPO with an opportunity to be fully included into Mamontov's ensemble of singing actors, Nadezhda Zabela chose instead to hold to her concept of an operatic performer as a musician rather than stage artist, resisting with increasing hostility Mamontov's attempts to integrate her into the troupe. Despite mounting tension, she signed with the company for the second season. She had no choice: there was little hope for a job at the Imperial Theaters—a traditionally-minded institution clearly more suitable to her approach, but without a vacancy for her until 1904.[116] Zabela was forced to stay with the company whose leader, troupe, and mission she neither understood nor respected. When Rimsky-Korsakov asked her how to announce her at a concert of his works in which she was to participate, she replied: "When you announce my participation, it will be necessary to add 'an artist of the Moscow Private Opera' to my name. S. I. would never forgive me if I omitted this title of mine, in his opinion very prestigious, and in mine—rather sad."[117] Gradually, both Mamontov and his associates began feeling just as frustrated with her as she was with them. Mamontov's assessment of her in late 1899 was harsh, yet insightful: "Zabela is a 'star' with a crooked mouth; she is dramatically worthless, but the audience wants to believe she is good because she sings well."[118]

## THE BOUNDARIES OF INTERPRETATION: FEODOR CHALIAPIN

While Zabela's public success was founded on the high quality of her singing, Chaliapin's vocal ability was not the main reason for his enormous popularity. Initially critics attempted to analyze his performances in the same manner as those of other opera singers: they discussed the strength of his voice, its range, flexibility, and other fine points of singing technique. It soon became evident, however, that Chaliapin's power lay elsewhere—a fact reflected in the reviews. For instance, the *Novosti Dnya* article on *Boris Godunov* did not contain a single word on the vocal presentation of the title role; instead, the critic, Evgeny Rozenov, focused on the drama of the protagonist:

> Chaliapin in the role of Boris has achieved new heights of musical-dramatic performance, which has hardly ever existed on the operatic stage. In the monologue *Dostig ya vysshei vlasti* [*I Have Achieved the Highest Power*, act 2], he has reached such a high degree of artistry in his act-

ing, facial expressions, flexibility of intonation, variety of dramatic nuances, and strength of psychological characterization, that it remains for criticism merely to bow silently before the talent, joining the ecstatic crowd.[119]

Chaliapin's own memoirs, as well as those of his colleagues, reveal that he was a beneficiary of Mamontov's coaching. While the singer does not mention long study sessions with his mentor, recalling only the brief insightful comments that illuminated his understanding of major roles, other witnesses mention these sessions.[120] They were apparently no secret from the troupe, nor from Mamontov's close associates such as Stanislavsky, who, Kuznetsov claims, "was aware of Mamontov's intense rehearsal work with Chaliapin [and] attended their study sessions, exercising his right, according to the family tradition, to attend the other's rehearsals."[121] In his study of Chaliapin's early career, Gozenpud discussed Mamontov's coaching of the singer for his starring role of Boris: "He worked through the part of Boris with Chaliapin: the scenes with Shuisky, with the children, and the last tableau. Mamontov paid the closest attention to the psychological angle, the behavior of the characters."[122] As a result of Mamontov's guidance, as well as the personal artistic choices that brought Chaliapin to their study sessions in the first place, his understanding of the operatic genre as primarily powerful staged drama was diametrically opposed to Zabela's, which explains the difference in their standing within the troupe. Perhaps the most illustrative example of their divergent philosophies is the two singers' respective approaches to rendering a composer's score.

Zabela was well known for her meticulous attention to the score; this was one of the reasons she was so prized by Rimsky-Korsakov, who actively disliked any "interpreting" of his works. It was also a reason for the respect awarded to Zabela by researchers who follow a traditional musicological decree of sanctity of the authorial intent. Chaliapin, on the other hand, had to be defended, both by his contemporaries and by Soviet scholars, from accusations of taking significant liberties with the score. Zabela herself touched upon the subject while reporting to Rimsky-Korsakov on the premiere of *Mozart and Salieri*, an opera constructed around Chaliapin's character: "I was sitting next to Savva Iv[anovich], and we both reveled in the wonderfully elegant impression from [*Mozart and Salieri*]. That lucky Chaliapin phrases so wonderfully: his phrasing seems to have commas, semi-colons, and exclamation points, and at the same time, all this is within the limits of the written music, without changing a thing."[123] Seventy-five years later, Abram Gozenpud made essentially the same point regarding *Boris Godunov,* stating in particular:

> In literature on Chaliapin, one often sees remarks that the artist occasionally changed from singing to "speech." However, he himself vehemently denied it. The impression of changing to the "speech mode" was created by the unusually natural quality of his vocal inflection. Without an opportunity to ground himself in music, Chaliapin failed frequently (a recording of him declaiming a Knudsen poem leaves a sad impression, and seems a weak imitation of a poetry reading by a bad actor). Chaliapin asserted that he had always sung and never spoken over music. And it was true.[124]

The literature to which Gozenpud responded in his 1974 study was probably an article by Lev Lebedinsky titled "Stsena 'Chasy s Kurantami' v Ispolnenii Shalyapina" ["The Chime Clock Scene as Performed by Chaliapin"], published in the March 1959 issue of *Sovetskaya Muzyka.*[125] Lebedinsky's analysis of an extant Chaliapin recording of the Chime Clock scene (that is, the final hallucination scene) from act 2 of *Boris Godunov* points out numerous divergences from the written score. For example, the singer alters the text of the monologue, sometimes by replacing Musorgsky's libretto with original lines from Pushkin's play. Lebedinsky's transcription shows the speech mode used on several occasions when the composer prescribed definite pitch. The climactic moment of the scene, during which the character begins to hallucinate, is performed unaccompanied: Musorgsky's orchestra is silenced for two whole measures so that nothing detracts from the emotion in the voice. Overall, Chaliapin's intention, made clear by Lebedinsky's excellent analysis, was to change the musical character of the scene. The singer's part, conceived by the composer as bare-boned recitative that grows out of and follows the orchestra, is reshaped to become a dramatic, declamatory vocal line that dominates and is supported by the orchestral accompaniment.

My own study of Chaliapin's 1927 Covent Garden recording of the hallucination scene, recently restored and released on CD, suggests that the singer's daring went even further than Lebedinsky proposed.[126] While his transcription includes only a few unpitched notes and notes of indeterminate pitch, my analysis indicates a much wider use of these two kinds of singing. Indeed, it appears that Chaliapin is employing three distinct modes of sound production: singing, speech, and a kind of speech-singing.[127] He alternates among these different modes according to the dramatic situation as reflected in the text of the monologue: the more agitated the character becomes, the closer the singer moves toward the speech mode. Table 5.1 outlines the specific distribution of the three modes of sound production over the four sections of the scene, divided according to the psychological state of the protagonist: an opening contemplation, a description of his agitated state of mind, hallucinations, and a final prayer. While a precise gradation between the modes is impossible as they flow seamlessly into one another, sections of contemplation and prayer are mostly performed in the singing mode, while the description is overwhelmingly speech-sung. The hallucination section utilizes all three modes: for example, while pleading with the child ("I'm not your evildoer"), Chaliapin uses the singing mode; the description of the apparition is speech-sung, while the climactic points at the beginning and the end of the section are clearly spoken (see table 5.1 for details).

Indeed, the speech-singing and speaking modes would be used by Chaliapin to dramatize his roles beyond *Boris*. For example, they were to enhance his interpretations of Salieri in Rimsky-Korsakov's opera (*pace* Zabela) and Holofernes in Alexander Serov's *Judith*.[128] Nor was Chaliapin's approach unique within the MPO troupe. As early as October 1896, Gruzinsky complained in *Russkoe Slovo* about Anton Sekar-Rozhansky's use of the speech mode in the finale of *Carmen*, demanding that, whatever the justification with respect to dramatic interpretation might be, "the boundary dividing singing from common speech must never be crossed."[129]

Returning to Chaliapin's interpretation of the hallucination scene, my analysis of the recording concurs with Lebedinsky's assessment that the vocal line, contrary to Zabela's claims and Chaliapin's own assertions quoted by Gozenpud, varies substantially from the original, even in the sung sections, becoming even freer in the speech-sung and spoken episodes. A similar picture arises from the analysis of Boris's other monologues, particularly *I Have Achieved the Highest Power* in act 2, mentioned by the *Novosti Dnya* reviewer, and the death scene

Table 5.1. An Analysis of the Three Modes of Sound Production in Chaliapin's
Interpretation of the Chime-Clock Scene from *Boris Godunov*

| Section | Text |
| --- | --- |
| Contemplation | Ugh, *it's so hard!* Oh, let me *get some air* . . . |
| | I felt as if all my blood had rushed to my face |
| | And then heavily subsided. |
| | Oh, cruel conscience, how harshly *you* punish! |
| Description | **Yes,** if inside yourself |
| | A single stain, *a single one by chance appeared,* |
| | **Oh, then you are in trouble,** |
| | **You would like to run, but there is nowhere to run.** |
| | *Your soul will burn; your heart will be filled with poison.* |
| | *It will feel heavy, so heavy,* |
| | *Like hammer strokes* <u>*it's ringing in your ears*</u> |
| | <u>*With curse and* **condemnation**</u> . . . |
| | *And something is stifling you; you are suffocating,* |
| | *And your head is spinning,* |
| | ***And boys, yes, boys covered in blood, are in your eyes!*** |
| Hallucination | <u>*There, over there, what is that? There, in the corner?*</u> |
| | *It's quivering,* it's growing . . . |
| | *It's getting closer* . . . it's trembling and moaning . . . |
| | *Off, off with you!* . . . *Not me* . . . I am not your evildoer . . . |
| | *Off!* . . . *Off with you, child!* . . . |
| | <u>*Not me* . . . *not me,* **no** . . . ***not me,***</u> |
| | <u>***It was the will of the people!*** . . .</u> |
| | <u>**Off** . . . **Oh!** . . . ***Off, child, off with you!***</u> |
| Prayer | My Lord! You desire not the sinner's death; |
| | Have mercy on the soul of the criminal, Tsar Boris! |

*Note:* The translation of the monologue is mine; fidelity to the original Russian text rather than issues of musical prosody was the most important consideration in translation; the singing mode is indicated by normal type, the speech-singing mode by *italics,* and the speech mode by <u>*underlined italics;*</u> all extraneous text inserted by Chaliapin into the monologue as an expansion or substitution for the original is printed in **bold type.**

in act 4. Unlike Zabela, who never allowed herself to deviate from the authorial text, as her few extant recordings indicate,[130] Chaliapin was convinced that strengthening the drama of the score was worth violating its integrity.[131]

During his MPO years, Feodor Chaliapin was particularly engrossed in exploring the dramatic possibilities inherent in his characters; in the later revivals of the roles, his performances are reported to have mellowed somewhat. According to Kruglikov, who compared Chaliapin's renditions of the role of Salieri in 1898 and 1901, in the original production the singer acted more freely and speech-sang even the arioso sections, a practice he would later abandon.[132] Shkafer also suggested in his memoir that Chaliapin's interpretation of Salieri might have been infused with too much naturalism early on, and that he gradually softened his approach. This would certainly be in agreement with Mamontov's aesthetics. Similarly, the singer's initial portrayal of Ivan the Terrible in *The Maid of Pskov* was based on then-fashionable psychiatric evaluations of the tsar. Later in the season his naturalist stance relaxed, possibly under the influence of Mamontov who, as we have seen, detested unabated naturalism.

The comparison made here between Feodor Chaliapin and Nadezhda Zabela's approaches to their work reveals a portrait of an ideal Mamontov singer: a singing actor, capable of an interpretation blending drama with music. While Zabela did not share Mamontov's vision, Chaliapin proved to be his most talented student. The core of the repertory that the singer would take with him to the Imperial Theaters, and on which he would later build an international career, was developed at the MPO. In most of his classic roles, therefore, he followed the creative guidelines set up by his stage director Mamontov, whose artistic principles were thus disseminated through his student. Varvara Strakhova, Chaliapin's close friend and frequent partner on stage, confirmed as much when she wrote:

> It would be right to view the years that Chaliapin spent with Mamontov as the period of his highest spiritual exertion and greatest creativity, qualitatively and quantitatively. This was the moment of the wildest flowering of his genius. There he created his phenomenal stage characters; and particularly then and there Feodor Ivanovich became *the Chaliapin* whose very name later meant so much to the world.[133]

# SIX

# From Meiningen to Meyerhold

It is clear, I hope, from the discussion above that Mamontov's enterprise was run in many ways like a drama theater, with acting and stage directing concerns being equal to and occasionally superseding purely musical, vocal considerations. Despite the fact that acting was Mamontov's passion, and directing his favorite pastime, one cannot explain such a fundamental role of spoken drama practices at his company purely by the nostalgic desire to re-live the experiences of his youth. The uniqueness of the MPO among Russian opera houses of the 1890s, both state-owned and private, resulted partly from the influence of Western European drama troupes: never before had an opera theater been so inspired by its stage rival.

Extant archival documents reveal that the implementation of spoken drama principles was a deliberate, openly acknowledged practice at the MPO. Mamontov loved the Maly Drama Theater and insisted that his singers attend it. He also held the French dramatic tradition in the highest regard: we have seen him offer the Comédie Française, and great French dramatic actors such as Sara Bernhardt, Eleonora Duse, and Jean Monet-Sully, as models for his young troupe. But arguably, the most significant impact on MPO operations and Mamontov's own directing was created by an acclaimed German company that had made waves around Europe since the 1870s and toured Russia twice, in 1885 and 1890. This company was the Meiningen Court Theater, owned by Duke Georg II of Saxe-Meiningen, and directed by the duke himself, his actress wife, and his assistant stage director Ludwig Chronegk.

According to Gozenpud, Mamontov attended performances of the Meiningen troupe during both of their tours.[1] Stanislavsky in his memoirs also mentions attending Chronegk's rehearsals, which indicates that visitors were allowed to be present. Knowing Mamontov, it is inconceivable that he would have missed such an opportunity. His correspondence reveals a detailed knowledge of the German troupe's internal operations, making it evident that he was either personally present at rehearsals, and also probably talked to Chronegk, or at least received Stanislavsky's detailed reports. Mamontov's intimate acquaintance with the Meiningen Theater is equally evident in his own work as a stage director. Indeed, both the directing and the operational practices of the two companies were so similar that, considering Mamontov's documented access to the Germans, it is unlikely this was coincidental. In fact, Mamontov and his associates were fully aware of the artistic and organizational correspondences between the troupes. While some of these may be described as parallel trends rather than direct influences, others were discussed by members of Mamontov's team in terms of implementing, as Kruglikov once put it, "our Meiningen" on the MPO stage.[2]

This tantalizing Meiningen connection has so far attracted almost no scholarly interest.[3] Such a gap in Mamontov scholarship may have been caused by a variety of factors, including an ideological one—a reluctance to acknowledge a foreign influence over a stage director portrayed as a Russian nationalist. More importantly, the lack of research on the subject may be attributed to the dearth of relevant primary sources. While the directing practices of the Meiningen troupe are detailed in the duke's extensive diaries, no comparable material exists in Mamontov's hand.[4] Fortunately, I have discovered a previously untapped source of information on Mamontov's stage directing: an expansive archive of research notes and rehearsal books belonging to Pyotr Melnikov, which is preserved at the Rainis Museum in Riga, Latvia. While most of these materials are related to the years of Melnikov's work at the Imperial Theaters and the Riga National Opera, at least one set of documents can be dated earlier. These are the detailed director's notes on Tchaikovsky's *Eugene Onegin*, the work that Melnikov staged for Mamontov in the fall of 1898. While the materials on many other operas he first directed at the MPO and later recreated elsewhere cannot be incontrovertibly dated from the earlier time period, the *Onegin* notes correspond directly to

Melnikov's letter to Mamontov dated summer 1899, which refers to the 1898 production (see below).

The *Onegin* materials prove that Melnikov, a highly meticulous person, saved his research and staging notes made during his tenure with Mamontov, and used them in his later work at the Imperial Theaters, building on the earlier foundation. This opens up the possibility that the notes on some other Melnikov-directed operas preserved at the Rainis Museum may also contain traces of the original Mamontov productions. Using these materials as a basis and complementing them with Mamontov's own statements contained in his correspondence and observations on his productions in press reviews, we can paint a much more comprehensive picture of the MPO's spoken drama practices. Mamontov's intent to implement some of the Meiningen policies and procedures will then become even more evident. The areas of correspondence between the two companies, as well as the avenues of discernible Meiningen influence on the MPO, including historicism and authenticity, approaches to visual design, casting, rehearsal techniques, role rotation, and the treatment of crowd scenes, will be investigated below.

## HISTORICISM AND AUTHENTICITY

History was a specialty of the Meiningen Theater: some of its most acclaimed productions included Schiller's *Die Jungfrau von Orléans* and Shakespearean chronicles. Similar productions were equally prominent on the playbill of Mamontov's company, which fed its audiences a steady diet of Russian historical operas. It will be instructive, therefore, to analyze the correspondences in the ways the two troupes approached historical drama—their natural point of convergence, and a genre in which they both excelled.

As we have seen, Mamontov's work on an opera, particularly a historical opera, began with preliminary research. Since Melnikov was primarily responsible for this work, his notes are particularly helpful in understanding its scope and methodology. The research on productions portraying historical events included studying historical sources, geographical locations, and contemporaneous iconography, particularly to observe ways of wearing clothes, as well as the habits, mannerisms, and behaviors that would be appropriate for the characters on stage. In discussing with Mamontov the possibility of reviving *La traviata* as a powerful drama, rather than a worn-out concert in costumes, Melnikov insisted that "in act 1, real barons should be on stage, not a real mess."[5] This kind of painstaking research was quite unusual for the Russian theaters of the time. It was habitual, however, for the Duke of Meiningen, who was responsible for researching his company's productions. For instance, both directors were known to make trips to historical locations in order to envision and orient their sets correctly. For their respective representations of Joan of Arc's story, each journeyed to Domrémy, Rouen, and Orléans before making recommendations on sets and staging. They also paid particular attention to such details as the time of year when events reportedly occurred. Thus, the duke made his designer repaint the backdrop for *Wallensteins Lager* after learning that the action took place in December. Melnikov even requested a specific designer for *1812*, chosen according to his skill at rendering the autumnal colors needed for act 3. He wrote: "A bright set design of fall colors was a long time coming, having handy as we do the paintbrush of Kostya [Korovin], who senses those tones so strongly!"[6]

When working on an opera that, apart from representing a certain moment in history, was based on a particular literary work, Melnikov carefully studied the original text, in addition to historical sources. Just as Mamontov in his letters frequently discussed the staging possibilities of a new opera with reference to a libretto rather than a score,[7] his student was well known for basing his staging on a literary original rather than on a composer's adaptation of it. Melnikov's notes for *Onegin* and *May Night* are literally made up of excerpts from the respective printed editions of Pushkin and Gogol that he cut out and glued into his notebooks. The details of scenery, characters' movements, and objects in view are carefully underlined (see figure 1, p. 203), later to be utilized in staging notes and design requirements.

Peripheral characters present in the literary source but excised in the libretto were studied in order to be incorporated into the stage business delegated to choristers and supernumeraries. The country ball scene from *Onegin*, an acclaimed success of director Melnikov, was such a daring achievement that even Mamontov got worried. The scene was created by directly following the description of that event in the novel, as evident from Melnikov's margin notes, in which he penciled in the names of the extras who would be playing Pushkin characters absent in Tchaikovsky's opera (see figure 2, p. 204).

In a letter to Mamontov, Melnikov defended his work by filling the pages with quotations from the novel:

> You accused me of putting a stain on our cause by letting Vorontsov and Vanya the barber on stage in *Onegin*! But Vorontsov represented at my village ball the "provincial fop Pustyakov," and Vanya "my cousin Buyanov, in feathers and a cap (you all know him well, of course!)." If you know Vorontsov, he is a true "provincial fop" in life, and Vanya the barber, who had spent ten years in the dressing rooms of Yuzhin and Lensky, [also] gave such a Tugoukhovsky at the court ball that no chorister could have mastered.[8]

A faithful representation of the original source was a cornerstone of the historicist approach to staging with which both the MPO and the Meiningen Theater were associated. In fact, both companies at some point claimed authenticity as their highest goal. According to Osborne, "The Duke came to be widely acknowledged as a champion of the un-adapted word of a dramatist, and high, not to say extravagant, claims were made for his fidelity to authorial intention."[9] Mamontov's letter to Stasov, Russia's greatest champion of authenticity, contains the following assessment of the 1887 production of Dargomyzhsky's *Kamennyi gost* [*The Stone Guest*]: "Obviously, we made no cuts."[10] However, despite the rhetoric, both directors allowed themselves a certain freedom with the works they staged. The duke was known to have amended an original text to improve the historical accuracy of the drama if his research revealed a detail unknown to or ignored by the playwright. Texts could also be adapted to tighten the action and to accommodate the predominantly visual character of the mises-en-scène. Similarly, the operas staged by Mamontov and his crew were occasionally reshaped for similar reasons: to incorporate details excised from the original literary source, or to streamline the development of the drama. For example, the reviewers of the 1896 production of Alexander Serov's *Rogneda* discussed substantial changes made to the opera by Mamontov in cooperation with the composer's widow, Valentina Serova-Bergman (1846–1924), herself a composer: one tableau was cut, two others shifted to different places within the opera. The critics unanimously praised this radical reshaping of the work: the new scene arrangement tightened the action, eliminated delays, and revealed internal motivations and relationships between the characters obscured in the original libretto. Aesthetics aside, the excision of the Kromy scene from *Boris Godunov* might have served a similar purpose of strengthening the drama of the protagonist by eliminating a scene arguably peripheral to his plight.

## VISUALIZATION TECHNIQUE

The similarities in approach to historical research between the directors of the MPO and the Meiningen Theater do not in themselves prove the Germans' influence on Mamontov's work. More likely, they demonstrate a remarkably parallel thinking process, which Mamontov probably recognized when he first saw the Meiningen troupe, and which facilitated his study of their practices. This parallel thinking is also evident in the similarly visual approach taken by both directors to creating their productions. The visual approach revealed to audiences in picturesque mises-en-scène and particular attention paid to set and costume design was made known to performers at a much earlier stage in the preparation of a production. The extant archival documents show that in addition to verbal explanations, both the duke and Mamontov used what I would call a visualization technique: the use of images to create mises-en-scène, develop characters' movements, or communicate directing ideas to associates. Just as the duke's notes and letters contain numerous sketches of sets and accessories, so do Mamontov's. In a letter to Shkafer, he mentioned one such sketch: "Don't forget, there must be a richly carved, beautiful gold-plated box, and not a small one—remember my drawing?"[11] (see plate 28).

Sketching was also a natural way for Mamontov to communicate his intentions to the designers. In a letter to Polenov regarding *Orfeo,* Mamontov described the set for act 1 as follows: "Here's what the libretto states: 'Beautiful remote grove of laurels and cypresses. On a small clearing, surrounded by trees, is Euridice's tomb.' The tomb should be a beautiful Greek sarcophagus, surrounded by a single step on which Orfeo is prostrated."[12] The description is supplemented by a sketch of the laurel grove, and the rectangular tomb with the surrounding step to the left of center. Polenov's extant sketch (see plate 10) demonstrates that the artist followed Mamontov's instructions to the letter. While exercising his painterly imagination in creating the sections of the backdrop omitted in the director's description (for example, a distant mountain with a temple, and a winding path leading to it from the tomb), Polenov incorporated every single detail contained in Mamontov's original sketch.

It is characteristic that Melnikov used sketching with similar frequency in his directing work: his untraditional vision of Larina's house (*en face*, not profiled as it was usually positioned) heads the *Onegin* notebook (figure 1). The director's production notes preserved at the Rainis Museum are filled with sketches (see figure 3, p. 205), all intended for Konstantin Korovin, the designer who, as we know, worked exclusively with Melnikov for almost two decades, both at the Bolshoi and at the Mariinsky. The presence of sketches in Melnikov's notebooks is not surprising: apart from the fact that most of his directing techniques were inherited from his mentor, Korovin must also have become accustomed to visual cues after fifteen years of working for Mamontov.

Visualization technique was used not only for the sets and mises-en-scène, but also for shaping the work of individual performers. The duke was known to supply his actors with drawings of their characters to illustrate the correct way of wearing costumes. Mamontov's drawings also include details of costumes and accessories, but concentrate more on poses and movements of the characters, supplemented by precise instructions. "Don't let Melgunova gesticulate too much in portraying the drowned woman," he wrote regarding the staging of *1812*. "She should beckon *a little* with her hand, and all the time the eyes sparkle, the head is bowed low, and the hand is under the chin." The description is followed by a full-figure drawing of the character in the desired pose.[13]

Apart from having to learn drawing (an art that, as he confessed, had eluded him), Mamontov also utilized his substantial talent as a sculptor to direct scenes and shape the images of individual characters. Regarding the staging of a particularly tricky scene from *The Necklace*, he wrote to Shkafer:

> I have been working a lot lately, and my eyes were tired, but now they work well again, so I will probably illustrate this scene with either drawings or sculptures over the next few days. In my opinion, this method of creating a role may be even more serious than a live demonstration; there is an opportunity here to look and think deeply, and absorb more in depth the internal motivations of a depicted person. There is a reason, appar-

ently, that Sarah Bernhardt and Monet-Sully were both sculptors. This is *real* working-out. [My son] Sergei Savvich has some successful little wax figures of mine: 1) Iante in act I; 2) Sad Daphne in her first entrance; 3) Daphne turning to stone. Then there is a Kabil. All this I would ask Sergei Savvich to show Polenov and all the performers. This should add some inspiration.[14]

Mamontov's students, both singers and stage directors, absorbed this practice. It is well known that Chaliapin, a talented graphic artist, used to make detailed pencil sketches of his roles.[15] Melnikov, whose skill level at drawing the human body was closer to Mamontov's than Chaliapin's, included numerous rudimentary character sketches in his notebooks, such as his rehearsal book for *Siegfried* (see figure 4, p. 206).

It appears that unlike the Duke of Meiningen, Mamontov and his students used character sketches for much more than a fashion show: visualization technique revealed and helped develop a character's personality. In her letter to Mamontov from Paris, Chernenko discussed his idea of staging Rubinstein's *The Demon* with her in the title role originally written for a baritone. The notion was so experimental that visualization was necessary to conceptualize it. Chernenko wrote: "I am awaiting the drawings of the Demon from you, but not too many: that would be very bad, you would be spoiling me; I must search for myself. But a few—that would be very interesting and, most importantly, would inspire me very much."[16]

Beyond the image of a single performer, Mamontov might choose to illustrate a complete scene using visualization technique. In one of his letters, he included a series of sketches for the confrontation of Daphne and Kabil in act 1 of *The Necklace*—the moment eventually judged by critic Yuly Engel as the best in the production. The scene is dramatically challenging: during a seductive solo for the sorcerer Kabil, played by Shkafer, princess Daphne, portrayed by Chernenko, undergoes a transformation from grieving lover to jealous killer without uttering a sound. Mamontov supplied Shkafer with a detailed layout of the characters' poses, movements, gestures, and facial expressions throughout the entire scene, supplementing his description with several drawings (see figure 5, p. 207).[17]

It appears that *The Necklace* was Mamontov's first attempt at a completely visualized concept of a production. Even more than *Orfeo,* the opera was conceived as vocalized pantomime, choreographed down to every grouping, movement, and gesture. All was illustrated in what Mamontov called his *partitura* [full score]. That "full score" (which unfortunately did not survive) provided a detailed guide to the stage director, the performers, and even to the designer, who was to create sets and costumes following the director's plan. In a letter to Polenov, who was skeptical about the project, Mamontov urged the artist to consult the score:

> At Shkafer's (he is the stage director) you will find the detailed, worked out plans for acting and movement according to my drawings. Have a look at them, and this might help you make peace with the plot. In it, there should be an expression of the mystery of some unknown force living through the ages. . . . *The Necklace* should be *excellently acted out,* as if from a score. (And I have provided my fully detailed score—please have a look at it at Shkafer's.)[18]

It is unlikely that Mamontov was aware of the use of visualization technique by the Duke of Meiningen, although he might have heard about it from Chronegk. Indeed, he was convinced that the method he had developed was unique—to the operatic world, at least. He believed that it would ensure the success of the production, writing: "If you do everything according to my drawings and indications, [*The Necklace*] will be *big news on stage,* since no one works in this manner."[19] Moreover, as a part-time music publisher, Mamontov believed that in order to ensure the quality of future productions for a new opera, the director's "score" must be printed alongside the composer's. Thus, in a letter to Polenov regarding the publication of *The Phantoms of Hellas,* he wrote: "I will do everything in my power, for I am truly happy for the success of your work. *Hellas,* nicely printed, with *good drawings* as the director's production notes, would probably make me just as happy as it would make you."[20]

## THE END OF TYPECASTING

The approaches to historical and literary sources and the use of visualization technique seem to have been developed by Mamontov and his team independently of the Meiningen Theater. Let us now turn to other characteristic Meiningen traits, the MPO implementation of which may be more confidently attributed to direct influence. This applies, first of all, to the end of traditional casting methods. At both companies, attention to the artistic ensemble led to phasing out of the old *Fach* system, a method of casting by character or voice type followed by both drama and opera theaters of the nineteenth century.[21] Casting was individualized, with the performers' egos subordinated to the director's vision. At the same time, there was no set type of performer to portray a particular character. Mamontov's adventurous idea of casting Chernenko, a mezzo-soprano, in the baritone role of the Demon has already been mentioned. Another of his students, Anna Stavitskaya, wrote to her mentor in some confusion soon after starting her work for the company: "You have recommended all these dramatic parts to me. They seem to suit my temperament very much, but my voice is purely lyrical, and is hardly suitable to all those parts."[22] She would soon discover that it was not "parts" but "roles" that were recommended to her, and that voice type mattered to Mamontov very little. Her debut, witnessed by Zabela (see chapter 5), was in the dramatic role of Tatyana in Melnikov's *Onegin* production.[23]

It is characteristic that both Chernenko and Stavitskaya, with whom Mamontov could experiment most freely outside the *Fach* system of typecasting, were beginners—young singers fresh from the conservatory, in their first or second year of employment. Yet both were cast in leading roles, an unheard-of practice on the Imperial stage. Just as in Meiningen, there were no obstacles at the MPO to the immediate casting of promising new singers. Indeed it was encouraged, sometimes provoking resentment from the more experienced cast members who, as Zabela once bitterly put it, had "no life because of the newcomers" (as quoted in chapter 5, n.107).

Like the Meiningen Theater, Mamontov's company was struggling to reconcile its ensemble principles with the still predominant, audience-supported star system. Neither the Duke of Meiningen nor Mamontov completely rejected the star system, but both chose their stars carefully, making sure either that they rehearsed with the rest of the cast (like Chaliapin did) or that their alienation from the troupe enhanced, rather than ruined, the message of the work. As we have seen, visual appearance was particularly important in Mamontov's casting decisions. For instance, one of the reasons for the special position enjoyed by Marie van Zandt within his company was her unique visual suitability for her signature roles: with a tiny child-like figure and beautifully expressive eyes, she was a perfect Mimi, Lakmé, and Mignon. Similarly, French director André Antoine, an admirer and a follower of the Meiningen troupe, believed that "the principal criteria in the recruitment of actors [at the Meiningen Theater] seemed to be physical and visual, in particular the ability of the actor to display the Meiningen costumes to the best advantage."[24] And while costume wearing was not perhaps Mamontov's most important standard in choosing a performer for a particular role (nor was it, surely, for the Duke of Meiningen), the costumes played an important part in both directors' approach to their work.

## THE ROLE OF COSTUME IN CHARACTER DEVELOPMENT

Critics of the Meiningen Theater complained that its lavish, elaborate costumes drew a disproportionate amount of attention to themselves and away from the actors. Similar criticism would later be directed at Mamontov's company (and eventually, at Diaghilev's Ballets Russes). Indeed, both Mamontov and the duke were well aware of the attractiveness of their costumes and made sure to utilize them to the best possible advantage. More importantly, however, the directors made sure that the effects produced by the costumes enhanced the overall dramatic concept of a production. For example, both routinely disregarded the common stage practice that clad leading actors in costumes designed to flatter and separate them from the rest of the cast. Instead, the costume of Joan of Arc in Meiningen's *Jungfrau* was expressly designed to match those of the other performers. Similarly, Gozenpud notes that in Mamontov's production of *Prince Igor*, "[lead singer] Sokolov did not parade Igor's imposing appearance in his movements, makeup, or costume. In the prologue his helmet and chain mail were almost identical to those of his soldiers, while his clothes at the Polovtsy camp matched those of the other prisoners."[25] The Soviet scholar explained this directing decision as an attempt to humanize the title character and make him more sympathetic. What clearly needs to be considered as well is Mamontov's admiration for Meiningen's *Jungfrau* production. This admiration is also evident in the similarities between the costumes of the Germans' Joan of Arc and his own: a breastplate of chain mail over a plain white dress and leggings. Moreover, in both Mamontov's and Meiningen's versions of *The Maid of Orleans*, Joan's costume was designed to match those of the other soldiers. As Gozenpud noted, in the coronation scene, both her costume and her position within the stage space separated her from the king and his resplendent court, allying her instead with standard-bearing guards that surrounded the procession.[26]

Deliberately contrasting the lead's costume with those of the other characters on stage could also serve a dramatic purpose. For example, despite Chaliapin's objections, Mamontov approved Ilya Bondarenko's costume design for Boris Godunov in black silk with violet and silver patterns, instead of the traditional red and gold brocade (see plate 33). The idea was quite brilliant: dressing the tsar in dark clothing for his first entrance in a triumphal coronation scene underscored his alienation from the courtiers and the crowd, revealed in the opening monologue. As Mamontov explained to the singer, a familiar story would be presented to the audience as a "mourning for Russia's history."[27] Thus, at the MPO as in Meiningen, a costume did not merely support the artistic ensemble but could also emphasize a focal point of the drama by providing an opportunity for a director's commentary on a character wearing it.

As costumes played such a significant role in both Mamontov and the duke's approach to drama, both directors made sure their performers were completely comfortable in them. In order to achieve that, they insisted that costumes be worn well before the dress rehearsal. At the Meiningen Theater, this was in fact a formal requirement, recorded in the duke's own hand:

> In costume dramas, rehearsals with weapons, helmets, armor, swords etc. must take place at as early a stage as possible, so that in the actual performance the actors are not hindered by the unfamiliarity and the heavy weight of the equipment. . . . The actors should rehearse in costume— either in the actual one or, if this is not yet ready or has to be treated with special care, one of a similar cut.[28]

A similar desire to overcome the awkwardness of "dressing up" and increase the comfort level of his singers—and perhaps the experience of watching Chronegk rehearse—may have prompted Mamontov to give the following advice to Shkafer regarding his acting and directing work in *The Necklace*:

I advise you that, when you begin working on your scenes, especially those with Daphne, both of you should wear something approximating a costume. She needs it to get completely comfortable with a Greek dress (it lacks a corset, and requires attention to get used to the pleats and bare arms). This is very important for the scene; otherwise the enemies named "somehow" and "doesn't matter" may creep in. For your own part, you would need to get used to a wide-sleeved robe with the arms bare, so that the arm movements could be incorporated into the acting.[29]

## ROLE ROTATION

As we have seen, there is much similarity in the two companies' approaches to directing a solo performer, from casting principles to the use of costumes in character development. Moreover, there is clear archival evidence that Mamontov adopted—at least in theory—the Meiningen iron rule of role rotation; that is, a lack of casting hierarchy that separated the principals from the second-tier performers. In Meiningen, a leading actor could even be fired for refusing to do a cameo; according to the duke, each member of his troupe must "regard it as a matter of honor to take walk-on parts, for the battle cry of our members must be: all for one and one for all."[30]

Implementing such a strict policy at the MPO was extremely difficult, however. While Georg II of Saxe-Meiningen was not only the leader of his company but also a ruling prince, Mamontov needed to convince his singers to put their egos on hold for the sake of the cause. We have already witnessed Zabela's indignation at the prospect; many others were similarly skeptical. In a letter to Mamontov prior to the start of the 1897–98 season, the newly appointed repertoire director Kruglikov described a scene between himself and one of the singers, the tenor Inozemtsev. This remarkable letter is the only surviving document in which the implementation of a Meiningen policy at the MPO is directly addressed by a member of Mamontov's team. Kruglikov wrote:

Seeing in the repertory list I have prepared for him, apart from numerous large parts, also a host of various *messengers* and *choir soloists,* [Inozemtsev] made a pitiful face and started begging me quite sweetly to spare him from all that, which he used to sing at the beginning of his career. I pointed out to him our Meiningen principle, but apparently he was little consoled by it. This story with Inozemtsev got me thinking. Is not our Meiningen already on a shaky ground, and won't it completely go to hell at the beginning of the season, when it would be necessary to talk with this, that, and the other [singer], more talkative and less shy than your brown-noser Inozemtsev?[31]

Despite Kruglikov's apprehension, a large part of the troupe followed along with Mamontov's idea. For example, critics wrote with amazement about a tiny unison chorus of minstrels in *The Maid of Orleans:* normally sung by choristers, it was performed by six female principals.[32] Apart from Mamontov's own authority, the singers could also have been inspired by Chaliapin, who never shrank from episodic roles, particularly if their dramatic possibilities piqued his interest. One of his signature parts was that of Vladimir Galitsky in Borodin's *Prince Igor*—a role that, according to one critic, "is usually completely lost, or at least hides deep in the background."[33] Playing the leading role in *Boris Godunov,* he was always jealous of the singer cast in the secondary part of Varlaam and eventually learned it himself. Even more of a cameo was the role of the Varangian Trader in *Sadko* (plate 17), limited to a short song and participation in two ensemble finales. Yet Chaliapin's interpretation of this character prompted Stasov's famous panegyric to the performer, "Radost Bezmernaya!" ["Boundless Joy!"] (see chapter 7) in no less a measure than the singer's portrayal of the central character of Ivan the Terrible in *The Maid of Pskov.*[34]

The implementation of the Meiningen role rotation policy (although, one must admit, not always as successful as in the examples cited above) was unusual enough. But Mamontov went further: he wanted his soloists to follow the German company's rule of mandatory participation in crowd scenes—an unheard-of practice in conventional theater, in Russia or elsewhere. The duke, however, considered it quite necessary, writing:

> It is a regrettable error, which often has artistically damaging consequences, that the members of a company who are employed as "actors" have little esteem for such roles, or regard them as unworthy of a genuine artist; and that, whenever possible, they try to avoid such roles, or else, if they can be forced to perform them, make their reluctance all too apparent. In Meiningen, all the artists, without exception, are required to assume such non-speaking parts.[35]

Mamontov's first experiment in implementing this practice took place in the first new production of the 1897–98 season—the year when, judging by Kruglikov's letter quoted above, the MPO consciously began to adopt Meiningen policies. This production was Musorgsky's *Khovanshchina*, an opera in which the importance of crowd scenes cannot be overestimated. A *Novosti Dnya* correspondent present at the dress rehearsal reported his impressions as follows:

> The opera is staged very thoroughly, with the best forces of the troupe. A curious novelty is the participation of absolutely every member of the troupe, even those without separate roles; these artists, who normally perform leading roles, for the interest and enlivening of the production, will go on stage in the Streltsy chorus and in general crowd scenes. Such an innovation can only raise the quality of the performance.[36]

The same principle is also evident in the directing work of Mamontov's assistants. For instance, Shkafer's first officially independent production was Rimsky-Korsakov's *The Tsar's Bride*. And even though his authority was often usurped by the composer, the influence of his mentor Mamontov is evident in the following press report: "All the young forces of the troupe will participate in the oprichnik chorus, which will undoubtedly bring special interest to the production."[37] One is reminded of the fact that the first production on which Shkafer worked directly with Mamontov was, as it happens, *Khovanshchina*, in which this Meiningen policy was first put into practice. For his part, Melnikov used a similar idea in his glitzy restaging of the epilogue from Glinka's *A Life for the Tsar* in the 1913 production of that opera dedicated to the 300th anniversary of the Romanov dynasty. The scene recreated the historic 1613 coronation of the first Romanov tsar, Mikhail Fyodorovich. Soloists of the Imperial Theaters, both Mariinsky and Bolshoi, were present on stage in the non-speaking roles of the historical characters who originally took part in the coronation. Essentially, for the first and last time in their mature careers, these "stars" were used as extras.[38]

## CROWD SCENES

Participation in crowd scenes was perhaps the most unusual requirement to which Mamontov subjected his singers. This, however, was not an arbitrary demand stemming from the director's desire to, as Zabela

once put it, "take us all down a peg."[39] Instead, he realized that the soloists' involvement was essential to staging these scenes following the
Meiningen approach. The duke's crowd was not an amorphous mass
speaking with a single voice, but a collection of individuals and small
groups, each behaving according to their own temperament and agenda.
Trained actors appeared in these scenes either as separate personages, or
as leaders of the groups of extras. As the duke himself explained:

> The leaders are given written parts with cues in which those very general
> terms normally used by the dramatist, such as "noise," "uproar," "mur-
> muring," "shouts," "screams," and suchlike are expanded by the director
> into words, which must then be memorized by the appropriate extras. . . .
> This accounts for the quite startling effect created at the first appearance
> of the Meininger, which was achieved by the liveliness of the involvement
> of the masses, by the real participation of the crowd, which contrasted so
> starkly with the woodenness, awkwardness, and lack of interest that we
> had previously had to accept.[40]

The purpose of the individualized treatment of the crowd was to
create the illusion of a natural reaction to the events on stage, as realized
in each person or group's gestures and movements. As we know, stage
movement was an important part of Mamontov's directing as well, not
only in solos but also in crowd scenes. One such scene was a staged fight
occurring in act 3 of *The Necklace*. In a letter to Shkafer, Mamontov
instructed him to involve both solo singers and choristers in order to
break the crowd into small groups, thus making the scene appear more
realistic: "Continue with the fight. Work out the skeleton well, with
the separate fighting episodes—let the young people (Zina, Manya, and
anyone from the chorus who is into it) try to make it interesting."[41] In
the scenes involving the individual characters as well as the crowd, both
the duke and Mamontov had to break through the tradition of the mass
arranged in a neat semicircle facing the audience—a tradition as old as
the Greek chorus. The duke prescribed that

> the arrangements of actors and crowds should not produce frozen *tab-*
> *leaux,* which halt the action of the drama, and which are clearly posed for
> the benefit of the audience. They are designed to support the dialogue by
> completing it, by realizing what is implicit in it, or, if they do appear to
> distract from it, to emphasize the changes brought about by the dialogue
> in the relationship between the characters on stage.[42]

For example, in the Curia scene from a Meiningen production of *Julius Caesar*, the director demanded that, instead of exiting and leaving the stage to the leads, the populace should remain and listen to the proceedings, with their backs to the audience. In the Citizens' Assembly scene [Veche, act 2, scene 2] from *The Maid of Pskov*, which he personally staged, Mamontov issued a similar demand to his bewildered chorus. Platon Mamontov recalls:

> During early rehearsals, Savva Ivanovich was displeased with the way the chorus behaved on stage—it felt wooden, lifeless, and awkward; and as at the Bolshoi Theater, it even stared at the conductor's baton. Stopping the rehearsal, Savva Ivanovich ran up on stage and began personally to position individual groups, turning them to the messenger, and during Tucha's speech, facing him. In those positions, most of the chorus had their backs to the audience. I clearly remember Savva Ivanovich shouting loudly: "I need a crowd, movement of the people; a force of nature, not a church choir."[43]

Russian historical operas such as *The Maid of Pskov* and *Boris* particularly benefited from the Meiningen approach: mass scenes in these operas were originally conceived by their composers as choral dialogue, so the staging in this case realized the authorial intent. Interestingly, in discussing Mamontov's treatment of the crowd, Gozenpud invoked Stasov's comparison between Perov's depiction of the Russian populace and the choral pages of Musorgsky scores.[44] The scholar posited that Mamontov's approach to these scenes came from studying the canvases of Russian historical painters such as Surikov.[45] More likely, however, the idea came to him from watching Chronegk's troupe rehearse.

One of the most remarkable and widely acclaimed examples of Mamontov's Meiningen-style "crowd control" was his staging of *Sadko*. According to Strakhova, who performed the role of a bard, Nezhata:

> The famous Market scene was conceived and staged exclusively by [Mamontov], and the result was a masterpiece: the huge stage of the Solodovnikov Theater was bathed in sunlight (Mamontov was a sun worshipper), and filled with traders, noble guests, gusli players, and jesters. The whole tableau created an impression of a living piece of the Novgorod marketplace.[46]

In staging *Sadko*'s crowd scenes, Mamontov followed the path of *The Maid of Pskov* and later *Khovanshchina*. While in the opening feast scene and final glorification he portrayed the chorus as a single character with a unified reaction to events, the Marketplace featured the individualized crowd in the best Meiningen tradition. Each chorister received a specific task, and the general picture was constructed as a sum of these tasks. Evgeny Petrovsky noted the fresh and lively impression created by the staging of *Sadko* in his report for *Russkaya Muzykalnaya Gazeta:*

> Some figures are truly artistic. Two gloomy old men—the blind pilgrims led by a young boy—particularly attracted attention . . . ; they were even disturbing in their remarkable realism . . . Loving attention is paid to the acting of the extras and the chorus. Many choral groups were truly amazing in their expressiveness, unheard of in operatic choirs.[47]

Such detailed work was so unusual on the Russian operatic stage that it made a few critics uncomfortable. They recognized the Meiningen approach, but its suitability to opera was a matter of debate. Kruglikov, before his conversion to Mamontov's point of view caused him to join the MPO troupe, made the following comment regarding one of the crowd scenes in *The Maid of Pskov*—the finale of act 2:

> Everyone is trembling, standing as if sentenced to death, and here at the front, a silly old man with a stick, in a fur hat that he forgets to take off while bowing . . . is scolding misbehaving kids. This "Meiningenesque" detail could easily have been avoided, particularly since it contradicts the oppressive mood of the moment.[48]

While in some productions, the goal was to represent the crowd as a sum of individuals, in others the drama required a huge mass of the populace, quite unfeasible in the limited space of a theatrical stage. The duke devised a special technique for creating the necessary illusion, which he described as follows:

> If the impression of a great crowd is to be created on the stage, the groups must be so arranged that those who stand at the sides extend deep into the wings. From no seats in the auditorium should it be possible to see that the group is finite. On the contrary, the arrangement should permit the audience to have the illusion that there is an even greater mass of people behind the scenes.[49]

The MPO faced the "mass problem" numerous times: the stage of the Solodovnikov Theater was larger than that of the Bolshoi, yet the company employed a total of fifty-six choristers, versus Bolshoi's hundred-plus. Operatic scenes requiring a mass of people often looked awkward; the half-empty stage was commented upon, for instance, by the reviewers of *Boris Godunov*. In that opera, as you may recall, the staging of crowd scenes was left to Mikhail Lentovsky. Mamontov and Melnikov, for their part, had followed the Meiningen recipe for counteracting the dramatic disadvantages to the size of their chorus since the company's first season. In Gozenpud's discussion of their staging of the prologue to *Prince Igor*, the duke's technique is described to the letter—without any reference, however, to its source: "It was impossible to unfold expansive crowd scenes in the theater. Therefore, the mise-en-scène of the prologue was constructed in such a way that the audience only saw a section of the square, creating an impression that the majority of the crowd—the soldiers and the people—were backstage."[50]

Such unconventional use of the masses to hide the actual stage shape also met another objective. The directors of both companies utilized staging as well as backdrop design to reconceptualize stage space and free their productions from slavish adherence to its traditional rectangular shape. Mamontov, for instance, often chose to narrow the huge stage of the Solodovnikov for intimate chamber works such as *Mozart and Salieri*.[51] He would later use the same technique for *Miniatyury* [*Miniatures*]—a triple bill of one-act operas he staged in 1907; his letter to Polenov, who created the sets, contains a pointed reference to the unusually small size of the backdrop canvas.[52]

Alternatively, some productions required a sense of space beyond the limits of the stage. While in some productions, such as *Prince Igor*, this space was created by manipulating the positions of the chorus and extras, in other cases a director needed a designer's help. Meiningen backdrops were known for their utilization of special openings such as window, arches, and doorways that created the illusion of depth by affording a view beyond the confines of the set. A similar principle was employed in perhaps the MPO's most famous set, Vasnetsov's "Berendei's Palace" (plate 9), on which the rooftops of the village are seen through the arched windows of the tsar's palace at the foreground. The backdrop for the Market scene in *Sadko* (plate 36) features the sails of trader ships visible beyond the city walls. Melnikov's staging of the village ball scene for *Eugene Onegin* went further still, creating the much-discussed unfolding set, on which several rooms of the house were seen by the audience simultaneously, with the characters moving among them.[53]

Overall, among the various techniques characterizing the Meiningen directing style, its approach to crowd scenes was the most wholeheartedly adopted by Mamontov and his team, since it was particularly suitable for adaptation to Russian historical operas. According to press reviews, it was the crowd scenes in which the Meiningen influence on Mamontov's troupe was most evident to an outside observer. These scenes were universally viewed as the most innovative directing contribution of the German troupe, and equally acclaimed as the MPO's strongest staging asset.

Meanwhile, arguably the most important characteristic of the Meiningen Theater absorbed and (at least partially) implemented by Mamontov was never seen by anyone outside the company. This trait was at the very heart of its daily operations—specifically, the level of control exercised by the stage director over all aspects of a theatrical production. It was the duke's fabled iron grip on his employees that contributed so much to the birth of the "director's theater" that Mamontov was to import into Russia.

## DIRECTOR'S THEATER

In Meiningen, a strict system of rules and regulations covered every aspect of an actor's life, including casting, participation in walk-on roles, memorization of lines, and rehearsal attendance. Rule breaking could result in a fine, or even dismissal; indeed, as Osborne points out, "what the Duke was doing to his actors smacked of despotism."[54] This picture of unwavering authoritarianism hardly resembles the friendly, cooperative atmosphere at the MPO, where singers rarely required a written summons to show up for rehearsals, and where the rules were followed more out of enthusiasm for the cause than fear of unemployment. Nevertheless, despite the collaborative nature of Mamontov's creative process, at his company, just as in Meiningen, all aspects of a production were controlled by the director. Evidently, Mamontov did not view this as a contradiction to the collaborative method, but rather as an extension of it—an assurance that the process would yield results without dissolving into endless debate. "You are the director," he once wrote to Shkafer, "so do your job without discussion. Talk is a disgusting sauce that spoils any good meal."[55]

The director's control was barely noticeable to a person unfamiliar with the daily operations of the enterprise. For example, Stasov's essay on Mamontov's designers is characteristically oblivious to the unseen presence behind their work:

> While working for S. I. Mamontov's theater, [the designers] were not in anybody's employ, including Mamontov's, but they remained completely free, independent artists—each in their own field—who continued their own, non-commissioned work while working for S. I. Mamontov's theater. Besides, no one restricted the artists: there were no orders, no rules for them here; no corrections, no additions, and no subtractions. Is this not happiness and a huge advantage?![56]

It is true that Mamontov rarely invaded his artists' territory: he knew the quality of their work, and rarely interfered when sets were being painted. Yet his comments, while few, were typically to the point, and were respected accordingly. Bondarenko recalled: "He never gave advice to Vrubel, but sometimes he would say: 'Misha, this color—it is the wrong color.' [Vrubel] would look and say: 'You know, you are right,' for Mamontov never criticized needlessly."[57] However, at the initial stage, when the overall visual concept of a production was being decided, Mamontov closely supervised his painters, making sure his directing ideas were incorporated into their work. Examples of this control abound in his prolific, detail-filled correspondence with Polenov regarding the designs for *Orfeo* and *The Necklace*. In his letters, Mamontov laid out specific requirements for each scene, often accompanied by sketches. Some sets were apparently created in direct collaboration between Mamontov and his designers, including those for *Orfeo*'s second act, "The Underworld": "Korovin and I invented it together; it should be interesting," Mamontov happily bragged to Polenov.[58] Meanwhile, there was no dictatorial tone in Mamontov's correspondence with the painters. Instead, there seemed to be an unspoken agreement: despite occasional differences, these close friends and collaborators somehow always managed to find a compromise without encroaching on each other's visions. The true test of a director's character came when Mamontov had to deal with Rimsky-Korsakov: both were strong-willed artists who believed their own authority superseded any other; the roots of their conflict will be explored in chapter 8.

Unlike Mamontov, the duke, who mostly staged the classics, had no experience in dealing with live—and demanding—authors. Overall, however, both directors' control over their troupes covered the same important areas. It would be helpful to include here Osborne's comprehensive summary of the Meiningen operation within the framework of director's theater:

> The repertoire of the company was determined at directorial level, and within the constraints of the commercial theater it shows a high degree of coherence, both in its reflection of the artistic strengths and specialties of the company, and in its consistent national and educational orientation. The texts used in the productions were edited and prepared at directorial level, in accordance with principles, which also clearly reflect the overall artistic policy. Actors were carefully considered in terms of consistent criteria, before being engaged; they were prepared individually for their parts and required to take part in extensive rehearsal. Casting was not done by *Fach,* but by the director, taking into account the specific aims and requirements of the production and the strongly visual orientation of the style. Scenic design was the responsibility of the principal member of the directorial team, the Duke himself, and he supervised closely the execution of his designs by scene painters who were familiar with, and sympathetic to, the aims of the company . . . Costume design was also in the hands of the Duke, and the wearing of costume was controlled with great firmness and attention to its implications for the interpretation of the drama. Arrangements, crowd scenes, and stage business were worked out carefully at directorial level, were carefully rehearsed, and carried out according to plan. Off-stage control of the production was, in short, comprehensive and overwhelming.[59]

At the MPO, every single area of operations mentioned above as the director's responsibility was personally supervised by Mamontov (see chapter 7 for a discussion of repertoire policy). Unquestionably, the level of consistency and control practiced at the Meiningen Theater was never equaled at Mamontov's enterprise; indeed, it was unparalleled in theater history. Nevertheless, observing the Meiningen troupe probably introduced Mamontov to the concept of the director's theater, which he gradually began to implement in his own company. This process was never completed, as it was interrupted by Mamontov's essential removal from power over the 1899–1900 season. Instead, it was taken over by the young Russian drama troupes: the Moscow Art Theater, whose director Stanislavsky, as we have seen, was a devotee in equal measure of both Mamontov and Chronegk, and a host of experimental studios that flourished in the 1900s and 1910s. Particularly closely associated with the new method was visionary stage director Vsevolod Meyerhold, whose early career intersected in a fascinating manner with those of both Mamontov and Stanislavsky.

## STANISLAVSKY, MEYERHOLD, AND
## THE POVARSKAYA STUDIO

Until now, Stanislavsky's Moscow Art Theater has been traditionally viewed in the literature as the first Russian stage to have absorbed and implemented the lessons of the Meiningen troupe and their French disciple, André Antoine. Rudnitsky stated as much, adding: "At the Art Theater, a director for the first time in Russia became the true leader of a theater and the author of a production, the creator of a unified work of staged art, blending together the efforts of the dramatist, actors, designer, composer, and connecting his creation with modern life, and modern audience."[60] Rudnitsky's opinion is supported by the documents of the period. In his diary, the Bolshoi Theater administrator Vladimir Telyakovsky called Stanislavsky's troupe, albeit in a derogatory sense, "the Russian Meiningen."[61] Sergei Diaghilev noted in his well-known *Mir Iskusstva* review of the troupe's 1902 St. Petersburg tour that "the Moscow actors have succeeded in mounting a classic, and producing it in the most polished manner, such as befits a modern, a most modern spectator. [They] know what discipline is, and that . . . is what combines all the colors into a single painting."[62]

As we have seen, Mamontov and Stanislavsky, who cooperated and exchanged ideas from the start of their directing careers, most likely attended Chronegk's rehearsals together. The older director then seized an early opportunity to implement the Meiningen principles in a professional theater setting. Stanislavsky observed, learned from the experience, and later utilized the same methods in the Moscow Art Theater's inaugural production, Alexei K. Tolstoy's historical drama *Tsar Feodor*

*Ioannovich.* Mamontov served as an adviser to that production. In a letter inviting him to the dress rehearsal, Stanislavsky wrote: "We would be very happy to see you at the rehearsal as a man of the theater . . . and a great artist [bolshoi khudozhnik]. Help us correct the mistakes that have unavoidably crept into such a complicated production as *Tsar Feodor.*"[63] After the premiere, Mamontov received another note: "Can't wait to see you to hear your honest opinion about the production. Sincerely respectful, grateful Alekseev."[64]

While there were differences in Mamontov and Stanislavsky's views, they also agreed on much of what they liked about the Meiningen approach, as well as what they disliked about it. Specifically, both believed that implementing director's theater with the strictness displayed by the Germans led to a loss of creativity on stage, a neglect of acting in the traditional sense—as role interpretation through the genius of an individual performer. Stanislavsky believed, for example, that the Meiningen production of *Die Jungfrau von Orléans,* discussed earlier, revealed a wide discrepancy between the quality of the acting and that of the stage direction.[65] Both Mamontov and Stanislavsky watched with apprehension as director's theater gained currency in experimental drama theaters as well as opera troupes of the 1900s whose directors—among them Nikolai Arbatov, Konstantin Mardzhanov, and Pyotr Olenin—declared themselves followers of the Art Theater. Stanislavsky admitted as much in his autobiography, writing that Chronegk's impact on his own directing style created the new breed of Russian stage directors. "The directors of the new type," he wrote, "became mere producers who made an actor into a stage property on the same level with stage furniture—a pawn to be moved around in their mises-en-scène."[66]

Mamontov, who was dedicated to coaching actors and had experienced the genius of Chaliapin's interpretations in his productions, could not accept the new fashion either. He was particularly upset by the fact that the young directors used slogans he himself pioneered, such as "ensemble," while taking their meaning to the absolute extreme where he was never willing to go. His reactions are recorded in his nephew's memoirs:

> Uncle Savva was sincerely outraged at all the noise made by the innovative opera directors. They wrote: "Who cares who is singing and who

is acting! Ensemble is important. We don't need talents! We don't need artistic individuality! We need discipline." According to the innovators, theater needed only an author and a director; it needed only a faceless, unified mass, a tool in the hands of a decorator and a stage director. The crowd should present real life, and the soloists are just details against the backdrop of the crowd. Uncle Savva argued in print against these views, publishing several reviews of the productions that particularly outraged him.[67]

The overly strict implementation of director's theater probably contributed to the doom of a fascinating project that brought Mamontov and Stanislavsky together with an Art Theater alumnus, the young, audacious stage director and future leader of Russian theater, Vsevolod Meyerhold. Their joint venture, inaugurated on 5 May 1905, was a small, experimental drama theater, a Moscow Art Theater affiliate that became known as the Theater-Studio on Povarskaya Street. While his older colleagues were, as we shall see, involved with the Studio to varying degrees, Meyerhold, as its director, had a free hand in determining the direction of the work. From the first rehearsal of the as yet unopened studio, his firm conviction that the director should be the single, all-powerful master of a production was evident. The young director's vision required that the actors carry out relatively modest tasks, their individuality completely subsumed by the overall picture created and dictated by the stage director. After watching a dress rehearsal of Maeterlinck's *La Mort de Tintagiles*, Stanislavsky noted the same discrepancy between the genius of the director's concept and the lack of personal engagement on the part of the actors that he had observed at the Meiningen Theater. In his memoir he mentioned, however, that the dictatorship of the stage director might have served a practical purpose here: most Povarskaya Studio actors were novices, unable to comprehend Meyerhold's sophisticated vision of Maeterlinck's drama, and their inexperience was concealed by treating them like clay for shaping mises-en-scène.[68]

Whatever circumstances prompted it, Meyerhold's move toward absolute power of the director over the troupe, which would eventually lead to his revolutionary ideas of bio-mechanics, began to take shape at the Povarskaya Studio. The director's theater concept absorbed by Mamontov from the two Meiningen tours, and partially revealed in his own company's productions and the work of the newly opened Moscow Art Theater, was thus realized in its most extreme form by Meyerhold and other young stage directors of the 1900s. The journey Mamontov started would lead Russian staged art directly to modernism.

## FROM REALISM TO SYMBOLISM

At first glance, the end of the road Mamontov took has nothing to do with its beginning. The evidently great influence of the Meiningen Theater, a realist institution, on directing practices of the MPO seems to directly contradict everything we know about Mamontov's aesthetics. The Meiningen signature historicism is equally difficult to reconcile with Mamontov's experiments with decorativism, stylization, and other modernist staging and design techniques. The apparent contradictions are at the heart of Mamontov's enterprise: even more than in its designs that balanced achievements of realism with new modernist trends, in its approach to drama the MPO stood at a historic point of transition. In this respect, it was not unlike the Meiningen Theater, which, born at the dawn of naturalism in theater, combined the classicist love for striking tableaux vivant with the demands of onstage realism. Turn-of-the-century naturalist playwrights and directors would acknowledge the Meiningen influence while at the same time consigning the German troupe without regret to the nineteenth-century past. The MPO faced a comparable aesthetic dilemma, which, ironically, grew especially problematic as a consequence of the company's unique strength—the close collaboration between its stage directors and set designers.

As we have seen, in the late 1890s the Russian arts were ready to leave behind the confines of realism. However, for a short while, they found themselves traveling along separate aesthetic paths: while prose literature and drama reached even deeper into the human psyche, the visual arts and poetry tried to transcend human nature and penetrate the mind and eventually the divine through the intermediaries of myth and symbol. The most cutting-edge style in drama was naturalism; in painting, it was symbolism. Artistic attributes of both coexisted in Mamontov's productions, many of them historical operas that required appropriately Meiningen-style staging, whether or not it happened to coincide with the director's aesthetic views. Furthermore, since the company was so in touch with the current trends in spoken drama, it was bound to be caught up in the early stages of the next aesthetic revolution experienced particularly painfully by Stanislavsky's company.

Built on the Meiningen premise, the Moscow Art Theater achieved its early resounding success as a champion of naturalist art—and almost immediately found itself branded as conservative and irrelevant. As Valery Bryusov's "Useless Truth" article proclaimed from the pages of *Mir Iskusstva,* Russian arts were embracing symbolism, and the Art Theater was out of touch. Stanislavsky and his codirector Nemirovich-Danchenko quietly agreed with Bryusov, feeling that *Tsar Feodor* and other historical dramas they produced were taking them in the wrong direction. This was particularly hard on Nemirovich, himself a playwright disgusted with "tiresome realism." Stanislavsky also worried that his art was too tied up with "crude reality," afraid of becoming forever a "Wanderer of the stage."[69] The phrase could have been invented by Mamontov, who clearly shared the sentiment. Indeed, his ties to the visual arts made him suspicious of naturalism from the start. For Stanislavsky, the transition away from "a Wanderer of the stage" was assisted by the subtle art of Anton Chekhov's mood theater—itself a transitional style somewhere between realism and symbolism. Chekhov's belief that stage art required a certain *uslovnost* was reflected in his plays produced by the Art Theater in the early 1900s. Fellow playwright Maxim Gorky wrote to him at that time: "Do you know what you are doing? You are killing realism. And you will kill it soon—to the death, for a long time. This form has outlived its time—that's a fact! No one could go further than you have, on that path. . . . Most importantly, what you write does not look simple, i.e., does not look like truth. . . . And I am thrilled about it. Enough of [realism] already!"[70] It is no wonder, then, that a few months after Gorky wrote this letter to Chekhov, he asked Stanislavsky to introduce him to Mamontov. Stanislavsky obliged, sending his mentor the following note:

I have a favor to ask. Gorky (the writer) is very interested in you, and he is having lunch at our house tomorrow afternoon. Why don't you come? You would make my wife and me very happy. If you agree, we are expecting you around 4–4:30 PM, for at 7:00 PM everyone will be off to the theater to see [*Ivan*] *the Terrible;* maybe you would like to come with us.[71]

The title role in the play Mamontov and Gorky were invited to see, Alexei K. Tolstoy's *Smert Ivana Groznogo* (*The Death of Ivan the Terrible,* a prequel to *Tsar Feodor*), was performed by Vsevolod Meyerhold.

It was Meyerhold, not Stanislavsky or Nemirovich, who later made Chekhov's call for stylization the centerpiece of his essay condemning naturalism on stage.[72] The idea was lodged in his mind even when, after having left the Moscow Art Theater to launch his directing career in the provinces, he was justly accused of crude realism and what his critics dubbed "super-Meiningen-ism." Although he, like Mamontov, began his career as a realist, Meyerhold was soon dissatisfied, feeling constricted by an excessive grounding in the everyday. Yet his bold early experiments in stage symbolism, such as the 1904 staging of Stanislaw Przybyszewski's *Schnee,* failed spectacularly before his provincial audiences. Meyerhold needed help; he needed a new kind of theater, writing: "[We need] to strive for the Highest Beauty in Art, to fight the routine, to search constantly for new expressive means for the new dramaturgy that still does not have its theater, for it has moved too far ahead, just as modern painting has moved too far ahead of staging and acting techniques."[73] Luckily, his old mentor Stanislavsky was equally frustrated. After his tentative attempt at staging a Maeterlinck triple-bill at the Moscow Art Theater resulted in a rare, humiliating flop, Stanislavsky needed Meyerhold's fearlessness and fresh perspective just as much as his former protégé needed his clout and expertise. Meyerhold returned to Moscow; Russia's first symbolist theater, the Povarskaya Studio, was born. In his memoirs, Stanislavsky described the creed of the new venture as follows:

> Realism—the everyday—has outlived its age. The time has come for the unreal on stage. . . . One must represent not life itself, as it flows in reality, but how we vaguely sense it in dreams, visions, in the moments of sublime heights. This state of mind needs to be represented on stage, just as the new painters do it on canvas, the new generation of musicians in music, and the new poets in their verses.[74]

On the Povarskaya Studio personnel roster, Meyerhold and Stanislavsky are listed on the top of the page, right next to each other, as codirectors.[75] On the bottom of the same page there is another name, marked "consultant"—the name of Savva Mamontov. Clearly, he was not treated as the other directors' equal in the troupe's hierarchy. Yet his enthusiasm for the project knew no bounds. Now daily in the company of the Blue Rose painters, and hard at work on the libretto for *The Phantoms of Hellas,* he was as ready and eager as Stanislavsky to serve as a midwife to the new theater. He lent Stanislavsky his pet designers—Nikolai Sapunov, Sergei Sudeikin, and Nikolai Ulyanov, all Blue Rose members, and all trained by him in the craft of stage design. He organized a permanent exhibition of modern Russian sculpture in the theater lobby. He was the only person, apart from Meyerhold and Stanislavsky, invited to speak at the inaugural meeting of the troupe that took place at the Moscow Art Theater on 5 May 1905. His attendance at the first open rehearsal of the Theater-Studio on 11 August is documented in Stanislavsky's correspondence.[76] And although the fact that the rehearsal took place in the village by the name of Mamontovka, near Moscow, is merely a fun coincidence, it is tempting to view it as a symbol of Mamontov's profound engagement with the project. He even invited himself, rather unceremoniously, into the sacred world of hiring and casting, which made even the ever-deferential Stanislavsky feel a little claustrophobic.[77]

If even Stanislavsky, despite his admiration for Mamontov, tried discreetly to put some distance between his "teacher of aesthetics" and the Povarskaya Studio, what about Meyerhold? As far as we know, the young director never wrote to Mamontov, and no direct evidence places him at the MPO performances or rehearsals. Yet we also know that he was an admirer of Mamontov's company: in a 1921 discussion forum titled "Do We Need the Bolshoi Theater?" he cited the MPO as an ideal for which to strive, calling upon his listeners to "continue along the path taken by Savva Mamontov's opera theater where Rimsky-Korsakov was first staged, Vrubel worked, and Chaliapin started his career."[78] He also shared many of Mamontov's aesthetic principles, including his belief in the synthesis of the arts, which was reflected in his own work aimed at fusing together word, gesture, color, and sound.

More importantly, the productions that Meyerhold directed at the Povarskaya Studio exhibit certain characteristics familiar from Mamontov's MPO experiments. For example, one of the most distinctive attributes of his *La Mort de Tintagiles* was its carefully choreographed, deliberate stage movement—what Meyerhold would later come to call "motionless" [nepodvizhnyi] or "stylized" [uslovnyi] theater. The production's mises-en-scène distributed human figures around the stage in a manner reminiscent of ancient frescos and bas-reliefs, which, in Rudnitsky's words, revealed the characters' internal dialogue through the music of plastic movement: "Live reliefs were born. . . . The *uslovnost* of gesture was almost ritualistic. The director's notes are highly precise in relation to each actor's poses. Meyerhold dictates every single motion in advance."[79]

In his book on Meyerhold, Konstantin Rudnitsky essentially credited him with the invention of motionless theater. Yet Stanislavsky, in his symbolist productions of 1904, had already begun replacing the Meiningen realism with statuary devices à la Maeterlinck. And as we have seen, essentially the same concept was realized in the MPO productions of *Orfeo* and *Judith*. Rudnitsky never offered Mamontov's company as a possible model for the Povarskaya Studio experiments. He should have: both *Orfeo* and *Judith* were in the active repertoire of the MPO during the 1898–99 season when the Moscow Art Theater first opened. *Judith*, a much-acclaimed premiere that featured Chaliapin in a starring role, was the talk of the town that year. It is highly unlikely that either Stanislavsky or Meyerhold would have missed that production, striking in its motionless *uslovnost*.

The Povarskaya Studio never opened to the public. Officially, this was a result of the 1905 Revolution during which, as Stanislavsky wrote, "Muscovites no longer had any time for theater."[80] In reality, inherent stylistic contradictions of the project doomed it from the start: the highly decorative impressionist designs of Sapunov and Sudeikin could not be reconciled with the austerity of Meyerhold's symbolist mises-en-scène, while the young actors trained at the Meiningen-influenced Art Theater could not accept either style. After watching a dress rehearsal of *Tintagiles*, Valery Bryusov was categorical:

> In many respect, an attempt was made in this production to break away from the realism of the contemporary stage and bravely accept *uslovnost* as the principle of theater art. The movements were more about plasticity than imitation of reality; some groupings resembled Pompeian frescos represented in a tableau vivant. . . . On the other hand, the habits of stage tradition [and] the years of Art Theater training made themselves powerfully known. [The Povarskaya Studio] has demonstrated to everyone that it is impossible to rebuild theater on the old foundations. We should either continue building the theater of Antoine/Stanislavsky, or start from scratch.[81]

Meyerhold realized that the Povarskaya Studio was not to be the theater of his dreams. "Maybe Diaghilev would build a new theater,"[82] he mused, even entering into short-lived negotiations with the budding impresario about the possibility in 1907. Frustrated by contemporary spoken drama, Meyerhold also searched for answers among its sister arts. It seems almost inevitable that his next step, barely four years after the Povarskaya Studio, would be opera. Meyerhold believed that the operatic genre was ideally suited for the realization of his *uslovnyi* theater principles, because it was, by its very nature, "unrealistic": "*Uslovnost* is the basis of operatic art—people are singing; therefore, one should not bring the elements of naturalism into acting, for *uslovnost* that immediately stands in disharmony with the real reveals its apparent unsoundness, and thus, the foundation of art crumbles."[83] In addition, Meyerhold shared Mamontov's familiar vision of opera as a kind of vocalized pantomime that would adapt well to the plastic choreography he developed in *La Mort de Tintagiles*. His first chance to test that hypothesis was *Tristan und Isolde* (1909), his inaugural production as a Mariinsky Theater stage director.

Meyerhold's *Tristan* was unanimously hailed by his contemporaries as a masterpiece of symbolist theater; it is still viewed as such today. Yet, surprisingly, the production was directorially a stylistic mix: the motionless theater of the principals, whose movements were choreographed throughout, was framed by realistic crowd scenes that were, if anything, Meiningen-esque. The only other opera production of the time that exhibited the same unusual combination of static, relief-influenced choreography for the lead with individualized crowd of mass scenes was Mamontov's production of *Judith*, which similarly contrasted Chaliapin's character with the chorus. Therefore, it can be convincingly argued, I believe, that without the knowledge of MPO's *Judith*, Meyerhold's *Tristan* would have never been born.

In 1911, together with his Mariinsky designer, Abramtsevo alumnus Alexander Golovin, and Diaghilev's choreographer Michel Fokine, Meyerhold gave new life to yet another signature Mamontov work, *Orfeo*. The type of stylization used in that sensational production, highly praised by poet Mikhail Kuzmin and by Alexandre Benois, differed from Mamontov's: instead of a "divine ancient dream" with a complete uniformity of stage movement, the audiences saw the decorative neoclassicism of Gluck's theater. No trace of *Tristan*'s realistic crowd remained; Fokine-choreographed expressive gestures and movements of the singers mimicked those of the dancers.[84] The choice of *Orfeo* as the subject is significant, however: it may reflect Mamontov's early influence, in the same way that the tribute to *Orfeo* revealed that influence in Diaghilev's articles, while the Moscow Art Theater's 1900 production of Ostrovsky's *The Snow Maiden* with Vasnetsov's designs was Stanislavsky's open homage to his old mentor.[85]

As we have seen, Mamontov, Stanislavsky, and Meyerhold all went through the same stylistic transition in their approach to staged drama, gradually abandoning their Meiningen-esque realism for symbolist stylization. Meyerhold went further than his older colleagues did, but it was Mamontov's directing work that showed him the way. As in its approach to design, the MPO's directing practices were in a constant state of stylistic flux, with multiple conflicting trends of contemporary theater explored and (sometimes uneasily) reconciled in its productions. Shaped by Mamontov's intense fascination with spoken drama, his company created its own unique fusion of opera and drama, realism and symbolism, and in turn paved the way for modernist drama theater of the early twentieth century.

FIGURE 1. Pyotr Melnikov, "Eugene Onégin" notebook (page 1). RMLAH; used by permission.

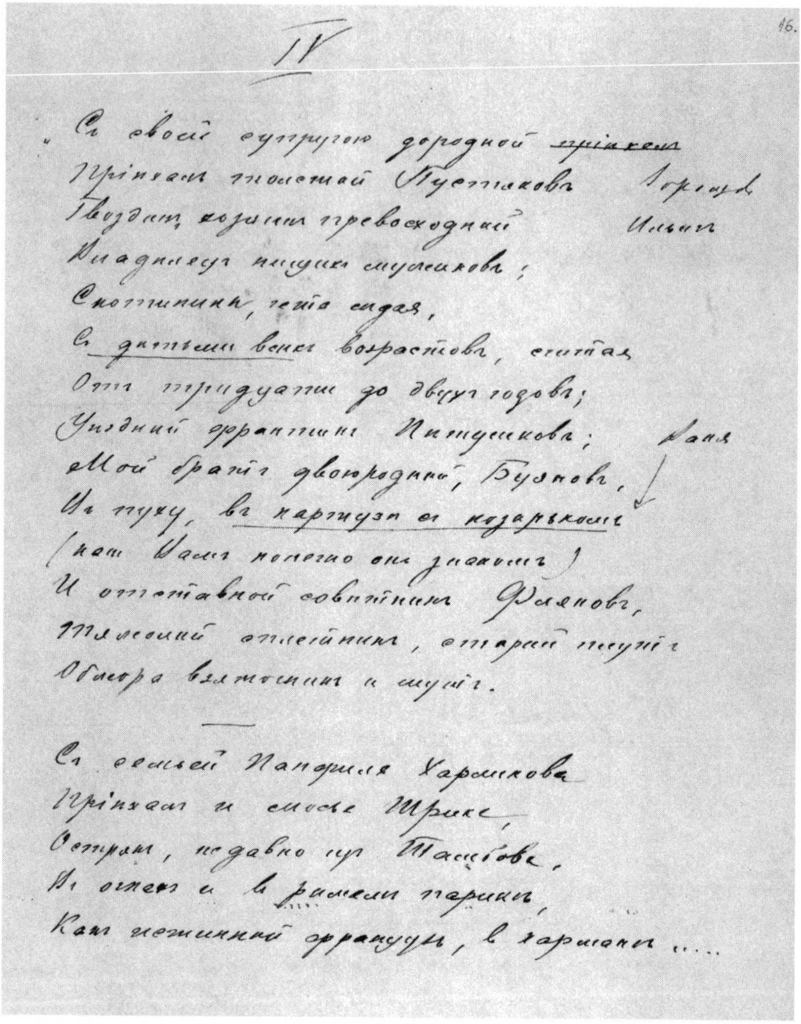

FIGURE 2. Pyotr Melnikov, "Eugene Onegin" notebook (page 16). RMLAH; used by permission.

FIGURE 3. Pyotr Melnikov, "May Night" notebook (insert). RMLAH; used by permission.

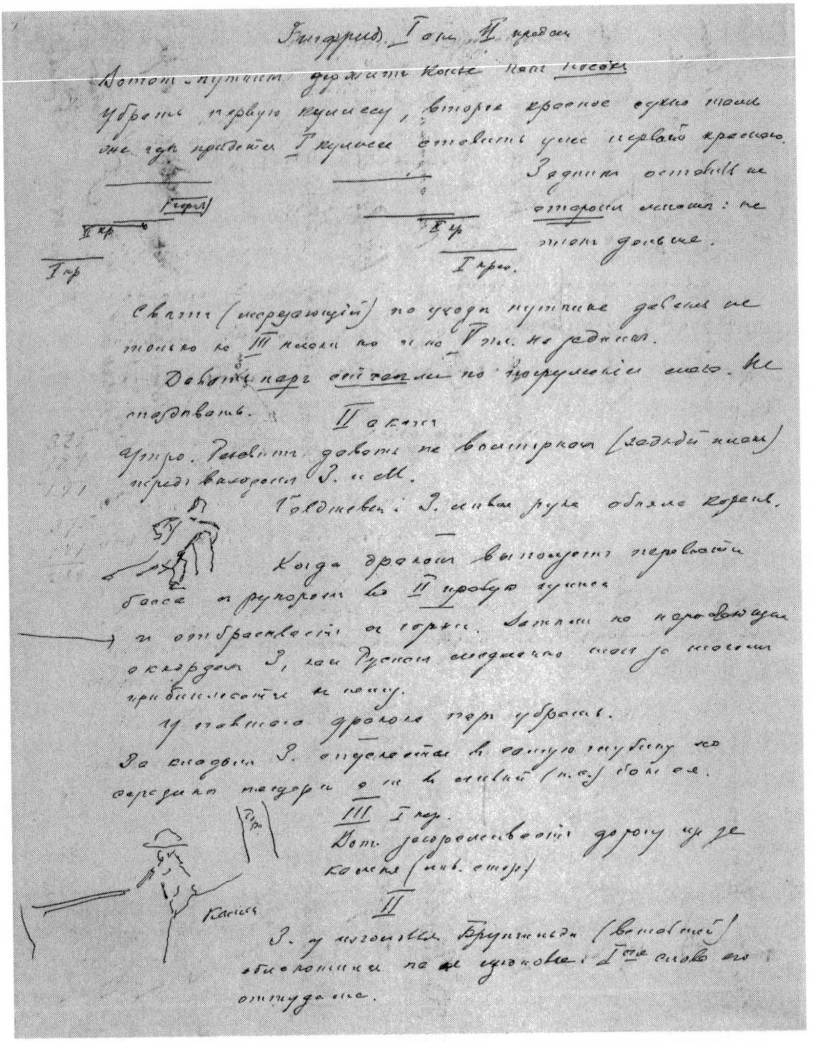

FIGURE 4. Pyotr Melnikov, "Siegfried" notebook (page 1). RMLAH; used by permission.

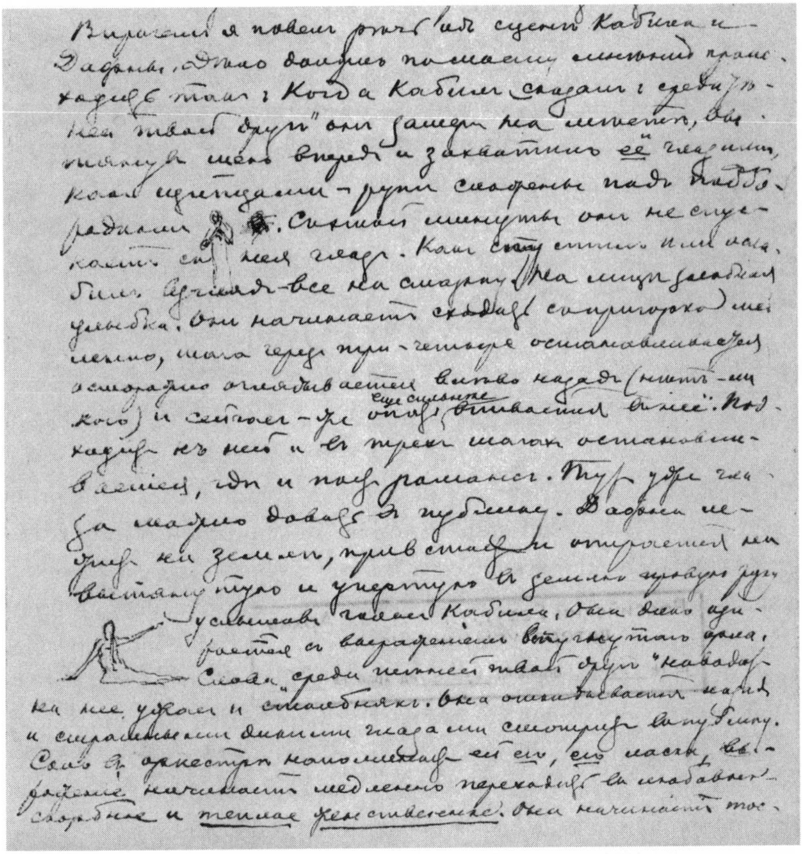

FIGURE 5. Mamontov's letter to Shkafer with drawings of Daphne and Kabil (fragment). RGALI; used by permission.

SEVEN

# Politics, Repertory, and the Market

Throughout this book, we have discussed Mamontov's aesthetic principles and their application to his innovative approach to the operatic genre, as staged drama realized through visual spectacle. Mamontov had a well-deserved reputation as a fountain of creative ideas, ranging from the reasonable and practical all the way to the wild, unachievable, and just plain ridiculous. Some succeeded brilliantly, making his company's reputation; others flopped spectacularly, either in rehearsal, or worse, in front of a live audience. Contemporary press reviews of MPO productions and initiatives are today the most accessible barometer of Mamontov's public triumphs and his equally public failures.

Ideologically biased, politically polarized, acolytes, foes, or allegedly neutral, dispassionate observers, Russian theater critics wrote constantly about the company. To this point, these writings have been invoked as a means of documenting which of Mamontov's ideas made it onto the MPO stage and became visible (and often controversial) enough to warrant mention in the dailies. Meanwhile, the creative process itself has been analyzed as a kind of art for art's sake—intensely focused on the nature and expression of its own artistry, impacted by a variety of aesthetic and performative trends in which its participants were involved, but seemingly unaffected by the "reality" of the company's existence: the constant fluctuations and attendant pressures of the theater market. Mamontov would have loved it, if only it were so. To his grudging acknowledgment and occasional dismay, the reactions of the public and the press intruded constantly on his decision-making process, as well as shaping the public face of his company and its historical legacy. The present chapter will examine MPO's often difficult relationship with the press as a reflection of the complex politics of the Russian opera market in the 1890s.

One October day in 1898, composer Nikolai Krotkov, an occasional visitor to these pages, sent a letter to his friend and collaborator, Mamontov, in which he outlined an idea for a fanciful project they might one day undertake together. He rhapsodized:

> Imagine a theater proscenium; behind it, there are two images of "something," one heavy, mediocre, but pompous; another young, full of genius, life, and high aspirations. . . . General character—fantasy, images—light, transparent, the colors of Goethe and Schumann. . . . The breadth and richness of your thought and imagination will find a suitable realization for these two main characters, and will surround them with other, secondary images full of poetry. These are the symbols of artistic growth on the stages of the Bolshoi Theater and the Private Opera. The parallels are masked. What do you think? The form is a one-act fantasy opera with your libretto and my music. Premiere in the near future.[1]

Had Krotkov truly intended to be cryptic with his allegory, few initiates would have been at a loss to penetrate such a thin disguise. From the moment its doors opened to the paying public, the Moscow Private Opera effectively announced its intention to be treated as a professional, commercial enterprise. As such, it was immediately placed in symbolic opposition to Moscow's most venerable operatic institution—the mighty Imperial Bolshoi Theater.[2] The Bolshoi had every advantage entering this competition: tradition; the prestige of a "model operatic stage" that attracted choice performing forces; an excellent building with superior acoustics; and, last but not least, the limitless financial resources of the Imperial court.

Mamontov was keenly aware that his fledgling company was viewed as a brazen upstart defying an operatic Goliath. Carefully and deliberately, he marketed the MPO's rebel image. The underdog status was relished, trumpeted, used to fire up the troops and shore up support—in a word, to take maximum advantage of the rivalry. His team truly believed they were fighting an uphill battle with the entire Imperial establishment; even the Maly Drama Theater would come under fire should it dare to stage a classical play with a suspiciously operatic subject. Apart from raising the troupe's morale, there were also commercial reasons for Mamontov to stoke the fire. After all, the Moscow theaters were ultimately competing for the same audience, as we can discern from the *Novosti Dnya* review of the opening night of Rimsky-Korsakov's *The Maid of Pskov:*

> There was a large audience despite the fact that on the same night at the Maly Theater, Moscow's favorite A[lexander] P[etrovich] Lensky unofficially celebrated his twenty-year anniversary as an actor of the crown stage, and quite officially premiered, for his benefit performance, a new play by Mr. Nemirovich-Danchenko. I will not reproach [the MPO] for taking such a big risk here, but note that, under different circumstances, the ticket sales for *The Maid of Pskov*'s opening night would have been even more brilliant.[3]

The critic's obvious disappointment notwithstanding, the "big risk" of putting an MPO premiere on a direct collision course with an acknowledged "event" in the cultural life of the city was a calculated one. It exposed a goal Mamontov set for his company from the start: to steal the spotlight permanently from its opposition and to become "the place to be" for Moscow's cultural and intellectual elite.

The goal was ambitious, to say the least, especially considering the violent prejudice against private theatrical ventures that dominated public opinion in the city. The history of Moscow's private enterprises prior to Mamontov's arrival was a never-ending tale of woe: none survived their first season. This includes an anonymous drama troupe mentioned by a *Russkoe Slovo* reviewer of the MPO's inaugural performance,[4] as well as numerous opera theaters, from the "sad productions" of Unkovsky and Ostrovidov,[5] to the venerable Pryanishnikov's company.[6] The latter reportedly inspired Mamontov to revive his Private Opera after his first failed attempt in the 1880s; he would also inherit Pryanishnikov's prima donna, Elena Tsvetkova. Yet despite the acknowledged quality and influence of Pryanishnikov's work, his troupe could not avoid adding bankruptcy to its list of accomplishments.[7] The market, therefore, did not look promising for Mamontov's new venture. As Garteveld succinctly put it in *Russkoe Slovo,* the MPO had to battle more than "its powerful neighbor across the street": it also had to face the "terrifying shadows of the past."[8]

## COMPETING ON AN EQUAL PLANE

The main danger posed by the "terrifying shadows" was a strong conviction held by most Russian intellectuals that a private company could not match the Imperial Theaters in production quality. Such evidently unequal competition would therefore be, as Nikolai Kashkin once declared in *Russkie Vedomosti*, "a truly unthinkable idea."[9] Only two strategies were viewed as capable of keeping a private opera company financially viable. One option was to turn it into what was called a *narodnaya opera* [people's opera house]—a theater whose cheap tickets attracted the cash-strapped lower classes that could not afford "real" (i.e., Imperial) opera, and whose repertoire pandered without reservation to mass taste.[10] Another was relying on the star power of contracted foreign singers. Mamontov had already tried the latter, back in the 1880s; the stars did keep his budget in the black, but the work gave him little artistic satisfaction.[11] Indeed, the MPO was an oddity among private enterprises Moscow had seen thus far: as we know, its commercial interests served an aesthetic agenda. As a result, fewer compromises were acceptable. To be taken seriously, the newcomer had to beat the Bolshoi Theater at its own game; the quality of the operatic experience simply had to be superior to those of its rival. Gradually, press reviews began to register the critics' astonishment: Mamontov's company was not only attempting but succeeding at something that, to quote Sergei Plevako of *Novosti Sezona*, "had never, ever been done by a private company."[12] A building that rivaled the Bolshoi in size and acoustics; substantial capital invested in each new production; the quality of the troupe, including chorus and orchestra; the splendor of the staging and visual design—all the factors that had reportedly sunk its predecessors[13] raised the MPO to a level "absolutely unthinkable for a private stage."[14]

Still, this was not enough. The most stubborn prejudice Mamontov faced was the belief that a private company could not compete with a crown theater on an even repertoire plane. That is, if the same opera were staged at the MPO and the Bolshoi, the "model stage" was presumed superior. Alexander Gruzinsky of *Russkoe Slovo* and other well-intentioned critics continuously advised the company to "avoid as much as possible the operas included in the Bolshoi Theater repertoire,"[15] particularly those staged there "with particular opulence, since these productions would inevitably invite comparisons not to the advantage of the Private Opera."[16] The cost of compliance would have been painfully high, however. The MPO would have lost the right to perform Glinka's classic *A Life for the Tsar*, a staple of the Bolshoi repertoire to this day; Gounod's *Faust*, arguably the most popular opera in Moscow at the time; and yet another crowd pleaser, Tchaikovsky's *Eugene Onegin*, since, according to Gruzinsky, that opera had already been performed at the crown stage more than a hundred times.[17] Perhaps more importantly, Rimsky-Korsakov's *The Snow Maiden*, the aesthetic manifesto of the Mamontov Circle, would have to be taken off the playbill as well. Indeed, a *Russkie Vedomosti* reporter considered the choice of *The Snow Maiden* for the company's opening night "a risky maneuver," because "it belongs to the group of operas that have been performed rather well at the Bolshoi Theater."[18] The critic's choice of words is significant: "rather well" is not exactly a ringing endorsement; yet, even a moderately successful production at the Bolshoi was expected to be a cut above the best attempt by a private enterprise.

The opinion of the press was clearly stated; Mamontov did not obey. Within two weeks of its opening night, the MPO unveiled its staging of *Eugene Onegin*—on the very same evening it was billed at the Bolshoi! The event occasioned a rather annoyed review from Semyon Kruglikov, a future ally but, for the moment, a skeptical columnist of *Novosti Dnya*:

> Tonight the public was given a choice between two *Eugene Onegins*. Without hesitation, we went to the Solodovnikov Theater. Our reasoning was as follows: we are long familiar with the performance of Tchaikovsky's popular opera by the crown troupe. But in [the MPO]'s production we clearly should expect to see something novel or at least outstanding, capable of completely overshadowing everything we know about *Onegin* from the Bolshoi Theater. Otherwise, it seemed to us, the private stage would not have dared to invite such a risky comparison.[19]

Kruglikov was disappointed. Tchaikovsky was not a Mamontov favorite; his involvement in *Onegin*'s staging had been marginal. Only in Melnikov's 1898 production would the opera become everything the critic had once hoped to see. But the very fact of pitting MPO's *Onegin* directly against the Bolshoi's was a clear sign: the new team would not be intimidated by its powerful neighbor. Within two months, the same daily, *Novosti Dnya* reviewed another opera from the Bolshoi repertoire, "performed at the Solodovnikov Theater with an ensemble so excellent that its like could rarely be heard on the Russian operatic stage, neither the private nor, truth be told, the crown one."[20]

Mamontov was determined to exploit to the fullest the clear advantage of a private venture over a large government department overburdened by bureaucracy: its flexibility in navigating the market. Initially, this was reflected only in the feverish pace of operatic performances: seven, sometimes eight a week against the Bolshoi's three or four. But more importantly, both critics and audiences expected it to facilitate the staging of so-called *novinki* [novelties]: premieres of new operas, or revivals of works neglected long enough to warrant the term. The press was relentless in its demands for the *novinki,* meeting each premiere of a familiar work, however well staged and performed, with open sarcasm. "The repertoire list of the Private Opera at the Solodovnikov Theater keeps growing, but unfortunately almost exclusively thanks to operas very renowned and very beloved," noted Kashkin in *Russkie Vedomosti,*[21] declaring ironically in another article that "no Russian operatic stage could survive without Gounod's *Faust,*" so the MPO "could not, of course, escape this common fate."[22] Meanwhile, Ivan Lipaev of *Novosti Sezona* also invited the company to get off "the diet of the tired and worn-out operas," and for goodness sake stage something new![23]

The critics' zeal was born of desperation. Responsible for their choice of operas to the Ministry of the Imperial Household, crown theaters authorized new productions rarely and reluctantly, with many interesting works from both Russian and foreign repertoire taken off the playbill as too difficult or too radical. As a result, the operatic press was faced with "the colorless repertoire that reigns on the Imperial stage in both our capitals lately."[24] Even St. Petersburg critics whined; and yet the Bolshoi fared immeasurably worse than the Mariinsky: on the rare occasions when new productions were authorized for Moscow, the process could literally take years. "The promised *Tannhäuser* was stuck in rehearsal for so long," reported *Novoe Vremya,* "that it was ready only in time for Lent, upon which a directive was sent down from Petersburg to delay it until the spring or even next season."[25] Premieres aside, a revival of Gounod's *Roméo et Juliette,* an opera hardly of Wagnerian complexity, took the Bolshoi long enough to occasion the following remark from

Kruglikov in a weekly *Semya:* "To be preparing a revival of an opera for two months truly means not to be in a hurry. But everything is relative. Wagner's *Siegfried* has been rehearsed at the Bolshoi Theater for about three years now. What is two months next to that? It looks like they are moving along with poor *Romeo* rather nicely."[26]

The sarcasm, however, did not help to mend the ways of the Bolshoi. And while *Novoe Vremya* was "gazing with hope toward Petersburg," calling for its "skillful and powerful hand [to] awaken the sleeping kingdom" and pointing to the touring Italian troupes as models of variety and efficiency,[27] other papers turned to their own Private Opera. To keep their attention, Mamontov's company had to offer an alternative to the two models of operatic enterprise already familiar to the Muscovites: a greedy private venture that sacrifices art for money, and a bureaucracy-laden "sleeping giant" resting on its laurels and not caring enough about art even to sell it. In other words, the MPO had to present itself publicly as a company that was highly professional, intellectually weighty, with its own original approach and cutting-edge artistic agenda, yet flexible, commercially viable, and attuned to the ideological and aesthetic concerns of its audience. The market craved such an institution desperately, and Mamontov, for his part, was determined to have the MPO fill that niche. To convince the cautious and prejudiced public, however, he first needed to woo the press—and not by blindly following its lead. He refused to cede the repertory staples to the crown and, as we shall see, would put out the novelties very much on his own schedule. Instead, he set out to manipulate the critics' disgust with the status quo and their natural curiosity about the newcomers to win support and publicity for his company. And, as with all great causes, before he could recruit, he had to advertise.

### MARKETING STRATEGIES

Advertising was crucial to Mamontov's success. It was the most effective means of manipulating the market, for it served two goals: disseminating information about MPO productions among educated opera lovers while courting the newspapers that, then as now, lived off the advertising revenues. The Moscow Private Opera advertised on the front pages of most major Moscow (and, during the tours, Petersburg) newspapers, and followed the common practice of supplying the press with advance notices of its premieres and weekly repertoire lists. In addition, in 1897 the company signed a contract with Semyon Kegulsky, the new editor of *Novosti Sezona,* the only Moscow daily that exclusively covered the theater. For a daily fee of twenty-five rubles, the contract stipulated the size and placement of the MPO ads in *Novosti Sezona* (front page; large type; page-wide spread above other ads), required Kegulsky to print 3,000 extra copies of his paper a day (1,000 to 1,200 copies were the norm), and specified the exact pattern of their citywide distribution, including hotels, restaurants, markets, department stores, waiting rooms of doctors and lawyers, government offices, and public buildings.[28] It was also quite common for Mamontov to plant advertisements in this and other newspapers, disguised as articles and reviews. Drafts of three such reviews (one of Verstovsky's *Gromoboi* and two of *The Necklace*) have been preserved among his correspondence, one with a note: "Give this to Kegulsky."[29] Apart from new productions, Mamontov advertised new singers joining his troupe: for example, the literary style of a *Novosti Sezona* evaluation of an Italian guest tenor who toured with the company in late 1897 unmistakably betrays his authorship.[30]

While paid advertising was necessary to ensure the newspapers' goodwill toward the company as well as its visibility on the theater market, it was perhaps no less important to court individual journalists, the opinion-makers whose remarks could make or break a show. Members of the press corps were used to receiving VIP treatment at the theaters they reviewed, including season tickets and free access to performers; when snubbed, they were known to retaliate. *Novosti Sezona* once publicly accused "certain newspapers" of systematically "dressing down" MPO productions in their reviews and even printing deliberate misinformation (an example was provided)—all because the company evidently "failed to provide these papers with advertising revenue and their reporters with season tickets."[31] Another way of courting the press and other members of the cultural elite was through charity performances whose proceeds, in full or in part, benefited a popular cause. The premiere of *Orfeo,* for example, was part of a larger event benefiting the Moscow Art Lovers Society, of which both Mamontov and Polenov were members.[32] During the company's 1898 Petersburg tour, a portion of the proceeds from the premiere of *Rogneda* was forwarded to the Help Fund for Writers and

Scientists, a popular charity supporting journalists and other workers of the quill. The gesture was apparently viewed by Mamontov's associates as a covert bribe intended to woo members of the press core still unconvinced of his company's merits.[33] Melnikov commented in a letter from Paris: "I can see that you have finally wormed your way into the editorial boards, and suspect the charity performance for the Literary Fund to be the sacrificial lamb."[34]

Still, Zabela's complaint to Rimsky-Korsakov that all the press was supposedly in Mamontov's pocket was clearly an exaggeration. Take, for example, *Novosti Sezona*—a newspaper that not only benefited from MPO advertising revenue and season tickets, but through its exclusive contract enjoyed direct financial support that almost quadrupled its circulation. Yet although Mamontov's investment bought exposure via advertising and reviews (often unsigned editorials), it gave him little or no control over editorial policy and personnel choices.[35] As we shall see, *Novosti Sezona* would use its MPO coverage to push a highly aggressive ideological agenda frequently to the detriment of his own: in pursuit of good publicity, Mamontov created a monster. And while *Novosti Sezona* critics, despite their partisanship, were sympathetic to his company's mission, as they understood it, there were plenty of negative reviews of MPO productions, even at the height of its success. Mamontov did not mind: any publicity was good publicity. What was more important is that the company was noticed, talked about, argued over, and valued for its contribution to the intellectual and artistic life of the city. The impossible was achieved: the Moscow Private Opera was in the spotlight of theatrical discourse.

## IN THE SPOTLIGHT

A good illustration of the MPO's new place in the cultural landscape of the old Russian capital was the public reaction to the disastrous fire that all but destroyed the Solodovnikov Theater on 20 January 1898. In their extensive coverage of that event, journalists assessed not only the damage that the fire caused the building, but also the damage that the possible loss of the troupe would cause the city. In its account, *Novosti Sezona* called the Solodovnikov "the best of our private theaters,"[36] while *Novosti Dnya* described the company as "the center of attention of theatrical Moscow."[37] Lest one wonder if the reports were merely a sympathy vote in the face of catastrophe, reviews of the company's activities during the following season leave little room for doubt. For instance, the 1899 premiere of *The Maid of Orleans* was characterized by *Novosti Dnya* as "one of the biggest events of the current musical season," a distinction almost never awarded to the Bolshoi.[38]

As newspapers frequently commented, the MPO developed its own stable, loyal, enthusiastic—and sizable—audience.[39] The company was enjoying more than critical acclaim; it was becoming ("what a scary thing to say!" Mamontov would exclaim) popular. Indeed, the 1898 Solodovnikov fire was a blessing in disguise, for it allowed the troupe to extend its influence beyond its native city toward the notoriously difficult, discerning, and fastidious theatrical elite of St. Petersburg. The MPO's first tour evidently caught Russia's northern capital unprepared. Despite earlier reports of Mamontov's exploits that occasionally appeared in its dailies, *tout Pétersburg* was in for a culture shock: an opera troupe from conservative Moscow, whose reputation as a cultural backwater was shared even by its own citizens and certainly by sophisticated Petersburgers, was suddenly the talk of the town. The opening night, featuring the St. Petersburg premiere of *Sadko* with the composer at the podium, created a furor, as reported to the Muscovites by a local correspondent for *Novosti Dnya*: "Rimsky-Korsakov's opera enjoyed brilliant success. The author was called for endlessly, after each tableau; the ovations were truly grandiose. It seems that no one expected such a high level of staging and performance for our excellent composer's magnificent creation. During intermissions, there was a buzz in the air; everyone was in an elated, celebratory mood—both the performers and the audience."[40]

Perhaps the most spectacular expression of that celebratory mood was Vladimir Stasov's immediately notorious essay "Boundless Joy!" which exalted Feodor Chaliapin's interpretation of Ivan the Terrible in Rimsky-Korsakov's *The Maid of Pskov*. Stasov's article seems to have been read by just about everyone in the city; it received an unprecedented number of commentaries from other critics.[41] The level of popularity it achieved (and the amount of scandalous publicity it generated for the MPO, to Mamontov's delight) can be illustrated by the fact that its title, "boundless joy," was soon transformed into a favored journalistic catchphrase. At first it referred only to Stasov's unbridled enthusiasm, as in the following commentary (notice the use of quotation marks): "'Boundlessly' and with purely youthful enthusiasm, he greeted the appearance of Mr. Chaliapin as 'boundless joy,' and dedicated to him in *Novosti* an entire panegyric that would be capable of embarrassing even a more experienced artist than Mr. Chaliapin."[42] Later, the catchphrase started being used, tongue-in-cheek, in cartoons and feuilletons to refer to Chaliapin's fame ("[Chaliapin's performance] is clearly 'boundless joy,' but the theater is as empty as ever"),[43] to the company itself ("last year's 'boundless joy' has subsided," wrote the same critic about the reduced attendance for its 1899 tour), and to the Kuchkist repertoire with which it was associated, thanks in part to Stasov's "youthful enthusiasm": "Of course, 'boundless joy' is a good thing, but the ecstasy of melodic recitative is completely lost on me."[44] The catchphrase was also used to refer to Stasov's other aesthetic crusades, not necessarily musical ones: for instance, a popular cartoon by the Old Judge that commented on one of Stasov's rare victories in his continuing war with Diaghilev's decadents was titled "Boundless Joy" (see plate 40). Finally, critics used the catchphrase to discuss subjects completely unrelated to opera, Stasov, or the arts—for example, in reference to the "boundless joy" of occult séances, an increasingly popular pastime of the Petersburg upper crust.[45] Evidently, not only the artistic activities of Mamontov's company but even the polemics they generated became a part of Russia's general cultural discourse of the late 1890s.

### GAINING THE UPPER HAND

As the above discussion demonstrates, thanks to a combination of innovative artistry and clever marketing, Mamontov's rebel theater earned a legitimate, respected place in the Russian operatic market in less than two seasons. It was seen as a viable competitor to the Imperial stage; its successes and failures were to be judged accordingly. In an 1899 interview with Petersburg-based César Cui, a *Novosti Dnya* critic casually referred to the "coexistence of two opera theaters, a crown one and a private one" as part of Moscow's artistic landscape.[46] Indeed, almost a year earlier, the normally cautious *Russkoe Slovo* columnist summarized the company's accomplishments thus:

The Private Opera has finally lived to see its time arrive, and its situation is clearly improving. The success is complete, both artistically and financially. The public dutifully applauds the performers; box office returns are brilliant.... Our Private Opera has finally lived to see its "lucky streak": even despite the guest tour by the Figners at the crown stage, the private one does excellent business and steadily attracts an audience! Its own repertoire, its own performing forces—these alone allow it to face the future with some confidence, and have practically no doubts about the possibility of a comfortable and deficit-free existence as a private opera theater *alongside* a crown one . . . Art is not afraid of competition.[47]

The last remark is, of course, somewhat idealistic: the spirit of competition underlined the relationship between the MPO and its crown adversary just as much in 1898 as in 1896. At the heart of that competition was the question of repertoire: premiering or reviving an opera overlooked by the Bolshoi was a sure way of attracting the attention of both the public and the press, and was used to full advantage even before Mamontov. As Kruglikov once noted, "the best operatic novelties, both Russian and foreign, are first presented to the Muscovites not by the Bolshoi Theater stage, but rather by private operatic stages." His examples included Pryanishnikov's 1892 Moscow premiere of *Prince Igor*[48] and Mamontov's productions of *The Snow Maiden* (1885) and *Samson et Dalila* (1896), the latter occasioning the article.[49] Every time an opera ignored by the Imperial Theaters was successfully staged at the MPO, the press could not contain its glee. For instance, not a single review of *Sadko* to be found in either capital failed to mention that Rimsky-Korsakov's opera was rejected by the Mariinsky repertoire committee, yet lived to see fifteen sold-out performances at the Solodovnikov in less than two months.[50] And in every article of this kind, the critics would drop not so subtle hints that the crown stage should begin a serious revision of its repertoire policy.

The Imperial Theaters were taking notice, if not of the press criticism, then of the public success of Mamontov's productions. Gruzinsky of *Russkoe Slovo* commented on the fact that, evidently, the triumph of *Rogneda* at the MPO had prompted a revival of that long-forgotten work at the Bolshoi the following season.[51] In its report on the proposed Mariinsky production of *Sadko* during the 1899–1900 season, *Novosti Dnya* attributed the decision to the "big success of Rimsky-Korsakov's opera" in Moscow.[52] Interestingly, *Rogneda* and *Sadko* were apparently not isolated incidents, but rather parts of a general trend. The list of operas either revived or premiered at the Bolshoi Theater within one or two seasons after their Solodovnikov productions also includes *Prince Igor* (MPO, fall 1896; Bolshoi, winter 1898), *Carmen* (MPO, fall 1896; Bolshoi, fall 1898), *The Snow Maiden* (MPO, fall 1896; Bolshoi, fall 1897), and *The Oprichnik* (MPO, winter 1897; Bolshoi, winter 1899), to name just a few. Critics noted the unusual situation of a "model stage" being led by the hand by a private company. Some voiced their appreciation of Mamontov's "courage to stage operas without a prior record of success" and, by implication, the Bolshoi's cowardice. In his review of the Bolshoi Theater's revival of *The Snow Maiden*, Gruzinsky mentioned the fact that this was only the thirteenth performance since the opera was premiered at the Bolshoi, adding that at the MPO it survived more performances over the single 1896–97 season.[53] Eighteen months later Andrei Kornev, Gruzinsky's replacement at *Russkoe Slovo*, commented cautiously:

> In most cases, our private operatic stage . . . has indirectly dictated the operatic repertoire of the Bolshoi Theater (the majority of the best . . . operas were first staged on our private stage, and then, after a significant time period, on the stage of the Bolshoi Theater, whose repertoire directors for a long time appeared to view the merits of these compositions with skepticism).[54]

The press also noticed a reversal in the attitude toward new productions at the Private Opera and the Imperial stage. In the newspapers, the Bolshoi Theater was chastised for staging Mamontov's hits "merely to satisfy the public demand, merely for the sake of staging" them—an attitude traditionally attributed to the greedy commercialism of private enterprises.[55] The MPO, on the other hand, was acclaimed for its "vigorous artistic spirit,"[56] great enthusiasm, and a "passionate love for the cause"[57] that set it apart from the businesslike atmosphere of the Imperial troupe. Anonymous leaders of the company were similarly praised for investing "not only their labor and money, but their very souls into the beloved cause,"[58] an assessment that mirrored the self-image lovingly constructed, sincerely believed in, and tirelessly promoted by Mamontov's team.

## APPROACHING NATIONAL REPERTOIRE

The differences observed by the press between Mamontov's enterprise and the Imperial troupe were understood as fundamental, going to the core of each company's structure and aesthetic platform. As a *Novosti Dnya* critic once put it, their divergent approaches revealed "their different operational principles; their different ideologies." As a crown institution, he continued, the Bolshoi Theater "has its own artistic goals, its own aspirations, its own understanding of the duties of an opera theater," distinct from those of the MPO. "Whether this understanding is right or wrong is another question," the reviewer concluded, but clearly, "the [Bolshoi's] directorate cannot waver from its predetermined path."[59]

Specific symptoms of the perceived ideological chasm included, among other factors, different levels of fidelity to a composer's published score and in-house rules allowing or prohibiting encores. Most critics, however, focused on the companies' repertoire policies, particularly with respect to national repertoire, as measured by the relative percentages of Russian and foreign operas on playbills. To the critics, this was evidently the main point of contention and the main point of comparison between the two troupes. Thus, at the end of each season, major Moscow newspapers featured lengthy statistical reports that measured and publicized the number of Russian and foreign works staged at the theaters, and even tallied the number of performances for every opera.

The first time the press was able to make a comparison between the Bolshoi and the MPO, the crown stage did not fare too badly: *Novosti Dnya* proclaimed the 1896–97 season "a great victory for Russian music" after reporting the roughly equal percentage of national and foreign works performed there (59 performances of Russian versus 58 of foreign operas). According to the report, in the earlier years Russian operas "constituted hardly a third of the repertoire."[60] The following season, the elated journalists reported that national works accounted for almost two thirds of the Bolshoi repertoire list (66 Russian versus 29 foreign operas). Meanwhile, the 1898–99 season proved disappointing to the press, with the balance returning to approximate parity (73 Russian versus 80 foreign performances). The situation that two years before was viewed as a "great victory" was now proclaimed intolerable; even a special Russian opera subscription series did not help the Bolshoi's sinking reputation.

Mamontov was partly to blame for this. Since its opening season, the number of Russian opera performances at his Private Opera consistently exceeded the number of foreign ones, which delighted the Moscow press. Moreover, with each passing year the proportion tilted more and more in favor of the national repertoire: 109 Russian operas versus 70 foreign performances were reported in 1896–97, 96 versus 43 in 1897–98, and finally, an overwhelming 94 versus 19 in the 1898–99 season.

These statistics seem to indicate a clear partiality toward local fare at Mamontov's enterprise, thus seeming to justify Western scholars' view of Mamontov himself as an integral part of the Russian nationalist revival movement. A thorough analysis of Mamontov's correspondence as well as the press coverage of his company's productions paints a much more complex picture of the political and ideological atmosphere in Russian society at the time. As we shall see, Mamontov's team started out as a willing participant in the press-led nationalist crusade, with its guaranteed exposure and preferential treatment, but soon found itself trapped in the aggressive rhetoric of rising nationalism and in its own good intentions.

## THE DIRTY WAR FOR "OUR NATIVE ART"

The Balkan war of 1875 proved a defining moment for the majority of Russia's liberal intelligentsia. The plight of their Southern Slavic brothers fueled an unprecedented upsurge in nationalist feelings in the country, which gradually began to infect its cultural and artistic landscape. The openly nationalistic Tsar Alexander III (1881–94) encouraged these feelings throughout his rule and promoted their expression in the arts via Imperial patronage.[61] The extent of the Tsar's support for national art became public knowledge after the Museum of Alexander III (now the State Russian Museum) opened in St. Petersburg in March 1898, just over three years after his death.[62] The new museum was to house the late tsar's collection of Russian paintings, primarily those of the Wanderers, gathered during the 1870s and 1880s. The widespread popular support for this project is indicative of a turn of the tide of public opinion toward was called *nashe rodnoe* ("our native"—i.e., Russian national) art. Similar tendencies began to develop in the music world, including opera theater.

A highly conservative institution by nature, enamored with Italian tunes and Italian stars, opera lagged a few years behind the other arts in adopting the nationalist cause. According to the press of Mamontov's time, which loved discussing the issue, Moscow audiences were solidly behind "our native art" by the early to mid-1890s. A *Novosti Sezona* editorial suggested that, by that time, Muscovites had finally "ended [their] blind attraction to the foreign. If there is a small group of people who still reject the significance of the Russian compositional school, the majority is now firmly convinced of the beauty and richness of Russian operas."[63] The true test of the strength of that conviction came with Mamontov's stage premiere of Musorgsky's *Khovanshchina*—a complex, difficult work by a Kuchkist composer, never before heard in the city. Kruglikov, in a rare appearance as a *Novosti Dnya* guest columnist, recalled a lukewarm reception for the opera's concert premiere in St. Petersburg in 1887. He blamed the critics' reserve on the fact that in the 1880s, opera theater's "bias toward Western, particularly Italian music was still very strong, while Russian music was hardly in favor at the time." Kruglikov observed: "A noticeable and long-desired turn in our society toward Russian national music, which brought back and offered an honored place in the repertoire to a host of compositions by Dargomyzhsky, Rimsky-Korsakov, Borodin, and [Alexander] Serov, had to have naturally initiated the staging of the unjustly suppressed *Khovanshchina*."[64]

In their reports on the anticipated *Khovanshchina* production, the Moscow critics never missed a chance to point out that the opera had never been staged by the Imperial Theaters; the St. Petersburg performance noted by Kruglikov was offered by a group of conservatory students and amateur musicians led by Rimsky-Korsakov.[65] By the late 1890s, the nationalists, for whom both the Art Academy and the conservatories had long symbolized Western dominion over Russian arts, evidently began to view the Imperial Theaters in a similar light—as a crown-sponsored institution whose policies deliberately suppressed Russian opera in favor of foreign repertoire. Press criticism of the Bolshoi Theater, even more cautious with respect to staging Russian works than the Mariinsky, turned particularly relentless after the appearance of the MPO and its successful productions of these works. For instance, the premiere of Rimsky-Korsakov's *The Maid of Pskov* occasioned the following outburst from Kruglikov in *Novosti Dnya*:

So, the Moscow premiere of *The Maid of Pskov* has finally taken place. Rimsky-Korsakov's eldest opera has waited its turn for a long time, but certainly not to be presented to the Moscow audience from the Bolshoi Theater stage. Why would they do that?! They have other things to do besides such trifles! They proudly leave all those [*Prince*] *Igors* and *Maids of Pskov* to private operatic enterprises.⁶⁶

An editorial of *Novosti Sezona* flatly accused the Bolshoi of stubbornly ignoring the *vox populi:* according to that paper, only under the pressure of competition did the theater finally decide to "break the seal of silence" and begin staging Russian operas:

But while starting to do so, they seem to have preserved their skepticism by announcing only two or three operas for this season. It is as if they are afraid that the cause will fail; that the audience reaction will prove negative, because the public taste may have already changed.⁶⁷

A more restrained commentator (and one less partial to the New Russian School than Rimsky-Korsakov's student Kruglikov), Nikolai Kashkin of *Russkie Vedomosti,* could not contain his sarcasm after the premiere of *Sadko:*

This great work by a Russian composer was rejected by the St. Petersburg [Imperial] Theater directorate, which preferred to stage Humperdinck's *Hänsel und Gretel,* a sentimental little operetta in which a few pages of pretty music hardly redeem the lowly flight of the whole. . . . During the premiere of *Sadko* on the stage of the Private Opera, the Moscow Bolshoi Theater once more offered its audiences Humperdinck's *Hänsel und Gretel:* so in Moscow the fates again brought these two works into competition with each other, but here Rimsky-Korsakov's music could finally speak for itself.⁶⁸

In an earlier article, Kashkin even complained about the lack of attention given to his late friend Tchaikovsky's works.⁶⁹ That was, perhaps, going a bit overboard: during the 1896–97 season Tchaikovsky was the most frequently staged Russian composer at the Bolshoi, leading the list with sixteen performances of two operas. At the same time, the representatives of the New Russian School were conspicuously absent from that list: no operas by Musorgsky, Rimsky-Korsakov, Borodin, or Cui were performed. In the mid-1890s, years after most of these operas were written, the Kuchkists were still known only to a narrow circle of enthusiasts, while the audience at large, with no professional training

to study published scores, had no access to them due to lack of performances. Ironically, wrote Kashkin, Musorgsky's name "has been more
familiar to the public from the press war on his account than from his
own works."[70] And indeed, the press war for access to and public recognition of Kuchkist operas raged on. Critics argued (quite correctly) that
by now these operas were better known in Western Europe than in their
own country, and tried to shame the crown theaters and the public into
taking an interest in them. Ivan Lipaev of *Novosti Sezona* wrote:

> While lectures on Musorgsky are delivered in Paris and Cui's operas are
> staged in Brussels, the majority of our citizens don't even suspect how
> much sympathy Russian composers inspire abroad. Before we open our
> eyes and awaken from hibernation, the verdict is already in over there,
> and we are left only to wonder how come we've never thought of it before.
> And in the meantime, a composer endures and suffers so much that the
> world grows dark to him, his inspiration grows cold, and the years lead
> him to his grave. It happened to Glinka; it happened to Dargomyzhsky.
> And later, the same fate awaited all those who cherished the ideals of those
> musical geniuses and followed in their footsteps, proving that the New
> Russian School of musical composition is not a bizarre, farcical invention,
> but a valuable national cause.[71]

The critic was right: the situation was becoming absurd. There was a
legitimate reason for the campaign waged by the press on behalf of national opera. However, in the best tradition of Russian musical journalism since the conservatory controversy of the 1850s and the Serov–Stasov
polemic over *Ruslan*,[72] theirs was a dirty war. The goal was worthy and
to them justified any means, including mudslinging, name calling, guilt
by association, and all other kinds of verbal abuse. Kashkin described
the beginning of this tradition as follows:

> In the old days of the 1860s, "when all impressions of everyday life were
> new to us," our musical press was quite bellicose. Thanks to the late [Al-
> exander] Serov, a bold and controversial decisiveness of verdicts could
> with equal ease raise a composer to the status of genius or attempt to
> erase him from the face of the earth as a mediocre nobody. Moreover, the
> same person could be proclaimed a genius or a mediocrity by different
> judges of his talent.[73]

This time, however—unlike in the 1850s and '60s when divergent points
of view were represented by equally powerful voices—the overwhelming

majority of critics, at least in Moscow, were in agreement on the issue, and the few dissenters among them were not so politely silenced. Particularly aggressive was *Novosti Sezona*. It accused the daily *Kurier* of ignoring its duty to society by not publishing a substantial enough report on *Khovanshchina*'s premiere. And after "a certain R.," a *Moskovskie Vedomosti* columnist, printed an unsympathetic review of that event, he was immediately branded "a staunch conservative, an ally of Ivanov, Baskin, Laroche, *e tutti quanti*, and just as solid and knowledgeable as the above-mentioned critics."[74] If even the sophisticated intellectual Hermann Laroche was branded an ignoramus, the St. Petersburg conservatives Mikhail Ivanov, Vladimir Baskin, and their supporters were treated with even less deference (although in fairness, unlike the elderly and sick Laroche, they did have an opportunity to respond in kind). For example, for disagreeing with Stasov over the infamous "Boundless Joy" essay, the conservative but astute Baskin was called a "quasi-critic." He was further advised that while "Mr. Stasov would always remain a true critic and a true preacher of Russian art," Mr. Baskin himself "never has been and never will be a critic, and will never be able to preach anything, except perhaps the world significance of Mr. Ivanov's feuilletons."[75]

While journalists could defend themselves through their respective newspaper outlets, the Moscow public did not stand a chance. The media, the most powerful weapon in any ideological war, gave it no choice: in their zeal to promote Russian opera, the nationalist press created a direct connection between musical style and patriotism. One of the most significant and attractive musical characteristics of an opera was now its "Russianness." According to *Russkie Vedomosti*, this quality was one of the best in *The Maid of Pskov*.[76] *Novosti Sezona* discussed *Khovanshchina* as a "splendid proof of Musorgsky's genius as a *national* composer,"[77] while Sergei Plevako in *Russkoe Slovo* chastised the listeners for their perceived indifference to its "wonderfully original Russian music" whose "Russian tunes, full of truth and sincerity, . . . spoke to the heart and, breaking it, awakened the memories of the immediacy of Russian life."[78] Any true Russian was now duty-bound to know and love Russian opera—at least according to one *Peterburgsky Listok* columnist, who stated as much in his review of *Sadko*: "Those who have not seen it, who have not heard its . . . magical music, are not acquainted with one of the capital creations of our national art. National indeed, since

*Sadko* is a purely Russian work from head to toe, and any real Russian who does not know it should be truly ashamed."[79] Love for Russian opera was promoted not only as a patriotic gesture but also as a "healthy habit," as the following pearl from *Novosti Sezona* indicates: "The need for healthy Russian creative works has been revealed ever more distinctly in our society; ever stronger rang its desire to return to native music, forgetting the pretty and lifeless music of Italian and French, Western composers."[80]

We should not be surprised by now that the juiciest, most incendiary quotes have been provided by *Novosti Sezona*. During the 1897–98 season, its contributing writers became the true leaders of the nationalist crusade. Using highly aggressive, unrestrained language, they proclaimed without hesitation that which was only hinted at in other publications. That is why a tinge of anti-Semitism and xenophobia—unfortunate side effects of the press war—are particularly noticeable in the *Novosti Sezona* editorials of that period. There, the works of the New Russian School were presented as the only "truly Russian" operas, while compositions by Russified foreigners such as Napravnik or Western-oriented locals like Tchaikovsky were branded "quasi-Russian."[81] Operas by Anton Rubinstein and other assimilated Jews were clearly labeled "foreign." "We do not dispute that the music of Meyerbeer, Rubinstein, Mendelssohn, and others is worthy of full respect and adoration, but would still ask Mr. Kugel and his associates to show at least a little indulgence to *Russian* composers as well."[82] "Mr. Kugel and his associates" were the editorial board of a St. Petersburg weekly, *Teatr i Iskusstvo*. The Western, contemporary music–oriented policy and the foreign-sounding name of the editor made this "puny little journal" *Novosti Sezona*'s favorite straw man. Responding to a reserved review of *Sadko* in *Teatr i Iskusstvo*, its editorial reads:

> This is not the first time Mr. Kugel allows himself such sneak attacks against everything Russian. Rather, he systematically advances such ideas. Mr. Kugel does not like Russian music; a Muscovite accent irritates his ear; Russian writers are illiterate, in his opinion; it seems the time is drawing near when Mr. Kugel will declare that Russia as a whole is not to his taste.[83]

Equating distaste for Kuchkist music with betraying one's country was a favorite weapon of the nationalist press, particularly *Novosti Sezona*.

Thus, despite the reliably Russian name of its editor, "everything Russian [was] alien and not at all dear" to poor *Moskovskie Vedomosti,* as evidently "to this newspaper the triumph of Russian music is undesirable." The following diatribe in its honor would have made Stasov proud:

> [*Moskovskie Vedomosti*] has always tried to prove the insignificance of real Russian music, which does not include works by Tchaikovsky and Rubinstein; but this paper has always considered these composers the only Russian composers while completely ignoring others, up to and including Glinka and his *Ruslan.*[84]

### THE "RUSSIAN OPERA" UNDER PRESSURE

Such was the ideological climate in Moscow as of 8 September 1896, the day Mamontov reopened his company under the name "Claudia S. Winter's Private Russian Opera at the Solodovnikov Theater." Initially, the "Russian Opera" part of that title had nothing to do with repertoire: it simply meant that the enterprise employed primarily Russian singers and, more importantly, staged its productions in Russian. This included foreign operas: until fairly recently, the custom of performing operas in their original languages was unknown in Russia. Typically, opera companies were identified by their linguistic affiliation: "Italian Opera," "French Opera," "German Opera," and so on; for example, the official name of the crown troupe housed at the Bolshoi Theater was "the Moscow Imperial Russian Opera." While opera companies filled their playbills with works in many national styles, their singers customarily performed in the language of the company irrespective of its repertoire. For example, a certain Italian Opera, which left St. Petersburg in February 1898, immediately prior to Mamontov's arrival, wrapped up its tour with Tchaikovsky's *Eugene Onegin*—in Italian, of course.

The MPO was a "Russian Opera." Foreign repertoire was typically performed in the Russian language, with meticulous attention paid to the quality of the translations. As a rule, Mamontov would translate each potential foreign premiere prior to making a decision whether or not it would even be included in the repertoire;[85] his translation of Puccini's *La bohème* is considered definitive to this day. Even operatic war horses readily available in Russian were retranslated before being produced by the company; and the requirement to know their assigned parts in authorized translations was included in each MPO singer's official contract.[86]

Meanwhile, the Moscow press, whose siege of the Bolshoi Theater repertoire committee had been producing meager results, was naturally thrilled to see the MPO inaugurate its opening season with *The Snow Maiden,* a rarely performed Rimsky-Korsakov masterpiece. The critics immediately set out to guide the new venture onto what they called "a correct path." What they meant was transparently evident in the early reviews of Mamontov's productions. From the beginning, these reviews contained hints that the company's repertoire policy, not merely its language of choice, should "justify the two words emphasized on its playbills by the drawn index fingers. These two words are *Russian opera.*"[87] "Mrs. Winter's enterprise appears to be on a correct path," wrote Kruglikov in *Novosti Dnya.* "One cannot but welcome the idea to create in Moscow an opportunity for relatively moderate-income folk to hear excellent examples of primarily Russian operatic art, which are rarely or never staged here."[88] Lipaev of *Novosti Sezona* reminded the new company that, traditionally, the commercial success of a private enterprise depended on its repertoire (and, as we have seen, duplicating the Bolshoi's playbill was considered unthinkable). "So far," he wrote, "the directorate appears to be following a correct path. Two out of three opening performances have been Russian operas—this is a good sign." The critic then continued lobbying for the national repertoire, linking it directly to the new venture's financial survival:

We should note that in Moscow, according to the most respected sources, Russian opera is desirable, and would inspire strong sympathy. Moreover, the majority of the public is inclined to demand it. If the directorate responds to this, it will profit, if not—then its activity would go against public opinion, and this in itself will not end well. It would be strange to adopt an idea of exclusivity, that is, that we insist only upon this one thing—give us only Russian opera. We simply view this as the main goal of the Private Opera, with no desire at all to lessen the significance of staging model examples of Western European operatic music. But Russian opera should come above all else.[89]

In his glowing report on the premiere of *Rogneda,* Lipaev called the production "a living proof of what the Private Opera should strive to achieve. The sooner it stages [other] Russian operas, the better off it will be."[90] Some of these "other" operas had been suggested back in September by Kashkin, who expressed "a wish that the Private Russian Opera keep moving in the direction revealed in its inaugural production," approved of the company's announced intent to stage Tchaikovsky's *The Oprichnik*, and hinted that "in the meantime, we would also like to hear Rimsky-Korsakov's *May Night*."[91]

By mid-October, reports on Mamontov's company showed traces of impatience, and even frustration: while performances were frequent and premieres numerous, no new Russian operas were among them (*Rogneda* would not be staged until 31 October). For instance, Gruzinsky publicly confessed in *Russkoe Slovo* that, "due to the frequent productions of worn-out operas from the Italian repertoire," he was "beginning to doubt the good intentions of our new private opera."[92] Even Kashkin's usually measured tone turned nastier, as in the following critique:

> Since 8 September, when the Russian Private Opera started its performances at the Solodovnikov Theater, this company has exhibited enormous activity, amazing at least in quantity. It is enough to mention that in less than six weeks, about forty opera performances were given, with twelve new operas staged. Despite such significant results (numerically), this theater still has no individual face, and as a result it has not won the decisive support of the audiences, which could have been expected given the size of its performing forces, and the financial means at its disposal. We greeted the launch of this likeable enterprise with great pleasure, but now anxiety unwillingly develops that this enterprise shall wither and die due to the lack of a specific plan and direction for its activities.[93]

The desirable "individual face" and "direction" is revealed toward the end of the essay, following a lengthy discussion of the rising level of artistic expectations among the most influential portion of the operatic audience—the intellectual elite. The critic expressed his hopes for the company's future as follows:

> The flourishing of Russian music over the last thirty years has naturally attracted the attention of the Russian audience, and there is no doubt that currently the majority is interested in the new Russian operas. The Bolshoi Theater has not been spoiling us in that regard, so if the Private Opera energetically takes up the cause of Russian opera, one could hardly doubt its success.[94]

Other newspapers echoed Kashkin's directive, urging the company to start "fulfilling its promises" by staging new Russian operas as soon as possible.[95] Several reviews of the *Rogneda* production concluded with explicit wishes that the company waste no time in preparing its next Russian premiere.

Meanwhile, staging exclusively or even predominantly Russian repertoire was not easy for a young company such as the MPO. To start with, it was a much more expensive exercise than staging foreign works, due to the unfair assignment of publishing fees and royalties that privileged the Imperial Theaters. The issue was addressed in *Novosti Dnya*, whose correspondent wrote:

> The process of staging Russian operas by private enterprises . . . is constantly hindered by music publishers who demand a much too high per-production fee for these operas. For example, Bessel receives 75 rubles per performance of Rimsky-Korsakov's *The Snow Maiden* from the directorate, beyond the author's per-act libretto royalties. Adding the libretto payment, the complete royalties for *The Snow Maiden* rise above 100 rubles per night. Given that crown theaters pay 10 percent of each night's box-office receipts in author's royalties, in order for the royalty payments by private theaters to equal those of crown theaters, the Private Opera's receipts must reach 1,000 rubles per night. Meanwhile, this number cannot be reached every night, particularly with cheap ticket prices.[96]

Per-performance royalties were indeed a heavy burden for Mamontov's young company.[97] But in the larger financial picture, they amounted to small change. More immediately, the MPO's market viability rested—as is typical of any private enterprise—on the speed with which new productions could be mounted. Yet Russian repertoire was notoriously difficult to stage. The operas were long; they included large choral scenes and numerous secondary characters, requiring much rehearsal time. The fact that they were so rarely staged helped with the marketing, but meant that the singers, not to mention the chorus and orchestra, were unlikely to be familiar with their parts. In addition, rendering the subtle, complex musical declamation of, for instance, Musorgsky scores required expertise that Mamontov's troupe was only in the process of acquiring. *Russkoe Slovo* guest columnist Victor Garteveld was virtually alone in acknowledging the difficulties Mamontov's company faced because of the pressure exerted by the press. He wrote:

It would of course be desirable for the enterprise to stage as many outstanding *Russian* operas as possible, since they are closer than most foreign operas to our public, in mood and spirit. But to stage exclusively Russian operas, particularly those by modern composers, is absolutely impossible for a private enterprise, for a number of reasons. First of all, any Russian opera is much more difficult to stage than most foreign ones (with the exception of Wagner, of course), and as a result, it requires numerous rehearsals. Let us take, for example, any Rimsky-Korsakov opera. The above-mentioned composer is probably the finest orchestrator in Europe today; he places great demands not only on his orchestra, but also on the soloists and the chorus. The difficulty of his writing and the complexity of his score have caused many opera theaters to think twice before agreeing to tackle such hard work. And everything said above about Rimsky-Korsakov also applies to Borodin, [Nikolai] Solovyov, Cui, [Alexander] Serov, and so on. So, if during the current season the Private Opera stages, as promised, three operas such as *Rogneda, Prince Igor,* and *The Oprichnik,* its heroism could only be truly appreciated by people familiar with the internal operations of the theater business.[98]

The majority of the Moscow press corps did not much care about any of that, however. The critics acknowledged the infamous challenges in staging native repertoire. They criticized the MPO for performing it without adequate polish (indeed, this was the tenor of many reviews throughout the 1896–97 season). But with the exception of Kashkin, they did not relent in pressuring it to stage more Russian operas. Instead, they seemed to be annoyed by the fact that valuable rehearsal time that should have been spent learning Russian repertoire was taken instead by foreign operas. This attitude is reflected, for instance, in Kruglikov's *Novosti Dnya* review of *La bohème,* in which he called this truly spectacularly staged opera "a real daughter" of the enterprise, as opposed to its "stepchildren," *Prince Igor* and *The Maid of Pskov.* "Would we see the same approach to the promised *The Oprichnik* and *Khovanshchina*?" he asked in conclusion.[99]

*The Oprichnik* was a disaster. Its premiere was announced for the current season; there were only two weeks of it left, so adequate rehearsal time was simply not available. Ready or not, the production had to run then, or be postponed until the fall, which surely would have attracted a storm of criticism. Interestingly, Kruglikov's main complaint was not that the opera was performed badly (a complaint which would have been justified), but that a Puccini opera was staged better than Tchaikovsky's:

> *The Oprichnik* was not lucky enough to become a favorite child of Mrs. Winter's enterprise: it is a stepchild of the company, just like *Igor* and *The Maid of Pskov*. Perhaps this is meant to emphasize that Tchaikovsky is closer to Rimsky-Korsakov and Borodin than to Puccini, but this is a confirmed fact anyway; it requires no evidence to support it.[100]

It is also notable that in his rhetorical zeal, Kruglikov managed to suppress any memory of his own reviews of *Prince Igor* and *The Maid of Pskov* just two months earlier. These reports hailed the great public success of both productions, supposedly "fully justified and well deserved" by their staging and performance.[101] Evidently, while the critics were not always satisfied with the quality and polish of the MPO's performances of the Russian repertoire, the ideological significance of these productions outweighed any objections as to their level of preparation. By mid-season, from around the time of *The Maid of Pskov*'s premiere in December 1896, the tone of the press reviews gradually began to change. At first barely perceptible, the shift was more pronounced by the opening of the 1897–98 season, even more so after the production of *Khovanshchina*, and fully apparent by the Christmas premiere of *Sadko*. Instead of hinting, pushing, or demanding Russian operas from the MPO, the press was now discussing Mamontov's "mission."

### THE MYTH OF MAMONTOV'S "MISSION"

Throughout this book, we have been paying close attention to the mission of the MPO as it was understood by Mamontov and his closest friends and associates. Below is the media's version of that mission as it was packaged and fed to the public in both capitals. As we shall see, the two mission statements are, to a large extent, incompatible. In their zeal to promote national music, the press effectively hijacked Mamontov's ideal of "serving art," and replaced it with its own cause, spelled out pithily by *Russkoe Slovo*: "to serve exclusively Russian music."[102] To summarize the critics' pitch, the company's sole goal was the cultivation of native music by staging Russian operas, either new ones or those previously neglected and little known to the public. Indeed, the "great, sacred cause" of propagandizing Russian works of art was allegedly adopted by the MPO's "enlightened leaders" from the very inception of the venture.[103] It "always" worked hard for Russian art and Russian composers, approached the production of their works with special care, and served as "the hotbed of Russian music," inspiring love for Russian composers and operas in society, and never betraying "its banner on which the memorable words *Native Art* are carved in golden script." Critics also emphasized the important educational and ennobling influence the company's "mission" had upon the public. They reminisced nostalgically about the crowds of thousands that gathered within the Solodovnikov walls for its Russian opera performances, and suggested that both the public, "long fed up with barbers and traviatas," and Mamontov's young troupe were thus steered "toward national musical self-awareness." *Novosti Sezona* even managed to fuse Mamontov's ideals with its own by describing "the new, disinterested cause of the individuals not officially named" as "the love of everything beautiful, and the enlightened desire to carve a worthy and deserved place for our national music."[104]

In response to the noble, nationalist mission that the MPO now supposedly had, the reviews of its performances were filled with exclamations like "glory and honor" and expressions of gratitude for its great service to Russian art, which history would never forget. Each Russian opera premiered or revived by the company was declared to have been extracted from oblivion, to which it was originally condemned by "our stale and backward musical institutions" (read: the Imperial Theaters) that should therefore answer to future generations for their crimes against art. In the hands of the Private Opera, of course, the rescued masterpieces "could not have wished for a better fate."[105] Meanwhile, the Bolshoi was continually accused of turning a deaf ear to the demands of the public and the press, and ridiculed for "the cult of [Trubetskoy's opera] *Melusina,* so valiantly and so unsuccessfully propagandized" from its stage.[106] As Kashkin put it, "without private initiative, Moscow would sink to the level of a distant province, where artistic news arrives late and mostly by accident." But since Mamontov "rose to the defense" of Russian opera, it had a chance not only to appear on the crown playbills, but even to "sneak out to foreign countries, so it might be possible one day to hear it in Berlin or Vienna."[107]

The more assured the Moscow critics became of the realization of their own prognoses, the more disappointment they voiced with the perceived MPO policy shift during the 1899–1900 season, which saw the revival of several foreign operas. A *Russkoe Slovo* columnist wrote:

> The turnaround in the direction of our Private Opera . . . is now completely defined. With their latest productions of *Les Huguenots, Lakmé,* and the projected revival of *Rigoletto,* the former defender of the interests of our national art has clearly stepped onto the path of ordinary associations, with their complete lack of any definite direction and complete dependency on the taste of the mass audience.[108]

The critics attributed the changes to Mamontov's forced absence from the company's helm that season (see n.102). However, while the ever unpopular (and Jewish) Meyerbeer was indeed news on the MPO stage, this was not the case with *Rigoletto* and particularly *Lakmé.*[109] Delibes' delicate opera, one of Mamontov's personal favorites, premiered in the fall of 1896 to glowing reviews. Yet, as his company's supposed nationalist cause became fully solidified, the foreign repertoire that previously received its share of attention from the press was routinely ignored, censured, or explained away. For example, as he chastised the Bolshoi Theater for staging *Hänsel und Gretel* and neglecting *Sadko,* Kashkin failed to mention that the MPO also had Humperdinck's opera in its repertoire; indeed, it gave its Moscow premiere. The company was criticized as being unfaithful to its motto for opening the 1897–98 season with *Faust,* instead of a Russian opera. *Novosti Sezona* actually refused to consider that performance its "true opening night," opting instead for the matinee of *A Life for the Tsar* the following day. Indeed, that newspaper made it a special point to rationalize any appearance of a foreign opera on Mamontov's stage. Excuses varied from lamentable yet unavoidable commercial compromises ("in the theater business, one must often stage not what is desirable or necessary, but what is expedient due to various external circumstances")[110] to the following puzzling commentary: "While non-Russian operas did appear, they were performed rarely, and represented mere episodic occurrences of foreign music, highlighting even better and more sharply the significance of Russian music. Between 3 October and 2 November, the Russian Private Opera gave thirty performances, twenty of them Russian operas and only ten foreign."[111]

Perhaps the most creative justification for the presence of foreign works in Mamontov's repertoire was offered by Vladimir Stasov, who suggested that while "S. I. Mamontov sometimes also presents foreign operas on his stage," he does so purely as an act of kindness to "the weakest and most backward" part of his audience that is still in the "initial stages of their education" in true, Russian music.[112] One can imagine, therefore, that the presence of Gluck's *Orfeo* on the company's playbill during its 1898 St. Petersburg tour would have been challenging to Stasov the nationalist on ideological, as well as aesthetic grounds—another reason he might have chosen conveniently to forget all about it when writing about Mamontov's work.

The Moscow critics, however, had no such luxury. When *Orfeo* first appeared on 30 November 1897, it was a spectacularly produced, significant premiere, with all proceeds from the opening night going to charity; it had to be reviewed. Yet the press was clearly confused: as Gruzinsky noted, "It is rather difficult to imagine the same operatic troupe performing Musorgsky's *Khovanshchina* and Gluck's *Orfeo;* there is an enormous chasm between the goals and objectives of the two operas."[113] The Moscow public's indifference to *Orfeo* seemed to have vindicated the critics, who ironically believed that it represented a betrayal of Mamontov's mission, as they understood it. Kashkin grumbled that the time wasted on the "ill-fated *Orfeo* caricature" would have been better spent rehearsing Rimsky-Korsakov's *May Night.*[114] Indeed, any foreign influence on the "hotbed of Russian music" was viewed as a dangerous precedent and discouraged. This was particularly true of guest tours by European stars, who tended to add insult to injury by singing their parts in foreign languages. Therefore, while "obliged to the directorate for the great aesthetic pleasure" provided by the fabulous Marie van Zandt—in the role of Lakmé, no less!—*Novosti Dnya* still insisted that "a Russian opera company must be independent" of foreign aid.[115]

It is clear that the increasingly unforgiving attitude demonstrated by the press toward the foreign presence on Mamontov's stage did not have aesthetic considerations at its core. The company was seen—and marketed to the public—not as an artistic venture, but rather, to quote *Novosti Sezona,* as "a purely ideological institution that pursues only the triumph of Russian art."[116] However justified was the crusade for public recognition of Musorgsky, Rimsky-Korsakov, Borodin, and other

Russian opera composers, the myth of the MPO as a "defender of our native art" created by the press had little to do with music. Instead, it had everything to do with politics. Unheard went the wise and lonely voice of Garteveld, who wrote in the conclusion of his *Russkoe Slovo* op-ed: "An opera theater is not a political or administrative institution, in which a certain 'face' should be clearly expressed, but rather an artistic institution that should primarily possess a 'beautiful face.' In other words, it should be placed above partisanship."[117]

Instead, the repertoire of Mamontov's enterprise was portrayed as a realization of the party line. Constructed by both critics and apologists, this piece of historical fiction quickly developed a life of its own. As a part of the Mamontov legend, it unfortunately penetrated not only public perception, but also scholarly literature, where it persists to this day. This stubborn myth is responsible, for example, for completely unsubstantiated claims made by several researchers about Mamontov's alleged concern about a non-Russian conductor's ability adequately to perform Russian operas.[118] Such concern was never voiced by Mamontov or his associates; indeed, it was never even advanced by their contemporary press. Instead, it was imposed as an afterthought by scholars who bought into the myth of the MPO as a staunch defender of "our native art." An in-depth look at Mamontov's approach to compiling repertoire, as reflected in his correspondence and realized in decision-making, reveals that myth to be in part true, in part the result of the critics' own campaign, and in part their wishful thinking.

## MAMONTOV'S REPERTOIRE POLICY

In his study of the Meiningen Theater, Osborne defined three major principles guiding that company's repertoire policy: political (plays that glorified the country and its rulers), stylistic (plays that supported the company's aesthetic agenda and showed the talents of its troupe to the best advantage), and commercial (plays most likely to sell tickets).[119] These categories may prove equally useful for analyzing Mamontov's approach to compiling a playbill, as his reasoning seems to have followed along similar lines. As we shall see, an opera could be selected for the quality of its score, its aesthetic message, the dramatic possibilities inherent in its plot, and/or an opportunity it provided to showcase the company's famed ensemble and the principles of a synthesis of the arts to which it aspired. Yet politics and market trends also factored strongly in the selection process. Indeed, political and commercial considerations often overlapped, due to the prevailing nationalism of a large number of opera-going Muscovites, the corresponding backlash against the Italians, and the public sentiments evoked by Russia's changing relationships with its European neighbors—Germany and France.

Even a superficial perusal of the MPO repertoire list reveals that the great majority of the works staged were recognized masterpieces of Russian and Western European music. The musical qualities of an opera undoubtedly played a role in its selection. Other factors proved at least as (if not more) important, however. For instance, *Orfeo* was evidently chosen first and foremost for the aesthetic message of eternal Hellenic beauty contained in its plot.[120] A significant attraction of the fairy tales, like *The Snow Maiden* and *Sadko,* as well as the historical pageants, such as *The Maid of Orleans* and the proposed *Les Huguenots,* would have been their inherent potential as stage spectacles that promoted the company's goal of a synthesis of the arts. But the most overwhelmingly important consideration proved to be the dramatic possibilities provided by the storyline. To illustrate, in a letter to Mamontov regarding the proposed staging of Cui's *Angelo,* Melnikov noted: "The drama presents a certain interest. Written following the strict rules of ancient dramas, it offers good material to the actors; all the roles are interesting." The musical setting is barely mentioned in the letter; evidently, directing opportunities offered by the libretto, and the "roles" it provided for the company's "actors" were what attracted Melnikov to the score. For another amusing yet characteristic example, in a letter that responded to Mamontov's new libretto for *1812* that he had just received, Melnikov spent four pages dissecting the plot, the roles, and the mises-en-scène; then he finally remembered to ask: "Who is composing the music?"[121]

Melnikov was writing to a sympathetic addressee: as we have already witnessed, Mamontov did tend on occasion to discount the quality of the musical setting as a factor in a new opera's stage success. On the other hand, when writing a libretto for a work that he would later produce, he aimed from the beginning to build the drama into the score. This way, the blending of acting and singing he required from his troupe would naturally result. A letter to Shkafer shows him practically salivating over the dramatic possibilities of an "evil" leitmotif in *The Necklace,* which would transform as it traveled through the opera, and which he demanded that Krotkov incorporate into his setting.[122] Meanwhile, when faced with staging a musically inferior composition (as *The Necklace* turned out to be), Mamontov's goal was to employ the power of drama (and when available, the distraction of visual effects) to counterbalance the weakness of the music. "If there are weak points in the opera," he wrote to his singers, "you must carry it with the *strength of acting* and *movement.*"[123]

Whenever possible, of course, Mamontov chose works that combined strong drama with good music. This quality may have particularly attracted him to Musorgsky's works, and helped him make peace with at least some aspects of the pressure to stage Kuchkist operas. Indeed, a *Novosti Dnya* reviewer of *Boris Godunov* stressed the fact that "by and large, this production was practically no longer an opera, from a typical point of view, but rather a drama, merely strengthened and deepened with the emotions evoked by the music."[124] One of the main attractions of the Kuchkist operas for Mamontov was their emphasis on musical declamation—the fusion of opera and drama that provided rich opportunities for his singing actors. Melnikov wrote:

> I understand *Angelo* as a true music drama; that is, it is the same drama we see at the Comédie Française, with every actor meticulously, clearly, and unhurriedly singing the poetry of his role. . . . Cui, just like Musorgsky in *Khovanshchina,* comes to an actor's rescue, and weaves the fabric of musical declamation; but still the declamation should be placed *above all else.*[125]

An opportunity to showcase the achievements of his "school" was clearly an important consideration for Mamontov in his repertoire choices. In fact, some in the press believed that a unique, synthesized approach to opera production practiced by his troupe and its particular attention to stage drama were the reasons that it could tackle many operas that were never successful elsewhere.[126] As Rozenov once pointed out in *Novosti Dnya,* typical operatic fare did not necessarily require "specially developed and trained singing actors," and stage directors with "encyclopedic knowledge." Russian historical operas, on the other hand, needed special expertise, without which they were performed "partly the Italian way, partly on gut instinct."[127] Musorgsky again presented a particular challenge: apart from purely technical, vocal know-how, performers required extensive knowledge of history and literature in order to penetrate the psychological complexity of their characters. No vocal prowess could redeem a weak actor in these roles, as Rozenov observed in another article:

> *Khovanshchina* does not require anything special from the voices of its performers, but it demands much from their artistic understanding. Perhaps that is the reason it has not yet appeared on crown stages. Routine manners of the Italian school, attention to fermatas on high notes, and showpiece arias on the proscenium lose their value here, while distorting the very essence of the opera beyond recognition. A Musorgsky opera demands a completely new, unheard-of level of intellectual and spiritual development from its performers.[128]

As we know, Mamontov's teaching methods were specifically designed to raise the level of "artistic understanding" in his troupe, as well as foster ensemble acting. A telling example of an opera chosen primarily to showcase the company's ensemble approach is the Russian premiere of Puccini's *La bohème*—a work staged despite the unanimous condemnation of the press, and made a success "despite our audience's aversion to lyrical operas."[129]

To say that Russian music critics took a dislike to *La bohème* would be an understatement. There literally was no media outlet in either Moscow or St. Petersburg that failed to publish a lengthy report on the new opera, and there was no review to be found that missed a chance to abuse Puccini's music. Kashkin, for example, confessed to having no inclination to discuss the work altogether "due to a feeling of shock, mixed in part with indignation, disgust, or something like that."[130] Lipaev of *Novosti Sezona* offered the following assessment of the score:

> The orchestral fabric is too thick, so the voices are barely heard; consumptive Mimi sings better than a healthy person; healthy painter Marseilles is virtually constantly slithering in the low register, like a sick man; the musical description of the crowd is artificial, affected, and reveals a kind of thoughtlessness—we confess, it was difficult to sit through the performance until the end.[131]

The complexity of the score and the composer's apparent disregard for the sacred rule of traditional Italian opera that privileged a coherent, easily comprehensible vocal line, clearly proved problematic to the press. It was incensed about the impressionist parallel triads and indignant about the use of polytonality in the depiction of the crowd in act 2. Puccini was accused of crossing the limits of the aesthetically possible, and—predictably—labeled a decadent. Only toward the end of the season, perhaps due to the fact that by that time it was selling out the house, did the critics warm somewhat to "this graceful and poetic opera."[132]

The press reviews of La bohème also contain notes on the opera's staging. It is described, uniformly (and according to Kashkin, "regret-tably") as beyond reproach; the ensemble as flawless. The reviews further include some analytical commentaries that may explain Mamontov's interest in this work. Kruglikov's review—in comparison with others only mildly disapproving—is particularly enlightening, due perhaps to its relative objectivity. The critic praised the engaging plot and excellent libretto of the opera as perhaps its most winning qualities. He also em-phasized Puccini's skill at constructing effective crowd scenes by divid-ing the chorus into small independent groups—the operatic equivalent of the Meiningen crowd that was a specialty of Mamontov's enterprise. Most importantly, however, Kruglikov noted that the composer of La bohème seemed to have a natural inclination to write for the stage:

> He senses the dramatic situations well, captures the emotions accurately, and hardly ever slows down the pace of dramatic action, which progresses in a lively fashion without being stuck in musical prolixity. Puccini is capable of expressing his ideas in a concise, laconic form, and his mu-sic, however weak on its own, somehow manages to be suitable to the moment.[133]

It was the opera's quality as a great stage drama that attracted Mamon-tov to it—the same quality that he found in Musorgsky and some other works from the Russian repertoire.

### RUSSIAN REPERTOIRE

The performance history of La bohème demonstrates that pressure from the press was not always a factor in Mamontov's repertoire choices. He selected operas—Russian or Western—that piqued his interest, and was perfectly willing to go against the grain and work on winning over his audience on the merits of a production. Furthermore, despite the press-constructed myth, his enterprise never intended to market itself as a "Russian" company. The production of *The Snow Maiden*, whatever critics believed, was not meant as a nationalist statement; it was an aesthetic manifesto of his troupe. However, in pushing the MPO to stage works from the Russian repertoire, the press had a very powerful ally, an ally Mamontov could not ignore—public opinion. The public voted with their wallets, and the vote was unanimous, according to the printed statistics. "Russian operas, *Rogneda* and *Prince Igor*, are selling out the house at the Solodovnikov Theater," reported *Russkoe Slovo*.[134] "Verdi's *Rigoletto* and *Un ballo in maschera* attracted a smaller audience to the Solodovnikov Theater than did the Russian repertory, a fact that very definitely characterizes the tastes and aspirations of the public," commented *Novosti Dnya*.[135] Three months into the company's opening season, several Moscow newspapers published the following announcement:

> It would be interesting to report some statistical data on the public attendance of Russian opera performances at the Solodovnikov Theater: *Rogneda* by [Alexander] Serov was given 10 times, attended by 19,800 people; Borodin's *Prince Igor*, 9 times, with 11,900 people; Rimsky-Korsakov's *The Maid of Pskov*, 6 times, with 12,700 in attendance. Altogether, these three operas were attended by 44,400 people. These numbers prove conclusively that the Muscovites are quite interested and attracted to Russian opera.[136]

The situation changed little during the following season. "*Khovanshchina* performances continue to sell out, despite frequent repetition and raised prices," wrote *Novosti Dnya*.[137] *Sadko*, as we have seen, sold out the Solodovnikov Theater fifteen times in less than two months. At the same time, according to *Russkoe Slovo*, by the third performance of Mamontov's beloved *Orfeo*, it "went on before the completely empty theater, clearly depressing the cast."[138]

The Moscow audience was a force to be reckoned with. It was increasingly clear that "native composers did best at the box office,"[139] and if the company were to carve a niche for itself in the Russian opera market and cultivate its own loyal following—in a word, to survive—it had to compromise. Aesthetic ideals had to be adjusted to the will of the public, and the nationalist card had to be played. From the beginning, this apparently caused great problems for Mamontov. Melnikov recalls him literally "running off to Paris," so as not to be present at the premiere of *Prince Igor*.[140] A brilliant businessman, Mamontov had to assess the situation realistically: as he once bitterly remarked, "we work here for the *Russian crowd,* and if we are to *survive and scrape the much-needed pennies together,* its peculiarities need to be taken into account."[141] Meanwhile, the artist in him undoubtedly found great joy and inspiration in staging masterpieces like *Sadko, The Maid of Pskov, Khovanshchina, Judith,* and *Boris Godunov.* He refused even to consider mediocre creations by Mikhail Ivanov and Nikolai Solovyov despite the fact that both composers were also syndicated critics of *Novoe Vremya* and *Peterburgskaya Gazeta* respectively, and their good will could have provided free publicity for the company. Instead, Mamontov's combative spirit attracted him to a different kind of free publicity—that generated by staging the still controversial Kuchkist repertoire, which placated the nationalist press, did wonders at the box office, and allowed him on occasion to smuggle in his own artistic agenda.

Nevertheless, over the years Mamontov became more and more concerned about the rising nationalist frenzy of his audience, and the increasingly nationalist image projected by the company itself as a result of complying with market demand. Melnikov made a similar observation in one of his letters from Paris, writing: "The Private Opera has now acquired a purely Russian physiognomy. If [we] begin producing foreign repertory now, it must be done with great care, for as you have seen for yourself, the audience does not respond as well to foreign repertoire as it does to Russian one."[142] The situation was aggravated by the fact that the 1898–99 season was to be Chaliapin's last with the company, so any projects conceived with the singer in mind would have to be implemented at that time. Since, as Melnikov pointed out in another letter, a large portion of the Russian operatic repertoire, from *A Life for the Tsar* on, was focused around a bass-baritone, rather than the more conventional tenor protagonist, the remaining Chaliapin projects would almost certainly be native works. Indeed, with ninety-four performances of local operas versus a mere nineteen of foreign ones, the company's third season proved to be its most "Russian" ever. It also proved its most successful one in monetary terms. Yet Mamontov apparently felt anxious and dissatisfied, addressing the issue in a much quoted and interpreted letter to César Cui, just prior to the company's second trip to St. Petersburg in the spring of 1899:

One can observe a significant fact: the audience clearly expresses its sympathies for Russian operas, and wants nothing to do with the foreign repertory except for *Faust* . . . A well-performed *Roméo et Juliette* or *Samson
et Dalila* barely fill half the theater. Last Sunday, even *A Life for the Tsar*
played to a full house. . . . At the Private Opera, Slavs, princes, boyars,
knights, boyarinas, peasants, and jesters never leave the stage. This is all
well and good, but sometimes it is suffocating. Is there no beauty in other
images, and in a more general, broader [artistic] sphere? Is it right to
pander, without question, to the tastes of the mass audience, and is it not
my duty as a leader of an artistic institution that has acquired some significance and power, in our multimillion-strong village named Moscow,
to push and promote other sounds and images, no less ennobling to the
soul? I did that. *Orfeo* is staged splendidly; it is being performed in a strict
style, but it is too naïve, so audiences got bored and are staying away; but
I still performed it, and made students listen to Gluck on mornings and
holidays. I wanted to produce *Alceste,* but didn't have the guts. I have not
touched Mozart yet. . . . The audience of the Private Opera (a good half of
it honest, sincere gray mass) obviously craves Russian epics; touching historical subjects; even *folk* operas. This is clear as the day. . . . Verstovsky's
wretched *Askold's Tomb* is selling out the house. It is pitiful and silly to
the point of a joke, but it succeeds through its sincerity, and the audience
is very happy. My God, this needs to be taken into account![143]

The letter to Cui offers us a glimpse into the heart of Mamontov's
internal conflict. His aesthetic principles were getting lost in the routine
of pleasing the public and the newspapers; he felt trapped in the web of
press-constructed mythology and his own publicity-seeking and good
intentions. The image of Mamontov revealed in this intense document
shatters his fictional portrayal as a nationalist. At the same time, the
letter is highly significant for understanding his aesthetic views and, as
such, cannot be ignored. This evidently presented a dilemma for both
Vera Rossikhina and Abram Gozenpud, the only Soviet-era musicologists who published in-depth studies of the MPO. Rossikhina opts not
to deal with the issue at all: in her book, she quotes sections of the letter
but omits all passages related to Mamontov's doubts, his desire to seek
beauty outside Russian opera, and his interest in foreign repertoire.[144]
Gozenpud does confront the problem in his study of Russian turn-of-
the-century opera theater, but attempts to explain it away. According to
the scholar, the letter reflected Mamontov's lack of comprehension of the
current social climate and the important task facing national operatic

art, as well as his fear of orienting the MPO's repertoire exclusively on historical subjects. On the other hand, Gozenpud continues, Mamontov understood the needs of his democratic audiences who thirsted for Russian opera. He eventually overcame his doubts—heroically, perhaps, as he went against his personal taste—and staged *Boris* instead of *Alceste*.[145] The researcher fails to mention, however, that the letter in question, although undated, is a response to Cui's missive of 23 January 1899;[146] its postscript indicates that it was written about a week before Lent. Thus, the letter represents Mamontov's musings at the conclusion of his company's most nationalist season. The consequences of the doubts expressed in it, therefore, should be sought not in the production of *Boris Godunov*, which occurred before the letter was written, but rather in the repertoire decisions made during the spring and summer of 1899 for the following, 1899–1900 season.

### THE REPERTOIRE CRISIS

By spring 1899, the MPO faced a repertoire crisis—another worry expressed in Mamontov's letter to Cui. The well of neglected native masterpieces had been drained. Promising young composers of both Moscow and St. Petersburg increasingly succumbed to the will of Mitrofan Belyaev, whose patronage, dispersed in the form of prizes, stipends, and publishing contracts, disproportionately privileged chamber and other instrumental music over opera, viewed as superfluous and outdated.[147] As a result, the only significant local composer still writing operas was Rimsky-Korsakov, who chaired Belyaev's Glinka Prize committee but himself was exempt from its patron's benevolent censorship. Rimsky-Korsakov's latest creation, *The Tsar's Bride*, was tentatively secured for the fall, but the MPO had no other Russian premieres scheduled for the upcoming season.

Mamontov decided to address the problem in two ways. To continue supplying the audience with new Russian repertoire, he commissioned two operas to be composed to his own libretti: the large-scale historical *War and Peace* clone *1812*, and the Greco-Roman myth-fantasy *The Necklace*. In retrospect, it seems ironic that the libretti were initially intended for, respectively, Rachmaninov and Rimsky-Korsakov; we wonder how Mamontov could have so egregiously misjudged these composers' talents. But there was clear logic to his choices. The most successful works of Rimsky-Korsakov to date were *The Snow Maiden* and *Sadko*, both fairy-tale fantasies in certain respects similar to *The Necklace*. And if we recall that the composer's operatic ventures immediately following *The Tsar's Bride* were the fairy *Tale of Tsar Saltan*, and then *Servilia*, set in ancient Rome, Mamontov's delusions suddenly appear much more insightful than they felt at first glance. As for Rachmaninov, during his Private Opera tenure his most successful work was a one-act opera, *Aleko*, whose style of poetic realism was not far removed from that required for *1812* (particularly its intimate "peace" scenes with the echoes of *May Night*). After both composers turned down the commissions, *1812* went to young Vasily Kalinnikov (1866–1901), a Kruglikov student raised on the ideals of the Kuchka, while *The Necklace* was entrusted to Krotkov, a one-time student of Brahms, whose compositional style, Mamontov hoped, would be suitable to a classical subject.

In addition to commissioning new Russian operas, Mamontov decided to turn Chaliapin's departure into an opportunity to restructure his company's repertoire policy, to provide for a better balance between local and foreign works. As early as spring 1898, according to Zabela's sarcastic comment to Rimsky-Korsakov, Mamontov was "digging up some ancient Italian operas and translating them into Russian, intent on refreshing our repertoire with them."[148] Melnikov's letters of 1898–99 are packed with comments on the newest creations of the French muse that would "lighten" the load of heavy Russian dramas. Mamontov's abandoned *Der Bärenhäuter* translation reveals his passing interest in contemporary German comic opera as well. Perhaps the most telling clue is a short announcement published in Moscow newspapers in April 1899, which offered the MPO's repertoire projections for the coming year.[149] The list included three foreign premieres: Wagner's *Die Walküre*, Offenbach's *Les contes d'Hoffmann*, and Otto Nicolai's *Die lustigen Weiber von Windsor. The Tsar's Bride*, still unconfirmed, was not mentioned; no other Russian operas were announced.

By the fall, the press began to comment on a sudden shift in the company's repertoire policy, but, as mentioned above, attributed it to Mamontov's absence. Yet it was likely that his continued influence behind the scenes steered the change of course. Indeed, this change should be perceived as neither sudden and unexpected, nor related solely to the frustration with the nationalist agenda expressed in Mamontov's correspondence. Throughout the company's existence he actively engaged with foreign repertoire, his choices again a reflection of both personal taste and sensitivity to market trends. As we shall see, the Muscovites' preferences in foreign fare were being shaped by a variety of factors. And while the city's boycott of Italian opera was a predictable result of the nationalist trend stoked by the press, its attitude toward other European operatic styles proved a rather unexpected consequence of a sharp change in the international policies of the Russian Empire in the mid- to late 1890s.

## THE DREADED ITALIANS AND THE FASHIONABLE FRENCH

In his memoirs published in a Riga daily *Segodnya,* seventy-year-old Pyotr Melnikov insisted on taking full credit for the "Russian direction" of the MPO, recalling that Mamontov infinitely preferred the Italian repertoire. However faulty his memory might have been at that point (and however tinged with wishful thinking), his mentor's passion for Italian opera is a historical fact. Between 1885 and 1892, Mamontov introduced Moscow to the cream of Italian operatic talent, featuring renowned stars such as Angelo Masini, Francesco Tamagno, and Antonio Cotogni on the playbills of his then Italian Private Opera.[150] Clearly, if his personal taste were the single decisive factor driving the repertoire policy, the high drama of Italian opera he loved would have been much better represented at his enterprise than it was.

Unfortunately, the press, campaigning for the national opera, chose to make the Italians its favorite straw man. *Novosti Sezona* declared Italian works tedious;[151] *Russkoe Slovo* protested any and all appearances of "operas from the worn-out Italian repertoire" on Mamontov's stage,[152] while *Novosti Dnya* suggested that *Un ballo in maschera* had no business being featured on the playbill of a "Russian" opera house.[153] Meanwhile, Kashkin thundered in *Russkie Vedomosti* that any operatic audience that preferred the repertoire with "the most vulgar plot and music imaginable" would demonstrate a deplorable lack of taste.[154] Even some foreign celebrities whose livelihood in the olden days depended on Verdi and Rossini joined the crusade against the fallen idols. For instance, in an interview with a Petersburg newspaper, the famous brothers de Reszke proclaimed: "Italian music has gone out of fashion; no one is interested in it; and there is no doubt that the music of our epoch is not Italian music."[155] The motivations for the juicy quote (unsurprisingly, it was picked up immediately by the Moscow press) might have been the desire partly to curry favor with the local critics and partly to promote the Wagnerian repertoire the brothers were in town to perform. Similarly, Russian anti-Italianism was in equal measure ideologically and commercially motivated. After all, the "barbers and traviatas" did more than lure audiences away from healthy nationalist values toward the cosmopolitan wasteland. Italian opera traditionally represented the main box-office competition to the native works touted by the critics.

As we have seen, the Moscow public—half bullied, half convinced by the media—flocked to Mamontov's Russian premieres. Meanwhile, with the single exception of *La bohème,* whose decadent appeal evidently made up for its dubious geographical provenance, Italian operas sold poorly. There was little choice but to limit the traditional Italian repertoire to a bare minimum, reserving it for van Zandt or another European guest star with enough clout to attract connoisseurs. Instead, Mamontov concentrated on exploring another foreign operatic style, less known in Russia and thus less of a target—late nineteenth-century French *opéra lyrique.*

Within a month of opening, the MPO playbill featured *Faust, Carmen, Mignon,* and *Samson et Dalila,* with *Lakmé* added on 5 November. While *Faust* and, to a lesser extent, *Lakmé* were known in the city through their Bolshoi Theater productions, the other three titles were relative newcomers. Even *Carmen,* incredibly popular in the provinces, was surprisingly never staged at the Bolshoi; like *Mignon* and *Samson,* it would occasionally be showcased by touring foreigners. Unless we count the unfortunate *Samson* experience at Unkovsky's company mentioned above, none of the three operas were ever performed in Moscow in Russian, by a Russian troupe.

Mamontov had big plans for the French repertoire. His knowledge of it was encyclopedic and his acquaintance with Parisian opera theaters intimate. He also had an enthusiastic ally in Melnikov, whose two-year Paris tenure made him a friend and devotee of Massenet, completely unknown in Russia at the time. In a letter dated 19 May 1898, Melnikov proposed that the MPO mount a Russian premiere of Massenet's *Thaïs,* taking it upon himself to guarantee the composer's attendance. To support his argument, he noted that the event would provide Mamontov with an occasion "to play once more on Franco-Russian sympathies."[156]

This mysterious remark referred to a rather unusual market situation Mamontov's company encountered at the start of its opening season. Finding itself at a low point in its tense relationship with Germany, Russia had recently signed an official friendship pact with France, a well-publicized event that enjoyed widespread popular support. As with any other mood of the Russian society, its sudden Francophilia was reflected in its artistic life. At the start of the 1896–97 theater season, Moscow newspapers reported packed houses at French drama and opera performances, accompanied by strong public displays of patriotism and French sympathies. This is an excerpt from a *Novosti Dnya* review dated early October 1896: "A display of Franco-Russian sympathies continues in our theaters. Every night during the shows, the public demands the performance of our anthem and *La Marseillaise,* which are being performed in all the theaters, accompanied by the enthusiastic ovations of audiences."[157] The Solodovnikov Theater was no exception: thus, at the premiere of *Carmen,* due to overwhelming public demand, the evening began with "the performance of the Russian anthem and *La Marseillaise,* both repeated three to four times, after which the opera itself was performed."[158] One could argue (and Melnikov's remark certainly points in that direction) that the appearance of a large number of French operas in the MPO's repertoire that fall was a shrewd response to the public demand occasioned by the signing of the Franco-Russian Alliance. On the other hand, it is also plausible that the public enthusiasm for all things French gave Mamontov an excuse to indulge his own interest in an operatic style whose lightness, grace, and elegance he admired, and even to teach his critics a little lesson in aesthetics.

Before Mamontov, the Moscow press tended to review French and Italian operas in more or less the same manner, making no distinctions between the two compositional styles. It was understandable: *opéra lyrique* was mostly known to the Muscovites via hastily assembled productions by Italian troupes, which themselves rarely differentiated between Verdi and Delibes.[159] After watching the MPO performances, critical comments on the quality of the prima's coloratura gradually gave way to observations of a different kind. Kruglikov's review of the premiere of *Mignon* is characteristic. After declaring the performance "smooth and polished, such as we rarely have the pleasure of seeing not only on a private, but also on a crown stage," he noted:

> The audience witnessed a harmonious, meticulous, and, most importantly, stylish rendition of a typically French opera in this best creation of Ambroise Thomas. A performer capable of penetrating its style must not only forget for a time all the devices used to realize a strong drama that lies at the foundation of a Verdi opera as well as a French opera *à grand spéctacle* (i.e., Meyerbeer and Halévy), but also develop a lighter, more intimate, so to speak, performing style, and a livelier manner of singing recitatives that should resemble real human speech as closely as possible, and should be as distant as possible from a singer's desire to show off the high notes.[160]

The critic concluded by praising "the conductor, Mr. Zelyonyi" for teaching the performers this characteristically French style of declamation. In reality, of course, their coach was Mamontov. Just as his appreciation of Italian opera stemmed from its high drama, not its high notes, he could not help but admire the great dramatic and ensemble possibilities of the French repertoire. He used operas like *Mignon* to train his singers in the craft of stage interaction, previously mastered only by spoken drama troupes—and only the best ones, such as the Meiningen Theater. The success of Mamontov's methodology is reflected in Kruglikov's review, in which the term "harmonious" refers specifically to ensemble strength.

## THE WAGNER WAR

If the French and Russian repertoires were the most fashionable commodities on the Russian theater market in the late 1890s, German opera, particularly Wagner's music dramas, was unquestionably the most controversial. While Wagnerian productions were increasingly being offered by touring German troupes and would soon find their way onto the Imperial stage, the critical response to them was nothing short of explosive. The disposition of the Wagner war reflects the ideological split within the Russian operatic press, divided into three main factions, to be labeled, for the purpose of this discussion, "conservative," "Kuchkist," and "modernist."

The "conservatives" preferred traditional Italian operatic forms (that is, "barbers and traviatas"), and eyed both Musorgsky and Wagner with suspicion. Characteristically, a conservative critic who wished to flatter Mamontov once compared his company to "our own Italian Opera."[161] The "Kuchkists" advocated the absolute primacy of Russian operas, primarily those by the New Russian School, and frequently took the familiar nationalist stand in their arguments. Stasov, for instance, contributed to the already elaborate Private Opera mythology by declaring that Mamontov's "dearest, most precious dream" was to turn the MPO into a specialized theater dedicated to national repertoire, with the goal of "performing all the operas from the Russian School that have so often been ignored and trampled into dirt by the crown theaters."[162] The third political faction of the operatic press were the "modernists," to whom the nationalist arguments of the Kuchkists were most frequently addressed. The modernists were distinguished by their Westernism, their Wagnerism, and their critique of the other two factions' equally old-fashioned idols. They were essentially absent in Moscow of the late 1890s, where they lacked a power base. In St. Petersburg, a small but aggressive modernist journalistic faction was led by Russia's single specialized music monthly, *Russkaya Muzykalnaya Gazeta,* founded in 1895.

Nikolai Findeizen and Evgeny Petrovsky, who ran *Russkaya Muzykalnaya Gazeta,* took upon themselves the responsibility for promoting Wagner's works, which were being decimated, in a rare show of unity, by both the Kuchkist and the conservative press. Even more than Puccini, Wagner was universally viewed in Russia as an unrepentant decadent. The conservatives dubbed his music "ultramodernist" and portrayed the "transcendental-philosophical" style of his mature operas as intellectually and emotionally barren, "its leitmotifs speaking naught to the heart."[163] A true star of the anti-Wagnerian campaign was César Cui, who from his syndicated *Novosti* pulpit proclaimed Wagner's theories unhealthy and his operas worthless and pretentious. His explanation for the public interest in them was the power of "Wagner's threatening name, which has hypnotized our music lovers and holds them in terror and slavish obedience,"[164] as well as the fear of the "so-called highest intelligentsia" that "some famous foreigner might suspect [them] of ignorance."[165] The radical Wagnerians responded with a scathing feuilleton by Evgeny Petrovsky, who claimed (correctly, perhaps) that the true motive for Cui's criticism was the professional jealousy of a "composer without an audience."[166]

As often happens, the very controversy around Wagner's name was attracting attention to his music, which was still, in the late 1890s, relatively unknown to Russia's mass audiences. Wagner was a hot commodity on the opera market, which undoubtedly contributed to Mamontov's interest in his works (see chapter 4). He knew how well controversy and scandal sold opera tickets. He probably also hoped that staging Wagner (or even a well-publicized intention of doing so) would dismantle the tired image of the MPO as the defender of native art in favor of a sharper, modernist guise.

As it turned out, instead of capitalizing on the Wagner war, his company was unexpectedly thrust into the thick of it the minute its unscheduled St. Petersburg tour began. On 22 February 1898, the very day Mamontov opened his Lent season at the Great Hall of the St. Petersburg Conservatory (formerly an opera theater), the illustrious "German Opera of Dr. Leve," featuring brothers Jean and Edouard de Reszke, the celebrated expatriate Félia Litvinne, and the esteemed conductor Hans Richter, inaugurated a series of Wagner performances literally across the street from the MPO, at the Mariinsky Theater. Both tours were highlights of the musical life in the Russian capital. Both troupes presented operas never before staged in the city. The rivalry between them was inevitable, and just as inevitable was the escalation of the Wagner war in the press, as both the Wagnerians and the anti-Wagnerians now had live, superior examples of their points of view readily available.

Everyone commented on the competition, and everyone saw it as primarily an ideological dispute that would inevitably result in a triumph for their side. This uncompromising partisanship may help explain why, in their MPO coverage, not a single St. Petersburg critic proposed a comparison, so obvious in retrospect, between Mamontov's synthetic conception of the operatic genre and Wagner's *Gesamtkunstwerk*. Cui and Stasov would certainly have never attempted it: these ardent nationalists considered any ideological affinity with Wagner an insult to Mamontov, whom they saw as an ally. Instead, both critics used their reviews of his tour to advance their aggressive anti-Wagnerian platform. For instance, in his comments on *Orfeo*, Cui offered a lengthy exposé on Gluck's "healthy" opera reform versus Wagner's "unhealthy" one.[167]

Stasov, in his polemics with Mikhail Ivanov of *Novoe Vremya* over the merits of *Sadko*, argued ferociously, and with a delicious disregard for logic, against any possibility of *Tannhäuser's* influence on the construction of the Market scene, which features a set of three songs by competing foreign traders.[168]

Smelling an opportunity for free publicity, Mamontov was delighted to fan the flames. Programming *Sadko*, *The Maid of Pskov*, and *Khovanshchina* against *Der fliegende Holländer*, *Lohengrin*, and *Die Walküre* was not enough. So, in a series of interviews that his lead singers, Feodor Chaliapin and Anton Sekar-Rozhansky, gave to the press in conjunction with the tour, both—supposedly independently and by their own volition—used a Wagnerian catchphrase, "music of the future" in reference to Rimsky-Korsakov and Musorgsky's approach to music drama. There is no concrete evidence to prove that Mamontov was behind it; yet these casual slips of the tongue are typical of the subtlety he often demonstrated in shaping public debate.

Predictably, the gamble succeeded, giving rise to a heated exchange in the press over the relative merits of the two "musics of the future." The conservatives begged to be excused from listening to either variety, as one critic wrote:

> They say that it brings us closer to the truth when one is speaking over the music rather than singing; this is possible. But what can I say: a pigeon house is closer to heaven than a *belle-étage*. But since it is not my destiny to touch the heavenly expanse with my essence, I would rather stay in a *belle-étage*, and won't climb up to a pigeon house. Music drama is basically a utopia anyway; so allow me to stick to the nicer, more pleasant forms of musical utopia.[169]

The Kuchkists, unsurprisingly, used nationalist arguments to further their cause against both the conservatives and the modernists. Typical is the following proclamation from Cui after the Petersburg stage premiere of *Khovanshchina*: "Glory and honor to the Moscow Russian Private Opera, which serves Russian art with such honesty and which brought us so much artistic pleasure last night, particularly after the foreign *Walküre*."[170] In his review of *Der fliegende Holländer*, Cui declared its music mediocre, traditional, and hardly deserving of "even the modest success that it has achieved here." He then concluded with yet another journalistic gem:

If a composer's name did not appear on playbills and was thus unknown to the listeners, how often the audience would be puzzled by a completely unexpected, unbelievable, fantastic result of such an innovation. Imagine, they could have disapproved of Wagner, and approved—of Musorgsky!![171]

The section of the audience specifically targeted by Cui's sarcasm was the so-called *tout Pétersburg*—the aristocratic and cultural (but not quite cultured, according to the critic) elite close to the Imperial Court; that is, the establishment, a long-standing foe of the Kuchka. Enraged with their preference, real or imagined, for the German troupe, he fumed:

Faced with a choice between a foreign and a Russian opera, between "the great Richard" (as [Alexander] Serov used to call Wagner) and some rejected local paper-stainer, between singing athletes and some Mr. Rozhansky, there could be no hesitation. *Tout Pétersburg* saw it as its duty to turn away from the national and bow to the foreign.[172]

Clearly, to Cui the Mamontov-Leve rivalry boiled down to the dichotomy of "Russian versus foreign." Yet Wagner's decadent creations apparently terrified some critics to such an extent that even foreign works on Mamontov's repertoire list scored unexpected support. Mostly this emanated from the conservatives: to them, even a Russian opera was preferable to Wagner; indeed, *any* opera was a blessing by comparison. In his review of *Orfeo,* a *Novoe Vremya* columnist wrote:

Despite the absence in its music of any drama or stage action, *Orfeo* offers a beautiful, serene impression, particularly after the ultramodern music of Wagner and his acolytes, willing and unwilling. . . . At the end of the performance, act 3 of *Faust* was given, and its music was again a breath of fresh air after everything we have heard this Lent.[173]

Meanwhile, there was a certain section of the press that preferred the Moscow troupe to the Wagnerians for yet another reason: to them, any opera would have been preferable to a German one. Portrayals of the competition as a Russian–German rivalry surfaced as early as the companies' opening nights, as we can discern in the following critique:

Music lovers were divided: while some, at the Mariinsky Theater, heard Wagner singing praises to German epic heroes in his *Lohengrin,* performed by the German troupe, others streamed to the neighboring former Bolshoi Theater where, for the first time on a Petersburg stage, a musical realization of the arch-Russian legend of the rich merchant Sadko was performed.[174]

Yet again, Mamontov and his troupe witnessed foreign policy intruding into matters of art. The political tension between Russia and Germany that occasioned the signing of the Franco-Russian Alliance appeared to have been resolved on a diplomatic level, and the Court, thanks particularly to the young empress Alexandra, born a German princess, was becoming quite Germanophile. The public did not forget, however, that only recently the country stood on the brink of war. As with the Francophilia of 1896, the anti-German sentiments of 1898 spread to opera theater. In some reviews of Wagner productions, these sentiments were hidden; in others, more openly displayed. For instance, a Petersburg correspondent of *Novosti Dnya* portrayed the atmosphere at the Wagner premieres as a defiant celebration of Germanness:

> Performances of the German Opera have attracted a choice audience: German dialect predominates, and the Petersburg children of the Vaterland—and legion is their name—feel like the true heroes of the day. Now at the Mariinsky Theater, the fanfares thunder, the brass roars, and Wagner's beloved leitmotifs resound with irritating fluidity on a daily basis, all to the glory of pure Wagnerism that has found many adepts here.[175]

With even more open hostility, another *Novosti Dnya* critic likened the arrival of the Wagnerian troupe to a foreign invasion, dropping satirical jibes on the court's Germanophilia and referring by name to the German commander whose untimely demise was widely believed to have saved Russia from catastrophe:

> The season has opened today on all fronts. I cannot remember ever having such a variety of entertainment as that expected this Lent. Particularly numerous are German entertainers: [they] are such a legion, it's terrifying. Had we not known that our relationship with the Germans was "most cordial," and that after the death of Moltke no new stratagems were being prepared, one could think that Landwehr battalions were infiltrating Russia disguised as opera singers, and that Wagnerian opera was the latest version of the good old Trojan horse.[176]

Whatever their particular problems with the Wagnerian troupe, the majority of St. Petersburg critics were delighted with the success of the MPO, which was apparently beating the Germans in their unexpected competition.[177] Quidam, the critic responsible for the Trojan horse essay, came up with a particularly colorful description of this battle, perhaps aided by the fact that his conservative tastes made him equally skeptical about both companies:

> The Wagnerian Germans sit gloomily on the riverbanks of the Fontanka and the Moika and cry: the competition between the two "musics of the future" is impossible, and one of them must perish. And at the time when "you cuckoo away, oh, dear cuckoo-bird" is thundering triumphantly from the Conservatory's Great Hall, a quiet and timid whisper is heard from the Mariinsky Theater, saying: "Ich bin so traurig, ja, ja, so traurig, ich wahr doch niemals so traurig wie heute. . . ."[178]

Newspapers reported with glee that the impresarios of the German troupe even petitioned the Russian government for taxation leniency, blaming the Muscovites for their financial woes. No one bothered to inquire whether the difficulties were real, or merely an excuse to exploit a loophole in the Russian tax code to increase profits. To find out, all the critics had to do was study the attendance figures for both theaters, which were regularly published in St. Petersburg dailies (see table 7.1).

As the table shows, Mamontov's troupe enjoyed a slight advantage over the Germans in terms of the number of tickets sold. It did succeed in turning the attention of the city's sophisticated audience away from the Wagnerian troupe, and thus, in some critics' view, won a certain moral victory. In purely monetary terms, however, while Mamontov did extremely well (enough to warrant a two-week extension of the tour), Leve's enterprise must have done substantially better. Ticket prices were never published, so a precise comparison cannot be made. However, critics did mention the MPO's affordable prices, as opposed to the Mariinsky's exorbitant subscription costs.

All this information was freely available; yet no member of the press chose to take advantage of it. No one cared: as usual, ideologically charged diatribes registered only those facts their authors wished to be acknowledged. The situation was not limited to St. Petersburg papers, or to the publicity that surrounded the 1898 tour. Indeed, the Wagner war offers us a glimpse into a larger picture of Mamontov's complex relationship with the press, a relationship that played a vital role in the fortunes of his company.

Table 7.1. Attendance Records of St. Petersburg Performances
by the Moscow Private Opera and Its Competition

Lent Season (NB: data on 16 Mar and part of 7 Mar not reported.)

| Moscow Private Opera Performance | Tickets Sold | Date | Wagnerian Troupe Performance | Tickets Sold |
|---|---|---|---|---|
| Sadko | 1,710 | 22 Feb | Lohengrin | 1,630 |
| The Maid of Pskov | 810 | 23 Feb | Holländer | 1,560 |
| Sadko | 760 | 24 Feb | Die Walküre | 1,620 |
| Khovanshchina | 780 | 25 Feb | Holländer | 1,420 |
| The Maid of Pskov | 810 | 26 Feb | no performance | — |
| Sadko | 1,300 | 27 Feb | Die Walküre | 1,620 |
| no performance | — | 28 Feb | Lohengrin | 1,140 |
| Rusalka | 1,900 | 2 Mar | Lohengrin | 1,750 |
| La bohème | 1,870 | 3 Mar | Die Meistersinger | 1,680 |
| May Night | 715 | 4 Mar | no performance | 1,420 |
| The Maid of Pskov | 810 | 26 Feb | no performance | — |
| Sadko | 1,900 | 5 Mar | Siegfried | 1,700 |
| The Maid of Pskov | 1,370 | 6 Mar | Holländer | 1,027 |
| The Oprichnik | 840 | 7 Mar | Tannhäuser | no info |
| no performance | — | 8 Mar | Siegfried | 1,100 |
| Faust | 1,830 | 15 Mar | Wagner highlights | 620 |
| The Snow Maiden | no info | 16 Mar | Cavalleria rusticana | no info |
| Sadko | 1,780 | 17 Mar | Tristan | 1,750 |
| Rusalka | 1,760 | 18 Mar | Faust | 1,470 |
| Rogneda | 1,730 | 19 Mar | Basso porto/ Die Walküre | 830 |
| The Snow Maiden | 860 | 20 Mar | Cricket/Meisters. | 730 |
| Khovanshchina | 380 | 21 Mar | Tristan | 1,000 |
| Orfeo/Samson | 598 | 22 Mar | Basso porto/ Die Walküre | 1,450 |
| Faust | 1,370 | 23 Mar | Huguenots | 1,235 |
| no performance | — | 24 Mar | Siegfried | 710 |
| Sadko | 1,900 | 25 Mar | Lohengrin | 1,610 |
| The Maid of Pskov | 770 | 26 Mar | Huguenots | 1,270 |
| Samson et Dalila | 538 | 27 Mar | no performance | — |
| **MPO total** | **26,631** | | **Wagner total** | **28,922** |

(continued on next page)

**Table 7.1. (*continued*) Attendance Records of St. Petersburg Performances by the Moscow Private Opera and Its Competition**

Easter Season (NB: data on April 10, 13–14, 18–19 not reported)

| Moscow Private Opera | | | Mariinsky Theater | |
| --- | --- | --- | --- | --- |
| Performance | Tickets Sold | Date | Performance | Tickets Sold |
| *Rusalka* | 1,070 | 8 Apr | *Ballet* | 1,750 |
| *Orfeo/Faust* | 810 | 9 Apr | *Roméo et Juliette* | 1,370 |
| *Sadko* | no info | 10 Apr | *Demon* | no info |
| *Mignon* | 940 | 11 Apr | no performance | — |
| *Orfeo/Life f. Tsar* | 1,420 | 12 Apr | *Mlada* | 1,050 |
| *Snow Maiden* | no info | 13 Apr | *Samson* | no info |
| *Faust* | no info | 14 Apr | *Ruslan* | no info |
| *Sadko* | 740 | 15 Apr | *Ballet* | 1,120 |
| *Mignon* | 895 | 16 Apr | *Aida* | 1,750 |
| *Rogneda* | 460 | 17 Apr | *Onegin* | 1,670 |
| *Hänsel/Orfeo* | no info | 18 Apr | no performance | — |
| *Sadko* | no info | 19 Apr | *Ballet* | no info |
| **MPO total** | **6,335** | | **Mariinsky total** | **8,710** |
| **MPO grand total** | **32,966** | | | |

Source: *Novosti i Birzhevaya Gazeta*, February–April 1898.

## MAMONTOV AND THE PRESS

Russian journalists wrote often and passionately about Mamontov's enterprise. As we have seen, not all reports were enthusiastic; in fact, some were largely negative. However, writings by both MPO supporters and detractors reveal that there was more at stake for their authors than the fate of a particular premiere. Indeed, more often than not, a review of a company production merely provided a pretext for initiating broader arguments on opera politics and aesthetics, in which the reviewer's agenda was promoted, accompanied by enthusiastic stone throwing at his opponents.

The ideological biases of the critics were reflected in everything they wrote about the troupe, from extended policy essays to dry unsigned notes in the daily chronicles. For example, while discussing ticket sales for the 1898 tour, the company's supporters would tout a sold-out performance but avoid commenting on a poorly attended one. Critics from the other camp did the opposite: kept quiet about a packed house and noted empty seats. Such willful blindness is particularly remarkable when the comments refer to the same evening, as we can observe in the press response to the premiere of *Khovanshchina*. In the conclusion to his report, the *Sankt-Peterburgskie Vedomosti* critic expressed "regret that our public does not attend these performances too well: the theater was largely empty."[179] Meanwhile, César Cui in his rave review of the same premiere (see above) recorded excellent opening-night attendance. In reality, the exact number of sold tickets for the *Khovanshchina* premiere totaled 780, which would have filled about half the theater.

This metaphor of a glass half-empty or half-full seems to imply that the critics who covered the MPO performances were divided into two groups—friends and foes. Gozenpud offers just such an appraisal, opposing "progressive" Stasov, Cui, and Findeizen to the "representatives of the reptile press," Ivanov, Solovyov, Baskin, and Burenin.[180] Let us put aside the questionable belief adopted by Soviet musicologists from biased Kuchkist critiques that a conservative viewpoint necessarily implies professional incompetence. What is particularly noteworthy is Gozenpud's unusual grouping of the company's "friends." Indeed, as we have seen, the conservatives, the Kuchkists, and the modernists all at one time or another expressed their support for Mamontov's company. Yet they expressed little support for each other or their respective agendas, as the Wagner war clearly reveals. Moreover, while the company's supposed "enemies" frequently backed its activities, its "friends" just as frequently criticized them. *Pace* Gozenpud, Russia's opera politics, particularly in St. Petersburg, was never two-dimensional. It was three-dimensional at the very least; and the MPO, right at the epicenter of the ideological storm, was very careful not to align itself directly with the conservatives, the Kuchkists, or the modernists, while taking full advantage of the publicity their charged coverage offered it.

The three factions' divergent approaches to the Russian repertoire staged by the MPO are also illustrative of the delicate balance Mamontov aimed to preserve with respect to the nationalist crusade. As we have seen, the Kuchkists hailed his repertoire policy when it aligned with their nationalist agenda, criticized or dismissed any deviation from the "correct path," and enthusiastically participated in the creation of the Private Opera myth. The conservatives, for their part, viewed Mamontov's playbill as radical due to the prominence of operas by Kuchkist composers, and the company's controversial anti-establishment stand. Yet, the modernists saw the very same playbill as essentially conservative, built as it was on twenty-year-old works that to them represented an old-fashioned, outdated set of values—the realist truth. Their position is elucidated in a review of the MPO's 1899 St. Petersburg tour published in Diaghilev's *Mir Iskusstva*, an increasingly influential voice of the modernist press. The critic, Andrei Koptyaev, wrote:

> The activities [of the MPO] are commonly labeled radical. But this is radicalism *faute de mieux*. Judge for yourself. Apart from the fact that this label is given to any enterprise that risks staging Russian operas, the national repertoire in itself is unthinkable without the operas of our leading innovators of the 1870s: Musorgsky, Borodin, and Rimsky-Korsakov. Without Kuchkist operas, there is nothing to stage: the audience cannot really be kept forever on a diet of Glinka, Dargomyzhsky, and Tchaikovsky. [However], the views on musical radicalism have considerably changed today, compared to the '70s, and we must admit that in many respects, the works of our innovators demonstrate touching conservatism.... The Moscow troupe has allowed the long-ignored operas of Rimsky-Korsakov, Borodin, and Musorgsky to see the light of day. Glory and honor to it for that; and it is not its fault that these works have already lost their *flavor of the moment,* and much in them—that which only responded to the combative mood of the '70s—is already foreign to us.[181]

The conflicting views of the MPO repertoire policy reflected in the press coverage again reveal Mamontov's company to be a product of its time—the time of an aesthetic shift on the Russian stage. Mamontov's market was poised at an aesthetic crossroads: three different concepts of an operatic genre—the traditional Italian model of middle-period Verdi, Kuchkist realism, and emerging modernism, represented to Mamontov's contemporaries by Wagner and Puccini—coexisted in the same market and competed for the attention of the same audience. The company's popular success, both in Moscow and St. Petersburg, was aided by its press-constructed status as a nationalist *cause célèbre*. Yet as we have seen, that success was secured, perhaps in equal measure, by clever marketing—Mamontov's uncanny ability to manipulate the press coverage to assure free publicity and to promote his own aesthetic agenda. Responding to the political and ideological realities of the time, he skillfully navigated Russia's treacherous operatic world to cater to his increasingly polarized audience during a time of both political and aesthetic instability.

# EIGHT

# Faces of the Enterprise

Throughout this book, it has become evident that Mamontov's Private Opera embodied a bewildering array of contradictions. Ideologically, realist trends, modernist innovations, radical nationalism, and operatic tradition battled each other in the minds of the troupe, its leaders, and its audiences. In each production, an elusive balance of visual spectacle, high drama, and flawless musical execution was a goal always striven for, yet rarely reached to every collaborator's satisfaction. Most crucially, the vision of what the MPO ultimately represented was always fluid: part temple of high art, part commercial market venture; part popular education initiative, dedicated to imparting the basics of stage aesthetics to the gray masses, and part teaching workshop committed to raising well-rounded, thoughtful, enlightened singing actors. Such a multivalent self-image could not help but impact the operational practices and internal power structure of Mamontov's company. Indeed, it led to the creation of a new type of "enterprise," recognized as distinctly different from its predecessors and most of its contemporaries, and a model for the modernist theater of the near future.

## MONEY MATTERS

After the government monopoly on theatrical productions was lifted in the early 1880s, Russia's theater world found itself populated by an ever greater variety of state and private companies with diverse and often confusing goals and repertories. To make sense of that increasingly diversified market, critics and audiences relied to a large extent on money matters: a company's ticket prices, its box office receipts, and its resulting overall financial health. Ticket prices offered the most public, easily available, and arguably the most telling piece of the money puzzle: they elucidated a company's target clientele and its self-representation as a "high art" theater for educated (and well-to-do) elite as opposed to a "people's theater" with the goal of entertaining the lower classes. As we shall see, MPO price policies proved resistant to such easy rich-versus-poor interpretations.

When the Solodovnikov Theater first opened its doors in September 1896, early critics found its ticket prices to be *obshchedostupnye*—literally, "affordable to all." The new company was immediately proclaimed to be an *obshchedostupnyi teatr*—a theater that survives on sales volume rather than production quality and critical success, but also serves the public by providing it with access to an otherwise unaffordable art form.[1] Indeed, sympathetic members of the press corps praised Mamontov's low-price policy as a vehicle of public education, aiming to spread cultural enlightenment and, of course, "love for Russian music" in layers of society normally unable to attend opera theater for financial reasons.[2] The critics had a point—cheap opera was rare. The Bolshoi Theater had few truly affordable gallery seats available, while most touring companies kept their prices high in order to survive. The advantage of the Solodovnikov was its large seating capacity (at ca. 2,200 seats, roughly comparable to the Bolshoi) that assured a reasonable financial return even though the gallery seats for evening performances started at twenty-three kopecks, and matinees cost half of these already "bare minimum" prices.

Having pigeonholed the MPO as a "people's theater," the press aimed to perpetuate that status by issuing dire warnings to the company's leaders not to forget their duty to art and to the public "in pursuit of profit."[3] The warnings fell on deaf ears, however: by the end of the calendar year, *Novosti Dnya* already complained about the fact that the company had "raised the prices for the new operas mid-season."[4] Indeed, according to extant financial records, from 1 January 1897 the complete MPO price scale was noticeably raised and kept at that level through the end of the following season.[5] In addition, during the company's stay at the Hermitage Theater in October 1897 and at the International Theater in

February 1898, the prices went up even more, occasioning complaints from the press.[6] Finally, during the 1898–99 season, even the most biased critics could not have possibly called the Solodovnikov Theater prices *obshchedostupnye*.

As we have seen, Mamontov shared, to an extent, the press belief in the MPO's mission of enlightenment. Affordable tickets could have provided a natural way of attracting to the Solodovnikov the widest possible audience that would benefit from his lessons in aesthetics. If so, why did Mamontov decide to raise the price scale three months into the opening season? I would argue that his reasoning had to do with the significance of ticket prices for the company's image. Prices were more than a financial issue, or an issue of access; they were an issue of prestige. The price scale at the Imperial Theaters was kept traditionally high, projecting the public face of a valuable, high-minded artistic institution that served a select group of sophisticated intellectuals. It was that mantle of artistic excellence that Mamontov intended to appropriate, not only with superior production quality and imaginative repertoire choices, but also with a comparable public image as projected through the price scale. While affordability brought popularity and, as many critics noted, higher financial returns from the sheer volume of sales, high prices brought the respect and approbation due an established, serious institution. They reflected an air of quality, stability, and tradition previously afforded exclusively to the Imperial stage. It was the image that the Moscow Private Opera aspired to achieve—at any cost.

Similar considerations likely prompted Mamontov to raise prices significantly for the company's second St. Petersburg tour in the spring of 1899. The increase that put the company's price scale virtually on par with the Mariinsky Theater, and that the local daily *Peterburgsky Listok* called "completely unjustified," could have been partially responsible for lower attendance compared to the first tour and, as a result, a rumored financial deficit.[7] On the other hand, according to the same daily, the tour attendance might have been affected by "audience apathy": after the action-packed spring of 1898, all Petersburg theaters reported lower attendance than the previous Lent season. Both the press and the audiences seemed bored: the Mariinsky was presenting its usual medley of guest stars in a typically eclectic repertoire; the aura of scandal surrounding the competition between the MPO and the Wagnerian troupe

**Table 8.1. Attendance Records of St. Petersburg Performances by the Moscow Private Opera and the Mariinsky Theater**

| Moscow Private Opera Performance | Tickets Sold | Date | Mariinsky Theater Performance | Tickets Sold |
|---|---|---|---|---|
| Boris Godunov | 930 | 7 Mar | Aida | 1,750 |
| Sadko | no info | 8 Mar | Lohengrin | no info |
| The Maid of Orleans | 930 | 9 Mar | no performance | — |
| Mozart and Salieri/ Orfeo | 785 | 10 Mar | Onegin | 1,040 |
| Faust | 1,420 | 11 Mar | no performance | 925 |
| The Maid of Orleans | 460 | 12 Mar | Faust | 1,210 |
| Rusalka | 720 | 13 Mar | no performance | — |
| Sadko | 1,120 | 14 Mar | Judith | 1,750 |
| Faust | 700 | 15 Mar | Faust | 1,125 |
| Aida | 660 | 16 Mar | no performance | — |
| Vera Sheloga/ The Maid of Pskov | 820 | 17 Mar | Judith | 640 |
| A Life for the Tsar | 760 | 18 Mar | Don Giovanni | 1,140 |
| Boris Godunov | 770 | 19 Mar | Judith | 617 |
| Aida | 220 | 20 Mar | no performance | — |
| Prince Igor | 1,150 | 21 Mar | Don Giovanni | 1,300 |
| Vera Sheloga/Orfeo | 210 | 22 Mar | Judith | 812 |
| Sadko | 830 | 23 Mar | Don Giovanni | 780 |
| Prince Igor | 1,270 | 25 Mar | Huguenots | 1,750 |
| Khovanshchina | 410 | 26 Mar | Don Giovanni | 735 |
| Faust | 1,270 | 28 Mar | Huguenots | 1,540 |
| Lakmé | 520 | 29 Mar | Onegin | 670 |
| Prince Igor | 740 | 30 Mar | no performance | — |
| Boris Godunov | 700 | 31 Mar | Tannhäuser | 890 |
| Mozart and Salieri/ La bohème | 470 | 2 Apr | Huguenots | 840 |
| Sadko | no info | 3 Apr | no performance | — |
| Rusalka | 860 | 4 Apr | Onegin | 940 |
| Scenes | 600 | 5 Apr | Tristan | 715 |
| A Life for the Tsar | 690 | 6 Apr | Onegin | 660 |
| Faust | 1,900 | 7 Apr | Tristan | 720 |
| Prince Igor | 430 | 8 Apr | no performance | — |
| Boris Godunov | 1,300 | 9 Apr | Tristan | 1,020 |
| **MPO total** | **23,685** | | **Mariinsky total** | **23,569** |

Source: *Novosti i Birzhevaya Gazeta*, March–April 1899; NB: data on 8 Mar and 3 Apr not reported.

was gone. Absent an ideological battle, no enterprising journalists were comparing the two companies' relative popularity. If such a comparison were to be made, however (see table 8.1), it would indicate that despite the slightly shorter tour, which would account for much of its reported 30 percent decline in attendance, Mamontov's troupe still beat—albeit just barely—its Imperial rival in the number of tickets they sold (23,685 vs. 23,569). With both prices and attendance records thus roughly comparable, Mamontov achieved a victory beyond profit and deficit: as in Moscow, so now in St. Petersburg his company claimed a place for itself in the public mind as the Imperial Theaters' equal.

Not that the issues of profit and deficit should be dismissed as peripheral. As we have seen, financial security—real or imagined—was an important part of the MPO's public image that Mamontov aimed to project in order for his aesthetic agenda to be taken seriously. After all, insolvency was the primary reason for the premature demise of his many predecessors in the extravagant and exorbitantly costly private opera business. The Moscow press corps was only too happy to point this out on a daily basis, as they tracked the company's reported expenditures during its first season. One *Novosti Dnya* article, after listing an enormous range of the company's expenses, including renting the hall (the actual cost of which was even higher than the newspaper projected), performers' wages, the cost of new productions, and so on, called for belt-tightening strategies. Specifically, it questioned the wisdom of keeping an expensive (and inferior) Italian ballet troupe in the city where, unlike in St. Petersburg, ballet was unpopular, and was cultivated at the Bolshoi "by tradition" and at the Private Opera "by delusion."[8] Evidently Mamontov agreed: by the following season, the Italians (except for their prima Iola Tornaghi, the future Mrs. Chaliapin) were sent home; separate ballets were no longer produced and all operatic dance scenes were performed by cheaper local performers.[9]

Another common fundraising tool available to Mamontov would have been the system of the so-called *benefisy* [benefits]—opera performances, part of the proceeds from which went to a star headliner popular with the public. The fans invariably flocked to their favorite's benefit, ensuring a full house, usually at raised prices. The benefits were a routine part of doing business at every Russian theater, from the Imperial stage to the tiniest private association. In fact, Zabela's correspondence with

Rimsky-Korsakov suggests that they were virtually a daily event at the MPO in the post-Mamontov era.[10] One could easily see, however, why the practice would have been abhorrent to him: with the rampant backstage drama it occasioned, it raised individual stars above their peers, to the detriment of the troupe's camaraderie and artistic ensemble. Thus, as the leader of the company, he sanctioned only two benefit performances: one in November 1897 for Elena Tsvetkova before her year-long leave of absence; another in February 1899 for Feodor Chaliapin at the end of his tenure. Both benefits were gestures of gratitude to the company's two brightest stars in consideration of their contributions, not a means of boosting the bottom line.

Meanwhile, Mamontov's company could have used the boost on more than one occasion. Beyond the necessary expenses, it was further financially burdened by a streak of annoying accidents and greater misfortunes that plagued it throughout its existence. For instance, apart from the fire that devastated the Solodovnikov Theater in early 1898, the ill-fated building was also the target of two separate lawsuits in three years. The lack of access to its regular stage resulted in shortened seasons and temporarily forced the troupe into smaller, less suitable, and more expensive buildings. The shorter seasons (particularly 1898–99, which started almost three months late) had an additional disadvantage: unlike a typical theatrical enterprise that hired its employees from the first through the last performance of a current season, Mamontov's company followed a long-term contract policy intended to be competitive with the practices of the Imperial stage. The stars of the company, Chaliapin and Sekar-Rozhansky, both had 3-year, 36-month contracts; other leading soloists signed 12-month or 24-month ones. Each contract ensured an employee a monthly salary, whether or not the theater was open for business. Singers of secondary roles were contracted from the opening to the closing day of the "official" season, regardless of whether the Solodovnikov opened on time. Chorus and orchestra were also employed seasonally, signed at half-pay until they were actually working. As a result, whenever a season started late (over ten weeks late in the fall of 1898) the whole troupe had to be paid out of pocket—a situation observed with some admiration by *Russkoe Slovo*.[11] The pocket, of course, was Mamontov's.

In his discussion of the company's financial fortunes, Gozenpud addressed the only official document ever published on the subject, which, as it happens, testifies to the Moscow Private Opera's solvency. Ironically, the document is indeed a testimony—a sworn statement by the company's administrator, Mrs. Claudia Winter, witness for the defense, read into the transcript of Mamontov's trial in June 1900. Confirming the deficit of 20,000 rubles resulting from the summer season at the 1896 Nizhny Novgorod Fair, Mrs. Winter stressed that the enterprise was now solvent and did not need Mamontov's financial support. Gozenpud questioned the veracity of the statement, which was aimed, after all, at dispelling accusations of squandering the shareholders' money on an opera company. "In reality," the scholar wrote, "the deficit stood not at 20,000 rubles but at an unaccountably larger sum; even afterward, Mamontov had to spend huge sums of money on the theater."[12] Gozenpud thus refused to entertain the possibility that the MPO ever became truly financially independent. Garafola agreed, although she did allow that the company was "conceived as a commercial venture."[13] Yet no Mamontov scholar has ever produced convincing evidence to resolve the issue one way or the other. The discussion below is based on the materials preserved at the Bakhrushin Museum.[14]

Due to the fact that only the first season's accounting records are available in full, with next to nothing preserved for the second and third seasons, this is what we can state with reasonable certainty about the MPO's finances. For the 1896–97 season, Mrs. Winter, the company's bookkeeper, reported an average per-performance return of 1,000 rubles, with average per-performance expenses equaling 1,394.90. By the end of the season, this discrepancy produced a deficit of just over 45,000 rubles.[15] Indeed, the records show that the deficit would have reached a staggering 65,000 rubles, were it not for Marie van Zandt's wildly successful guest tour, which produced 19,431.75 rubles of pure profit in five days. For its inaugural season, then, Gozenpud and Garafola's assertions about Mamontov's company are confirmed by documentary evidence.

Few financial records have been preserved for 1897–98; the newspapers at the end of the season reported, however, that were it not for the fire, the MPO would have undoubtedly shown a healthy profit. The successful St. Petersburg tour might have taken care of whatever the company had lost during the last winter month, but as mentioned above, no hard data is available.

Finally, the results of the third season are as follows. The press reported completely sold-out performances throughout the season, despite Chaliapin's frequent illnesses; under the new price scale (see above), per-performance return averaged 1,500 rubles. Even if average per-performance expenses remained at 1,394.90, the company would still show a profit of almost 12,000 rubles for the season. We can be certain, however, that the expenses must have gone down considerably: the 40,000-rubles/year ballet was gone, and the number of new productions stood at six, compared to twenty-five during the first season. As a result, the profit margin was undoubtedly higher, easily covering the late season opening (for which Mamontov's out-of-pocket expenses are recorded in Winter's book as 13,240 rubles) and whatever small deficit might have occurred during the spring St. Petersburg tour.

An in-depth analysis of all available evidence thus reveals that the fledgling company, despite the inevitable early setbacks, was at a minimum breaking even by its third year of operation and possibly even showing a profit. Financial independence for the MPO was unquestionably Mamontov's goal: with his own position rapidly deteriorating, he would not have been able to support it much longer. At the same time, while self-sufficiency was becoming a necessity, commercial success was never his main objective. A commercial enterprise was only one of the company's many faces. The idea of his venture turning a profit was attractive to Mamontov the railway tycoon; the vision of it as a temple of pure art appealed to his idealistic side. But to Mamontov the heart and soul of home theatricals, to Mamontov the member of the Sekretarev drama circle, who braved his father's wrath by almost becoming a professional opera singer—in a word, to Mamontov "the man of the theater" (as Stanislavsky called him)—the daily process of collective creativity was most likely the end in itself. Theater for its own sake was his highest goal, the *raison d'être* of his company's very existence—which leads us to an examination of yet another "face" of the enterprise, both public and private: the MPO as a studio theater.

## THE MOSCOW PRIVATE OPERA AS A STUDIO THEATER

"Studio theater" (sometimes also known as "laboratory theater") is a designation that has been applied to a wide range of experimental troupes that have proliferated around the world over the past century or so. The fascination with the concept parallels the rise in popularity of Stanislavsky's system of method acting developed in the confines of several Moscow Art Theater studios.[16] According to Stanislavsky, however, the term was coined by Vsevolod Meyerhold and first applied to the Povarskaya Studio, on whose official personnel roster their names, as well as the name of Savva Mamontov, are prominently displayed.[17]

As discussed in chapter 6, Mamontov's passion for the venture knew no bounds. The project was of tremendous importance for him—comparable to that of the journal *Mir Iskusstva* a few years earlier—and arguably held more significance for him than his sometimes excessively enthusiastic attention did for the Povarskaya's young troupe. As we have seen, Mamontov's support for Diaghilev's undertaking was based upon his recognition of *Mir Iskusstva*'s founding principle of collective creativity as a twin to the creative processes adopted by his own company. His involvement with the Povarskaya Studio was founded on a similar recognition of a shared creative principle; a desire, perhaps misguided, to resurrect the aspect of his now-defunct Private Opera that was most precious to him—not the glamor and success of a commercial enterprise, but the spirit of learning and experimentation of a studio theater.[18]

As a theatrical term, "studio" has been defined in two ways: as an experimental lab for advancing stagecraft, and as a training ground for theater personnel. For instance, in his renowned *Dictionnaire du Théâtre,* Patrice Pavis describes it as a laboratory theater "in which experiments on acting and staging are carried out with no concern for commercial profitability, and without even considering it essential to present a finished play to the general public."[19] Meanwhile, *International Dictionary of Theater Language* discusses the studio primarily as "a laboratory for the training of performers, directors, playwrights, designers, technicians etc.," although it goes on to acknowledge its predilection for "experiments and research."[20]

The concept of a teaching studio inherent in the latter definition readily applies to Mamontov's company: throughout this book, we have seen him train a generation of set designers, stage directors, and singing actors. More controversial is the idea of applying to the MPO the label "experimental laboratory," the most common definition of studio theater. This emphasis on experimentation was fundamental to Stanislavsky's understanding of the term when it was first applied to the Povarskaya Studio, as his memoir reveals:

> [Our ideas] demanded preparatory, laboratory work. There was no place for it at the theater with its daily performances, complex operations, and strictly parsed budget. For this, we needed a special kind of institution, which [Meyerhold] aptly dubbed a "theatrical studio." It is not a real theater, and not a school for beginners, but a laboratory for experiments by more or less accomplished artists.[21]

Yet although the term "studio" might have been new, Stanislavsky surely recognized its familiar premise. After all, he was a habitual observer of the MPO's daily life since its first "Italian" days back in 1885. Back then, two distinctly different approaches to new productions developed—likely due to the necessity of working with so many guest singers. The bulk of the star-driven repertoire was dealt with as in the "real" theater, with its daily performances and budget concerns. Yet certain productions—among others, *Rusalka, The Snow Maiden,* and *Die lustigen Weiber von Windsor*—were singled out for experimentation with mises-en-scène, set design, and stage movement. In these productions, much individual attention was given to acting by all members of the troupe, including the chorus; stage directing included a flexible mixture of techniques, combining collective creativity with the laws of director's theater.[22] Finally, the significance of the process—both the repertoire chosen and the manner in which it was staged—occasionally took precedence over the possibility of commercial success, as amply demonstrated by the sparsely attended performances of *The Stone Guest.* In other words, these few productions were approached in the manner of a studio theater.

In its second incarnation, Mamontov's troupe (now much larger and working in a much bigger building) demonstrated an admirable ability to integrate its commercial concerns with elements of a studio environment. Indeed, studio-like experimentation during production— individual coaching of singers, innovative approaches to movement, visual design, and stage directing techniques, daring, radical repertoire selections—underlay the box-office success of *Sadko, The Maid of Pskov, Khovanshchina, Boris Godunov, Judith,* and *The Maid of Orleans.* The studio approach is even more transparent, however, in Mamontov's so-called "failures." Rimsky-Korsakov's *Mozart and Salieri,* an intensely psychological chamber opera for two, with no arias to be found, proved commercially unsustainable, even with Chaliapin on the playbill; the cutting-edge operatic choreography of Gluck's *Orfeo,* a much more audience-friendly production, met with incomprehension, derision, and empty seats. Interestingly, the most common complaint about MPO productions throughout the company's existence—their "unfinished" quality, often believed to be the result of a "rush to print"—may also be viewed as an aspect of its studio environment; its unfortunate side effect, if you will, spilling over into the company's commercial universe. We have seen Mamontov's dislike of the drilling and polishing process necessary to complete a production; he would habitually dismiss his associates' concerns about the rough patches (as seen in Polenov's experience with *Orfeo*), or delegate the final stages of rehearsal to another. This nonchalant attitude reveals him to be a quintessential studio director, concerned with the process more than the product. As long as his artistic vision was made manifest, he almost did not care if anyone saw it or if it made any money for him. Granted, the businessman in him would not have permitted the MPO to become the glorious waste of effort that was the Povarskaya Studio, whose sparklingly innovative productions really were seen by no one at all. Yet the two companies had more in common than Meyerhold scholars—or Meyerhold himself, for that matter—might have realized. They were united by the shared premise of the laboratory theater, although in Mamontov's case his studio *avant le mot,* in yet another MPO contradiction, existed within and coexisted with a commercial enterprise.

During the early years of Mamontov's company, its studio-style productions were made possible by casting young Russian singers such as Nadezhda Salina, Tatyana Lyubatovich, and Anton Bedlevich. Relatively inexperienced, dedicated to the craft and their leader's vision, they personified the two interrelated aspects of the studio environment: the need for training and openness to experimentation. In the 1890s, a young singer with a fresh voice, adventurous spirit, willingness to stretch the limits of the profession, and few entrenched "performance traditions" became the MPO's ideal hire. The company's recruitment strategies were consciously based on identifying potential candidates among the senior classes of the Moscow and St. Petersburg conservatories, provincial singing schools, and even private studios. Once selected, the young recruits were auditioned (often informally, at Mamontov's house), then seduced and dazzled with a promise of a steady job, the opportunity to perform in the capital cities, personal attention, and most importantly, immediate access to leading roles.

That last provision would have been particularly tempting: fledgling opera singers were traditionally kept away from difficult and prestigious major parts. Instead, they were used as understudies to their elders or assigned cameo roles, with little onstage time and thus precious few opportunities to gain the kind of experience that would make them eligible for the leads in the future. This practice usually left most singers with two options: to move to a small provincial town where the employment standards were lower but the performance quality corresponded to those standards, or to resign themselves to walk-on roles and secondary parts for the rest of their careers. The MPO, then, offered them a unique third option: steady employment in a desirable location; a learning experience of singing the leads in a company with a high production quality; exposure to varied, innovative repertoire in a rare, artistic studio environment; and the extra bonus of Mamontov's tuition. As a result, the enterprise became a respected, publicly recognized graduate program, so to speak, for young vocalists with stage ambitions. *Novosti Dnya* called it "a school for Russian operatic forces that have grown considerably due to the development of music education in this country,"[23] while *Novosti Sezona* lauded "the new breed of opera performer" created by Mamontov's recruitment policy.[24] By its third season, the company had its pick of talented youngsters from across Russia, accepting into its troupe a tenor each from the musical colleges of Odessa and Tomsk, a baritone from the Kiev Conservatory, and the sopranos from those of St. Petersburg and Moscow.[25] Some new recruits fantasized about following in the footsteps of Chaliapin; all viewed employment at the MPO, if only for a year, as a smart career move. The graduates of Mamontov's studio were consistently winning lucrative contracts in the provincial theaters, the Imperial stage, and abroad; as Melnikov once proudly remarked, "These days it is not easy to compete with Private Opera alumni."[26]

Meanwhile, the administration of the Imperial Theaters paid increasingly close attention to the daily operations of its competitor in an attempt to explain and replicate the MPO's success. It was attributed to the very nature of Mamontov's company: smaller, bureaucratically unencumbered, and therefore flexible, with a young enthusiastic troupe performing in an unpretentious, intimate environment. We have already seen the Bolshoi begin to copy some of Mamontov's signature repertoire choices. In fall 1898, it attempted to copy the enterprise itself by creating the Novy [New] Theater, a smaller affiliate where alternating drama and opera performances were to be staged with the young forces of the Bolshoi and Maly theaters at reduced prices. The purpose of the Novy was to combine the flexibility and intimacy of a small company with the quality and unlimited resources of a crown institution, and therefore, to beat Mamontov at his own game. The plan failed: the new initiative was missing the two essential ingredients in Mamontov's recipe: a modern approach to staging and an innovative repertoire.

The opening of the Novy Theater coincided with major administrative changes at the Imperial Theaters; among them the appointment of Vladimir Telyakovsky as the manager of the Bolshoi. The savvy Telyakovsky was not involved in the creation of the Novy. He immediately recognized the futility of the new undertaking without a major shift in approach to repertoire, production techniques, and personnel. Instead of mimicking the MPO, he aimed to merge the best attributes of the two companies by thoroughly reforming the production practices at the Bolshoi while sparing no expense in hiring Mamontov's alumni—and not just the stars, Chaliapin and Korovin. After his appointment as the general manager of the Imperial Theater system in 1901, Telyakovsky stepped up the hiring process, and in 1906, in an ultimate gesture of acknowledgment, he invited Mamontov himself to become the chief stage director at the Bolshoi. His offer was declined. Pyotr Melnikov then took the position—according to the latter, upon Chaliapin's recommendation, but perhaps as a result of Telyakovsky's wish to have Mamontov-trained stage directors working for him. After all, Vasily Shkafer was hired to direct productions at the Novy in 1904; in 1907, he was already at the Mariinsky, staging the world premiere of Rimsky-Korsakov's latest masterpiece, *Legend of the Invisible City of Kitezh*. At their respective posts, both stage directors were working with familiar faces: singers and designers trained at Mamontov's studio. Shkafer had the additional—and evidently terrifying—pleasure of working alongside Meyerhold, the Mariinsky's chief stage director, then in the middle of creating his signature symbolist *Tristan und Isolde*.

Mamontov rejoiced in his former employees' infiltration of the enemy bastion: "Your place is at the Imperial Theaters," he once wrote to Shkafer.[27] After his trial and subsequent bankruptcy, his business empire was in tatters, and he was badly in need of a new project to embrace. Why then did he refuse Telyakovsky's flattering offer to get back to the theater life that he loved? The reason for Mamontov's decision had to do with the role he played within the Moscow Private Opera.

### STRUCTURE, HIERARCHY, AND ISSUES OF AUTHORITY

The image of Mamontov the philanthropist, millionaire patron of the arts, but not an artist, persists to this day. In a recent book, Murray Frame places him among a group of "merchant entrepreneurs who financed theatrical enterprises" such as the notorious conservative anti-Semite Alexei Suvorin (1867–1912), the owner of the Maly Drama Theater in St. Petersburg, or Mamontov's namesake Savva Morozov (1862–1905), a fellow tycoon, aspiring revolutionary, and the money bag behind Stanislavsky's Moscow Art Theater.[28] Throughout this book, we have observed a different Mamontov—the sculptor, the litterateur, the stage director, and the spiritual center of his company; the source of its creative energy, not merely its finances. This Mamontov was a theater man, passionately involved in every aspect of his company's operations, from voice coaching to the use of electricity. He commanded unprecedented respect as a teacher and mentor. Indeed, the theater itself, with its precarious amalgam of conflicting methods and approaches, such as the democracy of collective creativity and the hierarchy of director's theater, seems to have molded itself in the image of its creator, whose unique personality was an inherently controversial blend of autocrat and bohemian. Mamontov's greatest talent was that of organizer and coordinator, capable of bringing together diverse creative minds and making them work as a team, as he inspired and guided them toward the realization of the overall aesthetic goal he envisioned for each production. Nikolai Krotkov, a collaborator on two operas, *The Necklace* and *The Scarlet Rose*, once wrote to Mamontov: "I cherish your special ability to make me work as if taking dictation from you. You have many creative ideas, and you are able to present them in such a palpable way that what remains is only to transfer them to paper using correct symbols—notes in music, words in literature."[29]

Of course, taking Mamontov's "dictation" presupposed, together with the benefits of his inspiration and famously acute artistic judgment, allowing him a certain level of control over the end result of the creative process, a control Mamontov clearly cultivated, as his recruitment policies suggest. Had he accepted the job at the Bolshoi, working in this manner would no longer have been possible—very likely the reason for his refusal. As Gozenpud argues, Mamontov's inability "to submit to another's authority" might have prevented (aesthetic differences notwithstanding) the possibility of his collaboration with Stasov on the production of *Khovanshchina*. The researcher even attributes the departure of Rachmaninov from his post as an assistant conductor to the clash of creative wills,[30] a more controversial hypothesis that may or may not be sustainable.[31] Nevertheless, it is clear that Mamontov found it difficult to collaborate with any talented and strong-willed creative personality unless a certain division of labor was established between them—the path he chose in working with Melnikov, for instance. The internal organization of his enterprise could thus be understood as a concentric structure, with himself at the center, surrounded by a "committee" of select collaborators and advisors hand-picked for a particular production, and a larger group of students and colleagues comprising the outer layer. All levels of this structure were tightly connected and interrelated, and permeated both by centripetal forces carrying ideas from the outer circles to the center, and centrifugal ones spreading inspiration and energy from the center to the periphery.

Without ever holding an official title, Mamontov was what we today would call the artistic director of his company. The concept was unknown in turn-of-the-century Russia, so it is understandable that the contemporary press, while increasingly aware of Mamontov's connection to the MPO, did not immediately realize the extent of his involvement. Stasov was the first to forge a direct link between Mamontov's name and his company by openly referring to it as *mamontovsky teatr* [Mamontov's theater]. In Stasov's writings, Mamontov was portrayed as the company's creator and patron; he was also given full credit for establishing its repertoire policy, however partisan the critic's interpretation of it. Yet Mamontov's direct, personal contribution to the creative process remained unrecognized. Stasov credited him, for example, with involving his painter friends in designing sets for the company, but not with establishing the overall concept of those designs. In the critic's view, Mamontov's role with respect to his theater compared to those of Pavel Tretyakov and Mitrofan Belyaev, his fellow capitalists, who impacted the creation of topical Russian art, in painting and music respectively, through their targeted patronage. The unique nature of Mamontov's artistry thus appeared to have escaped Stasov, just as it escaped Murray Frame, who simply chose a different group of tycoons with which to align him.

The appearance of the term *mamontovskaya opera* [Mamontov's opera theater], coined a year after Stasov's essay by *Peterburgsky Listok*, does not prove that the press was now seeing more than financial support in Mamontov's involvement.[32] There are other hints, however, of the shift in critical perspective. For instance, in October 1899 *Novosti Dnya* published a satirical limerick that portrayed the stiff competition between Moscow's opera theaters during the 1899–1900 season as a horse race. Titled "Theatrical Races," the poem opened with a humorous portrait of the Bolshoi that, with all due pomp and circumstance, declared itself big (i.e., "bolshoi"). Yet size and grand traditions were proclaimed to be useless to what was essentially a "department of music" (in this case, a government bureaucracy). Nevertheless, the Bolshoi was considered the favorite to win the race due to the recently acquired thoroughbred "Chaliapin, bred in the stables of S. I. Mamontov."[33] The author thus gave Mamontov full credit for discovering the great singer and molding his talent, joining a widespread consensus within the operatic community. Mamontov's separation from the MPO in the wake of his arrest made his true position within the company even more evident to the press. In his review of the troupe's "unsupervised" revival of *Lakmé* in November 1899, *Novosti Dnya* columnist Evgeny Rozenov made the following observation: "Overall, one must note that the number of artistic blunders at the Private Opera has increased considerably since it lost its talented leader."[34] In this short sentence, without his name even being mentioned, Mamontov's role as artistic director of the MPO was thus publicly acknowledged for the first time.

Rozenov's statement is particularly fascinating since it reveals his own belated enlightenment on the subject of Mamontov's involvement. In an extended policy essay published at the start of the 1897–98 season, the critic praised "an experienced, thinking, and sensitive leader" whose recent addition to the troupe was to "breathe fresh power" into it.[35] Since Mamontov was at the head of the company from the beginning, the critic evidently meant Semyon Kruglikov—musician, critic, and Rozenov's predecessor at *Novosti Dnya,* who left his position as a regular columnist in order to join the MPO with the fancy title *rukovoditel khudozhestvennoi chasti,* literally translated as a "leader of the artistic aspect," that is, artistic director. In reality, according to his correspondence with Mamontov, Kruglikov viewed his role primarily as repertoire advisor: his knowledge of music being weaker than that of the visual arts, Mamontov must have wanted an experienced musician on his staff. Kruglikov also participated in contract negotiations with singers and conductors, hired chorus and orchestra, and accomplished similar tasks that, while administrative in nature, required auditions and artistic judgment. The two men shared a passionate interest in the artistic mission and success of the company: as Kruglikov once put it, "you and I share a lover, but we do not seem to fight over her."[36] Their collaboration was facilitated by having much in common in their aesthetic views, including Kruglikov's unwillingness, despite his Kuchkist ties, to surrender the MPO to the nationalist cause. He wrote:

> I see the objectives of *Russian Private Opera* broadly, and not at all from the *kvas* [i.e., nationalist] angle. Russian art should remain first for our mutual lover, but particularly to serve it well and sensibly, she must serve art *as a whole,* keenly listening to all its currents in the sense of trends, epochs, and nationalities, and capably separating the talented from the mediocre.[37]

Despite Kruglikov's importance to the company, however, it was Mamontov's opinion that determined the final course of action. Before making a decision, he frequently chose to listen to other advisors, even on the matters Kruglikov viewed as his responsibility, complaining of being slighted: "I felt many times during the season that you were not always pleased with me, especially when, in some musical questions, you found it more convenient to confide in someone else rather than in me. It was very painful to me."[38] Clearly, it was not Kruglikov but Mamontov who was in fact the artistic director of the MPO. He delegated some responsibilities to Kruglikov, but the latter was not essential to daily operations. It is possible that the primary reason Kruglikov was invited to join the team were his connections—in the press as a music critic, in the artistic circles of Moscow through his work for the Philharmonic Society, and, most importantly, to his former teacher, Rimsky-Korsakov. The wisdom of Mamontov's choice was revealed almost immediately, after Kruglikov had successfully lobbied the distrustful composer to secure the MPO's greatest coup to date—the production rights for *Sadko*.

As a leader of an opera theater that prided itself on the originality of its repertoire, and as a businessman with a keen understanding of the rules of publicity, Mamontov valued and cultivated connections to contemporary opera composers, both Russian and foreign. He knew Puccini, encouraged Melnikov's friendship with Massenet, and advised Shkafer on how best to capitalize on Saint-Saëns's impending visit to Moscow. Among Russian composers, Mamontov's most important collaborator was, of course, Rimsky-Korsakov: nine of his operas were staged at his company, six of them world premieres and five written expressly for the theater. In a sense, Rimsky-Korsakov's music held the same iconic, defining place at the MPO that Stravinsky's did at the Ballets Russes.

It is unquestionable that Mamontov realized Rimsky-Korsakov's significance as Russia's greatest living composer, respected his opinion, and appreciated his special relationship with his enterprise. After all, the composer's continued good will was vital to the company's prestige, as well as ensuring its financial survival. Nevertheless, the relationship between Mamontov and Rimsky-Korsakov suffered whenever Mamontov felt that the composer was beginning to usurp his authority as the producer of his operas, the creator of their staged versions. A complete breakdown in their collaboration occurred in the spring of 1899 over *The Tsar's Bride*. Prompted by Zabela, Rimsky-Korsakov wrote Mamontov a letter in which he outlined a set of conditions for the production, including casting, an issue vital to Mamontov's own artistic vision. The composer went as far as threatening to revoke the opera's production rights in rehearsal should his conditions not be met.[39] Mamontov was not amused by the ultimatum. Typically a prompt, polite, and prolific correspondent, he refused to answer the letter, thus quietly making his position known. Rimsky-Korsakov might not have changed his mind, but he clearly backed down, writing to Zabela:

> You are writing that [Mamontov] is unhappy with me and says that he has had enough of courting me; it's time for me to court him. But the thing is, I really don't ask for any courting. . . . And as for myself, I don't plan to

court him either, and if I—naively, perhaps—occasionally imposed myself on him, wishing to look after the production of my own pieces and help him—that is in the past, and will not happen again. . . . Anyway, it seems to me that the issue of courting is absolutely pointless. Nobody should court anyone. If composers didn't write operas, entrepreneurs would have nothing to produce; and if there were no operatic stages, there would be no need for composers to write operas. And operas should be staged the best way possible, and the author is the best judge and the best advisor even to the best stage director in Russia.[40]

According to Gozenpud, it was Mamontov's synthesized approach to opera production that served as the basis for his conflict with the composer, who believed in the absolute dominance of the musical aspect.[41] Indeed, as we have witnessed, the two rarely saw eye to eye on matters of stage aesthetics. Rimsky-Korsakov was either oblivious to or unconcerned with many of Mamontov's goals, as is evident in his off-hand dismissal of the significance of *Orfeo*.[42] Still, whatever their aesthetic differences were, it was clearly the issue of authority that separated them the most. While Rimsky-Korsakov believed the composer to be "the best judge" in all matters related to the production of his operas, Mamontov asserted and guarded his own authority as the company's artistic director, his own creative ownership of the works he staged, and he refused to relinquish these to anyone, even to the author. As the story of his conflict with the composer makes clear, he was willing to risk everything—including alienating his company's most important asset— in order to safeguard his creative autonomy. When *The Tsar's Bride* was finally staged, the only concession Rimsky-Korsakov received was the one Mamontov was willing to grant him from the beginning—Nadezhda Zabela singing the title role. As a result, a prolonged chill ensued in the relationship between the composer and his director, a fact responsible for a rather unflattering characterization of Mamontov in the *Chronicle of My Musical Life*.[43]

Fifteen years later, the leader of another theatrical venture would face a similar conflict regarding the staging of a Rimsky-Korsakov opera. This leader, of course, would be Sergei Diaghilev, and the conflict would revolve around the daringly unauthentic 1914 Paris production of *Le Coq d'Or*. Nadezhda Rimsky-Korsakov, the composer's widow, was incensed by what she called Diaghilev's "mutilation" of the opera, and even publicly threatened legal action.[44] Diaghilev was undeterred. The staging of *Le Coq d'Or* was in fact the second time his artistic ideas had clashed with Mrs. Rimsky-Korsakov's vision of her late husband's legacy. The first such clash occurred in 1910 over *Schéhérazade,* a ballet staged using a heavily edited score, with the composer's original program abandoned for a racier harem extravaganza. In an open letter published in a St. Petersburg daily *Rech* that responded to Mrs. Rimsky-Korsakov's attack on that production, Diaghilev defended his position against the accusations of "immorality" and "disrespect." He argued: "Defending the rights of [the authors] should not mean protesting against any artistic phenomena connected with their names, when these phenomena could only be faulted for the novelty of their idea and the boldness of its execution."[45] Like Mamontov before him, Diaghilev viewed the principle of collaborative creativity in very practical terms, as benefiting from the diverse talents of team members, but possible only under the firm leadership of an artistic director. As such, he was determined to protect his right to conceptualize a stage production in his own way, irrespective of authorial intent and the wishes of the composer's family. The comparison made here is not accidental. As I will argue below, Diaghilev's attitude stemmed directly from his acquaintance with and admiration for Mamontov's methods of organizing his enterprise, his marketing strategies, and his role as the company's artistic director.

## MAMONTOV AND DIAGHILEV REVISITED

Diaghilev's correspondence provides little insight into Savva Mamontov's role in shaping his early career. He mentioned him sporadically in his letters throughout 1898–99, and after Mamontov's sponsorship of *Mir Iskusstva* ended in late 1899, not at all. Diaghilev never wrote a memoir in which he would, like Chaliapin, Salina, and Shkafer, publicly acknowledge his debt to his mentor. One could argue, therefore, that Diaghilev's relationship with Mamontov could have been purely businesslike, just as with many other financial backers Diaghilev encountered during his career, and that the correspondences in their aesthetic views, while inspiring Mamontov to help Diaghilev, meant little to the latter. Lynn Garafola disagrees with this hypothesis, pointing to the memoirs of Diaghilev's close friend of that period, Walter Nouvel, dictated to Arnold Haskell. According to Nouvel, the young Diaghilev was "full of admiration for Mamontoff."[46] Nouvel's recollection, apart from being the only direct eyewitness report on the subject, is noteworthy for another reason: as the head of *Mir Iskusstva*'s music division, he was responsible for the coverage of the MPO's activities and thus must have had more occasions than anyone to discuss the matter with Diaghilev, his editor-in-chief. Garafola suggests that meeting Mamontov marked a turning point in Diaghilev's career, setting it firmly on a course of entrepreneurship. She writes:

> Mamontov turned the dilettante of art into a builder of artistic empires. [He] opened the eyes of the Westward-gazing Petersburger to the artistic riches of Moscow; introduced him to many of the painters who would figure in his activities during the next fifteen years; instilled in him a regard for collaborative relationships; steered him, in fact, toward the theater.[47]

In light of the discussion undertaken throughout this book, it is hard to disagree with Garafola's statement. However, the scholar never specified the causes and methods responsible for the remarkable transformation she described. Clearly, a few brief meetings and a hefty check would not have been able to accomplish it. I believe that the convergence between them was facilitated by Mamontov appearing in Diaghilev's life at exactly the right time, a moment filled with bitterness and frustration over the direction of his artistic endeavors and the attitude of his closest friends.

In a letter from Paris in the spring of 1897, Alexandre Benois harshly criticized the results of twenty-five-year-old Diaghilev's first attempt at organizing an art exhibit. In response, Diaghilev wrote:

> I am aware that my nature and my activities (if they could be called that), Lord knows, are not that profound; I do not possess a philosopher's nature, and am little inclined to that all-pervading atmosphere of skepticism. But the only thing I value and love in the people around me, *c'est quand on me prend au sérieux*, and that I cannot find in those precious few to whom my soul is drawn the most.[48]

A thirst to prove himself and to be taken seriously was foremost on Diaghilev's mind during the year he met Mamontov. By this time, his aspirations as a composer had been thwarted by Rimsky-Korsakov's uncompromising criticism.[49] His lack of painterly talents made him feel inferior to his artist friends Benois, Eugene Lanceray, Léon Bakst, and

Konstantin Somov, while their condescending attitudes caused his self-esteem to sink even lower. With the preparations for the Mir Iskusstva exhibition and the journal well underway, Diaghilev still felt that he was not doing anything artistically worthwhile. He saw himself not as a writer but as a bookseller, so to speak; not as a star but, in his own words, merely "an accompanist," forced to swallow his pride as he acceded to the demands of real artists.[50] Diaghilev's attempts to organize a new society of young artists that would have sponsored the 1898 Mir Iskusstva exhibition were unsuccessful: the painters refused to take any financial risk, suggesting instead that he bankroll the event out of his own pocket. Diaghilev was furious, writing to Benois: "No one has breadth and nobility of feeling. Everyone mistakes his wallet for his artistic principles."[51]

It was at that moment that Diaghilev met Mamontov. Not only did Mamontov share many of his aesthetic views, he was justifiably renowned for habitually placing his artistic principles above his financial interests. But perhaps Mamontov's position within his opera company would have intrigued Diaghilev the most; it certainly seems to have had the most lasting influence on him. Mamontov's role as the artistic director of the MPO was an example of what Diaghilev wanted to become. Without being a narrow specialist in any branch of the staged art, Mamontov was sufficiently well-rounded and authoritative to be able to conceptualize the complete artwork of an operatic production, and then to assemble a committee of specialists to implement it. He was more than an impresario; he was, in his own field, an artist—a role ideally suited to Diaghilev's own combination of talents. This was the position that he, from that moment on, must have aspired to achieve within his own circle.

During his frequent visits to Moscow in the fall of 1897 (see chapter 4), Diaghilev had ample opportunity to observe the main organizational principles and daily operating methodology of the MPO. Among several pieces of evidence documenting his presence at the theater, there is witness testimony of a young mezzo-soprano, Varvara Strakhova, who had just been accepted into Mamontov's troupe and was hard at work on her first leading role—Marfa in *Khovanshchina* (plate 22). In her memoirs, Strakhova described the structure of the company as concentric (similar to the model discussed above), writing: "At the center [of the circle] stood S. I. Mamontov, who was surrounded by outstanding people of art, including Polenov, V. Serov, M. Vrubel, S. Kruglikov; sometimes we would see Antokolsky, Pavel Trubetskoy, Diaghilev, K. Korovin, Rimsky-Korsakov, Glazunov, Rachmaninov, and Cui."[52] One should of course make allowances for the passage of time and Strakhova's later familiarity with Diaghilev's name (after emigrating in 1917, she settled in Paris). Nevertheless, it is enlightening to see that his name is listed next to those of Korovin and Rachmaninov, both of whom in the fall of 1897 were Mamontov's closest associates and full-time employees. Strakhova's memoirs indicate that, during his visits to Moscow that fall and possibly later, Diaghilev took full advantage of Mamontov's generous open-door policy by frequently and routinely attending the company's performances and rehearsals. Overall, the evidence suggests that Diaghilev must already have been familiar with the MPO's internal structure and management principles by the time of its 1898 Petersburg tour, during which Mamontov became the official co-publisher of *Mir Iskusstva*.

Earlier in this book, we touched upon the unusual circumstances of Mamontov's decision to sponsor Diaghilev's journal, and the aesthetic, rather than purely philanthropic, foundation for this decision. It is interesting to note that the contemporary press apparently viewed their collaboration in a similar light, as evident from a clever *Novosti Dnya* feuilleton that satirized a stereotypical Moscow capitalist wasting his millions on worthless projects undertaken by unscrupulous St. Petersburg entrepreneurs. Despite the essay's sardonic tone, the MPO and *Mir Iskusstva* were viewed by its author as exceptions from the described tendency; both were presented as serious institutions based on similarly noncommercial principles that left him at a loss.[53] It is unsurprising that the unique connection between Mamontov and Diaghilev, while attracting the attention of both critics and scholars, has never been adequately explained. Even Diaghilev's closest friends, including his self-proclaimed mentor, Alexandre Benois, had difficulty comprehending the true nature of his relationship with Mamontov.

In his published articles and memoirs, Benois discussed Mamontov's achievements very little. He compared the creation of the Moscow Private Opera, along with the Moscow Art Theater, to his own Pickwick Club on the Neva (an idea also explored by Garafola), but offered no assessment of its value.[54] He acknowledged attending the 1898 St. Petersburg tour, but discussed only his impressions of Chaliapin and the designers.[55] He appreciated the role of the enterprise in the development of modernist theater design, but attributed the concept of a unified visual impression to Korovin alone, while avoiding the issue of Mamontov's role within the company.[56] Furthermore, in his monumental *Istoriya russkoi zhivopisi v XIX veke* [*History of the Russian Painting in the 19th Century*], Benois described Mamontov as "an artist by nature and inclination who, in a whirlwind of events and projects, never managed to create anything," and assigned him a venerable but passive role as "the Tretyakov" of modernist art.[57] Mamontov's artistic contribution to the MPO, therefore, passed either misunderstood or unacknowledged by Benois the art critic. Moreover, whenever Mamontov is mentioned in Benois' private correspondence or memoirs, the overall impression created is that of the wariness and dislike of a refined Petersburg esthete for a wild, unpredictable Muscovite invading his pure and orderly artistic world. In Benois' recollections about the early days of the Mir Iskusstva group, the appearance of Mamontov is depicted as follows: "We could not stop talking about the journal during the whole period of preparation for the exhibition, and particularly after the opening. Apart from [Princess] M[aria] K[lavdievna] Tenisheva, who thirsted for noble glory, the famous Moscow Maecenas, uncontrollable 'mad dog' Savva Mamontov, had now appeared on our horizon."[58] Apparently, Princess Tenisheva's thirst for glory did not worry Benois at that point: he considered her under his artistic influence, her desire for the spotlight easily manipulated. He was decidedly apprehensive, however, about Mamontov. This wild card, considering Benois' opinion of him, must have been brought into the project by Diaghilev; his immense energy, unpredictable and "uncontrollable," was perceived as a threat. Benois recognized the immense power of Mamontov's charismatic personality, and was worried that his influence on Diaghilev might counteract his own, particularly since Benois himself was in Paris at the time, growing ideologically and aesthetically apart from the *Mir Iskusstva* editorial board. Indeed, the very first article he submitted to the journal was rejected because its stand against art for art's sake conflicted with the aesthetic platform outlined in Diaghilev's "Complex Questions."[59] Benois' fear was expressed in a letter to Tenisheva's friend, Princess Chetvertinskaya, in which he wrote: "Lord, give [Diaghilev] strength to withstand the pressure from Mamontov who, while magnificent and venerable, is also quite lacking taste and very dangerous."[60]

Benois had good reasons to worry. The evidence suggests that Diaghilev's personal relationship with Mamontov quickly reached the level of intimacy typical of friends and colleagues rather than merely that of a publisher and an editor. This development was facilitated by the fact that their approach to art, and particularly their preferred methods of promoting it, had much in common, especially at a point where they diverged from Benois' own. For example, Benois was apprehensive about confronting the group's ideological enemies in public, and constantly worried about "offending someone," as Diaghilev pointed out in one of his letters.[61] In order to keep the peace, he was willing to compromise to the point of joining an art society headed by his brother, Albert Benois, despite its establishment roots and disdain for young painters.[62] Diaghilev, on the other hand, rejoiced in the idea of an open press war and used scandal and bad publicity to promote his journal, deliberately seeking and even initiating it, as Taruskin has demonstrated in relation to the *Mir Iskusstva* polemics with Stasov.[63] This famously successful tactic could easily have been learned from Mamontov, who, as we have already observed, frequently used controversial repertoire and ideological debate for promotional purposes. Perhaps the earliest time Mamontov utilized negative publicity that way was during the 1896 Nizhny Novgorod Exhibition, in order to promote the works of Vrubel rejected by the selection committee (see chapter 4). Diaghilev must have been aware of this, since Mamontov's maneuver directly affected his own 1898 Mir Iskusstva exhibition, at which Vrubel's works were first presented to the St. Petersburg public. In the advance press coverage, the still unknown Moscow painter was introduced in terms of the scandal his decadent panels had created in Nizhny Novgorod. For example, a correspondent of *Peterburgskaya Gazeta,* in his article covering the opening of the Mir Iskusstva exhibition, recounted with much enjoyment the story of Vrubel's eviction, *mit Trommel und Trompeten,* from the Nizhny Novgorod Fair. The critic then suggested that Vrubel's paintings, "unbelievable trash [with] no picture and no thought," must have been exhibited this time "in order to prove how right the selection committee was to begin with."[64] And, just as in Nizhny Novgorod, the negative publicity served only to attract more spectators' attention to Vrubel.

Whether Diaghilev was aware in advance how the negative publicity would work in Vrubel's case, or was able to appreciate it after the fact, he certainly acquired a taste for Mamontov's method of promotion. He used it repeatedly and successfully to benefit the journal, and gleefully reported the results to his mentor. In the single surviving letter from Diaghilev to Mamontov, dated 1 December 1898, among various business matters we find the following remark: "Have you read Burenin yet? What great advertising!"[65] This phrase refers to a lengthy review of the inaugural issue of *Mir Iskusstva,* published three days earlier by the art columnist of *Novoe Vremya.* Despite what Diaghilev's comment might suggest, the article was not a panegyric: Burenin characterized the contents of the journal as "insolent decadent lies of our ignorant aesthetes," and had the following to say about the editor personally: "The above-quoted nonsensical blabbering of the newly self-declared prophet of his age and his generation represents a product of pride-induced insanity, 'one of the biggest characteristics' of which is an ego rising to the state of megalomania precisely as a result of its own worthlessness [and] internal inadequacy."[66] Diaghilev's short letter has the feeling of a muted conversation between two coconspirators. The lack of explanation for his remark about great advertising and the lack of quotation marks indicating irony clearly suggest that Diaghilev expected full comprehension from his addressee. The writing style is also noteworthy: it is markedly different from the style used in the journal's official correspondence, as well as from the formal language found in correspondence between Mamontov and the journal's assistant editor, Dmitry Filosofov.[67] Diaghilev did use the second person plural to address a man thirty years his senior, but so did Mamontov and his close associates such as Melnikov and Shkafer, who all used this respectful form in their correspondence. This is why the signature of Diaghilev's letter is particularly noteworthy: instead of a more formal option, he used "I shake your hand," the same phrase found in his letters to Benois and other close friends.

There is little direct evidence of Mamontov's continued mentor-student relationship with Diaghilev after the fall of 1899, when he terminated his sponsorship of *Mir Iskusstva* as a result of his arrest and bankruptcy. What we can prove is that Mamontov stayed in touch with Diaghilev and continued moral, if not financial, support for his activities for at least the following five years. For example, Mamontov continued to introduce him to the young artists he discovered, as revealed in a letter to Diaghilev from symbolist painter Victor Borisov-Musatov, dated

1904. He wrote: "On my arrival in Saratov, I found here a Scarlet Rose exhibition organized by Kuznetsov and Utkin, both of whom you know through Mamontov."[68]

Furthermore, in the famous 1899 caricature of Diaghilev as a milkmaid milking Tenisheva the cow, which provided a pretext for the princess cutting off her support for *Mir Iskusstva,* the cartoonist known as The Old Judge depicted a mammoth (in Russian, *mamont,* i.e., Mamontov) looking on approvingly at the milking process (see plate 39). And while Mamontov's prominence in the original cartoon is easily explainable by its date, it is rarely noted that a year later, The Old Judge published another Diaghilev cartoon dedicated to the fallout between *Mir Iskusstva* and Ilya Repin (see plate 40). The cartoon portrays Stasov in a peasant costume dancing a folk dance in front of a kneeling, penitent Repin, while Diaghilev the milkmaid watches defiantly, hands on hips. Tenisheva the cow, so prominent in the earlier image, is now a tiny figure on the horizon; Mamontov the mammoth, however, is depicted in the same prominent dimensions and in the same place, the upper right corner of the cartoon. Accidentally or not, he is now standing just behind Diaghilev.

Finally, Mamontov was one of only three people invited to make official speeches at a dinner party honoring Diaghilev after the closing of the 1905 exhibition of the Russian historical portraits—Diaghilev's last official "campaign" in Russia before he moved his activities abroad.[69] We do not know what Mamontov said; but we do know what Diaghilev would do. Indeed, we shall see that while Diaghilev's road to Paris was not necessarily suggested to him by Mamontov directly, it certainly followed his example.

### THE ROAD TO PARIS

Mamontov always dreamed of taking his troupe to Paris. He conceived of the idea as early as 1888, during his company's early days, and, unsure of himself, asked Stasov and Rimsky-Korsakov for their advice on the viability of a Paris tour during the 1889 International Exhibition. In response the two discouraged him from pursuing it, pointing to a Parisian opera company's plans to stage *A Life for the Tsar,* wondering about the impact that such a "small enterprise" could have during the World Fair, and worrying about compromising the cause. In truth, with everything they knew about Mamontov at that point, they had no reason to think he could pull it off.[70]

The Paris dream was resurrected ten years later. And while there is no direct evidence to prove that Mamontov discussed his plans with Diaghilev, there was no need. Within two weeks of the 1898 St. Petersburg tour, the news hit major newspapers of both capitals. *Novosti Dnya* reported:

> The success of Rimsky-Korsakov's new opera *Sadko* in Moscow and St. Petersburg has inspired the creators of the Moscow Private Opera to take the whole troupe to Paris in 1900, during the World Exhibition, with the following operas in its repertoire: *Sadko, May Night, The Maid of Pskov,* and *The Snow Maiden* by Rimsky-Korsakov, *Igor* by Borodin, *Rusalka* and *The Stone Guest* by Dargomyzhsky, as well as Glinka's *Ruslan*.[71]

The papers were known to print advance notices of MPO events that were not in fact taking place: the premiere of *Mozart and Salieri* was announced for mid-March, but would not occur until November that year. However, in a letter from Paris the following summer, Shkafer described the preliminary scouting of the operatic market that he, Melnikov, and other members of the troupe had been conducting there, and expressed confidence that his mentor's "secret intentions" of conquering the world's reigning cultural capital would meet with great success.[72]

While under house arrest in late 1899 (see chapter 4, n.63), Mamontov evidently delegated his work on the Paris tour to Melnikov, who took upon himself the delicate negotiations with Prince Tenishev, Maria Tenisheva's husband and the head of the Russian Section at the 1900 Exhibition, who had the power to approve or veto the participants.[73] The negotiations either never reached the paperwork stage, or the paperwork did not survive. They were, however, public knowledge among the intimates of the company, enough to have been the subject of correspondence between Rimsky-Korsakov and Zabela. In his letters from January 1900, the composer expressed essentially the same sentiment about the proposed tour that he had held back in 1888, voicing his skepticism about the idea and wariness of "Melnikov's intrigues."[74]

Meanwhile, only the reality of his bankruptcy in the aftermath of the June 1900 trial stopped Mamontov on his road to Paris. His plans were fated forever to remain his "secret intentions." He did, however, attempt to send an aesthetic message to Paris in 1907, when, at Rimsky-Korsakov's personal request, he agreed to advise the Opéra Comique on its planned production of *The Snow Maiden*. Initially he expected to go to Paris personally in order to stage the production, but no such invitation was extended by the theater's director, Albert Carré. Mamontov had to limit his participation to overseeing *The Snow Maiden*'s visual design; Vasnetsov's sketches of sets and costumes were duly dispatched to Carré, evidently making quite an impression.[75] Interestingly, after the news of Mamontov's participation hit Parisian newspapers, an enterprising correspondent solicited an interview with Carré's main competitor, Diaghilev, whose spectacular *Boris Godunov* was to be premiered simultaneously with Rimsky-Korsakov's opera. The interview contains yet another hitherto overlooked testament to Diaghilev's appreciation for Mamontov's expertise: while commenting on the *Snow Maiden* production team, Diaghilev publicly took full credit for recommending Mamontov to Carré.[76] We will likely never know whether or not he was telling the truth; it is, after all, possible that both he and Rimsky-Korsakov made similar recommendations to the Opéra Comique. But knowing Diaghilev's personality, we can be certain that he would never have made such a statement if he had any doubts about the level of artistry Mamontov's participation would bring to the project, and the consequent boost to his own reputation as a talent scout who had "discovered" him for Paris.

The fate of *The Snow Maiden* was a monument to bad marketing: poor advertising, backstage warfare, and, most importantly, competition provided by Diaghilev's *Boris* effectively demolished any chance of it rising beyond a *succès d'estime*. Mamontov's son Sergei, who witnessed the premiere, testified in *Russkoe Slovo* that the Paris newspapers unanimously praised the production, yet "the success of Musorgsky's *Boris* has been incomparably greater."[77] Mamontov's bitterness over the impending fiasco might have been a reason for some rather unpleasant remarks he made in a 1907 interview, in which he accused Diaghilev of squandering government funds for his and Chaliapin's personal glory.[78] In reality, the motivation behind both men's intent to conquer Paris was remarkably similar. In a letter to Albert Carré, Mamontov wrote: "I would very much like to be useful to you, in order to make the true poetry of Russia, the *delicate* sentiments of our people, known in France. They believe us to be drunken peasants. Well, that is not true."[79] Diaghilev, in turn, expressed his life's ambition in a letter to Benois, saying: "I want to pamper Russian art, to clean it up and, most importantly, to offer it to the West, to exalt it in the West."[80]

Ultimately, it was not the Moscow Private Opera but Diaghilev's Ballets Russes that, absorbing the most talented minds and innovative practices of Mamontov's enterprise, offered their shared aesthetic dream to Paris and the world. It was the Ballets Russes that with productions such as Le Coq d'Or completed the journey of Russian operatic staged art away from the nineteenth century toward the artistic and operational principles of modernity. Yet at the root of that historic triumph lies an unacknowledged but essential truth. As in his understanding of a synthesis of the arts achieved through collaboration and his adoption of the creative mantle of artistic director, so in his vision for the future of Russian modernist staged art Sergei Diaghilev was guided by Savva Mamontov.

Chaliapin's artistry, Korovin's two-dimensional backdrops, Stanislavsky's system of method acting, Meyerhold's motionless mises-en-scène, and the Gesamtkunstwerke of Diaghilev's Ballets Russes have all been acknowledged in both scholarly discourse and popular imagination as the faces of Russian modernist theater. All made a profound impact around the world that can still be felt today. All testify to the genius of their creators. And as I hope to have proven in the present study, none would have been possible without Mamontov's golden touch—his money, yes, but more importantly his contradictory, irrepressible, brilliantly exasperating inspiration. Rarely does one man make such a mark on history. Savva Mamontov's own artistry and the ideas he implanted in his students in his search for modernism in Russian theater would forever change the world of art in the twentieth century.

APPENDIX A

# Brief Chronology of Savva Mamontov's Life and Career

1841    3 October: Savva Ivanovich Mamontov born in Yalutorovsk, Siberia, a second son of millionaire wine seller, first-guild merchant Ivan Fyodorovich Mamontov.

1848    The Mamontov family moves to Moscow. Savva is educated at home with a German tutor, later at private schools in Moscow and St. Petersburg.

1859    Savva enters Moscow University.

1862    Savva leaves the university at the insistence of his father, because of his involvement with the Sekretarev drama circle as well as his suspected sympathies for liberal student groups. He is sent to Baku and later to Iran on business.

1863    Savva is sent to Italy to study the silk trade. He neglects his duties in order to study *bel canto* singing and is recalled to Moscow by his father just as he is about to sign a contract with one of Milan's opera houses.

1864    Mamontov returns to Moscow to work in his father's business. He joins the Moscow Art Lovers Society.

1865    25 April: Mamontov marries his cousin Elizaveta Sapozhnikova, whom he had met in Italy and who shares his interest in the arts. The couple honeymoons in Rome where they befriend the members of the expatriate colony of Russian artists.

1868    Mamontov's father dies; Savva takes over the family business, including a position as the majority stockholder and chairman of the board in the Moscow-Yaroslavl Railroad Company.

1870    March: Savva and Elizaveta Mamontov buy the Abramtsevo estate near Moscow from the Aksakov family.

| | |
|---|---|
| 1873–75 | Most of the Russian Romans return permanently to Russia; their close association with Mamontov continues, including prolonged stays at his Moscow mansion and at Abramtsevo; the beginning of the Mamontov Circle. |
| 1877–79 | "Mamontov Drama Nights," regular gatherings of the Circle devoted to reading and discussing plays. All participants are required to prepare their assigned roles. |
| 1878 | The first theatrical production of the Mamontov Circle: a series of *tableaux vivant—Demon and Tamara, Apotheosis of the Arts, Judith and Holofernes.* |
| 1879 | The first staged production of the Mamontov Circle: act 2 of Apollon Maikov's *Dva Mira* [*Two Worlds*]; sets and music by Vasily Polenov. |
| 1882 | Alexander Ostrovsky's *The Snow Maiden* is staged by the Mamontov Circle; sets and costumes by Victor Vasnetsov. |
| 1883 | The first opera production of the Mamontov Circle: Gounod's *Faust* (act 3); sets by Polenov, piano accompaniment by Professor Fitzengagen of the Moscow Conservatory; Mephistopheles—Savva Mamontov. |
| 1884 | Mozart's *Don Giovanni* is staged by the Mamontov Circle; Don Giovanni—Pyotr Melnikov, Zerlina—Alevtina Paskhalova. |
| 1885 | 9 January: The first incarnation of the Moscow Private Opera opens under the name Krotkov's Private Opera (with a mixed Russian-Italian cast, it would operate full-time through the end of 1886–87 season); the history of the MPO begins. February–March: The Meiningen Theater troupe tours St. Petersburg and Moscow. |
| 1888–92 | Mamontov's opera company is known as the Moscow Italian Opera; it operates during Lent only, with performances in Italian and mainly touring foreigners in solo roles. Guest singers include Angelo Masini, Francesco Tamagno, Antonio Cotogni, Marcella Zembrich, Sigrid Arnoldson, Marie van Zandt, Antonio and Francesco d'Andrade, Maria Duran, Adelaide Borghi, Giuseppe Kaschmann, Jules Devoyod, and other leading European stars (some past their prime), as well as Nikolai Figner and Medea Mei-Figner from the Imperial Mariinsky Theater in St. Petersburg. |
| 1892–93 | Ippolit Pryanishnikov's private operatic enterprise performs in Moscow; the company is bankrupted by the end of the season but is generally considered to have sparked Mamontov's interest in reviving the MPO with a full-time Russian troupe. |

1894    April: The First All-Russian Congress of Artists is held in Moscow, to coincide with the opening of the Tretyakov Gallery. The event is dedicated to building bridges between the older and the younger generation of artists. Mamontov supervises the art program, which includes a tableau vivant *Aphrodite* (text and stage direction by Mamontov, sets and music by Polenov; Agasandre—Stanislavsky), and the premiere of Anton Arensky's opera *Raphael*. Mamontov and Polenov participate in the establishment of the Moscow Association of Artists.

1894–95    Claudia Winter's opera company, tacitly sponsored by Mamontov, operates at the Panaev Theater in St. Petersburg. Singers include Feodor Chaliapin, Nadezhda Zabela, and Tatyana Lyubatovich; sets and costumes by Mikhail Vrubel.

1896    May–August: The All-Russian Exhibition in Nizhny Novgorod; Mamontov supervises the arts program, exhibits the crafts of the Abramtsevo workshops, creates an exhibition dedicated to the development of the Russian Northern region, and builds a special pavilion to exhibit Mikhail Vrubel's mosaic panels rejected by the selection committee. The MPO is revived and performs in Nizhny Novgorod throughout the summer. 8 September: The MPO opens its winter season at the Solodovnikov Theater in Moscow under the name of Claudia S. Winter's Russian Private Opera, with Mamontov as the undeclared artistic director (it will operate under his management through the end of 1898–99 season).

1898    20 January: Fire at the Solodovnikov Theater; the troupe is moved to the International Theater. February–April: The first St. Petersburg tour of the MPO.

1899    March–April: The second St. Petersburg tour of the MPO. Summer: An audit reveals a serious discrepancy in the finances of the Moscow-Yaroslavl Railroad Company; Mamontov steps down as the chairman of the board. 12 September: Mamontov is arrested on a charge of embezzlement; initially in solitary confinement at the Taganskaya Prison, he is later released under house arrest due to his failing health. He continues to direct the MPO activities through third parties.

1900    May–June: Mamontov's highly publicized jury trial takes place in Moscow (see introduction, n.8). 8 June: Mamontov and his codefendants are acquitted of all criminal charges, and the case is transferred to civil court, which would subsequently declare Mamontov bankrupt.

1900–1901    The MPO operates officially as an "association" (a company owned by its employees), unofficially as a commercial enterprise run by Claudia Winter and Mikhail Ippolitov-Ivanov; Mamontov's participation is irregular, and his authority is shaky. There is no information of his involvement with the company after this season.

1903    Summer: Mamontov leads an operatic enterprise at the Hermitage Theater in Moscow; sets by the Blue Rose artists Nikolai Sapunov, Sergei Sudeikin, and Pavel Kuznetsov; tenor Dmitry Smirnov (later with the Imperial Theaters and Diaghilev's Russian Seasons) makes his debut in Eugenio Esposito's comic opera *Camorra*.

1904    The MPO is dissolved at the end of the 1903–1904 theatrical season. The majority of the troupe, including Ippolitov-Ivanov, joins the new Zimin's Private Opera, which would operate continuously until 1917, mostly at the Solodovnikov Theater. Several MPO productions are revived with their original sets and costumes. Director and patron of the company, Sergei Zimin views it as the descendant of the MPO and counts its history from 1885.

1905    May: Stanislavsky and Meyerhold found an experimental affiliate of the Moscow Art Theater, the Povarskaya Studio. The Studio intends to house several troupes (one of them operatic) that would perform both classical and innovative repertoire alternatively in the city and the provinces. Mamontov serves as a consultant for the Studio and oversees its decorative aspect. Three productions are prepared, and open dress rehearsals are held starting in August; the Studio closes late in the year with the advent of the 1905 uprising (the revolution of 1905–1907).

1907    On Rimsky-Korsakov's request, Mamontov advises Albert Carré, director of the Opéra Comique in Paris, on the production of *The Snow Maiden* and supplies him with the set and costume sketches by Vasnetsov.

1918    24 March, Moscow: Savva Ivanovich Mamontov dies of pneumonia at age 76.

# Selected Premieres and Revivals at the Moscow Private Opera

| Year | Date | Title | Designer/s |
|------|------|-------|------------|
| 1885 | 9 Jan | Dargomyzhsky, *Rusalka* | Vasnetsov, Levitan |
| | 17 Jan | Gounod, *Faust* | Polenov |
| | 1 Apr | Verdi, *Aida* | Polenov, Korovin |
| | 18 Aug | Glinka, *A Life for the Tsar* | Levitan, Simov |
| | 8 Oct | Rimsky-Korsakov, *The Snow Maiden* | Vasnetsov |
| 1886 | 20 Mar | Krotkov, *The Scarlet Rose* | Polenov, Korovin |
| | 17 Dec | Dargomyzhsky, *The Stone Guest* | Korovin |
| | 28 Dec | Puccini, *Le villi* | Korovin |
| 1887 | 9 Feb | Wagner, *Lohengrin* | Korovin |
| 1889 | 27 Mar | Verdi, *Otello* | Korovin |
| 1896 | 17 May | Rubinstein, *The Demon* | Vrubel |
| | 8 Sept | Rimsky-Korsakov, *The Snow Maiden* | Vasnetsov |
| | 9 Sept | Verdi, *Aida* | Korovin |
| | 17 Sept | Thomas, *Mignon* | Korovin |
| | 18 Sept | Saint-Saëns, *Samson et Dalila* | Korovin |
| | 1 Oct | Bizet, *Carmen* | Korovin |
| | 3 Oct | Gounod, *Faust* | Polenov, Korovin |
| | 8 Oct | Humperdinck, *Hänsel und Gretel* | Korovin |
| | 31 Oct | Alexander Serov, *Rogneda* | Valentin Serov |
| | 5 Nov | Delibes, *Lakmé* | Korovin |
| | 15 Nov | Borodin, *Prince Igor* | Korovin |
| | 12 Dec | Rimsky-Korsakov, *The Maid of Pskov* | Korovin, Appolinary Vasnetsov |

| Year | Date | Title | Designer/s |
|------|------|-------|------------|
| 1897 | 11 Jan | Puccini, *La bohème* | Korovin |
|      | 23 Jan | Tchaikovsky, *The Oprichnik* | Malyutin |
|      | 12 Nov | Musorgsky, *Khovanshchina* | Appolinary Vasnetsov |
|      | 30 Nov | Gluck, *Orfeo* | Polenov, Korovin |
|      | 21 Dec | Verstovsky, *Askold's Tomb* | Korovin |
|      | 26 Dec | Rimsky-Korsakov, *Sadko* | Korovin, Malyutin |
| 1898 | 30 Jan | Rimsky-Korsakov, *May Night* | Korovin |
|      | 23 Nov | Alexander Serov, *Judith* | Valentin Serov |
|      | 25 Nov | Rimsky-Korsakov, *Mozart and Salieri* | Vrubel |
|      | 7 Dec | Musorgsky, *Boris Godunov* | Bondarenko, Korovin |
|      | 15 Dec | Rimsky-Korsakov, *Vera Sheloga* | Korovin |
| 1899 | 3 Feb | Tchaikovsky, *The Maid of Orleans* | Polenov |
|      | 22 Oct | Rimsky-Korsakov, *The Tsar's Bride* | Vrubel |
|      | 16 Nov | Kalinnikov, Prolog to *1812* | Vrubel |
|      | 21 Nov | Verstovsky, *Gromoboi* | Vrubel |
|      | 10 Dec | Cui, *Prisoner of the Caucasus* | Vrubel |
|      | 29 Dec | Krotkov, *The Necklace* | Polenov |
| 1900 | 9 Feb | Cui, *Mandarin's Son* | Vrubel |
|      | 21 Oct | Rimsky-Korsakov, *The Tale of Tsar Saltan* | Vrubel |
| 1902 | 12 Dec | Rimsky-Korsakov, *Kashchei the Deathless* | Malyutin |

# NOTES

## Introduction

1. Numerous examples of this popular view may be seen, for instance, on the pages of Richard Taruskin's *Stravinsky and the Russian Traditions: A Biography of Works Through Mavra* (Berkeley: University of California Press, 1996).

2. The term "Silver Age," coined years after the fact by that era's muse and icon, poet Anna Akhmatova, has become controversial of late, as is bound to happen to any overused historical label; see Omry Ronen, *The Fallacy of the Silver Age in Twentieth-Century Russian Literature* (Amsterdam: Harwood, 1997). However, it is still commonly used to designate both the time period and the cultural ideology of early Russian modernism, and will be used as such in the present study.

3. For recent examples, see Boris Gasparov, Robert P. Hughes, and Irina Paperno, eds., *Cultural Mythologies of Russian Modernism: From the Golden Age to the Silver Age* (Berkeley: University of California Press, 1992), Irina Paperno and Joan Delaney Grossman, eds., *Creating Life: The Aesthetic Utopia of Russian Modernism* (Stanford, Calif.: Stanford University Press, 1994), and Galina Rylkova, *The Archaeology of Anxiety: The Russian Silver Age and Its Legacy* (Pittsburgh, Pa.: University of Pittsburgh Press, 2007).

4. The word "artist" will occur frequently in the following discussion, particularly in the primary sources, and needs to be accompanied by a translator's note. What is translated into English as the word "artist" may in Russian mean "actor," both dramatic and operatic (a cognate, *artiste*), "painter" (*khudozhnik*), or—frequently, in relation to Mamontov—"a man of art," that is, an artist in spirit rather than occupation (in Russian, also *khudozhnik*).

5. On the Silver Age cabaret culture and its influence on Meyerhold, Evreinov, and other Russian modernist stage directors, see Barbara Henry, "Theatricality, Antitheatricality, and Cabaret in Russian Modernism," in *Russian Literature, Modernism and the Visual Arts*, ed. Catriona Kelly and Stephen Lovell (Cambridge: Cambridge University Press, 2000), 149–71.

6. For more information on *Victory over the Sun*, including costume sketches, see Camilla Gray, *The Russian Experiment in Art, 1863–1922* (London: Thames and Hudson, 1986), 158–59, 185.

7. For a standard biography, see Mark Kopshitser, *Savva Mamontov* (Moscow: Iskusstvo, 1972), and somewhat more fictionalized Ekaterina Kiselëva, *Dom na Sadovoi* [A House on Sadovaia Street] (Moscow: Moskovskii Rabochii, 1986); see also the chronology of Mamontov's life and artistic career in appendix A.

8. The circumstances of the trial are briefly as follows. Mamontov, together with several colleagues from the Moscow-Yaroslavl' Railroad Company, was accused of fraud and embezzlement of the company funds. Specifically, the prosecution alleged that Mamontov personally appropriated over a million rubles to support his exorbitant lifestyle; his involvement with the MPO was offered as an example of said excess. The defense team, headed by the legendary attorney Fyodor Plevako, argued that the missing funds had not been stolen for Mamontov's personal use. Rather, they were transferred from one of his enterprises to others; specifically, two Siberian factories purchased at the request of the government in order to keep them from being acquired by a German industrial conglomerate and used for military purposes. It was alleged (although never proven) that a loan arranged by the prime minister, Carl Witte, was supposed to cover the purchase and return the money to the railroad coffers, but the internal power struggle within the government led Witte to step aside and let Mamontov take the blame. While Mamontov's activities broke the rules of fiscal discipline, his motives were shown to be purely altruistic and serving Russia's best interests. His patronage of the arts and specifically the MPO was portrayed as equally unselfish; furthermore, it was proven that no company funds were used to support it. On 8 June 1900, after a two-week trial, the jury acquitted Mamontov and his codefendants of any criminal wrongdoing. The matter of the missing funds was left unresolved, pending a transfer of the case to a civil court, which declared Mamontov bankrupt later that year. For a full account of the proceedings, see "Delo Mamontova, Artsibusheva, Krivosheina i Drugikh: Polnyi i Podrobnyi Otchët" [The Case of Mamontov, Artsibushev, Krivoshein, and Others: Full and Complete Account] (Moscow, 1900), preserved as item 72, fund 155, BM.

9. The troupe and most of its assets were absorbed by the newly established Zimin's Private Opera (1904–17); for more information, see appendix A and Viktor Borovskii, *Moskovskaia opera S. I. Zimina* [Moscow Opera of S. I. Zimin] (Moscow: Sovetskii Kompozitor, 1977).

10. See Vera Rossikhina, *Opernyi teatr S. I. Mamontova* [S. I. Mamontov's Opera Theater] (Moscow: Muzyka, 1985).

11. Konstantin Sergeevich Stanislavsky (real name Alekseev): drama and opera director, cofounder of the *Moskovskii Khudozhestvennyi Teatr* (the Moscow Art Theater, or the MKhT), creator of the so-called "Stanislavsky system of method acting," a teaching methodology for dramatic actors still actively in use throughout the world.

12. Lynn Garafola, *Diaghilev's Ballets Russes* (New York: Oxford University Press, 1989), 15.

13. Vladislav Bakhrevskii, *Savva Mamontov* (Moscow: Molodaia Gvardiia, 2000).

14. For instance, when I applied to RGALI to begin my study of the Mamontov sources, the lead archivist remarked (politely) that I must be either ignorant or bored to concern myself with such an "old" subject.

15. Rossikhina, *Opernyi teatr S. I. Mamontova*.

16. Evgenii Arenzon, *Savva Mamontov* (Moscow: Russkaia Kniga, 1995).

17. Abram Gozenpud, *Russkii opernyi teatr na rubezhe XIX–XX vekov i Shaliapin, 1890–1904* [Russian Opera Theater of the Late 19th–Early 20th Centuries and Chaliapin, 1890–1904] (Leningrad: Muzyka, 1974).

18. Both Mamontov's and Diaghilev's ventures had "heirs" who professed artistic continuity and claimed the mantle of authenticity. Yet arguably, both Zimin's Private Opera and the Ballets Russes de Monte Carlo are quite separate artistic phenomena with their own independent accomplishments and histories, and should be viewed as such by their students, irrespective of (although not denying) any acknowledged influences.

19. Indeed, Rossikhina's 1954 dissertation, upon which her posthumously published monograph was based, specifically addressed the establishment of realism on the Russian operatic stage.

20. More recently, Arenzon, a former curator of the Abramtsevo museum, tentatively addressed Mamontov's connections with the Russian modernist movement in his book, despite its primarily nationalist slant and modest scope that did not allow for an in-depth exploration of the topic. This approach will be continued in the present study.

21. Stuart Grover, "Savva Mamontov and the Mamontov Circle, 1870–1905: Art Patronage and the Rise of Nationalism in Russian Art" (Ph.D. diss., University of Wisconsin, 1971).

22. César Cui, *La musique en Russie* (Paris: Fischbacher, 1880).

23. See, for instance, Gerald Abraham, *On Russian Music* (London: Reeves, 1939), Michel Calvocoressi and Gerald Abraham, *Masters of Russian Music* (London: Duckworth, 1936), and Rosa Newmarch, *The Russian Opera* (New York: Dutton, 1914).

24. Indeed, Mamontov's "campaign" for the elevation of Russian music was discussed in Soviet research as well: for example, Rossikhina's work emphasizes the "Russianness," as well as the realism, of the MPO playbill, while attempting to downplay its Western productions. On the origin of this view of Mamontov, see chapter 7.

25. Taruskin, *Stravinsky and the Russian Traditions*, 490–97.

26. It is illustrative of the relative significance Mamontov placed on his various artistic projects that the neo-nationalist haven of the Abramtsevo workshops was abandoned, soon after their creation, primarily to the care of Mamontov's estranged wife Elizaveta and her artist friends, Maria Yakunchikova and Elena Polenova, as Mamontov himself concentrated on the work of the MPO; for details see chapter 3.

27. That last technique, particularly rampant in the Soviet-era studies, would be especially misleading to a Western researcher without access to the archives, who would be forced to rely on these studies for information and have no choice but to accept their argument at face value.

28. Nikolai Rimskii-Korsakov, *Letopis' moei muzykal'noi zhizni* [A Chronicle of My Musical Life]; in *Polnoe sobranie sochinenii* [Complete Works], vol. 1 (Moscow: Muzgiz, 1955).

## 1. The Silver Age and the Legacy of the 1860s

1. Charles Harrison, "Modernism," in *Critical Terms for Art History*, ed. Robert S. Nelson and Richard Schiff (Chicago: University of Chicago Press, 2003), 195.

300 NOTES TO PAGES 16–21

2. While critics of the period never made it their goal to define these extremely complex and admittedly vague concepts, such definitions can be inferred and will be used as follows. *Truth* is a catchword that signifies the faithful representation of external reality in art, and through that representation, the usefulness of art as an ideological vehicle promoting moral and social causes. The art of truth tends to concentrate on "meaning," i.e., the content of art in direct relation to a contentious external world, rather than to its form and technique. *Beauty,* meanwhile, stands for the aesthetic quality of art, valued for its own sake, independent of any social agenda. The art of beauty tends to place a higher value on form and technique than on any external meaning. That is, the arrangement and intrinsic properties of word, color, and/or sound hold more significance than the relevance of their subject matter to contemporary social issues.

3. "Il n'y a de vraiment beau que ce qui ne peut servir à rien; tout ce qui est utile est laid . . . L'endroit le plus utile d'une maison, ce sont les latrines"; Théophile Gautier, Preface to *Mademoiselle de Maupin* (Paris: Charpentier, 1880), 22.

4. Matei Calinescu, *Five Faces of Modernity: Modernism, Avant-garde, Decadence, Kitsch, Postmodernism* (Durham, N.C.: Duke University Press, 1987), 55.

5. Quoted in Sergei Diagilev, "Poiski krasoty" [In Search of Beauty], *Mir Iskusstva* 3–4 (1899): 37–38. Diaghilev acknowledged Baudelaire as the author of the quotation but did not specify its precise source. My own thorough search did not reveal the origins of the quote either; it is possible that Diaghilev used a free paraphrase, as the sentiment occurs in a variety of Baudelaire's writings.

6. Dmitrii Sarab'ianov, *Stil' modern: istoki, istoriia, problemy* [*Style Moderne: Sources, History, Issues*] (Moscow: Iskusstvo, 1989), 33.

7. Valerii Briusov, "Nenuzhnaia pravda" [Useless Truth], in *Sobranie sochinenii v 7 tomakh* [Selected Works in 7 Volumes], vol. 6 (Moscow: Khudozhestvennaia Literatura, 1975), 64–65.

8. Briusov, "Kliuchi tain" [The Keys to the Mysteries], in *Sobranie sochinenii* 6: 80–81.

9. Lev Tolstoi, *Chto takoe iskusstvo?* [What Is Art?]; in *Polnoe sobranie sochinenii* (Moscow: Gosudarstvennoe Izdatel'stvo Khudozhestvennoi Literatury, 1951), 30: 177.

10. Ibid., 172–73.

11. Vladimir Solov'ëv, "Obshchii smysl iskusstva" [The General Meaning of Art], in *Filosofiia iskusstva i literaturnaia kritika* (Moscow: Iskusstvo, 1991), 74–75.

12. Nikolai Berdiaev, *Sub specie aeternitatis. Opyty filosofskie, sotsial'nye i literaturnye, 1900–1906* [From the Perspective of the Eternal: Philosophical, Social, and Literary Experiments, 1900–1906] (St. Petersburg: Izd. M. V. Pirozhkova, 1907), 31–32. Here and below, unless otherwise stated, the emphasis is in the original.

13. Bernice Rosenthal, "Theater as Church: The Vision of the Mystical Anarchists," *Russian History* 4, no. 2 (1977): 122.

14. See Calinescu, "The Idea of Decadence," in *Five Faces of Modernity,* 151–221.

15. Quoted in Calinescu, *Five Faces of Modernity,* 176.

16. John R. Reed, *Decadent Style* (Athens: Ohio University Press, 1985), 11.

17. Quoted in Reed, *Decadent Style,* 4.

18. Ibid., 10.

19. See Robert Morgan, "Secret Languages: The Roots of Musical Modernism," in *Modernism: Challenges and Perspectives,* ed. Monique Chefdor, Ricardo Quinones, and Albert Wachtel (Urbana: University of Illinois Press, 1986): 33–53.

20. Max Nordau, *Degeneration*, 8th ed. (New York: D. Appleton, 1896).

21. Quoted in Avril Pyman, *A History of Russian Symbolism* (Cambridge: Cambridge University Press, 1994), 1.

22. Reed, *Decadent Style*, 14–15.

23. For a more detailed discussion of this generational division, see Simon Morrison, *Russian Opera and the Symbolist Movement* (Berkeley: University of California Press, 2002), 2. Unlike the present study, the author goes on to focus primarily on the "mystic" generation.

24. Briusov, "Russkie simvolisty" [Russian Symbolists], in *Sobranie sochinenii* 6: 27.

25. Briusov, "Kliuchi tain," in *Sobranie sochinenii* 6: 81.

26. John Bowlt, "Synthesism and Symbolism: The Russian *World of Art* Movement," in *Literature and the Plastic Arts, 1880–1930*, ed. I. Higgins (New York: Harper & Row, 1973), 35.

27. The term *stil' modern*, translated here as "Russian *style moderne*," as used here and below, is a standard term in Russian art history and criticism. It refers to a variety of the early modernist trends in visual arts of the early Silver Age, and parallels such Western European developments as Jugendstil and art nouveau. Furthermore, as described in Sarabyanov's writings cited throughout this study, *style moderne* closely resembles Reed's definition of decadent art, which leads one to believe that the two discussed essentially the same phenomenon, a hypothesis also confirmed by reception history.

28. Sergei Diagilev, "Vechnaia bor'ba" [Eternal Struggle], *Mir Iskusstva* 1–2 (1899): 12–16.

29. Sergei Diagilev, "Nash mnimyi upadok" [Our Alleged Decline], *Mir Iskusstva* 1–2 (1899): 8–11. For a translated version, see Lynn Garafola and Nancy Van Norman Baer, eds., *The Ballets Russes and Its World* (New Haven, Conn.: Yale University Press, 1999), 76–84.

30. Diagilev, "Nash mnimyi upadok," 11.

31. Dmitrii Merezhkovskii, "Prichiny upadka i novye techeniia v russkoi literature" [The Causes of the Decline and the New Trends in Russian Literature], cited in Fan Parker and Stephen Jan Parker, *Russia on Canvas: Ilya Repin* (University Park: Pennsylvania State University Press, 1980), 107.

32. Ibid.

33. Belinsky's views are summarized from Vissarion Belinskii, *Estetika i literaturnaia kritika* [Aesthetics and Literary Criticism], 2 vols. (Moscow: Gosudarstvennoe Izdatel'stvo Khudozhestvennoi Literatury, 1959).

34. Charles A. Moser, *Esthetics as Nightmare: Russian Literary Theory, 1855–1870* (Princeton, N.J.: Princeton University Press, 1989), 7–9.

35. James Billington, *The Icon and the Axe: An Interpretive History of Russian Culture* (New York: Vintage Books, 1970), 349.

36. Fëdor Dostoevskii, "G.-bov i vopros ob iskusstve" [G.-bov and the Question of Art], in *Dostoevskii ob iskusstve* [Dostoevsky on Art] (Moscow: Iskusstvo, 1973), 63.

37. *Dostoevskii ob iskusstve,* 67.

38. See Aleksandr Druzhinin, "Kritika gogolevskogo perioda russkoi literatury i nashi k nei otnosheniia" [Critique of the Gogol Period in Russian Literature and Our Relations to It], in *Literaturnaia kritika* [Literary Criticism] (Moscow: Sovetskaia Rossiia, 1983), 122–76.

39. *Dostoevskii ob iskusstve*, 58–60.

40. Moser, *Esthetics as Nightmare*, 6.

41. Ibid., 5–6.

42. Billington, *The Icon and the Axe*, 387–88.

43. For an exhaustive treatment of the group's activities, see Elizabeth Valkenier, *Russian Realist Art. The State and Society: The Peredvizhniki and Their Tradition* (New York: Columbia University Press, 1989).

44. Il'ia Repin, "Pis'ma ob iskusstve" [Letters on Art], in *Dalëkoe i blizkoe* [The Far and the Near] (Leningrad: Khudozhnik, 1986), 380–82. The nihilist Bazarov, a character in Ivan Turgenev's novel *Ottsy i Deti* [*Fathers and Sons*], is a literary prototype of the so-called "new people" who championed realist art.

45. Quoted in Vladimir Stasov, "Prosvetitel' po chasti khudozhestva" [A Man of Artistic Enlightenment], in *Izbrannye trudy* [Selected Writings] (Moscow: Iskusstvo, 1952), 3: 211.

46. For a more detailed explication of the term *Kuchka*, see Taruskin, "What is a *Kuchka*?" in *Musorgsky: Eight Essays and an Epilogue* (Princeton, N.J.: Princeton University Press, 1991), xxxiii–xxxiv.

47. In reality, as will become evident throughout this book, both the Wanderers and the Kuchka were complex phenomena, their aesthetics encompassing but not limited to the realist doctrine. The two groups are discussed here in their early formative stages when their ideological platforms were relatively unified. It is this brief period that would later be mythologized by critics like Stasov and thus enter and become embedded in the public consciousness, irrespective of the changing and ultimately diverse views of particular artists.

48. Stasov, "Perov i Musorgskii" [Perov and Musorgsky], in *Izbrannye trudy*, 2: 136, 143.

49. In Russian musicological literature, Alexander Dargomyzhsky is generally considered, chronologically speaking, the next great opera composer after Glinka (see, for example, Iurii Keldysh, "A. S. Dargomyzhskii," in *Istoriia russkoi muzyki* [History of Russian Music] (Moscow: Muzyka, 1989), 6:83–134). His opera *Rusalka* (1855) was hailed by the Kuchkists, who believed, nevertheless, that its scenes featuring realistic representation of characters and naturalist declamation outshined its more traditional portrayal of the fantastic (see the quote from César Cui cited in Keldysh, 6: 86–87). Dargomyzhsky's last opera, *Kamennyi gost'* [*The Stone Guest*], a revolutionary word-for-word setting of a Pushkin drama in verse, particularly impressed Musorgsky and other Kuchkists. The opera was completed, after its author's death, by Kuchka members César Cui and Nikolai Rimsky-Korsakov and first performed in 1872.

50. Musorgsky to Stasov, 18 October 1872; in *M. P. Musorgskii: Literaturnoe nasledie* [M. P. Musorgskii: Literary Heritage], ed. Mikhail Pekelis and Aleksandra Orlova (Moscow: Muzyka, 1971–72), 1: 141.

51. Valkenier, *Peredvizhniki*, 119.

52. Ibid., 57.

53. The term *sobornost*, first defined by early Slavophiles Ivan Kireevsky and Aleksei Khomyakov and later explored by Vladimir Solovyov, Nikolai Berdyaev, and Pavel Florensky, among others, emphasizes willing subordination of individuals to the absolute values (religious, philosophical, national, etc.) of their community;

searching for what people have in common rather than what divides them, in order to achieve societal unity and harmony. Although the idea of *sobornost* has Hegelian roots, it was believed to represent a uniquely Slavic mindset (steeped in Orthodox Christianity, as well as in the communal lifestyle of the peasantry), a superior alternative to the corrupt individualism of the West.

54. Billington, *The Icon and the Axe*, 374–75.

55. For details on Herder's philosophy as it was appropriated by the group, see Johann Gottfried Herder, *Against Pure Reason: Writings on Religion, Language and History* (Minneapolis, Minn.: Fortress, 1993), 38–98.

56. Ivan I. Baloueff, review of *Grigoriev, Apollon. Sochineniia. Kritika* [Works, Criticism], ed. V. S. Krupitsch; *Russian Review* 30, no. 1 (1971), 84.

57. Marcus C. Levitt, review of *Russia's Last Romantic, Apollon Grigoriev (1822–64)* by Robert Whittaker; *Slavic and East European Journal* 46, no. 1 (2002), 167.

58. Wayne Dowler, "Echoes of *Pochvennichestvo* in Solzhenitsyn's *August 1914*," *Slavic Review* 34, no. 1 (1975), 110.

59. Quoted in *Dostoevskii ob iskusstve*, 37.

60. *Dostoevskii ob iskusstve*, 80–81.

61. Arenzon, *Savva Mamontov*, 35–42.

62. Ibid., 13–17.

## 2. Serving the Beautiful

1. Arenzon, *Savva Mamontov*, 17.

2. Mamontov's importance in the development of Russia's industry and transportation system was first publicly acknowledged in an essay by writer and publicist Vlas Doroshevich, titled "Russkii chelovek" [A Russian Man], published in *RS* on 22 May 1915; quoted in Kopshitser, *Savva Mamontov*, 240–41.

3. See Grover, "Savva Mamontov and the Mamontov Circle," above.

4. The realist writers and critics such as Belinsky, Chernyshevsky, Dobrolyubov, and even Vladimir Stasov (prior to 1862, see chapter 3) were all avowed Westernizers; others, such as playwrights Ostrovsky and Pisemsky (see below) were connected to the Slavophile circles.

5. The Sekretarev circle gathered at the home of a Moscow *chinovnik* [bureaucrat] named Sekretarev.

6. Glikeriya Fedotova (née Pozdnyakova) was one of the finest actresses of the nineteenth-century Russian stage. She had worked for years at the Imperial Maly Drama Theater, where she created the title roles in Alexander Ostrovsky's plays, *The Snow Maiden* and *Vassilisa Melentieva*.

7. For instance, "Luch sveta v tëmnom tsarstve" [A Ray of Light in the Dark Kingdom], Dobrolyubov's essay on Ostrovsky's play *The Thunderstorm*, mentioned earlier, was essentially a review of the production that crowned Mamontov's acting career at the Sekretarev circle.

8. Repin, "Pis'ma ob iskusstve," in *Dalëkoe i blizkoe*, 381. Ivan Andreevich Krylov (1769–1844) was a Russian poet known for his witty, moralistic fables, some loosely based on Aesop and Jean de la Fontaine, others more original.

9. Mamontov to Polenov, 12 February 1874; item 2865, fund 54, STG.

10. Polenov to Mamontov, 6 April 1900; item 197, list 1, fund 799, RGALI.

11. Gozenpud, *Russkii opernyi teatr i Shaliapin*, 118.

12. Gozenpud, for instance, qualified the above-quoted description of Mamontov's aesthetic views by calling him naïve.

13. Polenov to Mamontov, 6 April 1900; item 197, list 1, fund 799, RGALI.

14. See, for example, Rossikhina, *Opernyi teatr S. I. Mamontova;* the monograph is based on the author's 1954 dissertation titled "Mamontov's Opera Company and the Establishment of Realism on the Russian Stage."

15. See Grover, "Savva Mamontov and the Mamontov Circle."

16. Mamontov to Shkafer [October 1899?]; item 23, list 2, fund 920, RGALI.

17. Melnikov to Mamontov, Moscow, [November 1898]; item 36, fund 155, BM.

18. Published in *RS* 9, 13 January 1910, 5.

19. "Teatral'naia khronika" [Theatrical Chronicle], *ND* 5847, 5 September 1899, 2.

20. Vasily Safonov was the director of the Moscow Conservatory in the late 1890s, and as such was one of the people Mamontov held personally responsible for the status quo.

21. Mamontov to unknown person [Fall 1899?]; item 23, list 2, fund 920, RGALI.

22. Melnikov to Mamontov, 8 July 1899; item 170, list 1, fund 799, RGALI.

23. Mamontov to Shkafer and Chernenko [November 1899?]; item 23, list 2, fund 920, RGALI.

24. Mamontov to Shkafer [October 1899?]; item 23, list 2, fund 920, RGALI.

25. See for example, Fëdor Shaliapin, *Stranitsy iz moei zhizni* [Pages from My Life], in *F. I. Shaliapin: Literaturnoe nasledstvo* [F. I. Chaliapin: Literary Heritage], ed. Ekaterina Grosheva (Moscow: Muzgiz, 1959), 1: 126; Nadezhda Salina, *Zhizn' i stsena* [Life and Stage] (Moscow: Vsesoiuznoe Teatral'noe Obshchestvo, 1941), 63.

26. Musorgsky to Stasov, 18 October 1872; quoted in Taruskin, *Stravinsky and the Russian Traditions*, 438.

27. Mamontov to Cui [late April 1899?]; item 83, list 1, fund 786, RGALI.

28. Melnikov to Mamontov, 2 April 1898; item 21, fund 155, BM.

29. Mamontov to Shkafer [October 1899?]; item 23, list 2, fund 920, RGALI.

30. See, for example, an unusually exalted missive from a young soprano, Anna Stavitskaya, whose style normally avoids exclamation marks; Stavitskaya to Mamontov, 27 August 1899; item 237, list 1, fund 799, RGALI.

31. Shkafer to Mamontov, 11 September 1897; item 280, list 1, fund 799, RGALI.

32. Shkafer to Mamontov, 10 August 1898; item 280, list 1, fund 799, RGALI.

33. See introduction, n.8.

34. For instance, in the *Russkoe Slovo* coverage of the plans for constructing a new, permanent building for the Moscow Private Opera, the project is attributed to "one of Moscow's leading capitalists"; see *RS* 33, 2 February 1898, 2.

35. Il'ia Bondarenko, "S. I. Mamontov i ego opera" [S. I. Mamontov and His Opera Company], unpublished lecture at the Russian Theater Society (Vsesoiuznoe Teatral'noe Obshchestvo), 7 April 1941 (TS; item 24, list 1, fund 964, RGALI), 7.

36. Shkafer to Mamontov, 29 September 1898; item 280, list 1, fund 799, RGALI.

37. Soprano Nadezhda Salina, who had transferred to the Bolshoi Theater after three years with Mamontov, called her job at the Imperial Theaters *sluzhba* [a civil service job]; see Salina, *Zhizn' i stsena*, 100.

38. Shkafer to Mamontov, 10 August 1898; item 280, list 1, fund 799, RGALI.

39. Fëdor Shaliapin, *Maska i dusha* [Mask and Soul], in *F. I. Shaliapin: Literaturnoe nasledstvo*, 1: 242.

40. Shkafer to Mamontov, 10 August 1898; item 280, list 1, fund 799, RGALI.

41. Konstantin Sergeevich Alekseev-Stanislavsky was a cousin of Mamontov's wife, Elizaveta Mamontova (née Sapozhnikova); see also introduction, n.11.

42. Mamontov to Stanislavsky, 2 January 1908; item 9239, Stanislavsky fund, MATM.

43. Rossikhina, *Opernyi teatr S. I. Mamontova*, 64.

44. Mamontov to Shkafer [Fall 1899?]; item 23, list 2, fund 920, RGALI.

45. Mamontov to Stanislavsky, 15 October 1898; item 9235, Stanislavsky fund, MATM.

46. Shkafer to Mamontov, 25 December 1910; item 280, list 1, fund 799, RGALI.

47. Bondarenko, "S. I. Mamontov i ego opera," 25.

48. See, for example, Shaliapin, *Stranitsy iz moei zhizni*, in *F. I. Shaliapin: Literaturnoe nasledstvo*, 1: 126.

49. Pëtr Mel'nikov, "Moia pervaia vstrecha so Stanislavskim. Savva Ivanovich Mamontov—pokrovitel' khudozhnikov i artistov" [My First Meeting with Stanislavsky. Savva Ivanovich Mamontov, a Patron of Artists and Actors], *Segodnya* 334, [Riga, 1940]; item 282622, Mel'nikov fund, RMLAH.

50. Paskhalova to Mamontov, 17 July 1898; item 187, list 1, fund 799, RGALI.

51. Stanislavsky to Mamontov, 13 October 1908; item 236, list 1, fund 799, RGALI.

52. Paskhalova to Mamontov, 4 December 1898; item 187, list 1, fund 799, RGALI.

53. Alevtina Paskhalova's memoirs are preserved as item 13 of fund 200, GM.

54. See, for instance, a letter preserved in the Prakhov fund of the State Russian Museum that requests Mamontov's appraisal of a collection of ancient Greek coins; item 1027, fund 139, SRM.

55. Markiz Tuzhur-Portu, "Arabeski stolichnoi zhizni" [Arabesques of the Life in the Capital], *RS* 256, 16 September 1899, 2.

56. Rossikhina, *Opernyi teatr S. I. Mamontova*, 88.

57. Hellas—a poetic name for Ancient Greece; "Hellene"—a resident of Hellas.

58. See letters from Mamontov to Polenov, 3 June 1905 and [no date]; items 2891 and 2915, fund 54, STG.

59. See a letter from Polenov to the participants of the performance; item 1060, fund 54, STG.

60. Gozenpud, *Russkii opernyi teatr i Shaliapin*, 157.

61. Mamontov to Polenov, 9 November 1897; item 2884, fund 54, STG.

62. See a quote from Polenov's letter to his wife in Rossikhina, *Opernyi teatr S. I. Mamontova*, 114. Mamontov, incidentally, was not merely being stubborn: his reasons for casting Chernenko will be further discussed in chapter 4.

63. Shkafer to Mamontov, 29 September 1898; item 280, list 1, fund 799, RGALI.

64. Melnikov to Mamontov, 9 April 1898; item 23, fund 155, BM.

65. Stasov, "Vystavki" [Exhibitions], in *Izbrannye trudy*, 3: 218.

66. "Russkaia Chastnaia Opera" [Russian Private Opera], *NS* 420, 23 December 1897, 3. Indeed, throughout the late 1890s the Russian folk epic of Sadko, on which the opera is based, was commonly viewed as a native parallel to the ancient Greek myth of Orpheus (see Vladimir Marchenkov, "The Orfeo Myth in Modernity: Rimsky-Korsakov's Opera *Sadko*," in "The Orfeo Myth in Musical Thought of Antiquity, the

Renaissance and Modern Times," Ph.D. diss., Ohio State University, 1998). Remarkably, Mamontov staged *Sadko* less than a month after the premiere of *Orfeo*. One is tempted to speculate that their "mythological" connection did occur to him; there is no direct evidence, however, that he ever linked the two productions.

67. Consider, for instance, Mir Iskusstva's first, unrealized theatrical project, the ballet *Sylvia* (1901; see chapter 4), Léon Bakst's designs for the dramas of Sophocles (1904) and Euripides (1902), and his 1908 cult canvas, *Terror Antiquus*. The Ballets Russes productions *Narcissus* (1911), *Daphnis et Chloe*, and *L'après-midi d'un faune* (1912) also explore Greek myth as a subject matter.

68. Andrei Belyi, "Teatr i sovremennaia drama" [Theater and Modern Drama], in *Simvolism kak miroponimanie* [Symbolism as a Worldview] (Moscow: Respublika, 1994), 153–67.

69. See Rosamund Bartlett, *Wagner and Russia* (Cambridge: Cambridge University Press, 1995), 117–39.

70. Marchenkov, "The Orfeo Myth in Modernity," 162–63.

71. Andrei Rimskii-Korsakov, *N. A. Rimskii-Korsakov: Zhizn' i tvorchestvo* [N. A. Rimsky-Korsakov: Life and Works] (Moscow: Muzgiz, 1937), 4: 151–52.

72. See, for example, Vasilii Iakovlev, "*Boris Godunov* v teatre" [*Boris Godunov* in the Theater], in *Izbrannye trudy o muzyke* [Selected Writings on Music], vol. 3 (Moscow: Sovetskii Kompozitor, 1983), 235.

73. Gozenpud, *Russkii opernyi teatr i Shaliapin*, 214.

74. This classification of naturalism as an aspect of decadence was common in Soviet aesthetic vocabulary, as Gozenpud surely knew when he used the distinction in his defense of Mamontov.

75. Vladimir Artinov, "S. I. Mamontov o 'Svobodnom Teatre'" [S. I. Mamontov on Svobodnyi Theater], *RS* 233, 10 October 1913, 8.

76. P. S., "S. I. Mamontov o *Elene Prekrasnoi*" [Mamontov on *La Belle Hélène*], *Teatr* 366 (1913): 7.

77. Andrei Rimskii-Korsakov, *N. A. Rimskii-Korsakov*, 4: 152.

78. See Taruskin, *Musorgsky: Eight Essays and an Epilogue*, 23.

79. For a detailed treatment of Musorgsky's relationship with Stasov and Golenishchev-Kutuzov, a discussion of Kutuzov's aesthetic views, and significance of his memoirs, see Taruskin, "Who Speaks for Musorgsky?" in *Musorgsky: Eight Essays and an Epilog*, 3–37.

80. Mamontov to Shkafer [November 1899], item 23, list 2, fund 920, RGALI.

81. E. R., "Russkaia Chastnaia Opera: Oprichnik" [Russian Private Opera: The Oprichnik], *ND* 5170, 25 October 1897, 2.

82. S. K., "U Tsezarya Kiui" [At César Cui's], *ND* 5944, 11 December 1899, 3.

83. Vasilii Shkafer, *Sorok let na stsene russkoi opery* [Forty Years on the Russian Operatic Stage] (Leningrad: Izdanie Teatra Opery i Baleta Imeni S. M. Kirova, 1936), 132–33.

84. Vsevolod Meierhol'd, "K postanovke Tristana i Izol'dy v Mariinskom Teatre" [On the Production of *Tristan und Isolde* at the Mariinsky Theater], in *Stat'i, pis'ma, rechi, besedy* [Articles, Letters, Speeches, Conversations] (Moscow: Iskusstvo, 1968), 1: 144. Meyerhold's perception of Chaliapin is particularly interesting in light of the long tradition of viewing the singer as a proponent of realism; see chapter 4 on the modernist traits in Chaliapin's art.

85. Stasov, "Pokhod nashikh estetikov" [A March of Our Aesthetes], in *Izbran-nye trudy*, 3: 67–68.

86. Incidentally, Russian futurists and constructivists who advocated the presence of machinery on stage would have agreed with Mamontov's assessment, as they rejected the autonomy of art in favor of treating it as a weapon for reshaping the world.

87. Savva Mamontov, "O techenii opernogo sezona v moskovskikh teatrakh" [On the Progression of the Operatic Season in Moscow Theaters], draft article (1908); item 26, list 1, fund 799, RGALI. It is interesting that Yakovlev, who criticized Mamontov's production of *Boris Godunov*, considered the above-mentioned staging by Olenin exemplary; see Iakovlev, "Teatr Mamontova" [Mamontov's Theater], in *Izbrannye trudy o muzyke*, 3: 234. It is also worth noting that Musorgsky's opera held a special significance for Olenin: the role of Rangoni was his MPO debut (see plate 26).

88. Reed, *Decadent Style*, 14.

89. Sarab'ianov, *Istoriia russkogo iskusstva kontsa XIX–nachala XX veka* [History of Russian Art of the Late 19th–Early 20th Centuries] (Moscow: Moskovskii Universitet, 1993), 23.

90. For details, see chapter 4.

91. Diaghilev's attitude to modernity is often discussed in the literature; see for example *The Ballets Russes and Its World*, 160.

92. Mamontov to Cui [March 1899?], quoted in Rossikhina, *Opernyi teatr S. I. Mamontova*, 166.

93. Mamontov to Shkafer and Chernenko [November 1899?]; item 23, list 2, fund 920, RGALI.

94. E., "K 25-letiiu Chastnoi Opery. U S. I. Mamontova" [On the 25th Anniversary of the Private Opera. At S. I. Mamontov's], *Teatr* 568 (1910): 8.

95. Sh., "Beseda s Mamontovym" [A Conversation with Mamontov], *RS* 6, 9 January 1910, 5.

96. Kopshitser, *Savva Mamontov*, 235.

97. Shkafer, *Sorok let na stsene russkoi opery*, 162. Shkafer's description of his mentor as "the aesthete"—Stasov's favorite insult—also clearly aligns Mamontov with the decadent generation.

98. Kruglikov to Mamontov, 3 December 1898; item 145, list 1, fund 799, RGALI. A Musorgsky scholar will spot the Kuchkist slogan "to the new shores!" in Kruglikov's dithyramb; the man was, after all, a Rimsky-Korsakov student and, as we shall see, did not always see eye to eye with his boss, "the aesthete."

99. Mamontov to Shkafer, 27 July [1904?]; item 23, list 2, fund 920, RGALI.

100. Melnikov to Mamontov, 8 July 1899; item 170, list 1, fund 799, RGALI.

101. Mamontov to Shkafer [October 1899?]; item 23, list 2, fund 920, RGALI. For the details of Mamontov's arrest and trial, see introduction, n.8.

102. Mamontov to Shkafer [November 1899?]; item 23, list 2, fund 920, RGALI.

103. Vladimir Artinov, "Snegurochka v Narodnom Dome" [*The Snow Maiden* at the People's House], *RS* 287, 13 December 1913, 7.

104. Rosenthal, "Theater as Church."

105. Solov'ëv, "Obshchii smysl iskusstva," in *Stikhotvoreniia, estetika, literaturnaia kritika*, 134.

106. Varvara Strakhova-Ermans, "Vospominaniia o Shaliapine" [Recollections of Chaliapin] (TS; item 988, fund 468, BM), 5.

107. Stanislavsky's memoirs are quoted in Garafola, *Diaghilev's Ballets Russes*, 162.

108. Mikhail Vrubel', *Perepiska. Vospominaniia o khudozhnike* [Correspondence: Recollections of the Artist] (Leningrad: Iskusstvo, 1963), 154.

109. Mamontov to Shkafer [Fall 1899?]; item 23, list 2, fund 920, RGALI.

110. Mamontov to Stanislavsky, 22 August 1899; item 9236, Stanislavsky fund, MATM.

111. Shkafer to Mamontov, 29 September 1898; item 280, list 1, fund 799, RGALI.

112. Solov'ëv, "Prekrasnoe v prirode" [The Beautiful in Nature], in *Stikhotvoreniia, estetika, literaturnaia kritika*, 99–101.

113. Mamontov to Shkafer [December 1899?]; item 23, list 2, fund 920, RGALI.

114. Mamontov to Shkafer, 27 July [1904?]; item 23, list 2, fund 920, RGALI.

115. Mamontov to Stanislavsky, 17 May 1903; item 9238, Stanislavsky fund, MATM.

116. Mamontov to Stanislavsky, 22 August 1899; no. 9236, Stanislavsky fund, MATM.

117. Quoted in Konstantin Rudnitskii, *Rezhissër Meierhol'd* [Meyerhold the Director] (Moscow: Nauka, 1969), 37.

118. Rosenthal, "Theater as Church," 124.

### 3. Echoes of Abramtsevo

1. This, for instance, is a central focus of Dora Kogan's investigation of the Mamontov Circle; see her *Mamontovskii kruzhok* [The Mamontov Circle] (Moscow: Izobrazitel'noe Iskusstvo, 1970).

2. This tradition was especially strong among the merchant families of the Orthodox Old Believers, the denomination to which the Tretyakovs, Morozovs, and Kokorevs belonged; the Mamontovs, however, did not.

3. Konstantin Rudnitskii, *Russkoe rezhissërskoe iskusstvo, 1898–1907* [The Russian Art of Directing, 1898–1907] (Moscow: Nauka, 1989), 36.

4. Stasov, "Moskovskaia Chastnaia Opera v Peterburge" [The Moscow Private Opera in St. Petersburg], *NBG* 93, 4 April 1898, 2.

5. Unknown to Mamontov, July 1898; item 290, list 1, fund 799, RGALI.

6. Mamontov to Stanislavsky, 22 August 1899; item 9236, Stanislavsky fund, MATM.

7. Grover, "Savva Mamontov and the Mamontov Circle."

8. Shkafer, *Sorok let na stsene russkoi opery*, 167. Indeed, Grover's examples of Mamontov's exhibiting Serov and Korovin's paintings in his "Russian North" pavilion at the 1896 Nizhny Novgorod Exhibition, mounting Vrubel's majolica above the front entrance of the Metropol hotel, and his desire to decorate railway stations with works of art would rather suggest that Mamontov might instead have been using his businesses to promote the cause of art.

9. Bondarenko, "S. I. Mamontov i ego opera," 3.

10. Zabela to Mamontov, [Spring 1896?]; item 84, list 1, fund 799, RGALI.

11. Quoted in Nikolai Geineke, "Savva Ivanovich Mamontov i ego rol' v istorii russkoi opery" [Savva Ivanovich Mamontov and His Role in the History of Russian Opera], draft article, 28 February 1942 (item 20, fund 532, BM), 8.

12. Mamontov to Elizaveta Mamontova, Moscow to Rome, 23 February 1873; item 320, list 1, fund 799, RGALI.

13. Mamontov to Polenov, Moscow to Paris, 12/23 February 1874; item 2865, fund 54, STG.

14. Ibid.

15. Unless otherwise noted, all mentions of the family name "Serov" refer to painter Valentin Serov, not his father, composer Alexander Serov.

16. Kogan, *Mamontovskii kruzhok*, 6.

17. Repin to Serov, 1892; quoted in Arenzon, *Savva Mamontov*, 75.

18. Mamontov to Polenov, Abramtsevo, 23 August 1880; item 2870, fund 54, STG.

19. Mel'nikov, "Moia pervaia vstrecha so Stanislavskim."

20. Pëtr Mel'nikov, "Savva Ivanovich Mamontov i ego okruzhenie" [Savva Ivanovich Mamontov and His Circle], *Segodnya* 313 [Riga, 1940], 4; item 282623, Mel'nikov fund, Rainis Museum.

21. See, for example, Gray, *The Russian Experiment in Art*, 16–21.

22. Viktor Vasnetsov, "Vospominaniia o Savve Ivanoviche Mamontove" [Recollections of Savva Ivanovich Mamontov], in Vsevolod Mamontov, *Vospominaniia o russkikh khudozhnikakh* [Recollections of Russian Painters] (Moscow: Akademiia Khudozhestv, 1950), 65. Indeed, Vasily Polenov's activities as a composer that would result in the creation of *Aphrodite* and *The Phantoms of Hellas* could be traced to his experiences in Mamontov's theatricals.

23. Alexandre Benois, who in his memoirs described his disappointment with the theater design class he took at the Academy, also recalled his astonishment at Konstantin Korovin's ability to translate painterly techniques to the backdrop; see Aleksandr Benua, *Aleksandr Benua razmyshliaet* [*Alexandre Benois Contemplates*] (Moscow: Sovetskii Khudozhnik, 1968), 211.

24. Valkenier, *Peredvizhniki*, 128.

25. *Lubok* (pl. *lubki*)—a traditional handcolored woodcut print similar to the English chapbooks, produced in Russian towns from the seventeenth to the early twentieth century for circulation among the peasantry. *Lubok* subjects ranged from Bible illustrations to political satire; their style owed much to traditional icon painting and manuscript illustration in its disregard of proportion and perspective; see Gray, *The Russian Experiment in Art*, 97.

26. Kramskoy to Stasov, 27 July 1886; in Ivan Kramskoi, *Pis'ma. Stat'i* [Letters. Articles] (Moscow: Iskusstvo, 1965–66), 2: 252.

27. Kramskoy to Repin, 28 September 1874; in Kramskoi, *Pis'ma* 1: 268–69.

28. Fyodor Dostoevsky, "A Propos of the Exhibition," in *Diary of a Writer*, trans. Boris Brasol (New York: Braziller, 1954), 79–81.

29. Glenn Watkins, *Pyramids at the Louvre: Music, Culture, and Collage from Stravinsky to the Postmodernists* (Cambridge, Mass.: Belknap Press, 1994), 80. See also Glenn Watkins, *Soundings: Music in the Twentieth Century* (New York: Schirmer, 1988), 196–97.

30. Valkenier, *Peredvizhniki*, 58.

31. Repin to Kramskoy, 16 October 1874; in Il'ia Repin, *Izbrannye pis'ma v dvukh tomakh, 1867–1930* [Selected Letters in Two Volumes, 1867–1930] (Moscow: Iskusstvo, 1969), 1: 143.

32. See Stasov, "Priskorbnye estetiki" [Miserable Aesthetes], in *Izbrannye trudy*, 1: 287–95. Prakhov's article, under the tongue-in-cheek signature "Profan" [Ignoramus], was published in *Pchela* 45–47 (December 1876). The "barge haulers" mentioned in Stasov's article are a reference to Repin's painting *Burlaki na Volge* [The Volga Barge Haulers] (1873), the artist's first public success and the critic's favorite.

33. This work, incidentally, earned Antokolsky a gold medal from the Academy and a generous scholarship to Rome—a remarkable achievement for an unconverted Jew in Imperial Russia.

34. Antokolsky to Stasov, 9 March 1872; quoted in Andrei Lebedev and Genrietta Burova, *Tvorcheskoe sodruzhestvo: M. M. Antokol'skii i V. V. Stasov* [Creative Collaboration: M. M. Antokolsky and V. V. Stasov] (Leningrad: Khudozhnik RSFSR, 1968), 62.

35. Elizabeth Valkenier, *Ilya Repin and the World of Russian Art* (New York: Columbia University Press, 1990), 31.

36. Mamontov to Polenov, Moscow to Paris, 12/23 February 1874; item 2865, fund 54, STG.

37. Stasov, "Vystavki," in *Izbrannye trudy*, 3: 195.

38. Stasov, "Iskusstvo XIX veka" [Art of the 19th Century], in *Izbrannye trudy*, 3: 666–67.

39. Stasov, "Dvadtsat' piat' let russkogo iskusstva: Nasha zhivopis'" [Twenty Five Years of the Russian Art: Our Painting], in *Izbrannye trudy*, 2: 454. *Bogatyri* are legendary knights, the heroes of Russian epics and fairy tales, whose plots usually situate them at the medieval Kievan court of Prince Vladimir.

40. Stasov, "Dvadtsat' piat' let russkogo iskusstva: Nasha zhivopis'," in *Izbrannye trudy*, 2: 465.

41. Stasov, "Iskusstvo XIX veka," in *Izbrannye trudy*, 3: 667.

42. Valkenier, *Peredvizhniki*, 85.

43. Indeed, Camilla Gray contends that despite his frequent visits to Abramtsevo, Surikov cannot be counted among the members of the Mamontov Circle, because he did not participate in its communal projects—church construction, theatricals, and reading nights (on the latter, see chapter 5); Gray, *The Russian Experiment in Art*, 22.

44. Even in discussing paintings on mythological and Biblical themes, as well as on semi-legendary ancient subjects, Stasov demanded strict historical accuracy and realist depiction of the "real ancient world"; see his critique of Semiradsky that follows the discussion of Vasnetsov in "Dvadtsat' piat' let russkogo iskusstva: Nasha zhivopis'," in *Izbrannye trudy*, 2: 454–55.

45. John Bowlt, *The Silver Age: Russian Art of the Early Twentieth Century and the "World of Art" Group* (Newtonville, Mass.: Oriental Research Partners, 1982), 48.

46. Valkenier, *Peredvizhniki*, 131.

47. Diagilev, "Vechnaia bor'ba," 13.

48. Vrubel', *Perepiska. Vospominaniia o khudozhnike*, 59–60.

49. See Sergei Diagilev, "Pis'mo po adresu I. Repina" [A Letter Addressed to Repin], *Mir Iskusstva* 10 (1899): 4–8.

50. Valkenier, *Peredvizhniki*, 130.

51. Dmitrii Severiukhin and Oleg Leikind, *Zolotoi vek khudozhestvennykh ob'iedinenii v Rossii i SSSR, 1820–1932* [*The Golden Age of Artistic Associations in Russia and the USSR, 1820–1932*] (St. Petersburg: Izdatel'stvo Chernysheva, 1992), 133–35. The MAA would prove to be one of the most enduring exhibition societies in Silver Age Russia, surviving until 1924.

52. Bukva [I. F. Vasilevskii], "Peterburgskie nabroski: Dve vystavki" [Petersburg Sketches: Two Exhibitions], *RV* 66, 8 March 1898, 3.

53. Quoted in Arenzon, *Savva Mamontov*, 166.

54. Severiukhin and Leikind, *Zolotoi vek*, 133.

55. Arenzon, *Savva Mamontov*, 168.

56. Mamontov to Polenov [mid- to late 1900s?]; item 2911, fund 54, STG.

57. Mamontov to Polenov, 27 September [1907?]; item 2903, fund 54, STG.

58. Mamontov to Carré, Moscow to Paris, 17/30 November 1907; list 1, fund 799, RGALI. Notably, Carré was convinced—the *Snow Maiden* contract was taken away from Korovin and given to a French decorator who was required to execute the sets and costumes following Vasnetsov's sketches sent by Mamontov (see chapter 8 for details).

59. According to several eye-witnesses, after Mamontov's arrest, Korovin panicked and attempted to disassociate himself from the disgraced tycoon by destroying Mamontov's letters to him and all other personal effects that could prove that their relationship went deeper than that between an employer and an employee.

60. Sh., "Beseda s S. I. Mamontovym," *RS* 6, 9 January 1910, 5.

61. Artinov, "S. I. Mamontov o 'Svobodnom Teatre.'"

62. See, for example, a discussion of his polemics with *Zolotoe Runo* in Mark Etkind, *A. N. Benua i russkaia khudozhestvennaia kul'tura* [*A. N. Benois and Russian Artistic Culture*] (Leningrad: Khudozhnik RSFSR, 1989), 185–89.

63. Arenzon, *Savva Mamontov*, 180.

64. Platon Mamontov, "Savva Ivanovich Mamontov: Vospominaniia" [Savva Ivanovich Mamontov: Memoir], unpublished manuscript; item 4, list 2, fund 799, RGALI.

65. Gray, *The Russian Experiment in Art*, 33.

66. Dmitrii Sarab'ianov, "Russkii variant stilia modern v zhivopisi kontsa XIX–nachala XX veka" [The Russian Variant of *Style Moderne* in Painting of the Late 19th–Early 20th Centuries], in *Russkaia zhivopis' XIX veka sredi evropeiskikh shkol* [*Russian Art of the 19th Century among the European Schools*] (Moscow: Sovetskii Khudozhnik, 1980), 219.

67. See Vrubel's letter to the editor and Diaghilev's response in *Mir Iskusstva* 5 (1899): 40–41.

68. Gray, *The Russian Experiment in Art*, 35.

69. Grigorii Sternin, *Khudozhestvennaia zhizn' Rossii na rubezhe XIX–XX vekov* [Artistic Life in Russia of the Late 19th–Early 20th Centuries] (Moscow: Iskusstvo, 1970), 20–21.

70. Shaliapin, *Maska i dusha*, in *Literaturnoe nasledstvo* 1: 243.

71. The majolica works produced at Maria Tenisheva's Talashkino estate, which from its inception positioned itself as a rival to Abramtsevo, exhibit similar characteristics; however, Mamontov's and Vrubel's work with majolica predate that of its competition.

72. Gray, *The Russian Experiment in Art,* 32.

## 4. Visual Impressions

1. "Teatr i muzyka" [Theater and Music], *RS* 273, 11 October 1896, 3.

2. A. G., "Vozobnovlenie opery *Rogneda*" [A Revival of *Rogneda*], *RS* 295, 2 November 1896, 3.

3. Such catalogues are preserved, for example, in Pyotr Melnikov's archive at RMLAH.

4. Mamontov to Polenov, 5 October 1899; item 2888, fund 54, STG.

5. "Teatr i muzyka," *RS* 273, 11 October 1896, 3.

6. See Sarab'ianov, "Russkii variant stilia modern," 197.

7. "Teatral'naia khronika," *ND* 4907, 2 February 1897, 3. The decorators named were Carl Waltz, as well as Stavitsky, Smirnov, Sergeev, and Lebedev.

8. Note, for instance, the harmony of costume, makeup, and accessories used to create the image of Polovtsian Khan Konchak (*Prince Igor*), portrayed here by an MPO veteran, bass Anton Bedlevich, a member of the troupe from 1885 (see plate 25).

9. V. Baskin, "Teatral'noe ekho" [Theatrical Echo], *PG* 87, 30 March 1898, 3. The author of this critique invites a special comment: the conservative, ardently anti-Kuchkist Baskin had a bad reputation among Soviet musicologists, who followed the nationalist press of the 1890s in discounting his politically incorrect opinions by branding him an ignoramus (see chapter 7). However, I believe that his consistently conservative stand opposed to both the realists and the modernists gave Baskin (as well as his fellow conservatives Mikhail Ivanov, Nikolai Solovyov, and Victor Burenin) a unique voice in Russia's cultural landscape that surely deserves to be heard.

10. Arnold Aronson, "Scenic Design," in *International Encyclopedia of Dance,* 5: 541.

11. Serge Lifar, *Serge Diaghilev: His Life, His Work, His Legend; An Intimate Biography* (New York: Putnam, 1940), 130.

12. Aleksandr Benua, "Konstantin Korovin: Po povodu ego iubileia" [Konstantin Korovin: On the Occasion of His Jubilee], in *Aleksandr Benua razmyshliaet,* 211.

13. Salina, *Zhizn' i stsena,* 63–64. See also Rossikhina, *Opernyi teatr S. I. Mamontova,* 65–67.

14. Mel'nikov, "Savva Ivanovich Mamontov i ego okruzhenie." The short comments from the back of the auditorium described by Melnikov were also a characteristic feature of Mamontov's personal directing style (see chapter 5).

15. Abram Raskin, *Shaliapin i russkie khudozhniki* (Leningrad: Iskusstvo, 1963).

16. Arenzon, *Savva Mamontov,* 147.

17. "Teatral'naia khronika," *ND* 5849, 7 September 1899, 2–3.

18. V. Baskin, "Govoria o Fauste" [Speaking of *Faust*], *PG* 70, 13 March 1899, 3.

19. See Raskin, *Shaliapin i russkie khudozhniki,* 50–52.

20. At the same time, the date of Vrubel's *Faust* triptych, completed while he was directly exposed to Chaliapin's work on Gounod's opera, may also suggest that the painter's original vision may itself have been influenced by Chaliapin's artistry.

21. Zabela to Rimsky-Korsakov, 24 September 1901; item 907, fund 640, RNL.

22. Salina, *Zhizn' i stsena*, 118.

23. A feuilleton by Vlas Doroshevich that described the public's rediscovery of Vrubel as a result of Chaliapin's interpretation is quoted in Raskin, *Shaliapin i russkie khudozhniki*, 51. According to Salina, both the costume and the makeup à la Vrubel were created for Chaliapin by Konstantin Korovin.

24. A photograph of the sculpture can be found in Arenzon, *Savva Mamontov*, 149.

25. "Teatral'naia khronika," *ND* 5208, 1 December 1897, 3.

26. "Teatral'naia khronika," *ND* 5530, 21 October 1898, 3.

27. Sarab'ianov, "Russkii variant stilia modern," 197.

28. Nikolai Rimskii-Korsakov, *Letopis'*, 181.

29. Rimsky-Korsakov's own account of the incident can be found in *Letopis'*, 208–209.

30. Richard Taruskin, "Sadko," in *New Grove Dictionary of Opera* 4: 120.

31. Bondarenko, "S. I. Mamontov i ego opera," 15.

32. Shkafer, *Sorok let na stsene russkoi opery*, 141–42.

33. Bondarenko, "S. I. Mamontov i ego opera," 23.

34. It is notable that the memoirs on Diaghilev's Ballets Russes contain similar descriptions of his creative team living together as a large family (see below).

35. Bondarenko, "S. I. Mamontov i ego opera," 26.

36. Lentovsky to Mamontov, 31 March 1899; item 152, list 1, fund 799, RGALI.

37. Strakhova-Ermans, *Vospominaniia o Shaliapine*, 8.

38. Alexandre Benois, *Reminiscences of the Russian Ballet* (London: Putnam, 1941), 214.

39. Garafola, *Diaghilev's Ballets Russes*, 155.

40. Ibid., 155–56.

41. Quoted in Lifar, *Serge Diaghilev*, 130.

42. Mamontov to Shkafer, [November 1899?]; item 23, list 2, fund 920, RGALI.

43. Andrei Rimskii-Korsakov, *N. A. Rimskii-Korsakov*, 159–60.

44. See Rimsky-Korsakov to Zabela, 30 September 1900; item 796, fund 640, RNL. Nadezhda Zabela-Vrubel, MPO soprano from 1897–1902, was Rimsky-Korsakov's favorite singer and close personal friend. The composer idealized her voice, believed her to be the perfect interpreter of his operas, and created expressly for her the parts of Marfa in *The Tsar's Bride*, the Swan Princess in *The Tale of Tsar Saltan*, and the Princess in *Kashchei the Deathless*. For more information, see Liudmila Barsova, *N. I. Zabela-Vrubel' glazami sovremennikov* [N. I. Zabela-Vrubel' in the Eyes of Her Contemporaries] (Leningrad: Muzyka, 1982).

45. Quoted in Arenzon, *Savva Mamontov*, 153.

46. See Taruskin, *Stravinsky and the Russian Traditions*, 492.

47. Mamontov to Polenov, 24 November 1897; item 2885, fund 54, STG.

48. Mamontov to Shkafer, [Fall 1899]; item 23, list 2, fund 920, RGALI.

49. Artinov, "Snegurochka v Narodnom Dome."

50. A. G., "V Bol'shom Teatre" [At the Bolshoi Theater], *RS* 263, 1 October 1897, 3.

51. The reasons for Mamontov's relative neglect of the instrumental side of the operatic production are not entirely clear. Either he was less curious, or believed himself to be unqualified to offer an opinion: a trained singer and a reasonably competent pianist, he apparently could not read orchestral scores.

52. Rimskii-Korsakov, *Letopis'*, 209.

53. Rachmaninov would utilize the skills acquired at Mamontov's enterprise a few years later, when in 1904 he would take over the Bolshoi Theater orchestra; see Vasilii Iakovlev, "Rakhmaninov—Dirizhër," in *Izbrannye trudy o muzyke*, vol. 2 (Moscow: Muzyka, 1971), 372–90.

54. Rimsky-Korsakov, *Letopis'*, 209.

55. Nikolai Kashkin was one of several critics who complained about Mamontov's orchestra frequently being overworked and under-rehearsed; see N. K-in, "Psko-vitianka," *RV* 348, 17 December 1896, 3.

56. See Rimsky-Korsakov to Zabela, 12 May 1899; item 793, fund 640, RNL.

57. Indeed, the press commented on Ippolitov-Ivanov's appointment specifically in this light; see, for instance, an editorial "Chastnaia Opera" [Private Opera], in *NS* 617, 8 September 1899, 2.

58. Mamontov to Shkafer [Fall 1899?]; item 23, list 2, fund 920, RGALI.

59. "Khovanshchina," *NS* 390, 23 November 1897, 2.

60. V. Baskin, "Kniaz' Igor'" [Prince Igor], *PG* 79, 22 March 1899, 3.

61. Quoted in Gozenpud, *Russkii opernyi teatr i Shaliapin*, 154.

62. I. L., "Chastnaia Opera," *NS* 40, 10 September 1896, 2.

63. After his arrest on 12 September, Mamontov spent about two months in solitary confinement at Moscow's Taganskaya Prison; following a petition by family and friends, the fifty-eight-year-old tycoon was subsequently released and placed under house arrest due to health problems (for the details of the indictment, see introduction, n.8).

64. Mamontov to unknown and Shkafer [Fall 1899]; item 23, list 2, fund 920, RGALI.

65. "Teatral'naia khronika," *ND* 5960, 28 December 1899, 3.

66. Quoted in Lifar, *Serge Diaghilev*, 176.

67. Camille Mauclair; quoted in Aronson, "Scenic Design," 541.

68. Quoted in Janet Kennedy, *The "Mir Iskusstva" Group and Russian Art, 1898–1912* (New York: Garland, 1977), 343.

69. Peter Lieven, *The Birth of the Ballets Russes* (London: Allen and Unwin, 1936), 131. Taruskin signals his agreement with Lieven's assessment by not only quoting his description of *Petrushka* in *Stravinsky and the Russian Traditions* (see p. 661), but borrowing it for the title of the relevant section of the book.

70. See Bartlett, *Wagner and Russia*.

71. Bartlett, *Wagner and Russia*, 14.

72. A line from Alexander Serov's review of *Lohengrin*'s première, in which he publicly apologized to Wagner "for the Russian production's excessive realism . . . incompatible with the opera's mythical and mystical content" (quoted in Bartlett, *Wagner and Russia*, 38), serves as a remarkable illustration of the aesthetic incompatibility between Wagner's myth-laden staged dramas and the Russian realist doctrine.

73. Sergei Diagilev, "Osnovy khudozhestvennoi otsenki" [Foundations of Artistic Judgment], *Mir Iskusstva* 3–4 (1899): 52.

74. Kennedy, *The "Mir Iskusstva" Group and the Russian Art*, 100.

75. See Melnikov to Mamontov, Paris, 8/21 July 1899; item 170, list 1, fund 799, RGALI.

76. Sh., "Beseda s S. I. Mamontovym."

77. Rossikhina, *Opernyi teatr S. I. Mamontova*, 60. The researcher, however, refers only to the painters' stage-directing experience.

78. Taruskin, *Stravinsky and the Russian Traditions*, 488.

79. Quoted in Calinescu, *Five Faces of Modernity*, 166.

80. Taruskin, *Stravinsky and the Russian Traditions*, 437.

81. Rosenthal, "Theater as Church," 134.

82. Taruskin, *Stravinsky and the Russian Traditions*, 489.

83. Bondarenko, "S. I. Mamontov i ego opera," 15.

84. Quoted in Simon Morrison, "Scriabin and the Impossible," *Journal of the American Musicological Society* 51, no. 2 (Summer 1998): 292.

85. The anonymous author of the *Rannee Utro* article, "V tupikakh i osobniakakh" [In Mansions and Blind Alleys] ([1907]; item 15, list 3, fund 799, RGALI) briefly reports on "chatting" with Mamontov after a Scriabin concert. The topics of conversation (unfortunately, the journalist does not go into detail) included Emil Cooper's interpretations of Symphony no. 3 and *Poème d'extase*, Scriabin's compositional style, and the composer's recent interest in theosophy.

86. *Kurier*'s anonymous review, dated 1 December 1897, was also quoted in the press digest published in *NS* 399, 2 December 1897, 2.

87. Mamontov to Polenov, 17 August [1907?]; item 2902, fund 54, STG.

88. Mamontov to Polenov, 24 August 1907; item 2894, fund 54, STG.

89. See remarks quoted in Shkafer, *Sorok let na stsene russkoi opery*, 151.

90. It should be noted that "decadents" and "aesthetes" were discussed—and indicted—in the same chapter of Max Nordau's *Degeneration;* see Nordau, *Degeneration*, 296–337.

91. A. G., "Vozobnovlenie opery *Rogneda*."

92. Sternin, *Khudozhestvennaia zhizn' Rossii na rubezhe XIX–XX vekov*, 21.

93. In particular, Serov's modernist designs for *Judith* come to mind, to be discussed below.

94. Vrubel would take over as MPO's chief designer after Korovin's move to the Bolshoi in the fall of 1899, for the following three seasons (1899–1902). Among his finest achievements during this period are sets and costumes for Rimsky-Korsakov's *The Tsar's Bride*, *The Tale of Tsar Saltan* (see plate 38), and *Kashchei the Deathless*, all starring his wife, Nadezhda Zabela.

95. More anonymous but equally conspicuous was the work of architect Ilya Bondarenko, the author of the Solodovnikov Theater reconstruction project. Represented on the pages of this book primarily as Mamontov's close friend, archivist, and memoirist, Bondarenko is considered to be one of the most original and innovative architects of the Russian *style moderne*, an equal of Shchusev and Shekhtel; see Elena Borisova and Grigory Sternin, *Russian Art Nouveau* (New York: Rizzoli, 1988), 85.

96. Staryi Chelovek, "Za kulisami—VI" [Backstage—6], *ND* 5648, 17 February 1899, 3. The underlying assumption behind the joke, comprehended easily by readers, was a belief that any artist subscribing to the art-for-art's sake philosophy was by definition a "decadent."

97. See reviews in *RS* 342 and 343, 11 and 12 December 1899, respectively.

98. E. R., "Tsarskaia Nevesta v Chastnoi Opere" [*The Tsar's Bride* at the Private Opera], *ND* 5897, 25 October 1899, 3.

99. Novyi, "Otovsiudu" [From Everywhere], *RS* 254, 14 September 1899, 3.

100. "Teatral'naia khronika," *ND* 5208, 1 December 1897, 3.

101. A. Gr., "Orfei na stsene Teatra Solodovnikova" [*Orfeo* on the Solodovnikov Theater Stage], *RS* 323, 1 December 1897, 3.

102. "Teatral'naia khronika," *ND* 4857, 12 December 1896, 3.

103. Sergei Shchukin, Ivan Morozov, and other sophisticated collectors of modernist art who came out of Moscow's increasingly wealthy middle class cannot be considered representative of that group. The 2,200-seat capacity of the Solodovnikov Theater all but ensured that, even when in the audience, true connoisseurs of Korovin's and Vrubel's art would always be in the minority.

104. Repin's Impressionist Parisian works and some of Arkhip Kuindzhi's landscapes may be considered an exception; however, they do not display the radical approach to color evident, for instance, in Korovin's designs.

105. Twenty-five years earlier, a similar reaction was exhibited by the first audiences of the French Impressionists, as a response to their radically altered approach to the concept of "finished work."

106. A. G., "Khovanshchina," *RS* 306, 14 November 1897, 3.

107. "Teatr i muzyka," *NV* 7903, 26 February 1898, 3.

108. "Teatr i muzyka," *NV* 7913, 9 March 1898, 3.

109. Stasov, "Moskovskaia Chastnaia Opera v Peterburge."

110. The view of the historicist trend on the Russian stage as progressive was partially shaped by the success of the Meiningen Theater, which toured the country in 1885 and 1890; for an extended discussion of the Meiningen phenomenon and its impact on the MPO, see chapter 6.

111. Stasov himself, incidentally, did not use the term when discussing Mamontov's enterprise; but see a review in *NV* 8272, 9 March 1899, 3, in which sets and costumes for *Boris Godunov* are praised for their "archeological exactness." On the use of archeological exactness in the Western European drama theaters of the late nineteenth century, see Glynn Wickham, *A History of the Theater* (Cambridge: Cambridge University Press, 1985), 204ff.

112. Cf. Stasov's approach to historical painting outlined in chapter 3.

113. Stasov, "Opera Glinki v Prage" [Glinka's Opera in Prague], in *Izbrannye trudy*, 1: 157–58.

114. Stasov, "Moskovskaia Chastnaia Opera v Peterburge."

115. "Teatr i muzyka," *RS* 333, 11 December 1897, 3.

116. Platon Mamontov, "Savva Ivanovich Mamontov."

117. Briusov, "Nenuzhnaia pravda," 73.

118. Mamontov to Polenov, 5 October 1897; item 2881, fund 54, STG.

119. Mamontov to Polenov, 19 October 1897; item 2882, fund 54, STG.

120. Mamontov to Polenov, 21 September 1899; item 2887, fund 54, STG.

121. This in fact was a common practice for the MPO's historical productions such as *The Maid of Pskov*, whose sets were modeled after Pskov's traditional architecture.

122. Taruskin, *Stravinsky and the Russian Traditions*, 493. The scholar quotes a 1914 assessment of Vasnetsov's work by Sergei Makovsky, editor of literary journal *Apollon*.

123. Borisova and Sternin, *Art Nouveau*, 46.

124. A similar design had been used in the fabric for Boris Godunov's costume, reproduced on Golovin's 1901 portrait of Chaliapin; I am indebted to Myroslava M. Mudrak for this observation.

125. Borisova and Sternin, *Art Nouveau*, 24.

126. Ibid., 45.

127. Gray, *The Russian Experiment in Art*, 93–130.

128. The story of *Sadko* plays out in two locations: the medieval Russian city of Novgorod and the fantastic Underwater Kingdom. The tableaux are constructed symmetrically; secondary characters reflect on the fates of the central figures. The opera includes two bards (Sadko and Nezhata), two wives for Sadko (the human Lyubava and the Sea Princess Volkhova), and two moral authority figures (the Ancient One, representing Christianity, and the Sea Tsar, who represents the nature gods) whose confrontation leads to the resolution of the main intrigue and Sadko's return to the human world. For a detailed discussion, see Simon Morrison, "Semiotics of Symmetry, or Rimsky-Korsakov's Operatic History Lesson," *Cambridge Opera Journal* 13 (2001): 261–93.

129. In Rimsky-Korsakov's theory of harmony, a "tone-semitone" (i.e., octatonic) scale is classified as one of the "artificial" scales.

130. Incidentally, the first meeting between Rimsky-Korsakov and Nadezhda Zabela took place during a performance of *Sadko* that the composer attended at Mamontov's theater; Zabela performed the role of the Sea Princess in a costume designed by her husband, Mikhail Vrubel. To Rimsky-Korsakov, this would always be Zabela's signature part; in some of his letters he addresses her as the Sea Princess.

131. Rimsky-Korsakov to Zabela, 17 May 1900; item 795, fund 640, RNL.

132. Nikolai Kashkin, "Sadko," *RV* 7, 7 January 1898, 2–3.

133. "Orfei v Russkoi Chastnoi Opere," *NS* 399, 2 December 1897, 2.

134. For a discussion of Mamontov's application of the individualized crowd principle, see chapter 6.

135. Bondarenko, "S. I. Mamontov i ego opera," 23.

136. Gozenpud, *Russkii opernyi teatr i Shaliapin*, 189.

137. Sarab'ianov, *Istoriia russkogo iskusstva kontsa XIX–nachala XX veka*, 23.

138. Gozenpud, *Russkii opernyi teatr i Shaliapin*, 190.

139. "Teatr i muzyka," *RS* 84, 14 April 1909, 5.

140. Dmitry Smirnov's debut took place at the Hermitage Theater in summer 1903, in the leading role in Eugenio Esposito's comic opera *Camorra*, set to Mamontov's libretto. Mamontov staged the production and personally coached its young cast.

141. See Sanin's telegram in *RS* 13, 9 January 1910, 5, mentioned above. Sanin was also vocal about his debt to Mamontov in his private correspondence, as evident in his letter to Sergei Mamontov soon after his father's arrest, dated 15 September 1899; item 367, list 1, fund 799, RGALI.

142. Garafola, *Diaghilev's Ballets Russes*, 15.

143. Ibid., 151–52.

144. Eleonora Paston, "Khudozhestvennye printsipy mamontovskogo teatra" [Artistic Principles of Mamontov's Theater], in *Sergei Diagilev i khudozhestvennaia kul'tura XIX–XX vv.* [Sergei Diaghilev and the Artistic Culture of the 19th–20th Centuries] (Perm: Permskoe Knizhnoe Izdatel'stvo, 1987), 29.

145. See Aleksandr Benua, *Vozniknovenie Mira Iskusstva* [The Birth of Mir Iskusstva] (Leningrad: Komitet Populiarizatsii Khudozhestvennykh Izdanii pri Gos. Akademii Istorii Material'noi Kul'tury, 1928).

146. Diaghilev to Benois, 8/20 October 1897; item 939, fund 137, SRM; sections of the letter reprinted in Benua, *Vozniknovenie Mira Iskusstva*, 27–28.

147. Diaghilev to Benois, [November 1897]; item 939, fund 137, SRM; reprinted in *Sergei Diagilev i russkoe iskusstvo* [Sergei Diaghilev and Russian Art], ed. Il'ia Zil'bershtein and Vladimir Samkov (Moscow: Izobrazitel'noe Iskusstvo, 1982), 2: 30–31.

148. Ironically, Vladimir Stasov was supposed to have been a consultant for that production (see Gozenpud, *Russkii opernyi teatr i Shaliapin*, 158). The collaboration did not take place, more likely due to the distance between Mamontov's and Stasov's aesthetic positions, rather than the distance between their respective places of residence, Moscow and St. Petersburg. Indeed, it is illustrative of Mamontov's aesthetics that, instead of Stasov, the St. Petersburg observer of *Khovanshchina*'s staging turned out to be Sergei Diaghilev.

149. Sergei Diagilev, "Osnovy khudozhestvennoi otsenki," 52.

150. Rimsky-Korsakov to Zabela, 8 December 1898; item 792, fund 640, RNL.

151. See Aleksandr Benua, *Moi vospominaniia* [My Memoirs] (Moscow: Nauka, 1980), 2: 213.

## 5. Opera as Drama

1. This lack of an officially defined "job description" prevented Mamontov from rejoining the company after the conclusion of his 1900 trial; the new administration, well aware that the newly-bankrupt tycoon no longer held the purse strings, simply ignored him.

2. See, for instance, Strakhova-Ermans, *Vospominaniia o Shaliapine*, 5.

3. See Bondarenko, "S. I. Mamontov i ego opera," 25.

4. On Mamontov's financial relationship with the MPO, see chapter 8.

5. Sergei Rakhmaninov, "Vospominaniia" [Memoirs], in *S. Rakhmaninov: Literaturnoe nasledie* [S. Rachmaninov: Literary Heritage], ed. Zaruia Apetian, 3 vol. (Moscow: Sovetskii Kompozitor, 1978), 1: 55.

6. Mamontov to Shkafer, 28 October 1899; item 23, list 2, fund 920, RGALI.

7. For an illustration of the "stage manager" option, see Rossikhina's discussion of a stage director's role at the Imperial Theaters in *Opernyi teatr S. I. Mamontova*, 46.

8. In her dissertation, Lucinde Braun advances the venerable Mariinsky stage director Osip Palecek as a model of a "modern régisseur"; see her *Studien zur russischen Oper in späten 19. Jahrhundert* [Studies in Russian Opera of the Late 19th Century] (Mainz: Schott, 1999), 126–51. Palecek's attempts, however, were tentative and unsystematic, and they remained largely unacknowledged by his contemporaries; he is never mentioned in Mamontov's letters, or advanced as an example in any press reviews of the MPO.

9. On the "Mamontov Drama Nights," see Arenzon, *Savva Mamontov*, 75.

10. For more information on that production, including a glowing report on Mamontov's rehearsal techniques from lead actor Alexander Yuzhin-Sumbatov, see Arenzon, *Savva Mamontov*, 7.

11. Melnikov to Mamontov, [date?]; item 170, list 1, fund 799, RGALI.

12. P., "Moskovskaia Russkaia Chastnaia Opera: Sadko" [Moscow Russian Private Opera: Sadko], *RMG* 3 (1898): 290.

13. Quoted in Gozenpud, *Russkii opernyi teatr i Shaliapin*, 177–78.

14. Bondarenko, "S. I. Mamontov i ego opera," 24.

15. Platon Mamontov, "Savva Ivanovich Mamontov," 19.

16. Ibid., 119.

17. Shkafer to Mamontov, September 1897; item 280, list 1, fund 799, RGALI.

18. Indeed, so does the description of the first rehearsal of *Sadko* in his memoirs; see Shkafer, *Sorok let na stsene russkoi opery*, 141–42.

19. Ibid.

20. See Konstantin Stanislavskii, *Moia zhizn' v iskusstve* [My Life in Art] (Moscow: Iskusstvo, 1983), 86–87.

21. Shkafer, *Sorok let na stsene russkoi opery*, 154.

22. Melnikov to Mamontov, Paris, 19 May 1898; item 24, fund 155, BM.

23. The Melnikov fund at BM contains programs, reviews, and other materials related to the *La Scala* premiere, as well as a promotional booklet for the Paris Private Opera's 1928–29 season. The bulk of the materials connected to his work at the Imperial Theaters are preserved at RMLAH.

24. Melnikov to Mamontov, Paris, 19 May 1898; item 24, fund 155, BM.

25. Melnikov to Mamontov, Paris, 4 April 1898; item 22, fund 155, BM. "Barin"— noble, landowner, master (to a servant or a peasant on his land).

26. Melnikov to Mamontov, Paris, 8/21 July 1899; item 170, list 1, fund 799, RGALI.

27. Shkafer, *Sorok let na stsene russkoi opery*, 154.

28. Melnikov to Mamontov, Paris, 8/21 July 1899; item 170, list 1, fund 799, RGALI.

29. Shkafer to Mamontov, 11 September 1897; item 280, list 1, fund 799, RGALI.

30. Shkafer, *Sorok let na stsene russkoi opery*, 164.

31. For information on the Novy Theater, see chapter 8.

32. Shkafer to Mamontov, [1903?]; item 280, list 1, fund 799, RGALI. Shkafer's reference to "a year" in Mamontov's school means his first season of apprenticeship in 1897–98, before he was allowed to work independently.

33. See chapter 4: n.36.

34. Lentovsky to Mamontov, 31 March 1899; item 152, list 1, fund 799, RGALI.

35. On the realization of the artistic ensemble in Chaliapin's directing see Nikolai Kuznetsov, *Mamontov, Shaliapin, Stanislavskii—reformatory opernogo iskusstva v Rossii kontsa XIX–nachala XX vekov* [Mamontov, Chaliapin, Stanislavsky—Reformers of Operatic Art in Russia in the Late 19th–Early 20th Centuries] (Ph.D. diss., Moscow State Conservatory, 1996), particularly the eyewitness accounts quoted on pages 65 and 124–25.

36. For a discussion of the nontraditional application of the term "ensemble" to the MPO productions in the sense of artistic synthesis, see below and chapter 4.

37. As mentioned in the introduction, Mamontov's MPO initially operated between 1885 and 1892 and then was closed until 1896. For a detailed discussion of the role played by foreign stars during both periods of MPO's operations, see Olga Haldey, "Verdi's Operas in Mamontov's Theater: Fighting a Losing Battle," *Verdi Forum* 30 (2003–2004), 3–25.

38. N. K-in, "Boris Godunov," *MV* 339, 9 December 1898, 3.

39. Ts. Kiui [César Cui], "Moskovskaia Chastnaia Russkaia Opera" [Moscow Private Russian Opera], *NBG* 67, 9 March 1899, 3.

40. This method of star-centered directing was Mamontov's trademark from the early days of his company, leading to acclaimed successes such as *Aida* and *Otello* (see Haldey, "Verdi's Operas in Mamontov's Theater"). In the late 1890s, apart from the examples discussed, he demonstrated a similar example of creative directing in an acclaimed production of *Faust* with Chaliapin as Mephistopheles and Jules Devoyod guest starring as Valentin. Both singers, as undisputed stars with their own faithful followings, could not help but be drawn into an onstage competition: as a result, the antagonism between their characters became even more pronounced, strengthening the drama.

41. See, for instance, Rossikhina's monograph. Gozenpud's study also discusses the MPO almost exclusively from the point of Chaliapin's contribution. The author has even added the singer's name to the title of his monograph—in none of the other six books included in his series on Russian opera theater did he concentrate so much on just one personality.

42. Quidam, "Peterburg" [Petersburg], *ND* 5677, 18 March 1899, 3.

43. Shaliapin, *Stranitsy iz moei zhizni*, in *Literaturnoe nasledstvo*, 1: 128.

44. See, for example, "Chastnaia Opera," *RS* 262, 22 September 1899, 3. The article was occasioned by Chaliapin's final performance with the MPO (his contract with Mamontov officially expired on 21 September).

45. See, for instance, Gozenpud, *Russkii opernyi teatr i Shaliapin*, 226.

46. Cui to Mamontov, 23 January 1899; item 147, list 1, fund 799, RGALI.

47. Gozenpud, *Russkii opernyi teatr i Shaliapin*, 229.

48. See, for instance, Kashkin's review of *The Tsar's Bride* mentioned above.

49. "K zakrytiiu Moskovskoi Chastnoi Opery" [On the Closing of the Moscow Private Opera Season], *PL* 97, 9 April 1899, 3.

50. Staryi Chelovek, "Za kulisami—VI."

51. Shkafer, *Sorok let na stsene russkoi opery*, 163. One example of a clear misjudgment on Mamontov's part was his universally criticized invitation of a certain tenor Koltsov as an understudy for Sekar-Rozhansky's Sadko.

52. Stasov to Mamontov, 9 April 1898; item 239, list 1, fund 799, RGALI.

53. See, for example, Rossikhina, *Opernyi teatr S. I. Mamontova*, 128–130.

54. After all, Koltsov did not replace Sekar-Rozhansky in *Sadko* (see n.51 above).

55. Melnikov to Mamontov, Paris, 4 April 1898; item 22, fund 155, Bakhrushin Museum. "Tsvetok" [Blossom] or "Tsvetochek" [Little Blossom] was Tsvetkova's nickname in the troupe, derived from her last name.

56. Vsevolod Mamontov, "Chastnaia Opera S. I. Mamontova" (fund 155, BM), 160–61. In his own memoirs, Melnikov even hinted at a romance with his co-star during that production.

57. N. K-in, "Teatr i muzyka," *RV* 251, 11 September 1896, 3.

58. Gozenpud (see *Russkii opernyi teatr i Shaliapin*, 127) questions Kashkin's judgment, but since no recordings are available, this does not mean that the critic was wrong, or for that matter that Mamontov disagreed with him.

59. Zabela to Rimsky-Korsakov, 4 June 1898; item 905, fund 640, RNL.

60. Kruglikov to Mamontov, 24 June 1898; item 145, list 1, fund 799, RGALI.

61. Melnikov to Mamontov, Paris, 11 and 30 August 1898; item 35, fund 155, BM.

62. Melnikov to Mamontov, Paris, 13 July 1898; item 30, fund 155, BM.

63. Ibid.

64. Apart from Ermolova, Mamontov's inspiration was most likely the Meiningen Theater production of Schiller's play; it was a staple of the German troupe's repertoire during their two Russian tours (see chapter 6 for details).

65. Gozenpud, *Russkii opernyi teatr i Shaliapin*, 222.

66. Mikhail Ippolitov-Ivanov, *50 let russkoi muzyki v moikh vospominaniiakh* [50 Years of Russian Music in My Recollections] (Moscow: Muzgiz, 1934), 97.

67. Ibid.

68. See, for example, Mamontov's letter to Shkafer with advice for Vladimir Lossky, who was having trouble with Italian recitative in *Don Giovanni;* item 23, list 2, fund 920, RGALI.

69. Lyubatovich was the leading mezzo of the troupe during the 1880s; by the late 1890s, however, her voice was past its prime, and she moved to secondary, character roles in which her acting ability was an asset.

70. V. Baskin, "Orfei Gliuka" [Gluck's *Orfeo*], *PG* 81, 24 March 1898, 3.

71. See, for example, "Teatral'naia khronika," *ND* 4784, 1 October 1896, 2.

72. I. L., "Chastnaia Opera," *NS* 61, 1 October 1896, 2–3. This comment from Lipaev is particularly valuable due to the critic's overall interest in the "ensemble" quality of the company's performances.

73. V. Baskin, "Teatral'noe ekho."

74. Mamontov to Shkafer, [January, 1900?]; item 23, list 2, fund 920, RGALI.

75. Chernenko's name and signature appear on the 1896–97 choir rosters preserved in fund 155, BM.

76. Indeed, this questionable tradition was started by Princess Tenisheva, who in her memoirs accused Mamontov of ruining her budding operatic career. According to Tenisheva, her MPO audition had been deliberately sabotaged because Mamontov's lover, Tatyana Lyubatovich, "for whom he kept the theater," was allegedly afraid of the competition. See Maria Tenisheva, *Vpechatleniia moei zhizni* [Impressions of My Life] (Leningrad: Iskusstvo, 1991), 69–70.

77. Mamontov to Melnikov, 14/28 May 1898; item 36, list 1, fund 799, RGALI.

78. Arenzon, *Savva Mamontov*, 155.

79. Melnikov to Mamontov, Paris, 9 April 1898; item 23, fund 155, BM.

80. For details on such character analysis see, for example, Vladimir Lossky's recollections of his single study session with Mamontov dedicated to the image of Gounod's Mephistopheles; in Vladimir Losskii, *Memuary, stat'i i rechi* [Memoirs, Articles and Speeches] (Moscow: Muzgiz, 1959), 150.

81. Melnikov to Mamontov, Paris, 4 April 1898; item 22, fund 155, BM.

82. Paskhalova to Mamontov, [Summer 1898?]; item 187, list 1, fund 799, RGALI.

83. Mamontov to Shkafer, [Fall 1899]; item 23, list 2, fund 920, RGALI.

84. Mamontov to Shkafer [November 1899?]; item 23, list 2, fund 920, RGALI.

85. Mamontov to Melnikov, 14/28 May 1898; item 36, list 1, fund 799, RGALI.

86. Shkafer to Mamontov, Paris to Moscow, 10 August 1898; item 280, list 1, fund 799, RGALI.

87. Mamontov to Shkafer, [Fall 1899]; item 23, list 2, fund 799, RGALI.

88. Shkafer, *40 let na stsene russkoi opery,* 169.

89. Shkafer to Mamontov, 11 September 1897; item 280, list 1, fund 799, RGALI; for more colorful examples of "acting advice" to novice singers at the Imperial Theaters, see Chaliapin's memoirs.

90. Mamontov to Shkafer, [November 1899]; item 23, list 2, fund 799, RGALI.

91. Mamontov to Shkafer, [Fall 1899]; item 23, list 2, fund 799, RGALI.

92. Melnikov to Mamontov, Paris, 9 July 1898; item 29, fund 155, BM.

93. Shkafer to Mamontov, Paris to Moscow, 10 August 1898; item 280, list 1, fund 799, RGALI.

94. Rimsky-Korsakov to Zabela, 25 November 1898; item 792, fund 640, RNL.

95. For instance, stage director and musicologist Vladimir Pokrovsky, in his article on Chaliapin, noted that the singer never referred to "studying a part" but rather to "a role"; see: Vladimir Pokrovskii, "Chitaia Shaliapina," *Sovetskaia Muzyka* 11 (1968): 73.

96. Zabela to Rimsky-Korsakov, 28 October 1898; item 905, fund 640, RNL.

97. Zabela to Rimsky-Korsakov, 1 November 1898; item 905, fund 640, RNL.

98. Zabela to Rimsky-Korsakov, 31 August 1898; item 905, fund 640, RNL.

99. Zabela to Rimsky-Korsakov, 27 January 1899; item 906, fund 640, RNL.

100. Zabela to Rimsky-Korsakov, 5 December 1898; item 905, fund 640, RNL.

101. Zabela to Rimsky-Korsakov, 16 January 1899; item 906, fund 640, RNL.

102. Zabela to Rimsky-Korsakov, 28 February 1899; item 906, fund 640, RNL.

103. Zabela to Rimsky-Korsakov, 19 May 1899; item 906, fund 640, RNL.

104. Mamontov to Shkafer, [Fall 1899]; item 23, list 2, fund 920, RGALI.

105. Melnikov to Mamontov, 28 July 1899; item 39, fund 155, BM.

106. Zabela to Rimsky-Korsakov, 28 October 1898; item 905, fund 640, RNL.

107. Zabela to Rimsky-Korsakov, 21 November 1898; item 905, fund 640, RNL. Incidentally, Mamontov never cast Stavitskaya in the fiendishly complicated Rimsky-Korsakov parts. Zabela's comments demonstrate merely her personal bias, and a refusal to acknowledge Mamontov's ability to assess the vocal limitations of his singers with objectivity.

108. Zabela to Rimsky-Korsakov, [February 1899]; item 906, fund 640, RNL.

109. Zabela to Rimsky-Korsakov, 27 January 1899; item 906, fund 640, RNL.

110. *Angelo* was in fact on the repertoire list for the 1899–1900 season, and Mamontov personally pushed for its production, but the new administration of the company chose to ignore his advice, staging instead Cui's earlier—and weaker—opera, *Kavkazskii Plennik* [*Prisoner of the Caucasus*], in which Zabela did sing the lead.

111. Cui to Mamontov, 23 January 1899; item 147, list 1, fund 799, RGALI. The remark about Chaliapin refers to the fact that the singer, having already signed the contract with the Bolshoi, would not be able to participate in the rescheduled production.

112. Zabela to Rimsky-Korsakov, 23 November 1898; item 905, fund 640, RNL.

113. Zabela to Rimsky-Korsakov, 1 November 1898; item 905, fund 640, RNL.

114. Zabela to Rimsky-Korsakov, [March 1899]; item 906, fund 640, RNL.

115. Zabela to Rimsky-Korsakov, 11 December 1898; item 905, fund 640, RNL.

116. Interestingly, several of Mamontov's "homegrown divas" whom Zabela ridiculed in her letters (including Paskhalova and Gladkaya) made the Mariinsky Theater roster before she did.

117. Zabela to Rimsky-Korsakov, 9 December 1898; item 905, fund 640, RNL.

118. Mamontov to Shkafer, [October 1899?]; item 23, list 2, fund 920, RGALI.

119. E.R., "Boris Godunov," *ND* 5579, 9 December 1898, 3.

120. See, for example, Platon Mamontov, "Shaliapin i Mamontov" [Chaliapin and Mamontov], in *F. I. Shaliapin: Literaturnoe nasledstvo*, 2: 435–49.

121. Kuznetsov, "Mamontov, Shaliapin, Stanislavskii," 55–56.

122. Gozenpud, *Russkii opernyi teatr i Shaliapin*, 207.

123. Zabela to Rimsky-Korsakov, 26 November 1898; item 905, fund 640, RNL.

124. Gozenpud, *Russkii opernyi teatr i Shaliapin*, 189–90.

125. Lev Lebedinskii, "Stsena 'Chasy s kurantami' v ispolnenii Shaliapina" [The Chime Clock Scene as Performed by Chaliapin], *Sovetskaia Muzyka* 3 (March 1959): 33–45.

126. The recording used was *Iskusstvo F. I. Shaliapina: stseny i arii iz russkikh oper*, vol. 1 (Russian Disc RDCD00391, 1994). I had no access to the vinyl recording cited by Lebedinsky as his source (his article includes a serial number but no date or other details), but the Russian Disc recording used is the most accessible version in Russia, and was available in 1959. Thus, it could have been Lebedinsky's source. On the other hand, if the scholar used a different recording, this may account for some of the discrepancies described below.

127. While the effects of the speech-singing mode may be similar to the *Sprechstimme*, the techniques are essentially different: rather than hitting and then sliding off the suggested pitch, as Schoenberg proposed, Chaliapin's pitches fluctuate between definite and indefinite pitch in the general pitch area notated in the score. *Sprechstimme*, furthermore, suggests a reference to Schoenberg's style and, therefore, would not be appropriate.

128. See the discussion of Chaliapin's use of speech mode in *Judith* in Iu. E., "Iudif'" [Judith], *RV* 265, 25 November 1898, 3–4; and Justo, "Chastnaia Opera: Iudif' Serova" [Private Opera: Serov's *Judith*], *ND* 5566, 26 November 1898, 3.

129. A. G., "Teatr i muzyka," *RS* 265, 3 October 1896, 3.

130. See, for example, *Singers of Imperial Russia*, vol. 3 (Pearl, GEMM CD 9004-6, 1992).

131. Mamontov clearly shared this conviction. Aesthetic considerations aside, it might have contributed to his decision to excise the Kromy scene from his production of *Boris*, discussed in chapter 2. An even starker example is the reordering of the scenes in Serov's *Rogneda* (see chapter 6).

132. Gozenpud, *Russkii opernyi teatr i Shaliapin*, 197.

133. Strakhova-Ermans, *Vospominaniia o Shaliapine*, 10.

## 6. From Meiningen to Meyerhold

1. Gozenpud, *Russkii opernyi teatr i Shaliapin*, 222.

2. Kruglikov to Mamontov, 21 June 1897; item 145, list 1, fund 799, RGALI.

3. Prior to my own work, the possibility of a Meiningen influence on the MPO was acknowledged only by Arenzon, who limited his discussion of the topic, literally, to a footnote; see Arenzon, *Savva Mamontov*, 97.

4. Notable studies of the Meiningen Theater and its legacy include Max Grube's classic *The Story of the Meininger*, trans. Ann Marie Koller (Coral Gables, Fla.: University of Miami Press, 1963), Steven DeHart's *The Meininger Theater, 1776–1926* (Ann

Arbor, Mich.: UMI Research Press, 1981), and John Osborne's excellent *The Meiningen Court Theater, 1866–1890* (Cambridge: Cambridge University Press, 1988), which has been much utilized in the present study, particularly its extensive quotations from the Duke's diaries.

5. Melnikov to Mamontov, Paris, 9 July 1898; item 29, fund 155, BM; Melnikov used the word *kasha* (the closest English equivalent is "porridge").

6. Melnikov to Mamontov, 27 July 1898; item 33, fund 155, BM.

7. Mamontov to Shkafer, [Fall 1899]; item 23, list 2, fund 920, RGALI.

8. Melnikov to Mamontov, Paris, 8 July 1899; item 37, fund 155, BM. Alexander Lensky and Alexander Yuzhin-Sumbatov were two leading actors of the Imperial Maly Drama Theater; for more on Yuzhin-Sumbatov, see chapter 5, n.10. Tugoukhovsky is a comic character in Alexander Griboedov's play "Woe from Wit"; here, he is invoked as an easily recognized character type that also populated Pushkin's "Eugene Onegin" but was excised from Tchaikovsky's opera.

9. Osborne, *The Meiningen Court Theater,* 146.

10. Kopshitser, *Savva Mamontov,* 112.

11. Mamontov to Shkafer, [Fall 1899]; item 23, list 2, fund 920, RGALI.

12. Mamontov to Polenov, 19 October 1897; item 2882, fund 54, STG.

13. Mamontov to Shkafer, [October 1899]; item 23, list 2, fund 920, RGALI.

14. Mamontov to Shkafer, [November 1899]; item 23, list 2, fund 920, RGALI.

15. Pokrovskii, "Chitaia Shaliapina," 73.

16. Chernenko to Mamontov, [Summer 1898]; item 267, list 1, fund 799, RGALI.

17. Mamontov to Shkafer, [November 1899]; item 23, list 2, fund 920, RGALI.

18. Mamontov to Polenov, [October–November, 1899]; item 2912, fund 54, STG.

19. Mamontov to Shkafer, [October 1899]; item 23, list 2, fund 920, RGALI.

20. Mamontov to Polenov, 30 October [1907?]; item 2905, fund 54, STG.

21. The German term *Fach* can be translated as "profession" or "specialization."

22. Stavitskaya to Mamontov, 14 July 1898; item 237, list 1, fund 799, RGALI.

23. In her report to Rimsky-Korsakov, Zabela focused particularly on the drama in Stavitskaya's portrayal of the character—excessive drama, in Zabela's estimation. To her, Tatyana was a purely lyrical part.

24. Quoted in Osborne, *The Meiningen Court Theater,* 166–67.

25. Gozenpud, *Russkii opernyi teatr i Shaliapin,* 137–38.

26. Ibid., 222.

27. Ibid., 208.

28. Quoted in Osborne, *The Meiningen Court Theater,* 151.

29. Mamontov to Shkafer, [November 1899]; item 23, list 2, fund 920, RGALI. As was his practice, in this letter Mamontov again supplemented his writing with a sketch.

30. Quoted in Osborne, *The Meiningen Court Theater,* 142.

31. Kruglikov to Mamontov, 21 June 1897; item 145, list 1, fund 799, RGALI.

32. See, for example, Cui's article in *NBG* 69, 11 March 1899, 3. It is also characteristic of Mamontov's approach that the chorus originally written for male voices was performed by sopranos and mezzo-sopranos. The director did, however, approach a renowned Tchaikovsky specialist, critic Nikolai Kashkin, to ask his opinion on the switch.

33. V. B., "Kniaz' Igor'" [Prince Igor], *PG* 79, 22 March 1899, 3.

34. Casting Chaliapin in secondary roles had its drawbacks, of course, due to his "star" quality and magnetic stage presence. In *Prince Igor,* for example, his Galitsky completely overshadowed Borodin's rather one-dimensional protagonist—a fact commented upon in the press. Chaliapin's appearances as the Varangian Trader were rare, probably, for the same reason; in this case, the harmony of the artistic ensemble was more important than the rotation rule.

35. Quoted in Osborne, *The Meiningen Court Theater,* 152–53.

36. "Teatral'naia khronika," *ND* 5181, 4 November 1897, 3.

37. "Teatral'naia khronika," *ND* 5877, 5 October 1899, 3. One is left to wonder how Shkafer managed to slip the idea past Rimsky-Korsakov, who was maniacally strict in following the score. It is possible that the composer appreciated the stronger sound of the chorus when supplemented by the soloists' voices.

38. The role of the young tsar was performed by the Bolshoi's star tenor, Vasily Sobinov. Interestingly, according to Melnikov's account, Sobinov always regretted not accepting an invitation, straight from the conservatory bench, to join Mamontov's enterprise. Despite his respected position, fame, and a devoted fan club, he believed that working for Mamontov would have made him a better singer. See Mel'nikov, "Moia pervaia vstrecha so Stanislavskim."

39. Zabela to Rimsky-Korsakov, 28 December 1898; item 905, fund 640, RNL.

40. Quoted in Osborne, *The Meiningen Court Theater,* 152–53.

41. Mamontov to Shkafer, [Fall 1899]; item 23, list 2, fund 920, RGALI.

42. Osborne, *The Meiningen Court Theater,* 169.

43. Platon Mamontov, "Shaliapin i Mamontov," 441.

44. See Stasov, "Perov i Musorgskii."

45. Gozenpud, *Russkii opernyi teatr i Shaliapin,* 145–46.

46. Strakhova-Ermans, *Vospominaniia o Shaliapine,* 5.

47. E. Petrovskii, "Sadko," *RMG* 3 (March 1898): 288.

48. S. K-ov, "Pskovitianka" [The Maid of Pskov], *ND* 4860, 16 December 1896, 3.

49. Quoted in Osborne, *The Meiningen Court Theater,* 153.

50. Gozenpud, *Russkii opernyi teatr i Shaliapin,* 137.

51. Ibid., 196. Interestingly, a similar technique was also utilized by Gustav Mahler in his production of *Don Giovanni,* as well as in numerous *commedia dell' arte* and Baroque stylizations by Meyerhold.

52. Mamontov to Polenov, [1907?]; item 2915, fund 54, STG.

53. See, for example, Kashkin's review, "Novaia postanovka Evgeniia Onegina" [A New Production of *Eugene Onegin*], in *RS* on 29 October 1908, and Kruglikov's in *Golos Moskvy* for the same day. Both are preserved in the Melnikov fund of the Rainis Museum. It is notable that one critic attributes Melnikov's design idea to the influence of Stanislavsky's Moscow Art Theater, a company influenced in equal measure by the Meiningen Theater and the MPO.

54. Osborne, *The Meiningen Court Theater,* 141.

55. Mamontov to Shkafer, [Fall 1899]; item 23, list 2, fund 920, RGALI.

56. Stasov, "Moskovskaia Chastnaia Opera v Peterburge."

57. Bondarenko, "S. I. Mamontov i ego opera," 25.

58. Mamontov to Polenov, 19 October 1897; item 2882, fund 54, STG.

59. Osborne, *The Meiningen Court Theater,* 171–72.

60. Rudnitskii, *Rezhissër Meierhol'd,* 14.

61. Vladimir Teliakovskii, *Dnevniki directora Imperatorskikh Teatrov* [Diaries of the Director of the Imperial Theaters], vol. 1 (Moscow: Artist, Rezhissër, Teatr, 1998), 20.

62. *Mir Iskusstva* (1902); quoted in Lifar, *Serge Diaghilev*, 110 and Osborne, *The Meiningen Court Theater*, 142–43.

63. Stanislavsky to Mamontov, 12 October 1898; item 236, list 1, fund 799, RGALI.

64. Stanislavsky to Mamontov, 16 October 1898; item 236, list 1, fund 799, RGALI. As Mamontov and Stanislavsky's acquaintance predated the beginning of the latter's stage career, it was typical for Stanislavsky to sign his letters to Mamontov with his real last name, Alekseev (see introduction, n.11), rather than his stage pseudonym.

65. Stanislavskii, *Moia zhizn' v iskusstve*, 132.

66. Ibid., 134.

67. Platon Mamontov, "Savva Ivanovich Mamontov," 179–80.

68. Stanislavskii, *Moia zhizn' v iskusstve*, 293–94.

69. Ibid., 288.

70. Gorky to Chekhov, after 5 January 1900; in Maksim Gor'kii, *Sobranie sochinenii v 30-i tomakh* [Collected Works in 30 Volumes] (Moscow: Gosudarstvennoe Izdatel'stvo Khudozhestvennoi Literatury, 1949–56), 28: 113.

71. Stanislavsky to Mamontov, 27 September 1900; item 236, list 1, fund 799, RGALI.

72. Meierhol'd, "Naturalisticheskii teatr i teatr nastroeniia" [Naturalist Theater and Mood Theater], in *Stat'i, pis'ma, rechi, besedy*, 1: 120.

73. Vsevolod Meierhol'd, "K proektu novoi dramaticheskoi truppy pri Moskovskom Khudozhestvennom Teatre" [On the Projected New Drama Troupe Attached to the Moscow Art Theater] (1905), in *Stat'i, pis'ma, rechi, besedy*, 1: 89.

74. Stanislavskii, *Moia zhizn' v iskusstve*, 292.

75. A copy of the roster is preserved as item 226, fund 216, BM.

76. See Stanislavsky's letter to the Studio's administrator, Sergei Popov, dated 12 August 1905; item 248, fund 216, BM.

77. A conversation with Sergei Popov in which Stanislavsky searches for a way to decline Mamontov's proposal to hire a particular actress "without offending Savva Ivanovich" is related in Popov's "Vospominaniia o Teatre-Studii na Povarskoi" [Recollections of the Povarskaya Theater-Studio], TS, 8 August 1938; item 220, fund 216, BM.

78. Meierhol'd, "Nuzhen li nam Bol'shoi Teatr?" [Do We Need the Bolshoi Theater?], in *Stat'i, pis'ma, rechi, besedy*, 2: 486.

79. Rudnitskii, *Rezhissër Meierhol'd*, 51, 58–59.

80. Stanislavskii, *Moia zhizn' v iskusstve*, 294.

81. Avrelii [Valerii Briusov], "Iskaniia novoi stseny" [The Searches of the New Stage], *Vesy* 1 (1906): 72–74. Bryusov's reference to the "Antoine/Stanislavsky" theater alludes to the two directors' common admiration for the Meiningen troupe (for André Antoine, see chapters 5 and 6).

82. Meyerhold's diary; quoted in Rudnitskii, *Rezhissër Meierhol'd*, 73.

83. Meierhol'd, "K postanovke Tristana i Izol'dy v Mariinskom Teatre" [On the Production of *Tristan und Isolde* at the Mariinsky Theater], in *Stat'i, pis'ma, rechi, besedy* 1: 144.

84. Rudnitskii, *Rezhissër Meierhol'd*, 147–48.

85. Interestingly, Gorky's first meeting with Mamontov (see n.71) took place a week after the premiere of *The Snow Maiden*, the reason for the writer's visit to the city. Gorky was thrilled with the openly "unrealistic" play, with Vasnetsov's sets—and with Mamontov, writing to Chekhov: "Saw Mamontov—what an original character! I don't think he is a crook at all; it's just that he loves everything beautiful too much ... Still, is it even possible to love beauty too much?" (Gorky to Chekhov, between 1 and 7 October 1900; *Sobranie sochinenii* 28: 133; the comment about Mamontov being a beauty lover rather than "a crook" reveals some knowledge of the trial proceedings earlier that year; see introduction, n.8, above).

### 7. Politics, Repertory, and the Market

1. Krotkov to Mamontov, 25 October 1898; item 143, list 1 fund 799, RGALI.
2. This symbolic opposition was even reinforced geographically: Mamontov's building was located right across Theater Square from both the Bolshoi and its spoken drama counterpart, the Imperial Maly Theater.
3. S. K-ov, "Teatral'naia khronika," *ND* 4860, 16 December 1896, 3.
4. "Teatr i muzyka," *RS* 242, 8 September 1896, 3.
5. S. K-ov, "Teatral'naia khronika," *ND* 4773, 20 September 1896, 2.
6. Pryanishnikov, Ippolit Petrovich (1847–1921)—Russian baritone and impresario; trained and debuted in Milan (*Maria di Rohan*, 1876); as a Mariinsky soloist (1878–86), created the role of Mizgir in Rimsky-Korsakov's *The Snow Maiden*, and a number of Tchaikovsky characters, including Lionel (*The Maid of Orleans*), Mazeppa, and Eugene Onegin (in the St. Petersburg premiere of the opera); later worked in Tiflis (1886–89) and Kiev (1889–92), and for a single season, 1892–93, led a well-regarded private operatic enterprise in Moscow.
7. "Itogi sezona" [Results of the Season], *ND* 4931, 26 February 1897, 3.
8. V. Garteveld, "E può si muove," *RS* 289, 27 October 1896, 2–3.
9. Quoted in Vsevolod Mamontov, *Chastnaia Opera S. I. Mamontova*, 162.
10. "Chastnaia Opera," *RS* 262, 22 September 1899, 3.
11. For details of Mamontov's early efforts, see Haldey, "Verdi's Operas in Mamontov's Theater."
12. S. P., "Russkaia Chastnaia Opera" [Russian Private Opera], *NS* 428, 8 January 1898, 2.
13. "Itogi sezona," *ND* 4931, 26 February 1897, 3.
14. "Orfei v Russkoi Chastnoi Opere" [*Orfeo* at the Russian Private Opera], *NS* 399, 2 December 1897, 2.
15. A. G., "Teatr i muzyka," *RS* 261, 28 September 1896, 3.
16. "Teatr i muzyka," *RS* 257, 24 September 1896, 3.
17. A. G., "Teatr i muzyka," *RS* 253, 20 September 1896, 3.
18. K., "Teatr i muzyka," *RV* 250, 10 September 1896, 3.
19. S. K-ov., "Teatral'naia khronika," *ND* 4774, 21 September 1896, 2.
20. "Teatral'naia khronika," *ND* 4823, 9 November 1896, 2–3.
21. N. K-in., "Teatr i muzyka," *RV* 272, 2 October 1896, 3.
22. N. K-in., "Teatr i muzyka," *RV* 255, 15 September 1896, 2.
23. I. L., "Chastnaia Opera," *NS* 93, 2 November 1896, 2–3.

24. Ibid.

25. "Nam pishut iz Moskvy" [They Write to Us from Moscow], *NV* 7878, 1 February 1898, 4–5.

26. S. K-ov, "Muzykal'naia zametka" [Note on Music], *Sem'ia* 44, 3 November 1896, 14.

27. "Nam pishut iz Moskvy," *NV* 7878, 1 February 1898, 4–5.

28. The contract is preserved as item 71, fund 155, BM.

29. Mamontov to Shkafer, [December 1899]; item 23, list 2, fund 920, RGALI. The article "Ozherel'e" [The Necklace] was published in *ND* (see no. 5956, 23 December 1899, 3), signed S. K. Another *Necklace* advertisement appeared earlier in "Teatral'naia khronika," *ND* 5917, 14 November 1899, 3. I have not been able to trace the fate of the *Gromoboi* review.

30. "Russkaia Chastnaia Opera," *NS* 413, 16 December 1897, 2.

31. Ya., "Voprosy dnia" [Issues of the Day], *NS* 446, 29 January 1898, 2.

32. The "good cause" of the production was the single socially acceptable reason for Mamontov's name to appear on a theater playbill.

33. They would not have been surprised: Bondarenko's story of the rebuilding of the Solodovnikov Theater after the fire contains quite a few references to a "persuasion in an envelope" delivered to a variety of Moscow bureaucrats.

34. Melnikov to Mamontov, Paris, 9 April 1898; item 23, fund 155, BM.

35. Having learned from the experience, Mamontov's support for *Mir Iskusstva* would be much more targeted, as evident, for instance, in the emphasis on crafts during the journal's inaugural publication year.

36. "Pozhar Solodovnikovskogo Teatra" [Fire at the Solodovnikov Theater], *NS* 438, 20 January 1898, 2.

37. "Pozhar v Solodovnikovskom Teatre" [Fire at the Solodovnikov Theater], *ND* 5257, 20 January 1898, 2–3.

38. "Orleanskaia Deva" [The Maid of Orleans], *ND* 5633, 2 February 1899, 2.

39. See, for example, "Russkaia Chastnaia Opera," *NS* 534, 7 December 1898, 2; "Teatral'naia khronika," *ND* 5858, 16 September 1899, 2–3.

40. "Teatral'naia khronika," *ND* 5291, 23 February 1898, 3.

41. Indeed, it would initiate a vicious press war between the conservative and the nationalist press, with language on both sides bordering on the unpublishable—but more on that later.

42. A. S., "Muzykal'nyi Peterburg" [Musical Petersburg], *ND* 5296, 28 February 1898, 3.

43. Quidam, "Peterburg," *ND* 5677, 18 March 1899, 3.

44. Quidam, "Peterburg," *ND* 5675, 16 March 1899, 3. The "melodic recitative" discussed in the article refers to Musorgsky's style of musical declamation.

45. See, for example, a report in *ND* 5302, 6 March 1898, 3; note also a similarly tongue-in-cheek reference to a certain "learned professor Wagner."

46. S. K., "U Tsezaria Kiui," *ND* 5944, 11 December 1899, 3.

47. Novyi, "Otovsiudu," *RS* 328, 25 November 1898, 3. The Figners referred to in the article are Nikolai Figner and Medea Mei-Figner, the star tenor-soprano team from the Mariinsky Theater who created the leading roles in Tchaikovsky's *The Queen of Spades* and other operas.

48. In its 1892–93 season, Pryanishnikov's troupe also staged the Moscow premiere of Rimsky-Korsakov's *May Night* (like *Prince Igor*, a future staple of Mamontov's repertoire), as well as Leoncavallo's *Pagliacci;* see Gozenpud, *Russkii opernyi teatr i Shaliapin,* 111–12.

49. S. K-ov, "Teatral'naia khronika," *ND* 4773, 20 September 1896, 2.

50. See, among others, Ts. Kiui, "Moskovskaia Chastnaia Russkaia Opera," *NBG* 54, 23 February 1898, 3.

51. A. G., "V Bol'shom Teatre," *RS* 263, 1 October 1897, 3.

52. "Teatral'naia khronika," *ND* 5243, 6 January 1898, 3.

53. A. G., "V Bol'shom Teatre," *RS* 253, 21 September 1897, 3.

54. A. Kornev, "Muzykal'nye nabroski" [Musical Sketches], *RS* 40, 9 February 1899, 3.

55. "Igor' v Bol'shom Teatre" [*Prince Igor* at the Bolshoi Theater], *NS* 440, 22 January 1898, 2; the article collates and summarizes representative passages on the subject from all the major Moscow newspapers.

56. "Chastnaia Opera," *NS* 617, 8 September 1899, 2.

57. V. Ladov, "K otkrytiiu Chastnoi Russkoi Opery" [On the Opening of the Private Russian Opera], *PL* 64, 7 March 1899, 4.

58. Novyi, "Otovsiudu," *RS* 328, 25 November 1898, 3.

59. "Teatral'naia khronika," *ND* 5714, 25 April 1899, 3.

60. "Itogi sezona," *ND* 4931, 26 February 1897, 3.

61. Valkenier, *Peredvizhniki,* 125–27.

62. It is likely that Mamontov and his associates attended the grand opening of the Alexander III Museum on 7 March 1898, as the MPO was in the middle of its St. Petersburg tour, with Tchaikovsky's *The Oprichnik* on the playbill for that night (see table 7.1).

63. "Russkaia Opera" [Russian Opera], *NS* 318, 9 September 1897, 2.

64. S. K-ov, "Koe-chto o Khovanshchine" [Something about *Khovanshchina*], *ND* 5189, 12 November 1897, 3.

65. The only theater that showed any interest in staging *Khovanshchina* prior to 1897 was, unsurprisingly, Mamontov's company in its early years of operation. It is possible that Mamontov saw the St. Petersburg performance; in a letter to Stasov dated January 1888, he discussed his intention to produce the opera.

66. S. K-ov, "Teatral'naia khronika," *ND* 4860, 16 December 1896, 3.

67. "Russkaia Opera," *NS* 318, 9 September 1897, 2.

68. N. K-in, "Teatr i muzyka," *RV* 357, 28 December 1897, 4.

69. N. K-in, "Pskovitianka," *RV* 348, 17 December 1896, 3.

70. N. K-in, "Khovanshchina," *RV* 329, 27 November 1897, 3.

71. I. L., "Chastnaia Opera," *NS* 42, 12 September 1896, 2.

72. For a translated sample of articles discussing Anton Rubinstein's proposal to establish a conservatory in Russia, and arguing over the merits of Glinka's *Ruslan and Lyudmila,* see Stuart Campbell, *Russians on Russian Music, 1830–1880* (Cambridge: Cambridge University Press, 1994), 64–93.

73. N. K-in, "Khovanshchina," *RV* 329, 27 November 1897, 3.

74. "Pechat' o Khovanshchine" [Press on *Khovanshchina*], *NS* 381, 13 November 1897, 2.

75. "O chëm govoriat i pishut" [What Is Being Spoken and Written About], *NS* 464, 26 February 1898, 3.

76. R., "Teatr i muzyka," *RV* 340, 9 December 1896, 3.

77. "Khovanshchina," *NS* 384, 16 November 1897, 2.

78. S. P., "Iz pis'ma priezzhego" [From a Letter by a Tourist], *RS* 41, 10 February 1898, 3.

79. Iu. K., "Moskovskaia Opera" [Moscow Opera], *PL* 66, 9 March 1899, 3.

80. "Russkaia Chastnaia Opera" [Russian Private Opera], *NS* 342, 5 October 1897, 2. The journalist who advocated "healthy Russian creative works" as a part of one's cultural diet refrained in this case from creating an explicit dichotomy between "healthy" Russian and "unhealthy" Western operas. As we shall see, however, the missing label did exist, particularly for contemporary Western music; it was a familiar one—"decadence."

81. "Russkaia Opera," *NS* 318, 9 September 1897, 2.

82. *NS* 421, 24 December 1897, 2.

83. "O chëm govoriat i pishut," *NS* 431, 12 January 1898, 2.

84. "Posle spektaklia: Pechat' o Khovanshchine" [After the Performance: The Press on *Khovanshchina*], *NS* 382, 14 November 1897, 2.

85. See, for example, his correspondence with Shkafer regarding Siegfried Wagner's *Der Bärenhäuter*.

86. Such a contract is referred to in Kruglikov's letter to Mamontov, 19 June 1897; item 145, list 1, fund 799, RGALI.

87. A. G., "Vozobnovlenie opery Igor'" [Revival of the Opera *Prince Igor*], *RS* 310, 17 November 1896, 2–3.

88. S. K-ov., "Teatral'naia khronika," *ND* 4763, 10 September 1896, 2.

89. I. L., "Chastnaia Opera," *NS* 42, 12 September 1896, 2.

90. I. L., "Chastnaia Opera," *NS* 93, 2 November 1896, 2–3.

91. N. K-in, "Teatr i muzyka," *RV* 251, 11 September 1896, 3.

92. A. G., "Vozobnovlenie opery Igor'."

93. N. K-in, "Teatr i muzyka," *RV* 288, 18 October 1896, 2.

94. Ibid.

95. S. K-ov, "Teatral'naia khronika," *ND* 4831, 17 November 1896, 2.

96. "Teatral'naia khronika," *ND* 4789, 6 October 1896, 2.

97. Ironically, the situation would all but assure Mamontov's interest in the operas of Musorgsky. As Kruglikov once reminded him, the composer died without an heir, thus, both *Boris* and *Khovanshchina* could be performed royalty-free. See Kruglikov to Mamontov, 23 June 1898; item 145, list 1, fund 799, RGALI.

98. V. Garteveld, "E può si muove."

99. S. K-ov, "Bogema Puchchini" [Puccini's *La bohème*], *ND* 4890, 16 January 1897, 3.

100. S. K-ov, "Oprichnik Chaikovskogo" [Tchaikovsky's *Oprichnik*], *ND* 4901, 27 January 1897, 3.

101. See, for example: S. K-ov, "Teatral'naia khronika," *ND* 4831, 17 November 1896, 2.

102. "Teatr i muzyka," *RS* 215, 5 August 1900, 3. The author discusses the possibility of Mamontov's return to the enterprise after his acquittal in the embezzlement

case, and hopes that under his leadership the company would return to its "original mission."

103. The word "propaganda" here and below is used deliberately—both by the reporters who aimed to underscore the "ideological" nature of Mamontov's company as they saw it, and by this author who aims to preserve that connotation in the translation.

104. For the original sources of the digest offered here, see the following articles: "V Chastnoi Russkoi Opere" [At the Private Russian Opera], *ND* 5156, 10 October 1897, 3; "Russkaia Chastnaia Opera," *NS* 438, 20 January 1898, 2; "Russkaia Chastnaia Opera," *NS* 342, 5 October 1897, 2; Ts. Kiui, "Moskovskaia Chastnaia Russkaia Opera: Boris Godunov Musorgskogo" [Moscow Private Russian Opera: Musorgsky's *Boris Godunov*], *NBG* 67, 8 March 1899, 3; E. R., "Russkaia Chastnaia Opera: Oprichnik" [Russian Private Opera: *The Oprichnik*], *ND* 5170, 25 October 1897, 2; "Russkaia Chastnaia Opera," *NS* 371, 3 November 1897, 2; "Russkaia Chastnaia Opera," *NS* 534, 7 December 1898, 2; "Russkaia Chastnaia Opera," *NS* 367, 30 October 1897, 2; E. R., "Kavkazskii Plennik" [Prisoner of the Caucasus], *ND* 5943, 10 December 1899, 2–3, and 5946, 13 December 1899, 2–3; and "Russkaia Chastnaia Opera," *NS* 342, 5 October 1897, 2.

105. See Iu. K., "Moskovskaia Opera," *PL* 65, 8 March 1899, 3; Iu. E., "Orleanskaia Deva," *RV* 40, 9 February 1899, 3; E. R., "Kavkazskii Plennik," *ND* 5943, 10 December 1899, 2–3; and "Khovanshchina-IV," *NS* 380, 12 November 1897, 2.

106. See "Russkaia Opera," *NS* 318, 9 September 1897, 2; and N. K-in, "Teatr i muzyka," *RV* 343, 12 December 1896, 3.

107. N. K-in, "Sadko," *RV* 7, 7 January 1898, 2–3.

108. Vox, "Chastnaia Opera: Vozobnovlenie Opery Deliba Lakme" [Private Opera: Revival of Delibes' Opera *Lakmé*], *RS* 305, 4 November 1899, 3.

109. Still, we know that a revival of *Les Huguenots* was in Mamontov's mind at least since summer 1898, as evident from the vehement objections in Melnikov's letters of the period.

110. "Russkaia Chastnaia Opera," *NS* 342, 5 October 1897, 2.

111. "Russkaia Chastnaia Opera," *NS* 371, 3 November 1897, 2.

112. Stasov, "Moskovskaia Chastnaia Opera v Peterburge."

113. A. Gr., "Orfei na stsene Teatra Solodovnikova," *RS* 323, 1 December 1897, 3.

114. N. K-in, "Teatr i muzyka," *RV* 43, 12 February 1898, 3. A similar attitude to *La bohème* was noted earlier in Kruglikov's *Oprichnik* review.

115. "Itogi sezona," *ND* 4931, 26 February 1897, 3.

116. "Russkaia Chastnaia Opera," *NS* 342, 5 October 1897, 2.

117. V. Garteveld, "E può si muove."

118. See, for example, Kopshitser, *Savva Mamontov*, 188; Gozenpud, *Russkii opernyi teatr i Shaliapin*, 226.

119. Osborne, *The Meiningen Court Theater*, 145.

120. Similarly, in his search for operatic prospects, Mamontov scrapped the virtually completed translation of Siegfried Wagner's *Der Bärenhäuter*, which, to his disappointment, turned out to be a "pretentious piece of German trash," for the "beauty" of Saint-Saëns's *Proserpine*. See Mamontov to Shkafer, [October 1899?]; item 23, list 2, fund 920, RGALI.

121. Melnikov to Mamontov, Paris, 6 July 1898; item 26, fund 155, BM; Melnikov to Mamontov, Paris, 9 July 1898; item 29, fund 155, BM.

122. Mamontov to Shkafer, [Fall 1899]; item 23, list 2, fund 799, RGALI.

123. Mamontov to Chernenko and Shkafer, [November 1899?]; item 23, list 2, fund 799, RGALI.

124. E. R., "Boris Godunov," *ND* 5579, 9 December 1898, 3.

125. Melnikov to Mamontov, Paris, 24 June 1898; item 25, fund 155, BM.

126. I. L., "Chastnaia Opera," *NS* 93, 2 November 1896, 2.

127. E. R., "Russkaia Chastnaia Opera: Oprichnik," *ND* 5170, 25 October 1897, 2.

128. E. R., "Khovanshchina," *ND* 5194, 16 November 1897, 2–3. A translation of a large portion of this article may be found in Stuart Campbell, *Russians on Russian Music, 1880–1917* (Cambridge: Cambridge University Press, 2003), 124–28.

129. "Itogi sezona," *ND* 4931, 26 February 1897, 3. For a detailed examination of the production and its reception, see Olga Haldey, "*La Bohème à la Russe*, and Puccini Politics of Late Nineteenth-Century Russia," in *Opera Journal* 37, no. 4 (2004), 3–19.

130. N. K-in, "Teatr i muzyka," *RV* 21, 21 January 1897, 2.

131. I. L., "Po teatram" [Through the Theaters], *NS* 165, 16 January 1897, 2.

132. "Teatral'naia khronika," *ND* 4928, 23 February 1897, 3.

133. S. K-ov, "Bogema Puchchini," *ND* 4890, 16 January 1897, 3.

134. "Teatr i muzyka," *RS* 318, 26 November 1896, 3.

135. "Teatral'naia khronika," *ND* 4800, 17 October 1896, 2.

136. "Teatr i muzyka," *RS* 6, 6 January 1897, 3; reprinted in *ND, NS,* and other newspapers.

137. "Teatral'naia khronika," *ND* 5201, 24 November 1897, 3.

138. "Teatr i muzyka," *RS* 326, 4 December 1897, 3.

139. "Teatr Solodovnikova" [The Solodovnikov Theater], *RS* 272, 30 September 1898, 3.

140. Melnikov to Mamontov, Paris, 8 July 1899; item 170, list 1, fund 799, RGALI.

141. Quoted in ibid.

142. Melnikov to Mamontov, Paris, 4 April 1898; item 22, fund 155, BM.

143. Mamontov to Cui, [February–March 1899]; item 83, list 1, fund 786, RGALI.

144. Rossikhina, *Opernyi teatr S. I. Mamontova,* 166.

145. Gozenpud, *Russkii opernyi teatr i Shaliapin,* 203–204.

146. Cui to Mamontov, 23 January 1899; item 147, list 1, fund 799, RGALI.

147. On Mitrofan Belyaev's patronage and its consequences, see Taruskin, *Stravinsky and the Russian Traditions,* 47–71.

148. Zabela to Rimsky-Korsakov, 2 May 1898; item 905, fund 640, RNL.

149. This information was typically solicited directly from leaders of theater companies at the conclusion of each season.

150. For a detailed treatment of Mamontov's love affair with Italian opera, see Haldey, "Verdi's Operas at Mamontov's Theater."

151. I.L., "Chastnaia Opera," *NS* 93, 1 November 1896, 2–3.

152. A.G., "Vozobnovlenie opery Igor'."

153. S. K-ov, "V Teatre Solodovnikova" [At the Solodovnikov Theater], *ND* 4884, 9 January 1897, 3.

154. N. K-in, "Teatr i muzyka," *RV* 251, 11 September 1896, 3.

155. [n.a.], "O chëm govoriat i pishut," *NS* 464, 26 February 1898, 3.

156. Melnikov to Mamontov, Paris, 19 May 1898; item 24, fund 155, BM.

157. "Teatral'naia khronika," *ND* 4786, 3 October 1896, 2.

158. I. L., "Chastnaia Opera," *NS* 61, 1 October 1896, 2–3.

159. See, for instance, A. G., "Chastnaia Opera," *RS* 305, 4 November 1896, 2.

160. S. K-ov, "Teatral'naia khronika," *ND* 4770, 17 September 1896, 2.

161. "Teatr i muzyka," *NV* 7900, 24 February 1898, 4.

162. Stasov, "Moskovskaia Chastnaia Opera v Peterburge."

163. A. S-n, "Muzykal'nyi Peterburg," *ND* 5311, 15 March 1898, 3.

164. Ts. Kiui, "Opery Vagnera: Moriak-Skitalets" [Wagner's Operas: *Der fliegende Holländer*], *NBG* 66, 7 March 1898, 3.

165. Ts. Kiui, "Moskovskaia Chastnaia Russkaia Opera," *NBG* 54, 23 February 1898, 3. It is illustrative of Cui's elevated position in the Soviet musicology that Gozenpud judged his review to be "objective"; see *Russkii opernyi teatr i Shaliapin*, 180.

166. E. P-sky, "Iz chelovecheskikh dokumentov" [From Human Documents], *RMG* 4 (April 1898): 368–79.

167. Ts. Kiui, "Orfei Gliuka na stsene Moskovskoi Chastnoi Russkoi Opery" [Gluck's *Orfeo* on the Moscow Private Russian Opera Stage], *NBG* 83, 25 March 1898, 3.

168. Stasov, "Umoritel'nyi muzykal'nyi kritikan" [Hilarious Musical Criticizer], *NBG* 61, 3 March 1898, 2.

169. Quidam, "Peterburg," *ND* 5675, 16 March 1899, 3.

170. Ts. Kiui, "Moskovskaia Chastnaia Russkaia Opera: Khovanshchina" [Moscow Private Russian Opera: *Khovanshchina*], *NBG* 57, 27 February 1898, 3. *Die Walküre* was premiered at the Mariinsky on 24 February, the night before MPO's *Khovanshchina*.

171. Ts. Kiui, "Opery Vagnera: Moriak-Skitalets."

172. Ts. Kiui, "Moskovskaia Chastnaia Russkaia Opera," *NBG* 54, 23 February 1898, 3.

173. "Teatr i muzyka," *NV*, 11 April 1898, 4.

174. "Teatral'naia khronika," *ND* 5292, 23 February 1898, 3. A reference to the "former Bolshoi Theater" alludes to the St. Petersburg Conservatory's Great Hall, the MPO's location during the tour. In its former incarnation as an opera theater, it was known as the Grand [i.e., "The Bolshoi"] and housed the Imperial Russian troupe prior to its move across the street, to the refurbished Mariinsky.

175. A. S., "Muzykal'nyi Peterburg," *ND* 5296, 28 February 1898, 3; note a typically apocalyptic reference to the legions of the Antichrist.

176. Quidam, "Peterburg," *ND* 5292, 23 February 1898, 3.

177. This included *RMG*, which, despite its pro-Wagnerian position, reviewed both Russian and German performances with commendable objectivity.

178. Quidam, "Peterburg," *ND* 5302, 6 March 1898, 2; note the biblical imagery again, as well as a cleverly metaphoric usage of the operatic texts: the opening line of the tenor aria from act 1 of *The Maid of Pskov*, and a Wotan imitation that rings with authenticity.

179. M., "Russkaia Opera," *SPV* 56, 27 February 1898, 3.

180. Gozenpud, *Russkii opernyi teatr i Shaliapin*, 179.

181. A. Koptiaev, "Sezon Moskovskoi Opery" [The Season of the Moscow Opera], *Mir Iskusstva* 11–12 (1899): 127.

### 8. Faces of the Enterprise

1. The same label would be applied two years later to Stanislavsky's Moscow Art Theater, whose ticket prices were yet another aspect of its operations modeled on the MPO.

2. "Teatr i muzyka," *RS* 264, 1 October 1896, 3.

3. "Teatr i muzyka," *RS* 242, 8 September 1896, 3.

4. "Itogi sezona," *ND* 4931, 26 February 1897, 3.

5. For Moscow Private Opera's financial records see item 211, fund 155, BM.

6. "V Chastnoi Opere," *ND* 5157, 11 October 1897, 2. In all fairness, this specific price increase was a necessity, as both of these temporary locations had much smaller auditoriums than the Solodovnikov, which could have led to significant financial deficits had prices stayed the same.

7. "K zakrytiiu Moskovskoi Chastnoi Opery," *PL* 97, 9 April 1899, 3.

8. "Itogi sezona," *ND* 4931, 26 February 1897, 3.

9. Very little is known about the ballets staged at the MPO, or the dancers in-volved in them. Ballets were staged only during the company's first season; most were apparently *divertissements*, paired with shorter operas to provide a full eve-ning's entertainment. The only ballet performed independently seems to have been Delibes' *Coppélia*, premiered by the Italian troupe in Nizhny Novgorod on 22 June 1896, with Iola Tornaghi as both choreographer and soloist. Torhaghi was evidently tasked with overseeing all the MPO staged dances during the 1896–97 season, and most of the operatic dance scenes after the Italians were sent home and the Russian substitutes were hired in their place. Mamontov, whose keen interest in expressive gesture and movement, including "choreographing" entire productions, has been discussed throughout this book, rarely got involved in choreography proper. When he did, it was always with a specific visual and/or aesthetic goal in mind, as was the case with the seductive "serpantin" [serpent dance], fashionable in Russian variety shows, which he inserted into the Underwater Kingdom Scene of *Sadko*.

10. Zabela's situation exemplifies the most shameful aspect of the benefit system, as practiced at the post-Mamontov MPO: the beneficiary of the performance would be announced in the playbill to attract the fans, but the raised funds in fact went to the general operating budget rather than to the singer for whom they were supposedly in-tended. See Rimsky-Korsakov to Zabela, 15 January 1900; item 795, fund 640, RNL.

11. Novyi, "Otovsiudu," *RS* 328, 25 November 1898, 3.

12. Gozenpud, *Russkii opernyi teatr i Shaliapin*, 228.

13. Garafola, *Diaghilev's Ballets Russes*, 152.

14. Information is derived from items 205–211, fund 155, BM.

15. Indeed, the deficit would have stood at 65,000 if one includes the 20,000 rubles of left-over debt from Nizhny Novgorod. That debt, however, was not entered in the accounting book for the regular season and thus, as Mrs. Winter's trial testimony suggests, was in fact covered by Mamontov out of pocket; see "Delo Mamontova, Artsyusheva, Krivosheina i Drugikh."

16. For a specialized study of the Moscow Art Theater studios, see Rebecca B. Gauss, *Lear's Daughters: The Studios of the Moscow Art Theatre, 1905–1927* (New York: Peter Lang, 1999).

17. Baz Kershaw argues that the first studio theaters were created by the Western European stage directors of the 1880s, and names André Antoine's Théâtre Libre and

Frei Bühne by Otto Brahm as early examples; see "Studio Theater Movement" in *The Oxford Encyclopedia of Theatre and Performance*, ed. Dennis Kennedy (Oxford: Oxford University Press, 2003), 2: 1297-98; the Povarskaya Studio is, however, the first to bear the popular "studio" label.

18. Indeed, Mamontov evidently meant to resurrect that spirit literally. According to Sergei Popov's memoirs, Stanislavsky's plan for the Povarskaya Studio included creating several rotating theatrical troupes that would present their new repertoires alternately in the capital cities and the provinces. One of those troupes was supposed to be operatic—that is, Mamontov's; in fact, his protégé, soprano Tatyana Shornikova is listed on the studio roster.

19. See Patrice Pavis, "Laboratory Theatre," in *Dictionary of the Theatre: Terms, Concepts, and Analysis*, trans. Christine Shantz (Toronto: University of Toronto Press, 1998), 195.

20. [n.a.], "Studio Theatre," in *International Dictionary of Theatre Language*, ed. Joel Trapido (Westport, Conn.: Greenwood, 1985), 837.

21. Stanislavskii, *Moia zhizn' v iskusstve*, 290.

22. Which is not to say that Mamontov's star-driven productions lacked artistry of stage direction and set design; for instance, both were utilized to tremendous effect in the 1885 production of *Aida*. Involvement of guest soloists, however, naturally limited the ensemble possibilities of such productions; in *Aida*, only Lyubatovich (as Amneris) benefited from Mamontov's coaching (see Haldey, "Verdi's Operas at Mamontov's Theater," 11-12 for details).

23. "Teatral'naia khronika," *ND* 5847, 5 September 1899, 2.

24. "Russkaia Chastnaia Opera," *NS* 534, 7 December 1898, 2.

25. "Teatral'naia khronika," *ND* 5530, 21 October 1898, 3.

26. Melnikov to Mamontov, Paris, 30 August 1898; item 34, fund 155, BM. Interestingly, during its final years of operation the Meiningen Theater also came to be viewed as an actor's school where young performers would learn their craft before moving on and making their careers elsewhere.

27. Mamontov to Shkafer, [fall 1899]; item 23, list 2, fund 920, RGALI. Mamontov's negative attitude to Chaliapin and Korovin's "defection" to the Bolshoi had less to do with the events themselves than with being deeply offended by their behavior toward him after his arrest.

28. Murray Frame, *The St. Petersburg Imperial Theaters: Stage and State in Revolutionary Russia, 1900-1920* (Jefferson, N.C.: McFarland, 2000), 15.

29. Krotkov to Mamontov, Vienna, 17 May 1897; item 143, list 1, fund 799, RGALI.

30. Gozenpud, *Russkii opernyi teatr i Shaliapin*, 158.

31. Extant documents suggest that, although Mamontov recruited Rachmaninov to the company because of his respect for his prodigious talent, the young conductor was much too low on the food chain to wield any kind of authority that would have clashed with Mamontov's own. The reason for his resignation seems clear: the nervous breakdown in the wake of the fiasco of his First Symphony, which rendered him unable to write music and brought him to Mamontov in the first place, was over, and the company's insane rehearsal and performance schedule would surely have prevented him from resuming composition.

32. Iu. K., "Moskovskaia Opera," *PL* 65, 8 March 1899, 3.

33. Lolo, "Teatral'nye skachki" [Theatrical Races], *ND* 5875, 3 October 1899, 2-3.

34. E. R., "Lakme," *ND* 5906, 3 November 1899, 3.

35. E. R., "Russkaia Chastnaia Opera: Oprichnik," *ND* 5170, 25 October 1897, 2.

36. Kruglikov to Mamontov, 23 June 1898; item 145, list 1, fund 799, RGALI.

37. Ibid. "Kvas" is a lightly alcoholic, native Russian drink brewed from rye; as the favorite drink of the lower classes, its name is frequently used to denote grassroots, unsophisticated nationalism.

38. Kruglikov to Mamontov, 16 February 1898; item 145, list 1, fund 799, RGALI.

39. See Rimsky-Korsakov to Zabela, 12 and 20 May 1899; item 793, fund 640, RNL.

40. Rimsky-Korsakov to Zabela, 6 July 1899; item 793, fund 640, RNL.

41. Gozenpud, *Russkii opernyi teatr i Shaliapin*, 166.

42. See chapter 4, n.150.

43. See Rimskii-Korsakov, *Letopis'*, 209–12. The collaboration between Rimsky-Korsakov and Mamontov resumed in 1907 when the composer approached "the best stage director in Russia," asking him to consult on the Parisian production of *The Snow Maiden* (see below).

44. See "Vdova N. A. Rimskogo-Korsakova o Zolotom Petushke" [Rimsky-Korsakov's Widow on *Le Coq d'Or*], *Teatral* 133, 17 May 1914, quoted in: *Sergei Diagilev i russkoe iskusstvo*, 1: 466.

45. Sergei Diagilev, "Otvet N. N. Rimskoi-Korsakovoi" [Response to N. N. Rimskaia-Korsakova], in *Sergei Diagilev i russkoe iskusstvo*, 1: 222.

46. Arnold Haskell, in collaboration with Walter Nouvel, *Diaghileff: His Artistic and Private Life* (London: Gollancz, 1935), 55.

47. Garafola, *Diaghilev's Ballets Russes*, 150.

48. Diaghilev to Benois, spring 1897; item 939, fund 137, SRM.

49. See Taruskin, *Stravinsky and the Russian Traditions*, 461–62.

50. Diaghilev to Benois, December 1897; item 939, fund 137, SRM.

51. Diaghilev to Benois, 24 May 1897; quoted in Benua, *Vozniknovenie Mira Iskusstva*, 25.

52. Strakhova-Ermans, *Vospominaniia o Shaliapine*, 9.

53. Staryi Chelovek, "Za kulisami—XXI," *ND* 5688, 29 March 1899, 3.

54. Benua, *Aleksandr Benua razmyshliaet*, 506.

55. Benua, *Moi vospominaniia*, 4: 213.

56. Benua, *Aleksandr Benua razmyshliaet*, 211.

57. Aleksandr Benua, *Istoriia russkoi zhivopisi v XIX veke* [History of Russian Painting in the 19th Century] (St. Petersburg, 1902), 225.

58. Benua, *Vozniknovenie Mira Iskusstva*, 30–31.

59. The incident is described in Etkind, *Aleksandr Benua i russkaia khudozhestvennaia kul'tura*. Note the typically Soviet ideological approach evident in this description: Benois' position is depicted as progressive for promoting genre and representational painting, while Diaghilev's stand for "pure art" is considered reactionary.

60. Quoted in Benua, *Vozniknovenie Mira Iskusstva*, 32.

61. The letter, dated 2 June 1898, is quoted in Benua, *Vozniknovenie Mira Iskusstva*, 35. Interestingly, Benois cut this single phrase from an otherwise complete quotation; the full version may be found in item 940, fund 137, SRM.

62. See Diaghilev to Benois, 24 May 1897. Again, Diaghilev's criticism of Benois' position is not included in the published version, *Vozniknovenie Mira Iskusstva*, 25–26; it can be found in item 939, fund 137, SRM.

63. Taruskin, *Stravinsky and the Russian Traditions*, 429–37.

64. A. G., "Vystavka russkikh i finliandskikh khudozhnikov" [Exhibition of Russian and Finnish Artists], *PG* 15, 16 January 1898, 2.

65. Diaghilev to Mamontov, 1 December 1898; item 15, fund 155, BM.

66. V. Burenin, "Novye khudozhestvennye zhurnaly—II" [New Art Journals—2], *NV* 8173, 27 November 1898, 2.

67. For instance, despite the fact that Filosofov was certainly well acquainted with the copublisher of the journal he helped edit, his extant letter to Mamontov, preserved at BM (see item 49, fund 155), concludes with the highly formal *primite uvereniya v moyom glubokom uvazhenii* ("accept assurances of my deep respect").

68. Borisov-Musatov to Diaghilev, 1904; item 40, fund 27, SRM.

69. The others were Valentin Serov and the leader of the Moscow decadent symbolists, Valery Bryusov; the precise content of the speeches is unknown. Notably, Bryusov was well acquainted with the activities of the MPO and was one of the first to congratulate Mamontov, in an open letter, on his company's twenty-five-year anniversary (on the aesthetic convergence between Mamontov and Bryusov, see chapter 1).

70. Stasov to Mamontov, St. Petersburg, 12 April 1888; item 239, list 1, fund 799, RGALI.

71. "Teatral'naia khronika," *ND* 5306, 10 March 1898, 2.

72. Shkafer to Mamontov, Paris, 28 August 1898; item 280, list 1, fund 799, RGALI.

73. Arenzon suggests that Mamontov's decision to cosponsor *Mir Iskusstva* with Princess Tenisheva was an attempt to cultivate a relationship with her husband in advance of the World Fair; see Arenzon, *Savva Mamontov*, 170. While this was unlikely to have been his primary motivation, it is entirely possible that Mamontov expected to reap a fringe benefit from his decision to help Diaghilev.

74. See letters from Rimsky-Korsakov to Zabela dated 15 and 23 January 1900; item 795, fund 640, RNL. It is hard to believe that years of working with Mamontov did not improve Rimsky-Korsakov's opinion of him that he had formed in the 1880s without ever setting foot inside his theater. The composer's position may be explained by the fresh memory of his conflict with Mamontov, as well as an acknowledgment of the company's precarious position in his absence.

75. See Gregory Halbe, "Music, Drama, and Folklore in Nikolai Rimsky-Korsakov's Opera *Snegurochka*" (Ph.D. diss., Ohio State University, 2004), 34–38.

76. Sergei Diagilev, "Russkaia muzyka v Parizhe" [Russian Music in Paris]; quoted in *Diagilev i russkoe iskusstvo*, 1: 207–208.

77. Matov, "Snegurochka v Parizhe" [*The Snow Maiden* in Paris], *RS* 118, 22 May 1908, quoted in *Diagilev i russkoe iskusstvo*, 1: 417.

78. "V tupikah i osobniakah," *Rannee Utro*, 1907; item 15, list 3, fund 799, RGALI. On the other hand, the interviewer acknowledged that it was he who described to Mamontov the financial scandals around the *Boris* production that had just hit the Russian newspapers; given Mamontov's attitude toward "art for money's sake," his response might have been prompted by the one-sided information given to him.

79. Mamontov to Carré, 15 December 1907; list 1, fund 799, RGALI.

80. Diaghilev to Benois, 24 May 1897; quoted in Benua, *Vozniknovenie Mira Iskusstva*, 26.

# WORKS CITED

Abraham, Gerald. *On Russian Music*. London: Reeves, 1939.

Apetian, Zaruia, ed. *S. Rakhmaninov: Literaturnoe nasledie*. 3 vols. Moscow: Sovetskii Kompozitor, 1978–80.

Arenzon, Evgenii. *Savva Mamontov*. Moscow: Russkaia Kniga, 1995.

Bakhrevskii, Vladislav. *Savva Mamontov*. Moscow: Molodaia Gvardiia, 2000.

Baloueff, Ivan I. "*Grigoriev, Apollon. Sochineniia. Kritika*, edited by V. S. Krupitsch." *Russian Review* 30, no. 1 (1971): 83–84.

Barsova, Liudmila. *N. I. Zabela-Vrubel' glazami sovremennikov*. Leningrad: Muzyka, 1982.

Bartlett, Rosamund. *Wagner and Russia*. Cambridge: Cambridge University Press, 1995.

Belinskii, Vissarion. *Estetika i literaturnaia kritika*. 2 vols. Moscow: Gosudarstvennoe Izdatel'stvo Khudozhestvennoi Literatury, 1959.

Belyi, Andrei. *Simvolism kak miroponimanie*. Moscow: Respublika, 1994.

Benois, Alexandre. *Reminiscences of the Russian Ballet*. London: Putnam, 1941. *See also* Benua, Aleksandr.

Benua, Aleksandr. *Aleksandr Benua razmyshliaet*. Moscow: Sovetskii Khudozhnik, 1968.

———. *Istoriia russkoi zhivopisi v XIX veke*. St. Petersburg, 1902.

———. *Moi vospominaniia*. 5 vols. Moscow: Nauka, 1980.

———. *Vozniknovenie Mira Iskusstva*. Leningrad: Komitet Populiarizatsii Khudozhestvennykh Izdanii Pri Gosudarstvennoi Akademii Istorii Material'noi Kul'tury, 1928.

Berdiaev, Nikolai. *Sub specie aeternitatis. Opyty filosofskie, sotsial'nye i literaturnye, 1900–1906*. St. Petersburg: Izd. M. V. Pirozhkova, 1907.

Billington, James. *The Icon and the Axe: An Interpretive History of Russian Culture*. New York: Vintage, 1970.

Borisova, Elena, and Grigory Sternin. *Russian Art Nouveau*. New York: Rizzoli, 1988.

Borovskii, Viktor. *Moskovskaia opera S. I. Zimina*. Moscow: Sovetskii Kompozitor, 1977.

Bowlt, John. *The Silver Age: Russian Art of the Early Twentieth Century and the "World of Art" Group.* Newtonville, Mass.: Oriental Research Partners, 1982.

————. "Synthesism and Symbolism: The Russian *World of Art* Movement." In *Literature and the Plastic Arts (1880–1930)*, ed. Ian Higgins. New York: Harper & Row, 1973: 35–48.

Braun, Lucinde. *Studien zur russischen Oper in späten 19. Jahrhundert.* Mainz: Schott, 1999.

Briusov, Valerii. *Sobranie sochinenii.* 7 vols. Moscow: Khudozhestvennaia Literatura, 1975.

Calinescu, Matei. *Five Faces of Modernity: Modernism, Avant-Garde, Decadence, Kitsch, Postmodernism.* Durham, N.C.: Duke University Press, 1987.

Calvocoressi, Michel, and Gerald Abraham. *Masters of Russian Music.* London: Duckworth, 1936.

Campbell, Stuart. *Russians on Russian Music, 1830–1880.* Cambridge: Cambridge University Press, 1994.

————. *Russians on Russian Music, 1880–1917.* Cambridge: Cambridge University Press, 2003.

Cohen, Selma Jeanne, ed. *International Encyclopedia of Dance.* New York: Oxford University Press, 1998.

Cui, Cesar. *La musique en Russie.* Paris: Fischbacher, 1880.

DeHart, Steven. *The Meininger Theater, 1776–1926.* Ann Arbor, Mich.: UMI Research Press, 1981.

Dostoevskii, Fëdor. *Dostoevskii ob iskusstve.* Moscow: Iskusstvo, 1973. *See also* Dostoevsky, Fyodor.

Dostoevsky, Fyodor. *Diary of a Writer*, trans. Boris Brasol. New York: Braziller, 1954.

Dowler, Wayne. "Echoes of *Pochvennichestvo* in Solzhenitsyn's *August 1914*." *Slavic Review* 34, no. 1 (1975): 109–22.

Druzhinin, Alexander. *Literaturnaia kritika.* Moscow: Sovetskaia Rossiia, 1983.

Etkind, Mark. *A. N. Benua i russkaia khudozhestvennaia kul'tura.* Leningrad: Khudozhnik RSFSR, 1989.

Frame, Murray. *The St. Petersburg Imperial Theaters: Stage and State in Revolutionary Russia, 1900–1920.* Jefferson, N.C.: McFarland, 2000.

Garafola, Lynn. *Diaghilev's Ballets Russes.* New York: Oxford University Press, 1989.

Garafola, Lynn, and Nancy van Norman Baer, eds. *The Ballets Russes and Its World.* New Haven, Conn.: Yale University Press, 1999.

Gasparov, Boris, Robert P. Hughes, and Irina Paperno, eds. *Cultural Mythologies of Russian Modernism: From the Golden Age to the Silver Age.* Berkeley: University of California Press, 1992.

Gauss, Rebecca B. *Lear's Daughters: The Studios of the Moscow Art Theater, 1905–1927.* New York: Peter Lang, 1999.

Gautier, Théophile. *Mademoiselle de Maupin.* Paris: Charpentier, 1880.

Gor'kii, Maksim. *Sobranie sochinenii.* 30 vols. Moscow: Gosudarstvennoe Izdatel'stvo Khudozhestvennoi Literatury, 1949–56.

Gozenpud, Abram. *Russkii opernyi teatr na rubezhe XIX–XX vekov i Shaliapin, 1890–1904.* Leningrad: Muzyka, 1974.

Gray, Camilla. *The Russian Experiment in Art: 1863–1922.* London: Thames & Hudson, 1998.

Grosheva, Ekaterina, ed. *F. I. Shaliapin: Literaturnoe nasledstvo.* 2 vols. Moscow: Muzgiz, 1959–60.

Grover, Stuart. "Savva Mamontov and the Mamontov Circle, 1870–1905: Art Patronage and the Rise of Nationalism in Russian Art." Ph.D. diss., University of Wisconsin, 1971.

Grube, Max. *The Story of the Meininger,* trans. Ann Marie Koller. Coral Gables, Fla.: University of Miami Press, 1963.

Halbe, Gregory. "Music, Drama, and Folklore in Nikolai Rimsky-Korsakov's Opera *Snegurochka.*" Ph.D. diss., Ohio State University, 2004.

Haldey, Olga. "*La Bohème à la Russe,* and Puccini Politics of Late Nineteenth-Century Russia." *Opera Journal* 37, no. 4 (2004): 3–19.

———. "Verdi's Operas in Mamontov's Theater: Fighting a Losing Battle." *Verdi Forum* 30 (2003–2004): 3–25.

Haskell, Arnold, in collaboration with Walter Nouvel. *Diaghileff: His Artistic and Private Life.* London: Gollancz, 1935.

Henry, Barbara. "Theatricality, Anti-theatricality, and Cabaret in Russian Modernism." In *Russian Literature, Modernism and the Visual Arts,* ed. Catriona Kelly and Stephen Lovell. Cambridge: Cambridge University Press, 2000: 149–71.

Herder, Johann Gottfried. *Against Pure Reason: Writings on Religion, Language and History.* Minneapolis, Minn.: Fortress, 1993.

Iakovlev, Vasilii. *Izbrannye trudy o muzyke.* 3 vols. Moscow: Sovetskii Kompozitor, 1971–83.

Ippolitov-Ivanov, Mikhail. *50 let russkoi muzyki v moikh vospominaniiakh.* Moscow: Muzgiz, 1934.

Keldysh, Yuri, ed. *Istoriia Russkoi muzyki.* 10 vols. Moscow: Muzyka, 1987–2006.

Kennedy, Dennis, ed. *The Oxford Encyclopedia of Theatre and Performance.* Oxford: Oxford University Press, 2003.

Kennedy, Janet. *The "Mir Iskusstva" Group and Russian Art, 1898–1912.* New York: Garland, 1977.

Kiselëva, Ekaterina. *Dom na Sadovoi.* Moscow: Moskovskii Rabochii, 1986.

Kogan, Dora. *Mamontovskii kruzhok.* Moscow: Izobrazitel'noe Iskusstvo, 1970.

Kopshitser, Mark. *Savva Mamontov.* Moscow: Iskusstvo, 1972.

Korovin, Konstantin. *Konstantin Korovin vspominaet . . .* Moscow: Izobrazitel'noe Iskusstvo, 1990.

Kramskoi, Ivan. *Pis'ma. Stat'i.* Moscow: Iskusstvo, 1965–66.

Kuznetsov, Nikolai. "Mamontov, Shaliapin, Stanislavskii—reformatory opernogo iskusstva v Rossii kontsa XIX–nachala XX vekov." Ph.D. diss., Moscow State Conservatory, 1996.

Lebedev, Andrei, and Genrietta Burova. *Tvorcheskoe sodruzhestvo: M. M. Antokol'skii i V. V. Stasov.* Leningrad: Khudozhnik RSFSR, 1968.

Lebedinskii, Lev. "Stsena 'Chasy s kurantami' v ispolnenii Shaliapina." *Sovetskaia Muzyka* 3 (March 1959): 33–45.

Levitt, Marcus C. "*Russia's Last Romantic, Apollon Grigoriev (1822–64),* by Robert Whittaker." *Slavic and East European Journal* 46, no. 1 (2002): 166–67.

Lieven, Peter. *The Birth of the Ballets Russes.* London: Allen & Unwin, 1936.

Lifar, Serge. *Serge Diaghilev: His Life, His Work, His Legend; An Intimate Biography.* New York: Putnam, 1940.

Losskii, Vladimir. *Memuary, stat'i i rechi.* Moscow: Muzgiz, 1959.

Mamontov, Vsevolod. *Vospominaniia o russkikh khudozhnikakh.* Moscow: Akademiia Khudozhestv, 1950.

Marchenkov, Vladimir. "The Orpheus Myth in Musical Thought of Antiquity, the Renaissance and Modern Times." Ph.D. diss., Ohio State University, 1998.

Meierhol'd, Vsevolod. *Stat'i, pis'ma, rechi, besedy.* 2 vols. Moscow: Iskusstvo, 1968.

Morgan, Robert. "Secret Languages: The Roots of Musical Modernism." In *Modernism: Challenges and Perspectives,* ed. Monique Chefdor, Ricardo Quinones, and Albert Wachtel. Urbana: University of Illinois Press, 1986: 33–53.

Morrison, Simon. *Russian Opera and the Symbolist Movement.* Berkeley: University of California Press, 2002.

———. "Scriabin and the Impossible." *Journal of the American Musicological Society* 51, no. 2 (Summer 1998): 283–330.

———. "Semiotics of Symmetry, or Rimsky-Korsakov's Operatic History Lesson." *Cambridge Opera Journal* 13 (2001): 261–93.

Moser, Charles A. *Esthetics as Nightmare: Russian Literary Theory, 1855–1870.* Princeton, N.J.: Princeton University Press, 1989.

Nelson, Robert S., and Richard Schiff. *Critical Terms for Art History.* Chicago: University of Chicago Press, 2003.

Newmarch, Rosa. *The Russian Opera.* New York: Dutton, 1914.

Nordau, Max. *Degeneration,* 8th ed. New York: D. Appleton, 1896.

Osborne, John. *The Meiningen Court Theater, 1866–1890.* Cambridge: Cambridge University Press, 1988.

Paperno, Irina, and Joan Delaney Grossman, eds. *Creating Life: The Aesthetic Utopia of Russian Modernism.* Stanford, Calif.: Stanford University Press, 1994.

Parker, Fan, and Stephen Jan Parker. *Russia on Canvas: Ilya Repin.* University Park: Pennsylvania State University Press, 1980.

Paston, Eleonora. "Khudozhestvennye printsipy mamontovskogo teatra." In *Sergei Diagilev i khudozhestvennaia kul'tura XIX–XX vv.* Perm: Permskoe Knizhnoe Izdatel'stvo, 1987: 17–29.

Pavis, Patrice. *Dictionary of the Theatre: Terms, Concepts, and Analysis,* trans. Christine Shantz. Toronto: University of Toronto Press, 1998.

Pekelis, Mikhail, and Aleksandra Orlova, eds. *M. P. Musorgskii: Literaturnoe nasledie,* 2 vols. Moscow: Muzyka, 1971–72.

Pokrovskii, Vladimir. "Chitaia Shaliapina." *Sovetskaia Muzyka* 11 (November 1968): 71–83.

Pozharskaia, Militsa. *Russkoe teatral'no-dekoratsionnoe iskusstvo kontsa XIX–nachala XX veka.* Moscow: Iskusstvo, 1970.

Pyman, Avril. *A History of Russian Symbolism.* Cambridge: Cambridge University Press, 1994.

Raskin, Abram. *Shaliapin i russkie khudozhniki.* Leningrad: Iskusstvo, 1963.

Reed, John R. *Decadent Style.* Athens: Ohio University Press, 1985.

Repin, Il'ia. *Dalëkoe i blizkoe.* Leningrad: Khudozhnik, 1986.

———. *Izbrannye pis'ma v dvukh tomakh, 1867–1930.* Moscow: Iskusstvo, 1969.

Rimskii-Korsakov, Andrei. *N.A. Rimskii-Korsakov: Zhizn' i tvorchestvo.* 5 vols. Moscow: Muzgiz, 1937.

Rimskii-Korsakov, Nikolai. *Letopis' moei muzykal'noi zhizni*. In *Polnoe sobranie sochinenii: literaturnye proizvedeniia i perepiska*. Vol. 1. Moscow: Muzgiz, 1955.

Ronen, Omry. *The Fallacy of the Silver Age in Twentieth-Century Russian Literature*. Amsterdam: Harwood, 1997.

Rosenthal, Bernice. "Theater as Church: The Vision of the Mystical Anarchists." *Russian History* 4, no. 2 (1977): 122–41.

Rossikhina, Vera. *Opernyi teatr S. I. Mamontova*. Moscow: Muzyka, 1985.

Rudnitskii, Konstantin. *Rezhissër Meierhol'd*. Moscow: Nauka, 1969.

——. *Russkoe rezhissërskoe iskusstvo, 1898–1907*. Moscow: Nauka, 1989.

Rylkova, Galina. *The Archaeology of Anxiety: The Russian Silver Age and Its Legacy*. Pittsburgh: University of Pittsburgh Press, 2007.

Sadie, Stanley, ed. *The New Grove Dictionary of Opera*. 4 vols. New York: Grove, 1992.

Salina, Nadezhda. *Zhizn' i stsena*. Leningrad: Vsesoiuznoe Teatral'noe Obshchestvo, 1941.

Sarab'ianov, Dmitrii. *Istoriia russkogo iskusstva kontsa XIX–nachala XX veka*. Moscow: Moskovskii Universitet, 1993.

——. *Russkaia zhivopis' XIX veka sredi evropeiskikh shkol*. Moscow: Sovetskii Khudozhnik, 1980.

——. *Stil' modern: istoki, istoriia, problemy*. Moscow: Iskusstvo, 1989.

Severiukhin, Dmitrii, and Oleg Leikind. *Zolotoi vek khudozhestvennykh ob"edinenii v Rossii i SSSR (1820–1932)*. St. Petersburg: Izdatel'stvo Chernysheva, 1992.

Shkafer, Vasilii. *Sorok let na stsene russkoi opery*. Leningrad: Izdanie Teatra Opery i Baleta Imeni S. M. Kirova, 1936.

Solov'ëv, Vladimir. *Filosofiia iskusstva i literaturnaia kritika*. Moscow: Iskusstvo, 1991.

——. *Stikhotvoreniia, estetika, literaturnaia kritika*. Moscow: Kniga, 1990.

Stanislavskii, Konstantin. *Moia zhizn' v iskusstve*. Moscow: Iskusstvo, 1983.

Stasov, Vladimir. *Izbrannye trudy*. 3 vols. Moscow: Iskusstvo, 1952.

Sternin, Grigorii. *Khudozhestvennaia zhizn' Rossii na rubezhe XIX–XX vekov*. Moscow: Iskusstvo, 1970.

Taruskin, Richard. *Musorgsky: Eight Essays and an Epilogue*. Princeton, N.J.: Princeton University Press, 1993.

——. *Stravinsky and the Russian Traditions: A Biography of Works Through Mavra*. Berkeley: University of California Press, 1996.

Teliakovskii, Vladimir. *Dnevniki direktora Imperatorskikh Teatrov*. 3 vols. Moscow: Artist, Rezhissër, Teatr, 1998–2006.

Tenisheva, Maria. *Vpechatleniia moei zhizni*. Leningrad: Iskusstvo, 1991.

Tolstoi, Lev. *Polnoe sobranie sochinenii*. Moscow: Gosudarstvennoe Izdatel'stvo Khudozhestvennoi Literatury, 1951.

Trapido, Joel, ed. *International Dictionary of Theatre Language*. Westport, Conn.: Greenwood, 1985.

Turner, Jane, ed. *New Grove Dictionary of Art*. New York: St. Martin's, 2000.

Valkenier, Elizabeth. *Ilya Repin and the World of Russian Art*. New York: Columbia University Press, 1990.

——. *Russian Realist Art. The State and Society: The Peredvizhniki and Their Tradition*. New York: Columbia University Press, 1989.

Vrubel', Mikhail. *Perepiska. Vospominaniia o khudozhnike.* Leningrad: Iskusstvo, 1963.

Watkins, Glenn. *Pyramids at the Louvre: Music, Culture, and Collage from Stravinsky to the Postmodernists.* Cambridge, Mass.: Belknap, 1994.

———. *Soundings: Music in the Twentieth Century.* New York: Schirmer, 1988.

Wickham, Glynn. *A History of the Theater.* Cambridge: Cambridge University Press, 1985.

Zil'bershtein, Il'ia, and Vladimir Samkov, eds. *Sergei Diagilev i russkoe iskusstvo.* 2 vols. Moscow: Izobrazitel'noe Iskusstvo, 1982.

## Discography

"Iskusstvo F. I. Shaliapina—I. Stseny i arii iz russkikh oper." Russian Disc RCDC-00391, 1994.

"Singers of Imperial Russia," vol. 3. Pearl GEMM CD 9004-6, 1992.

# INDEX

*Locators in italics refer to figures (f), plates (pl), and tables (t). All plates appear between pages 129 and 130.*

Abramtsevo, 3, 6, 38, 67, 68–87, 120, 123, 127, *pl4*, 143, 201, 291, 292, 308, 310n43, 311n71; home theatricals at, 72–73, 92, 96, 99, 110, 131; workshops at, 10, 12, 74, 86, 119, 293, 299n26. *See also* Mamontov Circle (Abramtsevo Circle)

Abramtsevo Circle. *See* Mamontov Circle (Abramtsevo Circle)

Abramtsevo museum, 6, 96, 299n20

aestheticism, 20, 21, 25, 29, 32, 38, 56, 60; aesthetes, 23, 27–29, 32, 36–38, 58, 62, 75, 286, 307nn97,98, 315n90

Aksakov, the family of, 34, 38, 291; Sergei, 35

Alekseev, the family of, 34; Konstantin, 194, 298n11, 305n41, 326n64. *See also* Stanislavsky (Alekseev), Konstantin

All-Russian Congress of Artists, 49, 83, 89, 293

All-Russian Exhibition at Nizhny Novgorod. *See* Nizhny Novgorod Exhibition

Antokolsky, Mark, 37, 69, 70, 71, 77, 78, *pl12*, 283, 310n33

Arbatov, Nikolai, 55, 194

art for art's sake, 16, 22, 27, 30, 48, 51, 59, 67, 74, 75, 77, 78, 83, 126, 208, 284, 315n96. *See also* "beauty;" pure art

art nouveau, 20, 21, 301n27

art synthesis. *See* synthesis of the arts

*Arts and Crafts (Iskusstvo i Khudozhestvennaya Promyshlennost')*, 90, 129

Bakst, Léon, 99, 106, 120, 281, 306n67

Balakirev, Mily, 117

Ballets Russes, 5, 9, 59, 63, 125, 126, 278, 294, 299n18, 306n67, 313n34; *L'après-midi d'un faune*, 125, 306n67; *Cléopatre*, 106; collaborative methodology of, 99; *Coq d'or*, 279–80, 290; *Daphnis et Chloe*, 306n67; Diaghilev and, 6, 8, 105, 129, 181, 290; *Firebird*, 106; *Narcissus*, 306n67; *Petrushka*, 106, 314n69; *Schéhérazade*, 106; synthesis of the arts and, 106, 290; visual design at, 73, 89, 91–92, 120. *See also* Diaghilev, Sergei

Balmont, Konstantin, 22, 23

Baskin, Vladimir, 91, 94, 104, 153, 226, 259, 312n9

**Olga Haldey** is Assistant Professor of Musicology at the University of Maryland, College Park. She formerly taught music history and literature at the University of Missouri–Columbia and earned a Ph.D. in Musicology from Ohio State University.